FLESH AND GLORY

Flesh and Glory

Symbol, Gender, and Theology in the Gospel of John

DOROTHY LEE

A Herder and Herder Book
The Crossroad Publishing Company
New York

To the members of the
Phōs Hilaron Eucharistic group

The Crossroad Publishing Company
481 Eighth Avenue, New York, NY 10001

Printed in the United States of America

Library of Congress Cataloging-in-Publication Data

Lee, Dorothy A.
    Flesh and glory : symbol, gender, and theology in the Gospel of John /
Dorothy Lee.
        p. cm.
    "A Herder and Herder Book."
    Includes bibliographical references and index.
    ISBN 0-8245-1981-7 (alk. paper)
    1. Bible. N.T. John—Feminist criticism. 2. Symbolism in the Bible.
I. Title.
BS2615.6.S97 .L44 2002
226.5'064—dc21
                                                                                2002004684

1   2   3   4   5   6   7   8   9   10   06   05   04   03   02

Contents

Acknowledgments

I T IS IMPOSSIBLE TO IDENTIFY ALL THE PEOPLE who lie behind the making and shaping of a book. Some are academic colleagues, others friends and family. Still others are people whose opinions seem alien and disturbing; yet they too have as much influence as those whose views are more congenial. To all of these influences, friendly and hostile alike, I owe a debt of gratitude for helping to shape my thinking, my apprehension of the Fourth Gospel, my understanding of the centrality of theology and the vital need for a rethinking of Christian orthodoxy. Despite their influence, none is to be blamed for my wayward opinions.

Of my colleagues, I acknowledge gratefully the support of Peter Matheson, Christiaan Mostert, Muriel Porter, Robert Gribben, Rufus Black, Maryanne Confoy, R.S.C., and Eric Osborn. I would also like to thank Frank Moloney, S.B.D., whose own work on the Fourth Gospel has inspired me; Brendan Byrne, S.J., for his constant encouragement; and Morna Hooker, for her hospitality and graciousness, both academic and social. Grantley McDonald has been a learned and committed research assistant, whose flashes of humor have probably helped as much as, if not more than, his critical stance on all matters of (Latinate English) prose style. All of these, I hasten to add, reside in the friendly camp—yet each in their own way has challenged me (sometimes discomfortingly) to stretch my perspective beyond its natural timidities.

The Uniting Church Theological Hall, Melbourne, graciously made possible a period of study leave to complete the project, while Robinson College, Cambridge, gave me a hospitable home in a stimulating environment. I thank the Joint Theological Library, Melbourne, the Divinity Faculty Library, Cambridge, and Tyndale House, Cambridge. Queen's College, Melbourne, has been my abode for more than ten years and I am grateful to the community for its support. My involvement in the College—in the Chapel, the teaching, the social activities, and the replenishing of the fountain with fish—has given me a deep sense of home. I thank also my ecumenical colleagues and students within the United Faculty of Theology, Melbourne, as well as the staff, students, and colleagues in the Theological Hall. Paul McMahon and Michael Parker of Crossroad Publishing have been sympathetic, encouraging, and patient editors.

Some of the material in this book has been aired in earlier versions in *Pacifica* ("Abiding in the Fourth Gospel," "Beyond Suspicion? The Father of God in the Fourth Gospel," "Touching the Sacred Text"), and also *The Australian Biblical Review* ("Women as 'Sinners'"). Parts of chapter 5, on the Fatherhood of God, appeared in *Semeia* 85 (1999): 177–87 ("The Symbol of Divine Fatherhood"), and several sections of chapter 9, on Mary Magdalene, appeared in *Journal for the Study of the New Testament* 58 (1995): 37–49 ("Partnership in Easter Faith"). My views have developed in the intervening years, and I have come to a richer understanding of the Christian tradition and a more positive appraisal of its value for theology—including theology that wants to take seriously issues of gender.

There are those closer to home to whom I must render thanks: to Catherine Anderson, for teaching me (as only an architect could) the difference between ornament and decoration; to Neil Williams, for showing me that the gospel reaches even into the depths; to my sister, Ruth Lee Martin, for the courage and beauty of her music; to my daughters, Miriam and Irene, who interrupt, astonish, and occasionally inspire me; to my parents, Edwin and Barbara Lee, to whom I owe my life in more senses than I can say. Last of all, it would be remiss of me— and they would be deeply disappointed—to omit mention of my constant companions, Samuel and Portlee, small creatures with a flair for sympathetic listening.

QUEEN'S COLLEGE
UNIVERSITY OF MELBOURNE
FEAST OF THE ANNUNCIATION 2002

Symbol and Gender
in Johannine Study

T HIS BOOK IS A STUDY of symbolism in the Fourth Gospel. It is not intended to be comprehensive but exploratory, seeking ways of reading the biblical text that might avoid those presuppositions of Enlightenment thinking that are inimical to symbolic interpretation. The current crisis in biblical scholarship—the proliferation and dissipation of approaches to the text, the isolation of one reading from another, and the lack of a theological center conceded by too many—compels us to question where we have come, since the Enlightenment "liberated" biblical studies from captivity to church and dogma. The rationalism and objectivism of the Enlightenment carved the text into manageable pieces that were kept firmly apart from each other and equally distant from the community of faith and the interpreter. Attempting to move further, postmodern study of the Bible has seen an almost obsessive concern with methodology, often at the expense of theological exegesis. The result is that biblical exegesis is drowning in a surfeit of methods and methodology, while at the same time dying of thirst from the lack of a revivifying center. The deepening despair of locating meaning within texts has led to the conviction that interpreters can no longer speak across ideological divides, that texts cannot transform, that multiplicity and variance are the slender threads which alone can guide us through the labyrinth.

What has suffered most in these approaches to the text since the Enlightenment is the loss of awareness of the power of biblical symbolism: to touch the heart, to open worlds, to cross the divide of generations and cultures, to bring about transformation. Symbols where they are noted are generally treated as decorations or interpreted in an overly literal way that stifles the living flame that first ignited them. We are caught in a desert of relativism and banality that past generations would find astounding—a poverty that *is* astounding given the wealth of knowledge that has accumulated over the past two hundred years of biblical scholarship. Here is a tragic irony: all this knowledge and so little to nurture the soul. Even biblical studies is affected by the defining secularism of our age, which has been described as "soulless, aggressive, nonchalant and nihilistic."[1] The task of recovering biblical symbolism and theology is therefore compelling. We have reached a point of such skepticism in some quarters that the text with all its wealth of symbol has barely a redemptive word to say.[2]

We take instead a somewhat different route, a route that follows the symbols of the Gospel, convinced that their rereading will bring to life the ancient text across a multitude of difference. The symbols of the Fourth Gospel need such a hearing. On this symbolic journey through the Johannine narrative, we cross paths with the women of the Fourth Gospel at a number of points—not in an attempt to show their superiority or to set them apart from their male colleagues, but rather to explore the way in which symbol and character interact in their experience. The narratives that contain female characters are among the most beautiful and evocative of the Gospel and warrant study in their own right, apart from any pragmatic justification. There *is* justification, because women are now more than ever active readers and students of the text, in manifold ways. Such speaking in the end benefits women and men alike, opening locked doors in ancient walls that have been deemed irrelevant and covered in neglectful thickets of ivy. We have the freedom to rifle through the treasure box of tradition and perhaps find surprises that astonish and illumine us: in narrative and myth, in metaphor and symbol. We may find that, while some of the contents seem musty with age, others are surprisingly fresh, unlocking a mystery that is as dynamic today as it ever was in the past.

STUDIES ON SYMBOL AND GENDER IN JOHN

Johannine studies on both symbolism and gender have increased dramatically in recent decades. R. Alan Culpepper opened the door to literary studies of the Fourth Gospel with his pioneering work on the literary and narrative aspects of the Johannine text.[3] Using the insights of secular literary criticism, Culpepper applied them to John's Gospel in a comprehensive way, examining various literary devices and introducing students of the Gospel to new terminology and categories that have proved helpful in unlocking the Johannine text. Although Culpepper's is not a study of Johannine symbolism, it includes an important section on the symbols of the Gospel and encourages others to explore in more detail the sketchy outline proposed.[4] More recent commentators, influenced by Culpepper, have interpreted the Gospel from a literary and narrative perspective, examining also the role of the reader.[5] My own previous study of the Fourth Gospel analyzed the connection between narrative and symbol in several Johannine narratives from a theological viewpoint.[6] Craig Koester's study of Johannine symbols is perhaps the most comprehensive to date, examining a wide number of symbols in the Gospel from a literary perspective.[7] In her most recent monograph, as well as in a number of previous writings, Sandra Schneiders is unusual in combining a sensitivity to symbol with concern for issues of gender.[8] Most recently, Jan van der Watt has explored what he identifies as a metaphorical and symbolic field within the Fourth Gospel, focused around interlinked images of the family.[9] What these and other similar studies have done is threefold: they have opened up the symbolism of this most symbolic Gospel as the object of serious study; they have attempted to define symbol and metaphor in ways that emphasize their substantial rather than decorative nature; and they have endeavored to elucidate the theology of the Gospel by way of its symbolism.

Studies of women in the Fourth Gospel have likewise blossomed in Johannine discussions over the past few decades. These writings reflect a wider interest in bringing to the fore the female characters of the Bible, drawing them from the shadows of either the text itself or its many interpretations down through the centuries. The Fourth Gospel is particularly suited to such rereading, given the unusual prominence of women and the significant narrative roles they play as disciples and witnesses within the Johannine text. This focus of investigation was initiated in an early essay by Raymond Brown and was subsequently taken up by others building on his approach.[10] While there have been dissenting voices—such as the recent study by Adeline Fehribach[11]—for the most part there is a consensus that John's Gospel, while not by any means a "feminist" text in the modern sense, presents women in a remarkably positive way as disciples and leaders within the community of faith. The Fourth Gospel is generally recognized as the most sympathetic of all the Gospels in its portrayal of women. This work of retrieval has for the most part been fruitful, challenging the narrowness of previous interpretations and reversing the invisibility of women. These days it is difficult to read the Gospel without awareness of women's role, and without raising tantalizing questions about their place in the Johannine community.

Of special significance is the way in which key narrative moments in the Fourth Gospel are dependent on the discipleship of women. There are five women who play important roles in unfolding the Johannine narrative and theology: the mother of Jesus (2:1–11; 19:25–27), the Samaritan woman (4:1–42), Martha and Mary of Bethany (11:1–12:11), and Mary Magdalene (19:25–27; 20:1–18). There are two other women who appear only in the one episode at the foot of the cross, Jesus' mother's sister and Mary of Clopas (19:25b).[12] In addition, there is also the woman caught in adultery (7:53–8:11), who appears in a story that is probably not part of the Johannine text but a later addition.[13] The Johannine women "are presented in incomparably positive ways as persons who are closely linked to the self-revelation of Jesus and to the coming of his hour."[14] They are characterized in different ways throughout the Fourth Gospel, but there are common themes that run through each episode. Each of the five is presented as a disciple of Jesus in a relationship of mutual love, either in her initial appearance or by the end of the meeting with Jesus. Each has her own limitations and struggle, but remains open to faith so that her knowledge and experience are transformed through the narrative. Each witnesses to the significance and identity of Jesus, often proclaiming her faith to or on behalf of the community of faith and taking her place confidently within the "apostolic" life of the church.

Nonetheless narrative investigation remains a limited endeavor if it never moves beyond the women of the text. More is at stake than the presentation of female characters, whether they are portrayed positively or not. Writing from a feminist perspective, Adele Reinhartz argues that an authentic reading goes beyond "the words about and images of women" and attempts "to expose the question of liberation not only from the perspective of women qua women but from the point of view of the marginalized."[15] Apart from anything else, the women stand alongside the men of the Gospel, who are also capable of showing faith, playing a representative role, and engaging in apostolic leadership. Such qualities are not unique to women in the Fourth Gospel. What is perhaps extraordinary is the sense of mutuality in discipleship and ministry between women and men, and the partnership established between them.[16] Nevertheless, gender reading is not confined to female characterization but explores also the theological framework of the text: the way it comprehends human life in relation to God, and the centrality of Jesus for understanding both humanity and divinity.

If interpretation can unveil the hidden contours of female discipleship and ministry, what can a similar reading do for the Gospel's theology? What happens when women as well as men enter into dialogue, not just with the characters but also with the symbols and metaphors of the Gospel? It is this concern that impels the present study. For all the recent investigative work, the characters and symbols of the Fourth Gospel are far from being exhausted: they call for closer examination within the theological structures of the Gospel. Some symbols, such as the flesh, have not been analyzed symbolically in any depth; others remain peripheral, particularly those relating to female experience; still others, such as fatherhood, have been too readily dismissed in feminist theology. Questions of definition also need further clarification if symbol is to be taken seriously as the groundwork of Christian theology. If the Johannine text is to acquire new power, the symbols of the Gospel need to be highlighted, given prominence, drawn into the center of theological discourse. A focus on biblical theology and the symbols in which it is unfolded can open the reader to a rich vein of meaning,[17] even where women are not at the forefront of the text's intentions. The Johannine symbols have a vital role to play.

INTERPRETATION AND CONVERSION

Being concerned with the symbols of the Johannine text, the approach taken in this study is largely a literary one. This is not to discount alternative approaches to the text. There are other questions that bear on symbolic meaning: the background of thought and experience out of which the symbols arise, the cultural and social environment, the specific situation of the Johannine community, the influence of other texts, particularly the Old Testament and the Synoptic Gospels,[18] and the standard of interpretation used in the early Christian centuries in the construction of the canon. These are alluded to at different points in this study, even though the main concern is with the Johannine narrative in its own right. What lies behind the text is important, yet it is always dependent on, and secondary to, what lies within.

Awareness of the objectivity of the text is not ultimately separable from the Johannine author, generally referred to as the "evangelist" but also identified with the narrator of the Gospel. In this sense, we can speak of an intentionality to the Fourth Gospel, but chiefly as that resides within the text itself. Anything more about the original author is based on guesswork and surmises that, though useful, cannot be used as the basis of interpretation. The relationship between text and reader is more complicated, since there are three senses in which readership can be understood: the "implied reader," who is part of, and merges with, the text itself; the actual first-century audience of the Fourth Gospel; and contemporary readers, who read in their own ways and are not obliged to follow the reading path laid down by the implied reader. This study is concerned primarily with the former, the reader-within-the-text, while acknowledging the existence of a real readership in the first century. It is also aware that the evangelical purpose of the Gospel—and its purpose within the church's canon—is the transformation of real readers within the contemporary world.

A symbolic approach, as we will see in the next chapter, implies that meaning is referential but at the same time not easily captivated or contained. Symbols require readers (as well as authors) for meaning to emerge. The two-sided nature of interpretation implies that the Fourth Gospel does not possess a single, definitive meaning for all time, incontrovertible and fixed. The biblical text is, to an extent, polyvalent. This need not imply that its meanings are infinite or arbitrary; rather it contains what Paul Ricoeur calls a "surplus of meaning" or "excess of signification."[19] Readings that claim narrowly isolated or solitary meaning do not sufficiently account for the affective and noncognitive ways in which texts and readers interact. The freedom of "sacred reading" (*lectio divina*) cannot narrowly control and define the subjective apprehension of the reader. An approach that respects the surplus of meaning within the text knows that, while the range of interpretation is limited, it is also open to new horizons. Meaning requires both the objectivity of the text and the subjective experience of the reader.[20] Both are necessary: without the former, we are in danger of a "reader-text indeterminacy" that collapses into relativism, where the text has no distinct meaning;[21] without the latter, the role of the reader is reduced to that of passive recipient.

In biblical reading, the range of meaning is circumscribed by the wholeness of the text itself, by the community that interprets it, and by the "canon of truth" out of which the text is born. These factors possess a centripetal force, giving rising to the surplus of meaning in which the inspiring Spirit works, enabling the biblical text to become "word of God" in a dynamic interchange.[22] This understanding of meaning has important gender implications. The very openness of the text, within its own directionality, enables new readers to apprehend the text in new ways. Neither women's reading of the text nor our reading of women characters (whether by male or female) is confined to a single strand of meaning. The same is as true for interpretations that demean women or confine them to the shadows as it is for literalistic interpretations that search the text only in the light of questions of ideological decorum. Both are constrictive and coercive. Instead, the reader is "authorized" to engage in dialogue with the objective text, steering a way through a maze of "suspicion" to discover meaning and identity within the multifaceted symbols of the Johannine text. The symbols have the capacity to move out of the confines of the text and embrace the reader, gathering up his or her life into the larger narrative of Jesus, the Word and Wisdom of God.

At the same time as rediscovering the symbols, we need to find a model for appropriating the text that is more integrative than the historical-critical method alone. The dialectical process between explanation and understanding proposed by Ricoeur is particularly useful here.[23] He argues that, as readers, we begin to read a text naïvely, opening ourselves to its dynamic in the same way that children listen to stories; this first movement is a "naïve grasping of the meaning of the text as a whole."[24] Critical readings of any kind ought not to precede this initial response. The second movement, for Ricoeur, is explanatory. The reader steps back from the text and engages in the kind of research necessary for a deeper comprehension at a number of levels. Here the historical-critical method and related tools of biblical study play their part. This stage needs to include awareness of gender issues involved in the text itself and its interpretations. The final stage of understanding, without which the reading process is in vain, is a return to the openness of the reader's first engagement, but this time with a more sophisticated level of awareness: "a second naïveté beyond iconoclasm."[25] This stage involves empathy and a sense of the whole. Again the reader stands before the text, in an attitude of receptivity, discovering the "word of God" in a new way that embraces the whole person, as well the spirit of the whole text.

Ricoeur's "second naïveté" can be taken further. We need to incorporate the element of transformation into biblical interpretation, invisible perhaps to Western critical scholarship, but important to many generations of Christian readers, past and present. Writing from an Eastern Orthodox perspective, Theodore Stylianopoulos distinguishes a three-tiered interpretation: the exegetical level, using the insights of historical-critical scholarship; the interpretive level, where the reader is engaged by the text and evaluates its teaching and import; and the transformative or existential level.[26] In the case of the latter—a level largely absent,

according to Stylianopoulos, in Western interpretative theory—the reader is
 grasped by the text and transformed by its dynamic. This, the deepest level of
Scripture, is the level of experience, incorporating yet moving beyond the intellectual and theoretical, where the reader enters the transfiguring domain of the
spiritual. In this sense, the Holy Spirit is the true interpreter of Scripture within
the context of the community of faith, creating a living tradition that is able to critique the past and uncover new insights, consistent with revealed faith (John
14:26; 16:13). The remaking power of God, through the Spirit, continually forms
and reforms the church. Transformation is the end process of sacred reading:
without it, the other tasks are intellectual games, without ultimate significance.

THE SHAPE OF THIS STUDY

The following chapters explore these questions not in the abstract but from the
Johannine text and within its richness of symbolism.[27] Although this study may
not be the only way in which the text can be viewed, it does claim to be an authentic reading, even if it views the mountain from a limited number of angles. Yet—
to change the imagery—these viewings, even in their limitability, can act as
gateways leading the reader into the heart of a text that is vaster than any one symbol can contain. For this reason, the study of women is not intended for female
readers alone. Being representative characters, the women of the Fourth Gospel
have relevance also for men and possess the capacity to transform men's experience of faith and life as well as women's. In the end, all symbols, themes, perspectives, and interpretations lead to one place and one place alone, no matter how
variegated the paths or how difficult the journey: to the meeting with Jesus, the
Word-made-flesh, the divine Son, the giver of life, and Savior of the world.
Whether he is to be found in the temple, at the well, in the Galilean hills, at a fes-
tal dinner, in privacy with his friends, on the cross, or in the Easter garden, finally
makes no difference. The main point is that he becomes present in the place where
the reader is present, and that, through the symbols, the intersection discloses new
paths that lead assuredly to God.

This study engages feminist theology at a number of points, in a way that, without being uncritical, acknowledges the importance of its perspective. The very
term "feminist theology" is nonetheless problematic, suggesting that there is a
kind of theology for (certain kinds of) women that, while having its own contextual integrity, does not necessarily possess universal appeal. There is indeed difficulty in claiming that one's own theology is universal and that its framework
speaks for the Christian community worldwide. At the same time, the contextual
nature of *all* theology does not deny that theology also has the capacity (as does
great literature in all cultures) to speak across cultural, gender, racial, and other
barriers.[28] In the end, there *is* only "theology." Where women (and others) have

been excluded from speaking of God or hearing the divine word, and where the contextual realities and diversity of people's experience have been ignored, theology has failed to be what it truly is. Although using terms such as "feminist theology," therefore, this study is aware of the limitations and relativity of all such nomenclature. John's Gospel presents Jesus (to a woman!) as the Savior of the world, and the universal joy of this message has the capacity to leap across all the boundaries that lead to division and dissipation.

We begin with a definition of symbol (chapter 1), an important prelude to examining the symbols, since the language of religious symbol and metaphor is often employed loosely and uncritically. Thereafter we trace a number of symbols in the Fourth Gospel and their theological significance. Most important for John's theology is the symbol of the "flesh," both in its complex Johannine usage and its relationship to contemporary discussions on gender and Christology (chapter 2). The next two chapters examine symbols that extend across the Johannine narrative: the symbol of living water, with particular focus on the Samaritan woman (chapter 3), and the symbol of "abiding" as it unfolds the relational nature of Johannine theology (chapter 4). Parental imagery is the focus of the next two chapters: the symbol of divine fatherhood and its vital place in Christian theology, despite some feminist objections (chapter 5), and complex symbols of motherhood that relate to Jesus, the Spirit, and the mother of Jesus (chapter 6). This is followed by a discussion of sin in the Johannine narrative and its associated symbolism (chapter 7). From there, we move to symbols associated with Jesus' death and resurrection: the symbol of the anointing as its meaning unfolds in the evocative action of Mary of Bethany (chapter 8), the symbolism of Easter seen through the eyes of Martha of Bethany and Mary Magdalene, who share very different yet connected encounters with Jesus as "resurrection and life" (chapter 9). We conclude with a brief reflection on the relationship between symbolism and transformation, the latter being the goal of all "sacred reading" and the ultimate means of determining textual meaning.

CHAPTER 1

The Meaning of Symbol
in the Fourth Gospel

The symbol gives rise to thought.[1]

N O STUDY OF RELIGIOUS SYMBOLISM within a text such as the Fourth Gospel
can bypass the question of definition. The issue of how to interpret the Bible
is related directly to the way we believe symbolism operates within the biblical narrative. For all the advances in understanding Scripture arising from the
historical-critical method, there have been losses, particularly in the narrowing of
biblical interpretation and its disconnection from the community of faith. One of
the resultant problems of critical exegesis is the tendency to treat symbol and
metaphor—along with myth, narrative, and poetry—as secondary and derivative,
functioning only at a decorative level, thus disconnecting the reader from the text's
symbolic and transformative power. In this chapter we review briefly some of the
principles of patristic exegesis, since the patristic approach to Scripture is closer to
the symbolic apprehension of the fourth evangelist, in method if not in content.
From there, we move to a definition of symbol that coheres with the presuppositions of the first centuries of Christian interpretation and leads us into the Johannine text.

PATRISTIC PRINCIPLES OF EXEGESIS

The early church, with its strongly poetic and symbolic sensitivities, believed that
the Bible could be read at more than one level. Scripture was taken to be both
divine and human word: the witness to revelation, on the one hand, and its
accommodation to human limitability, on the other. Patristic exegesis—whether
in the so-called "allegorical" tradition (Alexandria) or the "typological" (Anti-
och)—believed it was both possible and necessary to interpret the text on the literal and spiritual levels, the one in some sense dependent on the other. The
fourfold sense of Scripture that became standardized by the Middle Ages consisted

of the literal, the allegorical (often linked to the church), the tropological (the personal or moral), and the anagogical (the ultimate or eschatological), and had its origins in patristic exegesis. Interpreters were free to move between different levels depending on the needs and context. There was also a freedom to move within similar fields of reference, even if that meant crossing between different biblical theologies, guided not by the thread of historical connectedness but by similar or related symbolism used in different contexts. By contemporary standards, it is true, the historical was insufficiently regarded and historicity presupposed in what we now consider an uncritical way. The "literal" level seems to us to be passed over too quickly and the deeper meanings embellished and spiritualized, especially in the allegorical tradition.[2] For modern exegetes, there seems too little discernible exegetical control.

The Antiochene tradition, with its preference for exploring patterns of promise and fulfillment within the diversity of the scriptural writings, was itself concerned with the danger of a tokenist attitude to the literal meaning of the text. This approach tends to regard the literal and the symbolic meanings as both having their own integrity, while the Alexandrian approach, typified in Origen, was less concerned with the "carnal" meaning and more concerned to identify allegorical meanings, whether in relation to the soul, the church, or eschatology. Caution is needed, however, in making simplistic distinctions between the literal, typological, and allegorical in this period. Frances Young has argued that modern exegesis is mistaken in regarding the Antiochene school as a precursor to the rise of biblical criticism. Young demonstrates that the difference between the two patristic traditions is much less than is generally conceded, neither being strictly interested in the literal level as we understand it with our primarily historical frame of reference.[3] Both traditions draw on the methods of interpretation taught in the classical schools;[4] both regard the text as "authoritative but far from binding";[5] both are concerned to identify and interpret the representative quality of Scripture (*mimesis*); both use the same hermeneutical keys to interpret the text; and both employ a similar range of reading strategies.[6] To some extent, both traditions interpret the text allegorically, though to different degrees and with a different approach to the literal level. Indeed, the difference between the allegorical (which was broadly conceived) and the literal is more a spectrum than an absolute distinction.[7] In any event, all patristic exegesis, of whatever school, takes seriously the symbolic import of the text and allows it to shape interpretation. As Sebastian Brock points out, "[t]he Patristic view . . . accords much greater significance to the symbol, whereas modern usage plays down the value of the symbol."[8]

Patristic interpretation was controlled by the Rule of Faith, which had grown alongside the canon and was, in a sense, the true canon, the basis on which the canon was formed. As a result, the Bible was seen as presenting a unified message of salvation. Writing from an Orthodox perspective, Theodore Stylianopoulos sets out the presuppositions of patristic exegesis, most of which would be unacceptable to contemporary, secular exegesis: the christocentric focus of all Scripture, the unity of Scripture (and therefore the principle of interpreting Scripture by Scripture), and the integration between Scripture and the sacramental, praying and teaching life of the church.[9] It must be borne in mind that patristic writers did not distinguish between biblical studies and systematic theology: *hermeneia* had a much broader meaning, from translation to exegesis to hermeneutics.[10] The interpreter was able to move between the textual and the theological in a way that is alien to modern scholarship, with its strict lines of demarcation between exegesis and dogmatics. All this is to say that the patristic writings read the biblical text from an overtly Christian perspective. The church's critical discernment was needed at every point: biblical statements that seemed to presuppose some kind of predestinarianism, for example, presented an image of God that was not theologically acceptable.[11] Within a symbolic understanding, Scripture, although authoritative and therefore divine in character, also had its human side.

Within its own framework, patristic exegesis interpreted the text with a remarkable degree of boldness and imagination—a freedom that was neither fanciful nor arbitrary.[12] Origen, for example, employs the allegorical tools of his day in an imaginative and creative way, yet is well aware of his own methodology and able to give a coherent account of it, using principles of interpretation that have continuity with both classical and Jewish readings of sacred texts. Young argues that, for Origen, there is already a polyvalence within the text itself which enables more than one meaning, or levels of meaning, to be discerned: "multiple meanings . . . are really multiple referents." Similarly, in the common patristic method of scattering interpretation with numerous biblical quotations and allusions, we find "an intertextuality of imaginative and creative play, far removed from the historicism of modern interpretation whether critical or fundamentalist." Indeed, the real difference between modern and patristic exegesis is not so much methodological as a fundamental difference of worldview: modern exegesis no longer interprets the text from within the imaginative freedom of a "sacramental" worldview, according to which the material world is "interpenetrated by another reality, which is transcendent and spiritual."[13] It is this perspective that explains both the controlling principles and the literary freedom and flexibility of patristic exegesis.

There is a further aspect of the patristic approach that is relevant here, the perspective of the interpreter. In none of the great patristic interpreters do we find any claim to a "neutral" or "secular" reading of the text. Certainly they knew they were dealing with critical questions of truth; yet they read the Scripture as Christian theologians, homilists, mystics, and pastors. The faith stance of the interpreter was crucial for right interpretation of the text. This was not merely a matter of correct doctrine—even where such things were hotly disputed—but a question of experience and interior knowledge. Sebastian Brock argues that a poet-theologian such as Ephrem the Syrian finds seriously inadequate the kind of inquiry that attempts either to subjugate the object of study or to find distance from it. The only true approach to theology is "that of engagement, an engagement above all of love and wonder."[14] During the early centuries, *theōria*, meaning spiritual receptivity and insight (literally, "sight," often used in the sense of gazing upon) was seen as an essential part of exegesis. Stylianopoulos defines *theōria* as "a prayerful sense of awe and wonder in the presence of God, his creation, the great acts of salvation, the Bible and all things."[15] In order to discern the *skopos* ("goal") of the text, which was the true task of the interpreter—discerning the ultimate meaning of a particular text in relation to the whole—such prayerful insight was vital. The very notion that the symbolic power of the text could be apprehended in a purely cerebral manner, and from a disinterested perspective, was foreign to the patristic mind. Ephrem, for example, comments on the paradise symbolism of Genesis 2–3 in a series of liturgical poems (as well as a prose commentary on Genesis), many of them addressing God directly. They move freely between the referential nature of the text and its symbolic associations in various parts of the Bible, on the one hand, and its subjective import, on the other—in ways that are sometimes deeply personal.[16] The whole person of the interpreter, heart and soul as well as mind, is involved in the act of interpretation. Indeed, more than that: individual interpreters were never finally separated from the communities from which they emerged and to which they, and the texts they interpreted, belonged.

The hermeneutical impasse in contemporary Western exegesis is due, in large part, to the loss of that rich, interpretative tradition which reads the text symbolically, theologically, prayerfully, and communally. Whether consciously or not, the Protestant Reformation began the move away from ecclesial to individualistic readings of the text, and to a focus (particularly in Calvin) on the literal meaning, although in other respects the Reformers themselves shared many of the patristic assumptions about interpretation and were deeply indebted to patristic exegesis. The rise of biblical criticism in the Enlightenment created, or at least exacerbated, a bifurcated worldview: between exegesis and dogmatics, individual and church, revelation and reason, heart and head. The Enlightenment came to regard Scripture as a loose collection of historical documents, rather than a carefully shaped collection of symbolic and theological writings held together by the faith of the community and a broadly conceived interior "logic." The Bible was now seen as historically and theologically disparate—no longer "the church's book." Divorced from its moorings in the community of faith and in the interplay of symbolic meanings, the study of Scripture ironically became less free and more constrained in its interpretation. The shift of focus to historical meaning, within a socioreligious setting, along with a belief in detectable authorial intention—very different from the patristic notion of the *skopos* of the text—meant that the Bible was no longer read in close proximity to literature, liturgy, and theology. As a result, biblical scholarship came to read the Bible in wooden and overly literalist ways, paying insufficient regard to its symbolic and sacramental import. The idea of the text possessing its own *skopos* to be discerned by prayerful study and by *theōria* was

polyvalence of symbol —
plentitude
of meaning

lost. In particular, scant attention was paid to biblical symbolism and the plenitude of theological meaning that symbolism contains. Stylianopoulous, with some justification, protests against "the presumptuousness of unbridled reason" in the Enlightenment, leading to either the relativizing or absolutizing of biblical authority—both, in his judgment, equally solipsistic.[17] The breaking apart of things that, in the early period of the church's life, were joined together more or less harmoniously, is one of the main causes of the current crisis in biblical studies.

Much contemporary feminist biblical scholarship is heir to this tradition, adopting Enlightenment presuppositions about the centrality of history and the focus on a single, intended, "literal" meaning. Suspicion itself is a tool of the Enlightenment, offering doubt and skepticism as the only alternative to misogynist authoritarianism. Even the notion of "reading against the grain," which is a subversive, feminist attempt to circumvent the problem of readings that are hostile to women, can sometimes be based on a curiously narrow view of what a text is and how it is to be read.[18] Various models have been suggested for women's reading of the text, but these include an almost mechanistic account: the presence or absence of women, the ratio of women to men, their political status compared to men, and so forth. Such statistics, while significant on one level, are not the only basis on which to evaluate a text. While interpretation is confined to the historical and sociopolitical, with little appreciation for the polyvalence of symbol or the theology and spirituality of the text, it becomes bound within the one "literal" level of reading. Instead of women readers asking questions about the *skopos* of the text and discerning new interpretations that are as generously embracing and transformative of women's experience as of men's, the feminist reader is caught in a secularist labyrinth from which there seems no escape. Reacting against the fundamentalism of past interpretations, the reader actively resists the text, afraid of its ability to co-opt and imprison, systematically unpicking its solitary meaning, until the evidence is found to confirm that Scripture is the real source of social and ecclesiastical misogyny. In a post-Christian stance, this is an understandable response, but within the guise of a Christian reading, it is tragic and incomprehensible. The irony is that everything is deconstructed in relation to the biblical text, except for the narrow and constrictive framework that Enlightenment scholarship has bequeathed us. The polyvalence of the text, its symbolic and unpredictable dance, its grounding in community and commitment, its holistic connection to all aspects of human life—all things for which feminist theology longs—are lost within the very paradigm that feminist exegesis does not appear to question.

It is vital that biblical studies, in all its dimensions (feminist or otherwise), recover a symbolic and theological approach to the biblical text. While it is undesirable and indeed unnecessary to turn back the clock, what is needed is the reconnection of exegesis to a more sensitive theological and symbolic mode of reading the text. One way to resolve the contradiction between ancient and modern ways of reading, and gain the best of both worlds, is to encourage a confluence between the two, allowing each to illuminate and "correct" the other: the historical and the symbolic. This would mean a new appreciation of the symbolic role that Scripture plays. Such a move would also need to involve recognition of the multivalence of the text and the two-sided character of biblical reading. At the same time, symbolic reading needs to be careful not to fall back into a naïve historicism that ignores the stylized nature of biblical narrative. Such confluence might give rise to a poetics of biblical reading beyond narrowly literal readings, including an understanding of how the text works at the narrative, mythic, and poetic levels. Overly literal notions of how the text affects the reader—whether in terms of authorial intention, gender identification, or power relations—must respect the numinous and imaginative character of biblical interpretation, acknowledging the unpredictable coalescence of spirituality and the symbolic text.

THE MEANING OF SYMBOL

Karl Rahner argues that any real theology must also be a theology of symbolism, since "all beings are by their nature symbolic" and "being is of itself symbolic."[19] Religious symbolism lies somewhere at the core of theology—as exemplified particularly in the Fourth Gospel. Paul Tillich, who is also concerned with theology and symbol, sees religious symbol as a "segment of the finite," used to speak of the divine. Such concrete symbols are necessary for religious discourse to speak about God. They are based in the *analogia entis,* the "analogy of being" that exists between God and the world—the resemblance between Creator and creation, even given the vast gulf between the divine and the human: "the symbol shares this '*analogia entis*' with being which it symbolises."[20] Tillich uses the same notion, which originates in Thomas Aquinas, not as a basis for natural theology (as Protestantism has tended to claim in its rejection of the concept[21]) but as the philosophical basis for speaking in any way about God. Symbols by their nature are two-sided, linked both to the infinite and the finite. They involve simultaneously the affirmation and the negation of the concrete image, in order that it may reach toward the infinite.[22] For Tillich, symbol is very different from sign and can be easily distinguished; the one is intimately connected to the infinite while the other has a more tenuous link:

> while the sign bears no necessary relation to that to which it points, the symbol participates in the reality of that for which it stands. The sign can be changed arbitrarily according to the demands of expediency, but the symbol grows and dies according to the correlation between that which is symbolised and the persons who receive it as a symbol. Therefore, the religious symbol, the symbol which points to the divine, can be a true symbol only if it participates in the power of the divine to which it points.[23]

The notion of participation is essential to Tillich's understanding of symbolism. In the same manner, he argues, that symbol participates in the reality to which it points, so "the knower participates in the known; the lover participates in the beloved."[24] This means that symbol is neither decoration nor fantasy, nor is it divorced from truth: "A symbol *has* truth; it is adequate to the revelation it expresses. A symbol *is* true; it is the expression of a true revelation."[25] In a similar way, for Rahner, the symbol intrinsically belongs to what it seeks to articulate; it "does not represent an absent and merely promised reality but exhibits this reality as something present, by means of the symbol formed by it." Even in eschatological terms, for Rahner, there is ultimately no access to God without symbol, particularly in relation to the humanity of Christ.[26] Revelation and symbol are not opposing categories, but, on the contrary, the one is expressed in the terms of the other: "'symbolic' is not at all opposed to 'real.'"[27] Symbol itself is revelatory and lies at the heart of the theological enterprise.

For Tillich, religious symbolism has a number of distinctive qualities. True religious symbols are figurative, perceptible to the sense or the imagination, possessing intrinsic power (as distinct from sign) and socially acceptable: that is, belonging to community.[28] The latter point is important because it stresses how symbols can die if they lose social acceptance. Symbols point beyond themselves to what cannot be directly grasped, while participating in that same transcendent reality; having a mediating and organic quality, they cannot simply be created by intentional decision. Thus they cannot be generated deliberately nor easily exchanged.[29] Tillich is aware also that symbols can be destructive as well as constructive, requiring careful interpretation. On this basis, there is a distinction to be made between different kinds of symbols: those that are primary and those that play a supporting role.[30] Symbols can also become idolatrous where there is "a confusion between themselves and that to which they point."[31]

According to Brock, Ephrem the Syrian is the most symbolic of all patristic theologians, since, for him, religious symbols and types are to be found everywhere in nature and Scripture, containing hidden aspects of a multifarious truth that can never comprehend the infinite God. These symbols represent both a ladder of descent from the divine to the human, in which the hidden God is made manifest—especially in the incarnation—and a corresponding ladder of ascent from the human to the divine, the latter dependent entirely on the former. This imagery shows that the function of symbols is both revelatory and performative. Christ himself, as Son, is "the Lord of symbols" who has "fulfilled all kinds of symbols at His Crucifixion." Moreover, the ultimate purpose of religious symbolism, for Ephrem, is eschatological, signifying both the veiling of that which is too bright for the human eye, yet also the restoration of paradise: the purpose of both symbols and types is "to entice humanity back from its fallen stage by offering innumerable glimpses of the glorious divine reality."[32]

Sandra Schneiders proposes a symbolic model for reading the Johannine text that belongs in the same philosophical framework. She defines symbol carefully, delineating five basic elements within symbol: "(1) a sensible reality (2) which renders present to and (3) involves a person subjectively in (4) a transforming experience (5) of transcendent mystery."[33] Drawing on this understanding of the relationship between symbol and reality, Schneiders describes Scripture as the "symbol of the Word of God" rather than the literal word of God itself.[34] This definition is helpful in distinguishing between sign and symbol. Schneiders argues that signs possess only the first element in the above definition: unlike symbols, signs cannot facilitate a subjective, transcendent experience that has transfiguring power.[35] They are signposts pointing in a certain direction but with an arbitrary quality to them, remaining essentially apart from that to which they point. Symbols, on the other hand, achieve much more: they not only point the way; they also take the reader/viewer there because—in Rahner and Tillich's terms—they participate in the reality to which they refer. In this sense, signs have a single, fixed meaning, whereas symbols are by definition multivalent, capable of more than one meaning, their referent unable to be fixed in as precise or logical a way. This perspective is vital for the Fourth Gospel, the most explicitly symbolic of all the Gospels. Indeed, the whole Johannine text is symbolic. In the very act of reading, the reader engages with another level of reality. Like parables, this symbolic Gospel draws the reader into the very experience which it describes. The symbols of the Gospel are not signposts pointing elsewhere, but vehicles of revelation.

Not all symbols, however, are of equal importance in the Fourth Gospel. Alan Culpepper makes a distinction between different symbols in John: some are personal, others impersonal; of those which are impersonal, some have core status within the text while others are peripheral or subordinate. For Culpepper, the three core (impersonal) symbols of the Gospel are light, water, and bread.[36] These are not static but rather "expanding symbols" through the narrative of the Gospel, developing in meaning and significance as the story progresses.[37] Jesus stands at the center of the Johannine symbols. According to Craig Koester, who follows Culpepper's distinction, the core symbols in particular are important in communicating the transcendent; other symbols have a supporting role. Thus, for example, while the changing of water into wine at the wedding at Cana is a core symbol, the stone water jars function as a supporting symbol.[38] What is most important for Koester is that the core Johannine symbols—which are often metaphors— bridge the gulf between heaven and earth: they "span the chasm between what is 'from above' and what is 'from below' without collapsing the distinction."[39]

METAPHOR AND SYMBOL

A symbolic understanding of the Fourth Gospel is essential for a new hermeneutic to emerge that opens the text as revelation to human experience. This includes, in particular, taking seriously the metaphors of the Gospel. Metaphor is best understood as a subset of symbol. Whereas symbolism covers a wide range of expressions—painting, sculpture, architecture, music, dance, dreams, actions, events—metaphor is a figure of speech, confined to the linguistic (whether verbal or written), being essentially a feature of discourse. Janet Martin Soskice defines metaphor as *"that figure of speech whereby we speak about one thing in terms which are seen to be suggestive of another."*[40] Metaphors function as more than a comparison between two entities; they do not merely substitute one element for another, nor do they function merely as affective channels. On the contrary, real metaphors have cognitive content as well as intuitive power, enlarging the reader or hearer's understanding. In this sense, they are neither decorations on the plain meaning of an utterance, nor pedagogical aids to sweeten the message. They are themselves constitutive of meaning, in whatever grammatical form they occur: an adjective, a phrase, a full sentence, a paragraph. By creating meaning, metaphors give rise to a sense of delight, surprise, or shock, taking the conventional and transforming it into something fresh and vital, so that "the power of the familiar is altered and a new potency infused."[41] Metaphors may be static or dynamic, single or composite, concerned with animate or inanimate objects, but, if they are effective, they share the same capacity to carry the reader "into the figurative or spiritual world" and to "transform realities."[42] Indeed Jan van der Watt proposes that a series of different metaphors can build up to a "metaphorical field," the example he uses being "the family of the King," where, through familial and related metaphors, "John creates what can be called a metaphorical network based on the social reality of family life."[43]

Metaphor is formed by bringing together two disparate elements: the tenor or object of the image and the vehicle or image.[44] The tenor may be apparent or submerged. In the Johannine metaphorical statement that Jesus is the light of the world (*to phōs tou kosmou*, 8:12; 9:5), "Jesus" functions as the tenor and "light" as the vehicle, creating new meaning within the Johannine text. While being grounded in Old Testament metaphors of either God or Torah as light (e.g., Pss 27:1; 36:9; 43:3; 119:105; Prov 6:23; Isa 60:1, 19–20), as well as the cultic framework of the feast of Tabernacles, the metaphor also possesses a universal quality.[45] It does not decorate the "plain meaning" of John 8–9, nor is it employed as a didactic tool to soften Jesus' teaching. In a real sense, the metaphor *is* the message. The reader or hearer is challenged to move from the literal level (the sun) to the metaphorical or spiritual meaning: Jesus gives human life its true meaning, providing spiritual guidance through self-knowledge and the knowledge of God. The movement from the literal to the metaphorical begins at the point where the reader recognizes the inadequacy or insufficiency of the literal level (in this case its absurdity, since Jesus is not literally the sun) and seeks a second-level meaning to make sense of the utterance, moving beyond the "is not" of the first level to the metaphorical "is." In order to perceive the metaphorical, however, the reader needs to retain a sense of the literal meaning.[46] Such "stereoscopic vision" enables him or her to grasp the figurative meaning without abandoning or "demythologizing" the original image.[47] Much of the misunderstanding of the Fourth Gospel is focused on the struggle of Johannine characters to grasp the metaphorical meaning. In some cases, the figurative is grasped; in other cases, the metaphor remains opaque and the characters become alienated from the Johannine Jesus and all he represents.

Another example of Johannine metaphor is the invitation of Jesus in 7:37–39, again in the context of Tabernacles: "Let anyone who is thirsty come to me." At first glance, the meaning of this utterance appears to reside at the literal level (although the reader is already aware of the metaphorical import of "living water" in 4:10–11[48]), but the metaphor begins to emerge in the parallel statement where "anyone who is thirsty" (7:37) becomes "the one believing in me" (7:38a). This is then followed by a further metaphorical dimension, "rivers of living water will flow from his belly" (7:38b), an assertion that is puzzling at this point in the narrative. That a deeper meaning is required is suggested by the scriptural reference. The metaphorical meaning relates to Old Testament depictions of God as the giver of water, both physical and spiritual (Exod. 17:1–7; Num. 20:1–13; Ps. 42:1–2; 63:1; 107:4–9; Isa. 55:1). In this case, the evangelist steps in to explain the metaphor (7:39): thirst, water, rivers, belly—all point to the need and longing for the divine Spirit who is given as an inner, saving gift by the glorified Jesus to those with faith, a gift that will flow out to others. This and similar metaphorical utterances serve to build a picture of the relationship between the Father, Jesus, the Spirit, and believers and the fundamental yet mysterious nature of the gift itself. It is not easy to translate these metaphors into plain speech for the simple reason that no such thing underlies them: the metaphorical medium is itself the message. To quote Northrop Frye's paradoxical reversal, in the deepest sense the literal meaning *is* the poetic meaning.[49] Through the careful buildup of such metaphors, John creates an integrated and engaging theology that embraces Christology, the Spirit, spirituality, and discipleship.

It is worth noting at this point that, despite attempts to differentiate them, metaphor and simile—at least in the latter's more intense forms—share a similar structure. Soskice argues that the most vivid similes have the same incremental nature as metaphor and function in a similar way, as opposed to those similes which are employed merely for their illustrative value.[50] The "like" or "as" of the simile in the former instance has no particular force, nor does it significantly change the meaning from metaphor. There are two similes in John's Gospel that possess such a metaphorical force. The divine glory of the Word-made-flesh is portrayed "as of the Father's only Son" (*hōs monogenous para patros*, 1:14). Later in the same chapter, John the Baptist describes the Spirit "descending as a dove" on Jesus (*katabainōn hōs peristeran*, 1:32). In neither case is the simile illustrative; on the contrary, the images function as metaphors, with an "is" and "is not" dimension. The Word is not biologically son of God, nor is the Spirit literally a dove. Yet both enlarge dramatically the reader's theological understanding: in the relationship between God and the Word, and in the role of the Spirit in the ministry of Jesus.

To a considerable extent, this outline of metaphor (and simile) correlates more generally with the symbols of the Gospel. Apart from actual metaphors, the symbols include the feasts of Judaism, the characters, the Johannine "signs" (miracles), and the images that emerge from the metaphors. As with metaphors, symbols in general require a second-level understanding for their symbolic nature to emerge, and this is the level of interpretation. From the analysis of dreams to the study of character to the interpretation of art and music, symbols operate on two levels: the perceptible and the imperceptible, the surface and the subterranean, the ordinary and the extraordinary, the palpable and the ethereal. Yet, as L. P. Jones points out in his study of water symbolism in the Fourth Gospel, there are some differences between metaphor and symbol: with symbols the tenor is not always easy to detect (think, for example, of dreams!), remaining elusive and "somewhat mysterious," and symbols tend to be recurring rather than single linguistic events.[51] Nevertheless the essential pattern is the same. Thus, for the fourth evangelist, the first-level meaning relates to material reality and a materialistic interpretation of the world. The second level is the symbolic level, which the narrator wants the reader to grasp and which the Johannine characters struggle to understand. The movement from misunderstanding to understanding is the movement, in literary terms, from the material to the symbolic. The tangible is the means by which the spiritual or symbolic is attained, the latter being impossible without the former. In Johannine theological terms, it is the movement from unbelief to faith.[52]

Sallie McFague argues against the equation of metaphor and symbol in this way. In her study of metaphor, McFague makes an appeal for the development of a metaphorical theology grounded in the parables of Jesus. Using a cognitive understanding of metaphor, McFague underscores the shocking and unconventional character of the parables, stressing that "metaphorical thinking . . . is not illustrative, ornamental, or merely heuristic, but essential."[53] Yet she draws a curious distinction between a symbolic apprehension and a metaphorical one, identifying the former with Catholicism (characterized by similarity, harmony, and continuity) and the latter with Protestantism (skeptical, stressing dissimilarity and discontinuity).[54] For McFague, the medieval worldview possessed a "symbolical mentality" based on a sacramental view of the world.[55] Grounded in the *analogia entis*, the "sacramental universe" presupposes that everything participates in Being and therefore that "everything in such a universe can be a symbol of everything else and, most especially, of God, who created everything out of divine plenitude as a mirror and a reflection of the divine self."[56] Against Tillich, who stresses both the affirmation *and* the negation of the concrete within symbol, McFague sees the symbol as lacking the "is not" dimension of metaphor. Whereas in her view symbol seems to be conservative, metaphor is radical, emphasizing disconnection and newness.

However, the distinction proposed by McFague—whatever it may say about denominational difference—is problematic. Symbol and metaphor cannot be so easily divided. The relationship between the literal and the figurative is not identical in every symbol or metaphor: for some more than others, the literal level retains a sense of its own integrity and meaning, whereas in others the literal level is entirely overtaken by the figurative. Moreover, despite her conviction of the cognitive element within metaphor, McFague's own use of metaphor seems to reduce it to an imaginative game with words and pictures, with minimal reference to external truth claims. Perhaps it is the separation of metaphor from symbol that suggests to her that metaphor possesses a fanciful, if not arbitrary, quality.

Furthermore, it is equally difficult to perceive the force of McFague's claim that the sacramental universe is no longer feasible—a perspective by which, in her own words, "the things of this world, its joys and catastrophes, harvests and famines, births and deaths, are understood as connected to and permeated by divine power and love."[57] Why it is impossible to "return" to such a worldview in which all things are connected to divinity and where the symbol "is neither literalised nor spiritualised" is not made clear.[58] Even taking into account the advances in scientific knowledge, it is hard to see how such a sacramental view of the world can be so lightly dismissed. Leaving aside the question of the "analogy of being," we might ask how the assertion of the "irrelevance" of the sacramental worldview is a strong enough basis for rejecting something so deeply ingrained within the Bible and subsequent Christian tradition; the question surely is one not of relevance but of truth. It is ironic that, in rejecting what is arguably as much part of the Johannine (if not biblical) worldview as it is of the medieval, McFague is compelled to invent the metaphor of the world as God's body, a similar but yet more theologically problematic version of the sacramental universe.[59] Yet, whereas in the New Testament the "body of God" relates specifically to the incarnate Christ and also to the life of the church, for McFague the conception is now located in creation, without an adequate theology of revelation and with a weak doctrine of redemption, cut off from its christological roots.[60] The disconnection between symbol and metaphor creates too many problems, both literary and theological. In the Johannine worldview, at least, the two clearly belong together.

SYMBOL AND ICON

The coherence between metaphor and symbol can be extended to include icons— like metaphor, another subset of symbolism. Indeed, the character of Johannine symbol may be understood more clearly through the role of icons in Eastern Christianity.[61] The Greek word *eikōn* is usually translated into English as "image."

Icons in Orthodox theology are thus pictorial *images* representing sacred events or persons either biblical or within the religious tradition. They are not decorations of the plain truth but visual symbols with cognitive content, the artistic equivalent of metaphors, closely interwoven with theological discourse, liturgy, and spirituality. By their nature icons make no claim to encapsulate or assimilate divine presence but convey a sense of profound attachment and open a pathway between human restlessness and divine love, without at the same time captivating the mystery which revelation itself does not dissolve.[62] They mediate a personal relationship between the viewer and the divine realm: God, Christ, the Theotokos, the communion of saints. Indeed, in Orthodox understanding, Christ is the original *Ikon*, the true *Image* of God, in whose *image* humankind is created (Gen. 1:26–27).

Historically, disputes over icons—particularly at Nicaea II in the eighth century and in the Protestant Reformation in the sixteenth—revolved around two theological issues: the conviction of divine immanence in the incarnation, on the one hand; and the fear of falling back into idolatry on the other. Theologically, disputes over icons have been the outworking of the ambiguity between image as creative symbol and image as propaganda. While the Ten Commandments forbid the making of "graven images" (Exod. 20:3–6; Deut. 4:15–20; 5:7–10), the Scriptures are full of anthropomorphic images of God. In the Jewish and Christian traditions, God is beyond all human attempts at portrayal, yet the efforts to describe God never cease. The problem is how to approach the God who is wholly other except through the symbols of creation. The tension is pertinent to a symbolic reading of the Fourth Gospel. In Johannine terms, symbolic portrayal is a way of drawing out the implications of the incarnation. At the same time, symbols can also become idolatrous: the projection of our own image onto the divine in unconscious and self-promoting ways. The Johannine understanding of symbol is located between these two paradoxical convictions: that God is invisible, unknowable, and unable to be captured in human signs (1:18, 6:46);[63] and that, through Christ, God has radically entered the material realm in human form (1:14).

This theological dialectic is present in the complex relationship between the icon-venerator (or iconodule) and the iconoclast. The argument for icons seems to flow straight from the pages of the Fourth Gospel. There is no such thing as an unmediated and unadulterated experience of God in this view; rather the mystical is engaged through the medium of the senses. This means that, whether pictorial, linguistic, or literary, the icon (like metaphor) is not identical with the reality it attempts to convey. An iconic understanding of the text—since words can operate as "verbal icons"[64]—offers a symbolic resemblance rather than a photographic equivalent, that contains an "is" and an "is not" dimension: "All visible signs *convey and conceal* within them the invisible grace of the operating Holy Spirit."[65] There is a fundamental awareness of divine presence that both contains and complements rational discourse. This is not to deny cognitive content but rather to confirm that the symbol conveys an intelligible yet ineffable sense of presence. The icon generates participation leading to transfiguration. It is precisely this sense of presence, participation, and transformation that lies at the heart of Johannine symbolism.

A further parallel with the symbolism of the Fourth Gospel is that icons are nondualistic, drawing "no sharp distinction between the sacred and the profane, between the physical and the metaphysical,"[66] and arising from an embodied understanding of spirituality. In the Fourth Gospel, the humanity of God hallows creation as the raw material of revelation. For Rahner, "the incarnate word is the absolute symbol of God in the world, filled as nothing else can be with what is symbolised."[67] As Schneiders expresses it, the Johannine Jesus is the "archetypal symbol of God" in the Fourth Gospel;[68] "the foundational symbol, the very revelation of God."[69] All other symbolic forms draw their character and inspiration from this core symbol.[70] Through the outer form, the inner meaning is disclosed: the icon is a window on the eternal, and its physical characteristics—form, shape, color, pigment, stylization, perspective—lead the viewer from one world to another. "Iconicity transcends physicality. It does not erase the physical but overwhelms it, drenching it with significance."[71] From this perspective, human experience is to be taken seriously: however fallible and partial, it is the vehicle of divine revelation. Thus an iconic and symbolic reading of the Fourth Gospel acknowledges the luminous presence of the divine within the contours of the human, endorsing the advent of God in the creaturely world. The Johannine text—itself a large "symbolic narrative"—is, in an iconic understanding, a profound yet also limited and culturally bound "stammering" at the edges of the infinite,[72] a series of partial images unfolding the economy of salvation within the character and purpose of God.

ICON, IMAGE, AND GENDER

There are two issues relating to this discussion of symbol and icon that have important implications for gender study. In the first place, it is not as clear as some feminists would like that women are seen as made (directly) in the image of God.[73] Christianity may claim superiority to Judaism by the fact that baptism, unlike circumcision, is equally available for females and males (see Gal. 3:28), but Christianity has itself questioned whether the divine image is directly present in females or only indirectly through some kind of male source or headship. In 1 Corinthians, for example, Paul seems to speak of a hierarchy that begins with God as the *kephalē*—head or source—of Christ, Christ as the *kephalē* of the man/husband (*anēr*) and the man/husband as the *kephalē* of the woman/wife (*gynē*, 11:3–4). A few verses later he speaks of the man/husband as being "the image and glory" of God (*eikōn kai doxa*), whereas the woman/wife is merely "the glory of man" (11:7). The fact that Paul himself seems confusingly to undercut this hierarchy a few verses later with awareness of a new dispensation, in which woman and man are seen in mutual relations "in Christ" and interdependent (11:11–12), does not resolve the problem of the opening verses.[74] In many respects, the early church was torn between what critical exegesis now regards as two separate creation accounts in Genesis 1–3: the first, which asserts the mutuality of man and woman in sharing the divine image (Gen. 1:26–27), and the second, which portrays woman as created second, for man and from his side (Gen. 2:7–25), the latter implying a hierarchy of relations, particularly if interpreted in the light of the after-effects of the Fall (Gen. 3:16). Paul's own confusion may go back to what appears to be the confusion in the opening accounts of creation. What results is a double message for women, which translates particularly into questions of ministry and leadership. Yet there is no doubt that the tradition at its best confirms the image of God in female as well as male, a point made clear in Augustine's own discussion of Paul's meaning: "Who is there then who will make women alien from this fellowship, since they are co-heirs of grace with us?" (*De trinitate* 12.12).[75]

Whether the Fourth Gospel shares this confusion is unclear, as the terminology of "image" is not used. Nevertheless, it is arguable that John does regard females as sharing in the divine image with males. As we will see in later chapters, the stories of the Samaritan woman and Mary Magdalene portray women in independent relationship to men, yet drawn into the orbit of Jesus' public ministry. The mother of Jesus is herself given an iconic role in the faith and life of the new community. Both Martha and Mary represent the community of faith in its confession of faith: one portraying its credal life, and the other the mutuality of love between disciples and Jesus. It is clear that these women share, with men, the status of being "children of God," a concept closely related to that of the image. Whether or not this mutuality translated into equality of status in leadership within the Johannine community is unknown: communities do not always reflect their own iconography or theology in practical realities. What is important is that, in this Gospel, believing women and men in their narrative portrayal share and reflect the divine image restored in the incarnate Christ. Their role, like that of men, is symbolic of that communion of persons which stems from the being of God.

Second, it must be admitted that modern feminist theology in its critique of the tradition would doubtless prefer to stand in the tradition of the iconoclasts rather than the iconodules— those who venerate the icons. Does this alienate feminism from the iconic perspective of the Fourth Gospel? It may be that, depending on how we interpret it, iconoclasm is not absent from this Gospel. The critique of "the Jews," for example, without denying its problems (if read only at the literal level),[76] is in one sense iconoclastic, representing an attack on religion that is self-serving and life-denying. The God of the Fourth Gospel cannot be encapsulated in any creaturely category, notwithstanding the legitimacy and centrality of its symbolic language—a perspective that, in its concern for divine transcendence, is also characteristic of iconoclasm.[77] It is possible, indeed, that we need to distinguish between iconoclasm and iconophobia—or at least speak of different kinds and degrees of iconoclasm. According to John of Damascus, the great champion of icons in the period of Nicaea II, the veneration of icons was not idolatrous but a gateway to God: the divine through the human, the glory through the flesh.[78] This viewpoint is undoubtedly closer to the Johannine view than that of the iconoclasts. Yet, for the iconoclasts on the other side, certain symbols—in whatever form—appeared like a retreat into idolatry. Is this necessarily the same as the violent opposition to icons (in any shape or form) that the church has witnessed in more than one controversy? Iconoclasm can have the positive role of idol- (rather than icon-) breaking, where the likeness between signifier and signified is so misleading that the connection between them needs to be severed. The iconoclastic dimension, in this sense, might operate not so much to exclude iconic expression as to confirm divine transcendence over against idolatry. More importantly for our purposes, the iconoclastic dimension, where it involves a critical engagement with the symbols and is concerned to avoid idolatry, may have a place. In one sense, it expresses the "is not" dimension of the symbols.

This dynamic is pertinent to women's rereading of the Christian heritage. In that feminist hermeneutics has identified itself with the iconoclasts over against those who venerate the "icons" within Scripture and tradition, there is a vital concern to reassert the mystery of God over against what is perceived as idolatry in parts of the Christian tradition.[79] Some forms of feminism would undoubtedly see an oppressive dogmatics at work in any interpretation that seeks to recover the tradition. Nevertheless, the critique of idolatry aimed at paternalistic power may allow the tradition to speak in new ways. The symbolic and iconic perspective of the Fourth Gospel can be interpreted to women's advantage, challenging perceptions of female invisibility in ways that ideological moralizing and political declamation cannot, and defining the core of faith as intrinsically hospitable to women, despite all attempts to say otherwise. Women belong within the iconographic structures of this Gospel: here, if nowhere else, their place at the core of faith is assured. In terms of gender reading, a symbolic and iconic reading offers a beneficial model for feminist theology that avoids the extremes of either reformist fundamentalism or post-Christian exile. The recovery of such symbolism opens the way for a radically new, yet also strong and ancient, iconography that draws women and men into the life of faith. Interpreted in this sense, iconoclasm and iconophilia are not opposites but exist in a dialectical relationship: both can be used to identify and purify the core symbols of faith.

SYMBOL AND REVELATION

As we have seen, the basic theological issue underlying symbolism and icons is how human beings, in human language, can name that which is transcendent and by definition beyond the forms of creaturely life. Frances Young discusses the problem in relation to patristic use of allegory and typology,[80] pointing out that the early fathers—especially Gregory of Nyssa and Athanasius—were aware of the problem of naming God and believed that earthly language could be "elevated" to speak of the divine, which is beyond all human categories.[81] As a consequence of this, Gregory states:

> While, however, we strenuously avoid all concurrence with absurd notions in our thoughts of God, we allow ourselves the use of many diverse appellations in regard to Him, adapting them to our point of view. For whereas no one suitable word [*onoma*] has been found to express the divine nature, we address God by many names, each by some distinctive touch adding something fresh to our notions respecting Him—thus seeking by variety of nomenclature to gain some glimmerings for the comprehension of what we seek. (*Contra Eunomium Libri* II.144–45)[82]

Thus God-talk is seen as a stretched form of language in which God is accommodated to human "signs." At the same time, the names are not arbitrary nor merely of human creation. Gregory himself distinguishes between those designations of God in Scripture that relate to the divine economy of salvation and those which have to do with divine essence. Scripture itself is seen as polyvalent and sacramental, communicating a sense of the divine that employs yet transcends the categories of human existence. God-language is referential but in a way that exceeds all linguistic utterance.[83]

Northrop Frye has proposed three phases or levels of language in order to illustrate the shift in linguistic understanding that separates us from the biblical and patristic periods. Frye speaks of the metaphorical phase, the analogical or sacramental phase, and the descriptive phase.[84] The first level, associated particularly with Homer, presupposes a poetic understanding of language in which words are concrete and seen as having dynamic power to bring into being; the second, beginning with Plato, arises from an intellectual understanding and a consequent degree of abstraction, in which words become "the outward expression of inner thoughts or ideas";[85] the third, which commences with the Renaissance and flourishes in the Enlightenment, is deductive, separating subject and object, treating language as primarily descriptive. These phases move from an understanding in which "the word evokes the thing" to the Enlightenment belief that "the thing evokes the word."[86] The Bible belongs to the first phase, the poetic—to which, for Frye, we need to return—and the development of Christian theology is located in the second, although Gregory of Nyssa and Athanasius belong somewhere between the first two phases. Within this schema, we might well argue that exegesis, for the most part, has located itself in the third phase—ironically, at greatest distance from the biblical understanding and use of language. In theological discourse, giving priority to the first phase of language, with recognition of the place of the second, means a return to a symbolic understanding of the naming of God and of the plenitude of meaning within symbolism. God's elusive, transcendent being, both revealed and concealed, calls for symbol and metaphor as that form of eloquence most suited to it.

What are the implications for our understanding of revelation in the Fourth Gospel? It is clear that poetic language, whether in metaphor, imagery, irony, metonymy or other figures of speech, has the capacity to create new meaning, conveying that which has its source in divine revelation beyond the material realm. Revelation is a given from this perspective: its symbolic meaning and structures are divinely shaped. The frame of reference in which revelation comes, through Scripture and tradition, is itself constitutive of theological meaning and Christian identity: "in the beginning was the Word" (John 1:1). This is the essence of Frye's first phase of language (or myth) in which the word, or symbol, "evokes the thing." On the other hand, in the Fourth Gospel symbol is also something that arises from human experience and creaturely existence ("and the Word became flesh," 1:14). Symbol can be seen paradoxically as the limited expression of a reality that transcends anything that human speech or imagination can articulate. Here we move closer to the second phase, with awareness of the distinction between form and content, language and reality. From this perspective, our experience of the transcendent (whether joyful or painful) is ineffable. It seems never large enough, never precise enough, never as profound as the experience demands: too banal, prosaic, sentimental, obscure, inaccurate, ponderous. The symbolism of the Fourth Gospel is always reaching beyond itself. There is a gulf between "signs" and reality, an awareness of an otherness that cannot be captured in human utterance. Gregory of Nyssa is himself conscious of the abyss between the divine and human which intrudes itself into theological language, even where it is most poetic and symbolic:

> But, as I am so taught by the inspired Scripture, I boldly affirm that He Who is above every name has for us many names, receiving them in accordance with the variety of His gracious dealings with us, being called the Light when He disperses the gloom of ignorance, and the Life when He grants the boon of immortality, and the Way when He guides us from error to the truth. (*Contra Eunomium Libri* III.8.10)[87]

Here the essence of God escapes our classification or inspection; yet the symbols themselves have the miraculous power to bring us into the domain of salvation.

In the Fourth Gospel, revelation is complex, having by definition a divine and a human dimension. Originating "from above" it discloses itself within the framework of that which is "from below," that being the source of its symbolic power. Comparing Jesus and John the Baptist (in a neutral way), the Johannine evangelist comments: "The one who comes from above is above all things; the one who is from the earth is from the earth and speaks from the earth" (3:31).[88] Earlier in the same chapter, Jesus draws a distinction between "earthly things" (*ta epigeia*) and "heavenly things" (*ta epourania*): if Nicodemus fails to understand the "earthiness" of the birth symbolism, how could he understand the "language" of heaven (3:12)? Revelation originates in the divine realm, "from above," but through the sending of the divine Word it is disclosed within the flesh, "from below," within the domain of the creaturely. "Only in *ta epigeia* are *ta epourania* revealed."[89] Symbols in this Gospel, like icons, are themselves the expression of the coming together of divine and human, the transcendent and the immanent, the spiritual and the this-worldly.

When, toward the end of the Farewell Discourse, Jesus promises to speak no longer to the disciples *en paroimiais* ("figures of speech"? "riddles"? 16:25), and the disciples claim at last to understand him because he now speaks "openly" (*en parrēsią*, 16:29–30), the evangelist is not implying that there is an accessible form of communication more basic or quintessential than symbol or metaphor. The "hour" to which Jesus alludes at 16:25 is the supremely *symbolic* moment of his exaltation on the cross and return to the glory of the Father. The point is that, as a result of this event, and with the consequential advent of the Paraclete, the disciples will finally understand the purpose of Jesus' coming and departure (16:28) and not be confused by its meaning. The symbols will be able to function as translucent symbols, not as opaque barriers, as the image of "birth" is for Nicodemus in John 3. The flesh will no longer be a closed door but will lead the believing community to the vision of divine glory.

Noting the symbolic nature of theological language thus has important implications. Because the theological referent of symbolic language is transcendent, more than one symbol (or set of symbols) is needed to express the breadth and depth of that which it connotes. Although meaningful in itself, no single metaphor, image, or icon is exhaustive of meaning. In biblical language, moreover, metaphors inhabit complex fields of reference. The "logic" of symbolic language is coherent but not necessarily linear. One can move within different constellations, maintaining an internal cogency that does not rule out other ways of expressing the same (or similar) realities. For example, it is possible to speak of the Johannine Jesus as "son" yet also in another sense as "mother." In a similar way, Ephrem can sing of the sword that excludes from paradise and the sword that pierces Jesus' side as being symbolically and theologically the same, despite the lack of connectedness from a strictly exegetical viewpoint: "Blessed is He who was pierced/and so removed the sword from the entry to Paradise" (*Hymns on Paradise* 2, response). In each case, the symbols belong within different fields of reference, in each of which meaning has internal coherence. It is possible to make the leap from one field to another, from one constellation to another, and to find in each a new set of metaphorical "rules." This need not imply that symbolic and metaphorical language is arbitrary and transmutable; on the contrary, the Fourth Gospel has a distinctive set of symbols that are integral to its evangelical and revelatory core. In the Johannine sense, "real metaphors are not translatable."[90]

In the end, symbols take us to the threshold of divine mystery: they reveal and conceal, convey yet do not capture, evoke without exhausting meaning. Mystical theology sees this recognition of the power yet limitations of symbol as the *apophatic*, the theological movement away from speech when faced with a reality that surpasses yet embraces the creaturely world. It is linked to the *via negativa* (negative theology) in which the divine is described in terms of what God is not, rather than what God is. God's being can never be appropriated or described directly: no human speech or symbol is adequate to contain it: "Whoever is capable of investigating becomes the container of what he investigates; a knowledge which is capable of containing the Omniscient is greater than Him, for it has proved capable of measuring the whole of Him."[91]

Yet such symbols are themselves the product of revelation, God's gracious self-accommodation to human finitude. A powerful symbol of this paradoxical dynamic in the narrative of the Fourth Gospel is the emptiness of the place where the body of Jesus has lain, guarded by angels at the head and foot (20:11–12). Here, as Mary Magdalene soon discovers, is an emptiness that paradoxically "announces the plenitude of God's presence."[92]

Finally, we observe that the pattern of symbol and icon operating through the medium of the material is inscribed in the Gospel's central theological conviction. The theological and literary character of the Fourth Gospel is grounded in the incarnation, as we will see in the next chapter, the union of literary form and theological meaning parallelling the union of divine and human in the person of Jesus. Just as the Synoptic parables consist of a metaphor, a narrative, and an outside reference point (the reign of God),[93] so the Johannine text has a similar dynamic between metaphor/symbol, narrative, and external reference point. The purpose of the Johannine narrative is to unfold the symbolism, and the emergence of the symbolism draws out the narrative, communicating "eternal life" (*zōē aiōnios*) to the reader of the Gospel. The process is similar to the way the hearer or reader of the parables comes face-to-face with the reign of God, even in the telling, so that the ordinary becomes revelatory of the extraordinary. Just as the Synoptic parables are intimately related to Jesus, so too with the narrative of the Fourth Gospel.

The symbolism of the Fourth Gospel is neither arbitrary nor decorative, but intrinsic to revelation. A symbolic and iconic reading will take us to the heart of this Gospel, as no abstract and disembodied theology or stolid exegesis can. The symbols are bearers of reality, yet even those closest to the core do not attempt to imprison or delimit that reality in constrictive ways. There is always a raggedness around the edges, an opening up to new meaning, a sense of reality expanding, an awareness of ineptitude. Symbols are efficacious and luminous yet also give rise to a kind of humility of the senses, taking us to the edges of a reality that is beyond the power of expression. They function as icons through which the reader (viewer) glimpses the glory of the eternal, a glory that is radiant in its capacity to generate life and love. In this worldview, imagination plays a key role. Once restored, imagination—which is closely allied to faith—enables the reader to enter the symbolic world of the Gospel with transforming effects. It is these symbols that give shape and substance to Christian faith, even though none is adequate to comprehend the ineffable God who chooses to be disclosed in the fragile beauty of the flesh. It is to this divine-human miracle that we now turn.

CHAPTER 2

Restoring Glory:
The Symbol of Jesus' Flesh

Love's will requires your own, that in
The flesh whose love you do not know,
Love's knowledge into flesh may grow.[1]

SYMBOLIC READING of the Fourth Gospel begins theologically with the Johannine understanding of the incarnation. The divine Word (*logos*), whose being is "turned towards" the Father in love and intimacy (*pros*, 1:1, 2),[2] and who created the universe, enters the world in human form at a specific point in history in order to communicate the life and love of God. With its complex background in Jewish and Hellenistic thought,[3] the image of Christ as the Word is essentially symbolic: the Johannine Jesus is the Symbol of God, the true Icon from which the other symbols of the Gospel derive meaning. The incarnation is the centerpiece of the Johannine symbolic universe, upon which all else is built.[4] It is not the maleness of Jesus that has symbolic significance in this worldview but rather his embodiment in material/human form. In this chapter, we turn to the Johannine language of incarnation, observing the way in which the symbolism of "flesh" (*sarx*) and its related imagery unfolds divine glory (*doxa*) in the person of Jesus, in order to restore glory to the "scattered children of God" (11:52).

In a number of important ways, the language of flesh in John's Gospel signifies far more than a reconstruction of the historical Jesus. The symbolism, without lacking historical foundation, draws out the significance of divine embodiment within the life, death, and resurrection of Jesus of Nazareth. We have already seen that symbol is not to be confused with decoration: very different from the common misconception that rhetorical figures function as "sweeteners" or pedagogical aids. Symbol and metaphor are concerned with the creation of new meaning. Being multivalent, they are not exhaustive but contain a "surplus of meaning" that leaves them open to new readers, new contexts, and new shades of meaning; but, having a referential quality, their range of meaning is not infinite. Symbols can be explained—indeed, they require explication at different points—but the paraphrase is never as powerful or meaningful as the original and cannot ultimately replace it. To speak of the incarnation in symbolic terms, therefore, is not to deny the affinity of the Johannine Jesus with the earthly Jesus; nor does it deny the truth-claims of the Gospel. Yet it is the symbolic import—both cognitive and affective—that has the capacity to engage the reader and lead to the revelation of glory.

Of its thirteen occurrences in the Johannine text, *sarx* occurs in five different contexts: the Prologue (1:13–14), the dialogue with Nicodemus (3:6), the Bread of Life narrative (6:51–56, 63), the Tabernacles Discourse (7:38; 8:15) and the Great Prayer (17:2).[5] In addition, there are other synonymous physiological terms that are part of the same semantic field: *haima* (blood), *sōma* (body), *koilia* (belly, womb), *kolpos* and *stēthos* (both meaning "breast"), *anthrōpos* (human being), Jesus' thirst (*dipsan*), the phrase *haima kai hydōr* (blood and water), the mark of the nails (*ho typos tōn hēlōn*) and the wounded side (*hē pleura*). Although *sarx* is the most significant word, it is not the only way of designating Jesus' humanity, and it is important to avoid a linguistic literalism that sees concepts or images residing only in particular words or expressions. We may also note the references to Jesus' home-town (1:45; 7:41–42), his parents (1:45; 2:1–12; 6:42; 19:25–27), his brothers [/sisters?] (2:12; 7:2–10) and his friends (11:1–3), all of which serve to establish his human identity.[6] At the same time, as we will see, the "signs" (*sēmeia*) of Jesus' ministry themselves have a material quality that connects them in a distinctive sense to the incarnation.

THE JOHANNINE PROLOGUE

The incarnation is first introduced in the Prologue to the Gospel (1:1–18). Literary studies have demonstrated that the Prologue is not just the beginning of the narrative but also the Gospel's "ground of being," pervading the story from beginning to end.[7] It is the key to the Gospel, setting out the major themes unfolded through the narrative: life, light and darkness, sending, witness, the world, authority, rebirth, enfleshment, glory, truth, revelation. It is often noted that other important terms are not found elsewhere in the Gospel—Logos (in its christological sense), fullness, grace—indicating that the Prologue had its origins in a hymn, possibly from the Johannine community.[8] Even if this is so, it does not mean that the incarnation, as with other themes and symbols of the Prologue, is alien to and therefore absent from the Gospel's conceptual framework.[9] Whatever its prehistory, the final author has made the Prologue the foundation stone of the Gospel.[10] The Prologue, with its theme of the divine Logos dwelling in intimacy with the Father yet entering the world in human form to forge the same intimacy with "his own" (1:11),[11] dominates the Gospel like a vast, Gothic archway, giving those who enter the sense of what they are to discover. Or, to change the metaphor, it is the hub to which the spokes forming the Gospel's wheel are all attached. It holds together the ensuing narrative, making sense of the whole.

The christological title "Logos," which is central to the Prologue, has rich connotations arising from the Old Testament within three main fields of reference. It is linked first of all to creation and the dynamic word of God which gives birth to the world. In the first creation account (Gen. 1:1–2:3 LXX), with its balanced symmetry and orderly progression of days, God *speaks* all things into being on each day of the first week (*kai ho theos eipen*), *names* each thing, *assigns* each its place and function, and *blesses* all that is made. From the darkness of chaos this creative word draws out order and being, variety and complexity, fecundity and beauty, activity and rest. On the fifth and sixth days, living creatures are formed beginning with the fish and birds (day 5), then the animals and humankind (day 6). The fertility of each is intrinsic, guaranteeing the flourishing of each kind, but to human beings alone is given "dominion" over other living creatures, because they are created in the divine image and likeness (*eikōn kai homoiōsis*, Gen. 1:26–28). In this context, the divine *logos* is the foundation of the world's being, cause of its fecundity, and source of its felicity: it has no animation—past, present, or future—apart from that creative word. This is foundational also for the Prologue, which refers both to creation and incarnation in the same terms and within the same frame of reference. The Johannine symbolism derives from the opening words of the Gospel, "in the beginning" (*en archę*), which are identical to the first words of Genesis in the Greek Old Testament (LXX).

Second, the divine *logos* in the Old Testament is prominent in the foundational events of Israel's history: in the call of Abraham and the promise of descent (Gen. 12; 17:1–18:15); in the painful blessing of Jacob and the giving of a new name, Israel (Gen. 32:22–32); in the revelation to Moses of the divine Name, which will effect the liberation of Israel from slavery and journey to the Promised Land (Exod. 3); in the giving of the Law (Torah) and the Ten Commandments (Exod. 20:1–17; Deut. 5:6–21); and in the prophets, where God addresses the word of judgment and salvation to Israel—judgment against idolatry and injustice, and salvation as the restoration of the covenant to which God alone remains faithful.[12] The word of judgment is purifying (e.g., Mal. 3:2–4), effecting a renewal of the covenant (Jer. 31:31–34), and the word of salvation brings consolation to the suffering people of God (Isa. 40:1–11). As with creation, this word brings life out of darkness, chaos, and nothingness: in the later context, it speaks from the experience of exile, suffering, infidelity, desolation, dispersal, and death. God's *logos* is the basis not only of creation but also of the covenant relationship with Israel, as God's people, God's children, God's chosen ones. The creative Word which judges and saves is vital for John's Christology, where the Logos is personalized in Jesus. What John reveals in the Prologue is that God's communication is no less than *divine self-communication in human form*: in continuity with God's communication to Israel, certainly, but intensified in the vehicle by which that communication is made. It is the same Word which judges and gives life in the Johannine Jesus.

In the Wisdom writings, there is a third dimension to God's creative and redemptive word that has significantly influenced the Fourth Gospel. This resides in the notion of wisdom (*sophia*), which is used synonymously with *logos* (Wis. 9:1–2). Studies over the last couple of decades have demonstrated the way in which *sophia* in the Old Testament and Intertestamental writings moves from being a quality necessary for a sensible and prudent life (where it is grounded in a theology of creation) to a more personified, if not personalized conception— partly under the influence of Hellenistic thought—until it evokes a dimension of God's own self, associated with creation and God's redemption of Israel.[13] Thus Sophia is portrayed (like Torah) as preexisting with God before creation and as leading Israel out of Egypt into the Promised Land.[14] The Prologue is profoundly influenced by this vision of Sophia, and it is a major, if implicit, source of John's Christology both in and beyond the Prologue. Elizabeth Johnson argues that "[w]hat Judaism said of Sophia, Christian hymn makers and epistle writers now came to say of Jesus," and demonstrates how the Fourth Gospel "is simply suffused with wisdom themes."[15] Like Wisdom, the Logos is preexistent, descends from above, is both hidden and revealed, is accepted by some and rejected by others, forms an intimate relationship with disciples, and reveals divine glory and life.[16] Jesus is presented in this Gospel as "Wisdom incarnate."[17]

The Prologue, despite some unevenness, has a concentric structure, the end returning to its beginning in the relationship between God and the divine Logos/Wisdom (1:1–2, 18). Yet the end is not identical to the beginning. Much has been revealed of the Logos in between, particularly in relation to creation: that he is its creator and source of its light and life, beyond all power of darkness (1:3–5, 9); that "the world" has failed to recognize him (1:10–11); that those who do recognize him enter into a new relationship with God through the same creative power (1:12–13); that the Logos has entered creation in material form and in that context revealed the Father's true nature (1:14, 16–18). In the last verse of the Prologue, the two dimensions of the Logos come together: like Janus, the Roman god of the door, he faces two directions at the same time, turned both to God and to the world, occupying a unique place as the gateway or bridge between heaven and earth. Dwelling in intimacy with the Father (1:18), he turns to face the world and discloses therein the Father's true nature. Similarly the ending of the Gospel will return to its beginnings, particularly in Thomas's declaration of the risen Christ as "my Lord and my God" (20:28).

"Flesh" appears twice in the Prologue in close proximity, setting out the core Johannine symbol of faith. Its background in Jewish and Hellenistic thought is surprisingly diverse. The word *sarx* has a range of meanings in classical thought and can refer to part or all of the body (human or animal), the seat of emotion and desire, or even the pulp of fruit.[18] In some contexts it can take on a distinctly negative connotation, in conjunction with a dualistic anthropology, where, particularly in Plato, it is seen as tainting or imprisoning the soul.[19] In the Old Testament (where it mostly translates the Hebrew *bāśār*), *sarx* is largely a positive concept, sometimes referring to the body itself or part of the body—for example, in circumcision (Gen. 17:11)—but more generally manifesting a holistic anthropology that does not strictly separate soul and body. Adam's response to the creation of Eve from his body, for example, is to declare that she is "bone of my bones and flesh of my flesh" (Gen. 2:23): as his desired partner, a role no other living being could play, she becomes in partnership with him "one flesh," an unashamed union of body, mind, and heart (Gen. 2:24–25). Similarly, the Psalmist speaks of the longing for God in parallel spiritual and physical terms that mean more or less the same thing: "my soul thirsts for you; my flesh faints for you" (Ps. 63:1). Often in the Old Testament and Judaism, the mortality and fragility of flesh contrast with the eternal being and power of God, a vital contrast for its influence on Johannine theology.[20] In a further sense, while uniquely possessing the divine image, Adam and Eve are not unique in being formed of flesh. Elsewhere in the Old Testament, flesh relates to all living creatures: "of every living thing, of all flesh, you shall bring two of every kind into the ark" (Gen. 6:19); "everything that opens the womb of all flesh, human and animal . . . shall be yours" (Num. 18:15); God is the one "who gives food to all flesh" (Ps. 135 [136]:25). John's Gospel is heir to these Old Testament traditions, without any indication of an anthropological dualism that sunders body and soul. Nor does "flesh" have the negative connotations sometimes found in the Pauline writings, where in some contexts it is symbolic of the Old Age with its self-destructive patterns of sin and death (e.g., Rom. 7:14–8:17; 1 Cor. 3:2–3; Gal. 5:16–26). John's use of *sarx* and other related terms reflects something of the same Old Testament diversity, although a unifying theology underlies his usage.

The first occurrence in the Prologue is in relation to human life, where rebirth is the action of God and not the result of flesh (1:13): "As many as received him he gave them authority to become children of God, to those believing in his name, who were born not of blood nor of the will of *flesh* nor of the will of a man but of God" (1:12–13).[21] It is hard to discern a clear distinction between the three phrases of 1:13, but they seem to cover the whole process of procreation and birth, with male and female elements. The reference to blood is in the plural (lit., "bloods") and probably refers in this context both to conception, which was often imagined in the ancient world as being caused by the mingling of female blood and male seed (see Wis. 7:2),[22] and childbirth itself.[23] The phrase "will of the flesh" refers to sexual desire but expresses also the human choice involved in procreation, particularly in producing an heir.[24] The "will of a man" reinforces this desire, but also points to the male initiative in reproduction, according to ancient biology, in which the seed is the source of life. The contrast, however, is not between body and soul, since the will (*thelēma*) as well as the body is involved in reproduction, but between human embodied existence and the divine realm—in Johannine terms "above" and "below." Through the divine Logos, God has created all things, including flesh (cf. 17:2), yet that same flesh does not possess the divine "authority" (*exousia*, 1:12) to bring about new birth. Although divinely fashioned, the flesh is ineffective to procure its own salvation: in between creation and God hovers the "darkness" that obscures the face-to-face relatedness of creation to its Creator (1:5). Only God, not flesh, can enable believers to become "God's kin-folk."[25] Rudolf Schnackenburg argues that, for John, *sarx* "expresses that which is earth-bound . . . , transient and perishable . . . , the typically human mode of being, as it were, in contrast to all that is divine and spiritual."[26] In a similar way, Rudolf Bultmann argues that *sarx* in the Fourth Gospel signifies the "transitoriness, help-lessness and vanity" of the world in relation to salvation, as opposed to "darkness," which denotes the world in its hostility toward God.[27] The transitory life of cre-ation contrasts with the eternal being of God, who is transcendently distinct from all created life.

The second occurrence of "flesh," in the next verse (1:14), brings us to what is arguably the central affirmation of the Prologue: "and the Word became *flesh* and dwelt among us" (*kai ho logos sarx egeneto kai eskēnōsen en hēmin*, 1:14a).[28] Flesh here is a form of metonymy, indicating the full humanity which the divine Logos assumes, a humanity that is embodied and spirited. From the perspective of the reader, this declaration is the last thing we expect to hear. The divine Word/Wis-dom as agent of creation may well enter the world but not surely in flesh—espe-cially since the weakness and fragility of flesh have just been contrasted with the dynamic power of God. The Logos, we would expect, belongs only on the other side, possessing that divine power which brings life from nothingness. Yet the cen-tral paradox of this Gospel is that the Logos crosses the divide and radically enters the domain of "flesh": "born yet not born, carnal yet spiritual, weak yet strong, dying yet living" (Tertullian, *Treatise on the Incarnation* 5.38–40). It is perhaps sur-prising—at least in retrospect—that the Prologue does not declare what we have come to assume: that God became "man" in the generic sense of "human being" (*anthrōpos*; cf. the Latin *homo*) as opposed to the male *anēr* (Latin *vir*), used in 1:13.[29] Rather it discloses that the divine Logos becomes flesh and in that flesh "we beheld his glory."

Glory is a central Johannine theme, appearing here for the first time but found throughout the Fourth Gospel, either as a noun (*doxa*)[30] or in its verbal form "to glorify" (*doxazein*).[31] For the most part, "glory" in the New Testament world, in common with its antecedents in the Old Testament—particularly the Greek ver-sion—is a theological term that is fundamentally concerned with God and only in a secondary sense applies to human beings. Glory in the biblical world signifies the powerful and radiant reality of God, both in its holy otherness and transcendence, and in its engaging nearness to human life. It expresses "the splendor or majesty or overwhelming weightiness of the divine presence."[32] This means, in effect, that *doxa* defines the divine being or essence "either in its invisible or its perceptible form."[33] The Johannine revelation of the glory, manifested through symbol, follows the same tradition: glory unfolds the divine being as radically loving, self-giving, and life-giving. Where the divine glory is manifest, there flourish love, friendship, truth, freedom, unity, joy, and peace. In the Fourth Gospel, glory is profoundly christological: Jesus himself is the revelation of the glory because the same radiance, that majestic yet intimate presence, is manifested fully in him, in his preexistence as well as his incarnation. The Johannine Jesus participates in that which is most characteristic of the divine realm and the divine being: "*doxa*, for John, means nothing other than Jesus' divinity."[34] Not only his incarnation but also his ministry, in its "signs" and works, represents the manifestation of glory; above all, the cross reveals glory because there God's true being is disclosed in its fullness. There is also a sense in which both Jesus and the Father are "glorified" throughout the Gospel: particularly in the passion, each is responsible for "glorifying" the other (13:31; 17:1–5). Jesus glorifies the Father by revealing God's true nature as loving and life-giving, whereas the Father glorifies Jesus in exalting him to his former glory. The cross becomes a ladder to heaven by which Jesus returns to his native abode and former glory, drawing all people (all things?) to himself as he ascends (12:22; cf. 1:51). In the same way, before the passion, Jesus prays for those with whom he has shared the glory (17:22).

In 1:14, the language of glory is dependent more specifically on Old Testament imagery associated with Mount Zion. The dwelling of the Logos in human form (*eskēnōsen*, literally "tabernacled" or "pitched his tent") parallels the tabernacle [*skēnē*] as the temporal dwelling-place of God's glory: "O Lord, I have loved the beauty of your house, and the place of the dwelling of your glory [*skēnōmatos doxēs sou*]" (Ps. 25:8 LXX).[35] For John, the divine indwelling is symbolized in the temple and points to the eschatological advent of the Logos in which God's glory now abides.[36] There are wisdom overtones in this language: Sophia is described as "a breath of the power of God, and an unmixed emanation of the glory [*doxa*] of the Almighty" (Wis. 7:25; cf. 9:8–11). In Wisdom's hymn of praise in Sirach, Sophia declares of herself that "the one who created me gave a resting-place for my tent [*skēnē*]. And he said, 'Dwell [*kataskēnōson*] in Jacob, and in Israel receive your inheritance'" (Sir. 24:8). What 1:14 discloses is the revelation of divine glory radiating from the flesh. C. K. Barrett describes this as "the paradox which runs through the whole gospel: the *doxa* is not to be seen *alongside* the *sarx*, nor *through* the *sarx* as through a window; it is to be seen in the *sarx* and nowhere else."[37]

The focus on christological identity is significant for its bearing on salvation. The "we" of 1:14 defines those who have received divine birth (1:12–13) with a sense of intimacy and belonging that points to the community of faith, from which the Gospel emerges and to which it is addressed.[38] The dynamic between "flesh" in 1:13 and "flesh" in 1:14 is a transfiguring, twofold movement: believers come to share in the divine nature, just as—and indeed solely because—the Logos comes to share in human nature. It may seem as if these verses ought to be reversed, if the effects of 1:12–13 are dependent on 1:14. John's logic, however, does not operate in a linear way:[39] the advent of the Logos in the world has already been alluded to in 1:9–11 and is implied in 1:5. While remaining transcendent, the Word/Son takes the form of the human and in doing so transforms humanity to become "children of God" (*tekna tou theou*, 1:12), resplendent with divine glory. Athanasius, as we will see, understands this in terms of the restoration of the divine image, given and lost in the opening chapters of Genesis. Throughout the Gospel narrative, many come to acknowledge Jesus as the Word-made-flesh, particularly in the crucifixion and resurrection narratives, where the divine glory is most poignantly seen and witnessed by the apostolic community. As Augustine points out, this "sight" is itself the result of divine healing (Augustine, *In Joannis Evangelium* 2.16). The "we" of 1:14 behold the glory in the flesh, confessing its "grace and truth" (1:17).

In this sense we can speak of "flesh" as a core symbol in the Fourth Gospel:[40] it bears and conveys divine glory just as metaphor operates to disclose new meaning. This meaning is primarily christological: it is the flesh of "Jesus Christ" (first named at 1:17), which bears the glory. Revelation thus has a paradoxical form, being divine in origin: "the only Son, God, who is in the embrace of the Father, has *revealed* him" (*exegēsato*, 1:18). Yet the preexistence of the Logos which signifies the eternal being of the Son is disclosed in the categories of space and time (cf. 1:30; 8:58; 17:5, 24). Revelation arises from within the structures and shape of human experience and materiality (*sarx*). Without the miracle of faith, made possible only through the advent of the Logos in human flesh, human beings of themselves are incapable of divine disclosure: they can barely recognize their own Creator. In the Johannine worldview, the symbol of the flesh revealing the divine glory becomes universal because it is first particular: only now, because God has taken on flesh, can all flesh disclose the glory of God. What is at stake is the reality of salvation.

ALLUSIONS TO FLESH IN THE MINISTRY OF JESUS

The incarnational and symbolic nature of John's Christology is evidenced in the "signs" (*sēmeia*) and works (*erga*) of Jesus' ministry. As the first "sign" at Cana makes plain, the purpose of the miracles is to reveal the divine *doxa* in order to lead the disciples to faith (2:11). The "signs" relate mostly to the healing or restoring of the flesh: the healing of the royal official's son and the disabled man at the Pool (4:46–5:9), the feeding of the hungry (6:1–15), the restoring of sight to the man born blind (9:1–41), and the raising of Lazarus from the dead (11:38–44). Udo Schnelle, who argues that John has an explicitly antidocetic purpose, says that "the miracle is the locus of revelation of the *doxa* of the fleshly Jesus"; the miracles are the deeds of the *logos ensarkos*.[41] In arguing that there is no antimiracle polemic in John, Schnelle stresses the importance of the *sēmeion* as "bound up with the earthly and subject to verification in space and time," unfolding Jesus' humanity and the *doxa* of his divinity.[42] Although we are not speaking directly of Jesus' flesh, there is, as it were, a fleshly quality to the *sēmeia*. Schnelle, like Marianne Meye Thompson, rightly sees a fundamental link between the "flesh" of Jesus and the tangible and corporeal nature of the miracles.[43] Nevertheless, what is important is not their miracle-working quality (as against Schnelle), but rather their christological significance: they are "not events referring or pointing to something extraneous to themselves; rather, in them *the doxa of the Christ actually takes place*."[44] The "signs" function as symbols,[45] taking the reader from the material to the symbolic, from flesh to glory, transfiguring the *sarx* to radiate the presence and power of divine glory.

The next explicit reference to the incarnation, in the cleansing of the temple, uses the term "body" (*sōma*) rather than "flesh." John speaks of the temple here as the antitype of the "body" of Jesus which will rise from the dead: Jesus, the evangelist tells us, "was speaking of the temple of his body" (2:21).[46] The change of terminology should not be overemphasized; the full significance will not emerge until the passion narrative. Yet the symbolic meaning already begins to appear in the reference to the temple, establishing a connection with the verb used in 1:14 (*eskēnōsen*). The flesh/body of Jesus reveals the divine glory, just as the temple revealed the glory of God for Israel (cf. Isa. 6:1–5). Now the symbol of Jesus' humanity expands to include his risen presence. The reference here is proleptic: the reader will not understand until the passion and resurrection narratives, when we will bear witness to Jesus' "body," crucified and risen.

In John 3, Jesus uses the word "flesh" in the context of the symbol of birth, responding to Nicodemus's misunderstanding of his challenge to conversion.[47] Nicodemus's failure to comprehend birth as a metaphor of entry into eternal life is clear from his assumption that the adverb *anōthen* means "again" in a literal, biological sense rather than the spiritual meaning it has for John. The primary meaning of *anōthen* in the Fourth Gospel is "from above," which is a direct reference to the Spirit, although it also has the secondary meaning of "again" in a metaphorical sense.[48] Jesus' two parallel solemn sayings to Nicodemus (3:3, 5) set out the conditions for entry into the new order: "seeing" the reign of God, which is synonymous with "entering" it; and birth, which is "from above" and "of water and spirit." The latter probably refers to the waters of childbirth, interpreted metaphorically of birth in the Spirit.[49]

The new order which requires new "birth" has already been indicated symbolically by the miracle at Cana (2:1–12) and the cleansing of the temple (2:13–22). Both stories signify, for the evangelist, the eschatological transformation that is the purpose of Jesus' coming, explicated in the metaphor of birth: the transfiguration, in each case, of a lesser substance to something that supersedes it in quality—water into wine, the mortal body of Jesus into his resurrected body (2:19–22). Transfiguration is imaged now as "birth": the movement from one location to another, from one form of life to another. Only by being born "from above" can Nicodemus enter into that new reality that the Johannine Jesus both brings and embodies. Yet to Jesus' surprise, Nicodemus, "the teacher of Israel" (3:10), is unable to comprehend what is required of him—unlike John the Baptist, who, later in the same chapter, yields (like the water for purification in the stone jars at Cana) to that which is greater: "he must increase, but I must decrease" (3:30).

In this context the Johannine Jesus speaks of the flesh. In order to unfold the symbol of birth, Jesus distinguishes between the parallel spheres of flesh (*sarx*) and spirit (*pneuma*), comparing and contrasting human birth with divine birth: "that which is born of the flesh is flesh, and that which is born of the Spirit [*pneuma*] is Spirit" (3:6). The distinction between the two is not pejorative but descriptive, distinguishing the two different but connected domains. They are not separable because the bridge linking them is the common notion of birth, the one necessary to lead to the other. Yet they are as distinct as the figure of Adam made from clay before and after the breath of God is breathed into his body (Gen. 2:7). New life is given by the breath of the Spirit: the creative processes of the divine Logos are one and the same. Those who receive divine birth are defined, in the terms of the Prologue, as those who "are born not of blood nor of the will of flesh nor of the will of a man but of God" (1:13). As we have seen, before any mention of the incarnation in the Prologue, "flesh" is introduced in what might at first seem to be a hostile way, as in 3:6. In both cases, the same contrast is operative; it will appear again, in starker form, in 6:63. There is no polemic against the flesh, however: it is not evil but powerless. For all the generativity that human beings possess—a power bestowed on them, and on all living creatures, by God in creation (Gen. 1:22, 28)—none can perform the needed transformation. Only the divine voice can pronounce, "Let there be light"; only the One who generated creation's own generativity can re-create its life in so radical a way. None of this is to disparage the life of creation. As Augustine perceives in more than one homily on John, underlying the Fourth Gospel is a confirmation of creation—indeed a continuity and contiguity between the two spheres of flesh and spirit.[50] Transfiguration is not the movement from one disconnected form of life to another: on the contrary, the new draws out the inner meaning of the old.

There is a helpful parallel with the story of the man born blind in John 9. Though the language of flesh and spirit is not explicit there, similar imagery is present, including parallels with Adam.[51] The man's eyesight is not restored but created: he is born blind and has never possessed the gift of sight (9:2). He is healed by the use of water and dust, both images linked to creation (9:6–7), and his identity as well as his body undergo transformation (9:8–9). Indeed, the authorities' attempt to cast doubt on his identity pushes him unwittingly toward his healer (9:24–34), until finally he sees Jesus for the first time, both literally and symbolically (9:35–38) and is vindicated (9:3, 39–41). Flesh is the medium that leads to spiritual illumination. The metaphor of Jesus as the light of the world makes possible the transformation—indeed at some level *is* the transfiguration, as the literal level opens up before the symbolic. What Nicodemus is offered and fails to grasp (at least in John 3) is comprehended by others. Again and again the experience of birth "from above" is witnessed in the Johannine narratives, even finally in the story of Nicodemus himself (19:38–42).[52]

The story of the Samaritan woman makes references to Jesus' hunger (4:8, 31–34) and thirst (4:7). Although these are not developed at this stage, the symbolic significance of Jesus' humanity is suggested by the way in which Jesus' thirst opens up the dialogue between Jesus and the woman. We are not told whether Jesus does drink from the water jar—only that the Samaritan woman later abandons it (4:28)—but John is more explicit about the significance of Jesus' hunger. In response to the disciples' misunderstanding of his conversation with the woman, Jesus reacts to their offer of food by speaking of his "true" food: "my food is to do the will of the one who sent me and to accomplish his work [*ergon*]" (4:34). Once again we are not told whether or not Jesus eats, but what is clear is that food has become metaphorical for something more fundamental that is taking place in the narrative. It could be argued that if Jesus has had no real need to quench his thirst or fill his hunger in a physical sense, then the genuine nature of his humanity is in doubt. Is John guilty of a "naïve docetism" that denies the reality of the flesh and presents Jesus as seeming to be human but not really subject to bodily needs and desires?[53] Yet the symbolic significance of Jesus' hunger and thirst only works if the human needs of Jesus are genuine. Through it the narrator establishes a bond between the humanity of Jesus and that of the woman, making possible the ensuing self-disclosure.[54] Once more, the full meaning of this will only become plain in the passion narrative.

The Bread of Life narrative offers a further perspective on flesh, explicating the significance of the incarnation for the life of the community. There is also reference to discipleship and faith that echoes the contrast of 1:12–13. The discourse is firmly attached to the story of the feeding (6:1–15), with its imagery of bread in the context of Passover (6:4), the symbolic meaning of which is gradually unfolded. Both become symbols in the dialogue that ensues, following Jesus' miraculous appearance on the sea (6:16–21). In the feeding story, Jesus acts as host at the meal, even to the extent of distributing the loaves himself.[55] In the dialogue between Jesus and the crowds/"Jews,"[56] the symbolic meaning is gradually unfolded while those present become more and more alienated. Brown speaks of the whole sequence as dividing into two segments, word and sacrament, but this is an artificial division, influenced by later liturgical practice.[57] The gradual revelation of Jesus as the true Bread incorporates both the sapiential and the eucharistic throughout.[58] In 6:51–58, where Jesus speaks at greater length of eating and drinking (though it has already been alluded to in the first "I am" saying in 6:35), it is not a new dimension that is introduced but rather a return to the beginning:

the full symbolic significance of the feeding story is now disclosed. Jesus is the Bread of life on which/whom believers must feed in order to have life. Those aspects of his identity that denote his earthly life—his parents, his birth-place, his brothers ([sisters?] 6:42; cf. 1:45–46; 2:1–12; 7:2–10)—are inadequate of themselves to encompass his identity, although they point symbolically to it. The one who is "the son of Joseph" from Nazareth is also "the Bread which has come down from heaven" (6:41).

At this point the concept of flesh becomes explicit (6:51). The context is the fourth "I am" saying of the chapter (cf. 6:35, 41, 48), summing up what has gone before and also opening up, more explicitly, the emphasis on the symbolic act of eating (and drinking).[59] Once again, the text refers back to the feeding, where it is clear that the "sign" points symbolically to Jesus as both the host (cf. 6:11 and 6:52: "the bread which I myself will give") and also the food itself ("I am the bread come down from heaven"). The giving of the flesh "on behalf of the life of the world" (cf. "giving life to the world," 6:33) expresses the universalism of the Johannine Gospel, yet it is also an indication of Jesus' own death, by which the gift will be given. This takes further the Sophia overtones that are present in the language and imagery (Prov. 9:2–5; Sir. 15:3; 24:21): Jesus' self-giving, which brings life to believers, is accomplished paradoxically through his death (cf. 12:24).

In this and the following verses, the Johannine Jesus sets out in uncompromising terms the necessity of eating his flesh and drinking his blood, without which eternal life is impossible (6:52–58). The word *sarx* is mentioned six times in all, accompanied by four references to "blood" (*haima*), and is interchangeable with "me" (6:57), making it clear that the phrase "flesh and blood" refers to Jesus himself. The addition of "blood" draws out the eucharistic significance within the context of faith, imagery that has echoes of the wedding at Cana, where Jesus provides the "best wine" (2:1–11), and also the symbolism of water and thirst (4:1–42; 6:34; 7:37–39). The latter, however, is symbolic of the Spirit rather than Jesus himself in a direct way.[60] The divine self-giving in Jesus' death and in the Eucharist is one event, the two representing different dimensions of the one self-gift which is both human (of the "flesh") and divine (God's self-communication). The flesh of Jesus is that which dies and rises again, creating and sustaining life—not just physical life but also eschatological life ("eternal life," 6:54). This represents an expansion in the meaning of the *sarx* of Jesus (1:14). We are speaking not of the earthly Jesus, but rather of the presence of the risen Christ in the life of the community through the life-giving Spirit.

There are parallels here with the imagery of birth in John 3. In a similar way, without the symbol—birth, feeding—eternal life cannot be attained, just as birth and food (and drink) are essential to create and sustain physical life (note the Johannine contrast in 6:27 between the food that abides and the food that is perishable). Similarly, both passages have sacramental overtones inherent in their symbolism: in John 3 with reference to baptism and in John 6 in relation to the

Eucharist. The eucharistic language of John 6 derives from its symbolic and theological framework: just as the flesh of Jesus radiates divine glory, so too the material substances of bread and wine are transfigured in the Eucharist to become redolent of divine presence/glory. The core symbols associated with the sacrament involve the transformation of material reality to be the bearer of spiritual reality, while those who embrace the symbols are themselves transformed, like being drawn to like.

Despite the necessity of *sarx* as outlined above, John asserts a few verses later that the flesh is "of no avail" (6:63). Here the ineffectiveness of flesh is contrasted negatively with "the life-giving Spirit," appearing to countermand what Jesus has just said of the necessity of eating his flesh in order to gain life. It is unnecessary to resolve this seeming contradiction by interpreting 6:51–58 as a later addition to the text by an alien hand.[61] The point is that flesh *of itself* has no power to give eternal life.[62] Only the Spirit, who is the Giver of life, possesses such power. This does not imply an ontological dualism in which "flesh" is intrinsically evil. Working through the flesh, the Spirit vivifies that which is useless or dead—in this context, the "flesh" of Jesus, which dies yet rises to life, above all in the Eucharist. In terms of the theory of metaphor, we have here the explication of the "is not" dimension: flesh is not literally to be consumed in a cannibalistic way. The metaphorical "is not" falls away to allow the "is" dimension to unfold. It is the "flesh" of the risen Lord that gives life through the transfiguring presence of the Spirit.

In the Tabernacles Discourse (John 7–8), there are two possible allusions to the flesh of Jesus. The first is controversial and depends for its meaning on the punctuation. Jesus invites people to come to him and drink, promising living water to those who respond. There are two alternatives for reading the text (7:37–38), both using the word *koilia,* which refers literally to the hollow part of the body—the stomach, belly or intestines, or occasionally the womb:[63]

- "If anyone is thirsty let him [her] come to me and let the one believing in me drink. Just as Scripture said, rivers of living water will flow from his belly."

- "If anyone is thirsty let him [her] come to me and drink. The one believing in me, just as Scripture said, rivers of living water will flow from his [her] belly."

Exegetically, it is possible to argue for either reading.[64] The second could be a restatement of Jesus' promise to the Samaritan woman of "a spring of water springing up to life eternal" (cf. 4:14).[65] Attractive as that reading is, however, it is less persuasive theologically than the first reading, assuming that the *koilia* refers to Jesus. In John's Gospel the life of the believer is entirely dependent on Christ, the Wisdom of God and source of living water (4:10; 6:35);[66] Christology, in other words, has priority over discipleship. In this interpretation, John foreshadows the flow of blood and water from the side of Jesus at the crucifixion and the giving of the Spirit, both of which are linked to the death/departure of Jesus. The Old Testament background is the flow of water from the rock in the wilderness (Num. 20:1–13; Ps. 78:16; Isa. 48:21) and the eschatological spring of water in the temple in Jerusalem (Ezek. 47:1–12; Zech. 14:8; cf. Isa. 12:3).[67] Although the meaning is still to be revealed, the iconography points to Jesus' humanity as the place of divine disclosure: it is from the "belly" of Jesus that the Spirit will come to give water to the thirsty and drink to those who believe. Once more the pattern of 1:14 is the interpretative lens for subsequent references to Jesus' incarnate flesh. John now begins to point forward to the glorification of the passion as the context for the giving of the Spirit, linked fundamentally to the flesh of Jesus.

Later in the Tabernacles Discourse, the phrase "according to the flesh" (*kata tēn sarka*, 8:15) is used more negatively within a forensic context to denote the willful misunderstanding of the Pharisees concerning Jesus' origins and destiny. Jesus' opponents make false judgments (in this case about Jesus), unlike Jesus himself, who makes no such judgment. This assertion, complicated because Jesus does have the role of eschatological judge in this Gospel (cf. 5:22, 27, 30),[68] follows the "I am" saying about Jesus as the light of the world. (It is in this context that later scribes placed the story of the woman caught in adultery [7:53–8:11] as exemplifying the saying in 8:15.[69]) As in 6:63, the context makes plain that "flesh" signifies that which is divorced from Spirit. In contrast, Jesus refuses to make such judgment—though if he were to do so, his judgment would be based on truth and proper witnesses (8:15b–18). In the hands of Jesus' enemies, flesh takes on a hostile meaning: the contrast here is between *sarx* represented by Jesus, which is life-giving, and *sarx* represented by his opponents, which is self-sufficient and ineffective. Being unwilling to open themselves to the revelation, those who judge "according to the flesh" finally turn to violence to eliminate the one who reveals to them the unbearable truth: that his own flesh is the medium of divine glory (8:59). Flesh stands over against flesh in this disputation. In the end it is Jesus' flesh that his opponents try to destroy. The two references to the flesh of Jesus in this discourse thus reflect the two distinct uses of *sarx* found in the Prologue.[70]

In this survey of physiological references to Jesus, it is also worth including the reference to the "breast" of Jesus at the Last Supper, on which the beloved disciple leans during the meal (*kolpos, stēthos*, 13:23, 25; cf. 21:20). The description comes from Jesus' prediction of his own betrayal, the resulting dismay of the disciples and Simon Peter's nonverbal request of the beloved disciple to inquire of Jesus for the identity of the betrayer. The literal meaning is that the beloved disciple's couch is nearest that of Jesus, on the right side; he holds the place of honor at the banquet, in close enough physical proximity to be able to touch Jesus and converse discreetly with him (cf. Luke 16:23): "Reclining on his left arm with his head close to his Master's breast, he was consequently able to hold easy and quiet conversation with Him."[71] The intimacy is strengthened by the double description: "reclining . . . on the bosom of Jesus" (13:23) and "having reclined on the breast of Jesus" (13:25). Yet the symbolic meaning is apparent also in the intimacy that the physical closeness denotes. This impression is strengthened by the use of *kolpos*—meaning the bosom, breast, or lap (and also, by extension, the fold of a garment)—which echoes the Prologue and the description of the Son as "turned toward God" and lying in the *kolpos* of the Father (1:18).[72] The beloved disciple shares the same intimacy with Jesus that Jesus shares with the Father. While the reference in the Prologue is metaphoric of the spiritual intimacy between Father and Son, the reference in 13:23 takes on a distinctly physical as well as symbolic meaning on account of the incarnation. Intimacy with the Father is made tangible through the flesh of Jesus; the closeness of mutual knowing is palpable and bodily. Jesus' flesh makes possible a divinely human love, functioning as the bridge between heaven and earth, and the beloved disciple exemplifies the place occupied by the believing community in its loving attachment to God.

The last explicit occurrence of *sarx*, though not directly in relation to Jesus, is found at the beginning of Jesus' prayer in John 17, which brings to a climax the Farewell Discourse. According to the chiastic structure of John 13–17 proposed by Wayne Brouwer, the prayer parallels the narrative of the footwashing (13:1–35) as the outer frame of the discourse, with the common focus on unity with Jesus, as expressed in terms of mutual love.[73] As the "prayer of the departing Redeemer,"[74] Jesus foreshadows his glorification or exaltation on the cross. The prayer is also performative: it effects that for which it asks. Indeed, at a deeper level, what is requested is *already* a reality, given that prayer is strictly speaking unnecessary for the Johannine Jesus (cf. 11:41–42; 12:28–30), the unity of will and purpose between Father and Son being so perfect as to leave no gap between the asking and the receiving.[75] In this sense, as Dodd points out, Jesus' prayer enacts the exaltation; it is already an *anabasis*, an ascent of the Son to the Father in an act of mutual glorification.[76] What it prays for, it effects: what it effects is an ontological reality into which the reader is drawn. The prayer divides into several sections: the introduction (17:1–5), in which Jesus gives a summation of his life and ministry centered on the key Johannine theme of glory; the prayer for the disciples, the purpose of which is to draw a protective circle around them in view of what is to come (17:6–19); the prayer for future believers (17:20–23), drawing them into the unity of Father and Son; and the conclusion (17:24–26), where Jesus as the Revealer again sums up the purpose of his coming and the destiny of the disciples.[77]

Within the opening section, the phrase "all flesh" (*pasa sarx*, 17:2a) is capable of being read in a narrow or broader sense: it could refer to humankind or all creation. If the latter, it denotes all living creatures and not just human beings—all that is formed by the divine Logos. There are a number of arguments to support this view, although commentators tend to favor the former.[78] Old Testament usage, where the phrase is common (note the Hebrew *kol-bāśār*), supports at least the possibility of such a rendition. In the flood story, for example, the phrase is frequent, in each case referring to all living creatures affected by the flood—animals, fish, and birds.[79] Although "all flesh" can refer to human beings (e.g., Jdt. 2:3; Ps.

64[65]:2; Isa. 66:23), nevertheless, in contexts where it is particularly associated with dominion, the phrase suggests all creatures over whom the Creator has authority—whether that dominion be exercised directly or handed over to Adam as God's agent (e.g., Ps. 135[136]:25; Sir. 17:3–4; Bel 5 LXX).

There is a further dimension to this question in John 17:2, obscured in translations such as the NRSV, which opts for human beings as the focus of Jesus' words. In the next phrase, the wording literally is "in order that, as to *everything which you have given him*, he might give them eternal life." This is paralleled later in the prayer by a similar use of the neuter: "Father, in respect to *that which you have given me*, I wish that where I am they too may be with me . . ." (17:24; cf. 10:29).[80] John uses the phrase "everything which" in one other context in the Fourth Gospel, where it is used in parallel with masculine forms:

> *Everything which* the Father gives me comes to me,
> and the one coming to me I will never cast out (6:37) . . .
> This is the will of the One who sent me,
> that *everything which* he has given me I will not lose from it
> but I will raise it up on the last day.[81]
> For this is the will of my Father,
> that everyone who sees the Son and believes in him
> may have eternal life,
> and I will raise him [her] up on the last day. (6:39–40)

It is possible to argue in both these contexts that the difference between the neuter and more obviously personal forms is stylistic.[82] A dynamic translation would therefore understandably (perhaps) wish to render all references in personal language. It is also possible, however, that the difference has more significance than the stylistic. One possibility for explaining the force of the neuter in 17:2, 24 (and in John 6) is that it points to the unity of the disciples: "that they may be *one*" (neuter, 17:21–23).[83] Yet it is also possible that the neuter suggests, as does "all flesh," a wider sphere than just the human.[84]

This interpretation is supported by the parallels between 17:1–5 and the Prologue:[85] glory, life, authority, preexistence, the intimacy between Father and Son. Here in 17:1–5 the Son is again "turned towards" God (cf. 1:1–2, 18), addressing the Father in intimate terms as the source of dominion and life, a power given to the Son through whom "all things came into being" (cf. 1:3). Thus the divine Word/Son "has authority over the whole world,"[86] the acknowledgment of which marks out the community of believers over against the "world" (*kosmos*). Reading the prayer in light of the Prologue thus makes a difference to the way we interpret 17:2. Apart from anything else, it is clear that there is nothing negative about the understanding of flesh as it is presented here. As with the Prologue, Johannine Christology is rooted in creation as the fundamental manifestation of the Son's dominion. Thus, while at one level, flesh in 17:2 refers to human beings and their capacity to enter a knowing relationship with God through Jesus, at the same time, understood more comprehensively, "all flesh" is synonymous with "all things" in creation, for which the Logos is the source of life.

In this sense, 17:2 needs to be read with both creation and incarnation in mind. There is a double connection operative within the text which the narrative has already supplied. The Son's dominion over "all flesh" in creation is set alongside the assertion that the Word/Son became flesh. The two seeming contradictions coalesce: the one who formed flesh is himself formed by flesh; the Creator of all living creatures becomes a living creature; flesh stands alongside flesh. The dominion exercised "from above" now arises "from below," out of the earth, bone of our bones and flesh of our flesh (Gen. 2:23). The fashioner of all things is himself fashioned. Divine glory radiates now not from heaven alone but from within the very core of earth. The Word/Wisdom/Son takes on the temporalities of speech, wisdom, and filiation: a limitable being, possessing cosmic authority, yet using that authority to "lay down my life in order that I may take it up again" (10:17–18). We cannot read the phrase "all flesh" on the lips of the departing Redeemer without awareness that it is the same creatureliness that the eternal, glorified Son shares: at one with all living beings. Flesh addresses flesh in this cosmic context. The Son who prays is the Son in whose mortal flesh the glory shines: in his life, in his death, in his final ascent. After this point, no further explicit reference to "flesh" is made. Yet in other ways, John pursues the incarnate theme to the end of the Gospel.

FLESH IN THE PASSION AND RESURRECTION NARRATIVES

The passion and resurrection narratives do not make direct use of the word *sarx*. Nevertheless, other terminology and imagery express the same concept. Most striking perhaps is the use of *sōma* ("body"), which overlaps with *sarx* though with a theologically less distinctive meaning. After the cleansing of the temple, *sōma* reappears only in the passion and resurrection narratives, where it refers to the dead body of Jesus, which seems to be the main focus of the word[87]—though once it includes those crucified with Jesus (19:31). In the burial scene, *sōma* is used three times (twice?) to refer to the deposition and interment by Nicodemus and Joseph of Arimathea (19:38, 40).[88] In the story of Mary Magdalene at the empty tomb, it is used in relation to the two angels guarding the stone slab "where the body of Jesus lay" (20:12). In both contexts, the body of Jesus is surrounded by the extravagant love and devotion of his disciples; its absence from the tomb is depicted with numinous signs. Having read the cleansing of the temple, the reader knows, as Joseph, Nicodemus, and Mary do not, that this same *sōma* is not destined to remain a lifeless corpse. The one who is himself "the resurrection and the life" (11:25) has divine authority (*exousia*) over life and death and is able to give up and take up his life (10:17).[89] The synonymous term *sōma* is another way of alluding to the mortality implied by the incarnation. Although it lacks eucharistic overtones, and is not explicitly linked to *pneuma* and *doxa*, the word *sōma* carries the sense of Jesus' mortality yet also the hope of resurrection. Whatever the reason that John employs *sōma* rather than *sarx* in this context[90]—and the reason may be stylistic—the effect is to confirm, almost from the beginning of the Gospel, that the suffering body in the passion narrative, crucified between two other "bodies" and buried in the tomb under a mountain of spices, is destined not for decay but for resurrection and life. The two words, flesh and body, thus have an overlapping though not identical range of meanings. Despite the difference of emphasis, there is continuity between them: the humanity of Jesus implies his physical death; the divine radiance revealed in his human flesh/body makes possible his bodily resurrection from the dead.

The passion narrative consists of a number of scenes or images that form a symbolic series, drawing out the theological significance of Jesus' death. In the trial scene, Pilate presents Jesus to "the Jews" in regal clothing, with the words, "Behold the man [human being]" (*idou ho anthrōpos*, 19:5). The expression indicates poignantly Jesus' humanity in the midst of suffering: the humiliation of being mocked and used as a political pawn, and the extremity of pain and exhaustion following the scourging, so that he presents a pitiable figure, probably hardly able to stand up. Yet, despite the signs of physical abuse—and despite Pilate's mocking—the word *anthrōpos*, in the context of the royal attire, points symbolically and ironically to Jesus' kingly status (cf. 18:36–37), his identity as Son of God (19:7) and the glorification that is the true meaning of the cross.[91] The two dimensions are seen in the one figure. In T. L. Brodie's words, Jesus "bears the marks of the world's confusion and reflects the reality of human misery and desolation." At the same time, "beneath the misery there is a divine element," articulated in the kingly garb in which Jesus goes to the cross.[92] This powerful icon displays "the hidden divinity of the earthly Jesus and the paradox that the one who is apparently humiliated on the cross is in reality the exalted and glorified one."[93] Not as a male (*anēr*) but as the royal *anthrōpos* does Jesus go to his death.

A similar paradox is present in the scene depicting Jesus' thirst and subsequent death on the cross, which are equally symbolic (19:28–30). At the physiological level, Jesus is experiencing the raging thirst which is the prelude to death. Yet John uses the reference to Scripture as a pointer showing the symbolic importance of Jesus' thirst (19:28; cf. Ps. 22:15). The short scene is bounded on either side by reference to "accomplishment": on the one hand, Jesus' knowledge that all things have been "accomplished" (*tetelestai*), including that of Scripture (*teleiōthē*, 19:28), and, on the other, Jesus' last utterance in this Gospel: "it is accomplished" (*tetelestai*, 19:30). The closest parallel is the hunger of Jesus in conversation with the disciples, after his conversation with the Samaritan woman, where "my food is to do the will of the one who sent me and to accomplish his work" (*teleiōsō*, 4:34). Jesus' thirst makes sense at the literal level, but it is also symbolic: Jesus, who remains in control of his own destiny, is ready now to lay down his life because he has achieved what the Father has given him to do. Once again, the reference is to glorification: by "thirsting" to fulfill the Father's will, the Son has glorified the Father, above all in his death. So thirst is symbolic not just of the Samaritan woman's need for "living water" (4:10) but also of Jesus' mission and of that unity of love and purpose binding together Father and Son. When Jesus drinks from the sponge filled with sour wine (19:29–30a),[94] the reader is reminded symbolically of the Father's cup, which Jesus has agreed to drink (18:11). Once more, in his human thirst and suffering, Jesus' flesh becomes symbolic of the glory of God.

The most powerful symbol of the life-giving significance of Jesus' flesh is the piercing of his side—arguably the climax of the passion narrative.[95] The dynamic of this episode is the same as for 1:14. The flesh that the Logos assumes is genuine because it is mortal: as Schnelle points out, the blood and water "constitute the human being" and are "intended to emphasize the reality of Jesus' death."[96] Nothing more powerfully expresses the palpable nature of Jesus' life, the materiality that he has so radically embraced. That John understands this dual imagery as symbolic is also clear: the reader knows already that the two elements point symbolically to life, blood and water being symbols of eternal life in this Gospel (3:5; 6:53–56; 13:1–13; 15:1–8), water in particular linked to the Spirit (7:37–39; cf. 19:30).[97] In a secondary sense, they are symbolically related to baptism and the Eucharist. However, that these two symbols flow from the dead body of Jesus is of equal significance. The imagery here, along with other, synonymous terms, reinforces the centrality of the incarnation in John's theological framework. The tangibility itself is, in any case, intrinsic to the sacramental power.[98] Here, perhaps more than anywhere else, the divine *doxa* pours forth from the *sarx* of Jesus. Once more we find flesh in its expanded meaning: the symbolic significance of flesh stretches to include the dead body, which becomes paradoxically an icon of the Spirit and life: here in the suffering, dying flesh the divine glory is powerfully manifest.

Yet John takes the iconography further. In the appearance of the risen Christ on Easter Sunday, first to the disciples behind closed doors (20:19–23) and one week later to Thomas (20:24–29), the wounds of suffering are shown to the disciples, leading them to Easter joy and faith (20:20, 25–28). There is more to this motif than a sign of recognition and continuity, or even an incentive to faith. The wounds represent the *sarx*, which is fundamental to the identity of the Risen One. As the expression of *sarx*, the wounds function symbolically to reveal the divine *doxa*. It is precisely the symbolic meaning which Thomas, for all his doubt, recognizes in his confession of faith, "my Lord and my God" (20:28)—a confession that brings the Gospel to a climax and points the reader back to the Prologue. The wounds are transfigured to become symbols not of death but of life, the life that comes from the death of Jesus. Yet the story of Thomas needs to be read in context. Mary Magdalene has not been permitted to hold on to Jesus because he is about to ascend (20:17);[99] and the Gospel, in its original form, concludes with a beatitude to those who "have not seen and have believed" (20:29). The whole narrative of John 20 functions to reassure the reader that the incarnation is still palpable, even if in a different way, through the life-giving presence of the Spirit-Paraclete activating the eucharistic life, love, and mission of the community. Once more, the significance of the flesh is expanded beyond the tangibility of the earthly Jesus.

SYMBOLIC SIGNIFICANCE OF FLESH

The significance of the flesh—in the language of *sarx* and other related terms—is unfolded symbolically throughout the narrative of the Fourth Gospel. Like other Johannine symbols, its importance is already signaled in the Prologue, so that while readers know that flesh is the locus of divine glory, they do not know the *how* of that divine self-manifestation nor its implications, especially for the postresurrection life of the community. What occurs in the Gospel is the outworking of what the Prologue asserts. Flesh throughout the Gospel expands in significance, filling with meaning the radical statement of divine humanity in the Prologue in 1:14, demonstrating both the contiguity of flesh with our materiality and the capacity of transfigured flesh to nourish and sustain the life of the spirit. In an illuminating article on the bodily reality of Christ in theology, Graham Ward speaks of the body of Jesus undergoing a series of "displacements" from its literal and specific humanity: in relation to eschatology, crucifixion, resurrection, and ascension.[100] While this flesh is like other flesh, it is also significantly different in its ability to be transposed, above all in the Eucharist, where "a new understanding of embodiment is announced."[101]

In asserting that the divine glory is manifest through the flesh, both in the Prologue and throughout the Gospel, the evangelist gives the flesh/body an extraordinary status. For John, the role of flesh in salvation is neither arbitrary nor incidental, but essential. It is the core Johannine symbol of salvation, in which the material realm becomes the bearer of divine reality. In the technical terms of metaphor, "flesh" is the vehicle and "glory" the tenor. Although, as we have seen, the Old Testament already interprets the divine glory as residing symbolically in the tabernacle/temple, that indwelling is now transferred to the person of Jesus, who is the preexistent Logos, belonging to the realm of glory and radiating divine light within his own being. In the incarnation, the symbolism shifts location: not a temple but a person; not bricks and mortar, but flesh and blood; not a fixed geographical location, but a cosmic humanity. The symbolics of incarnation in the Fourth Gospel are crucial for its theological meaning. In the Fourth Gospel, symbol, as we have noted, does not mean something arbitrary or merely subjective but implies that which is intrinsic, referential, ontological. The flesh of Jesus is not an evanescent or fanciful symbol that is dependent only on his mortal life. Throughout the Gospel it is seen to gain in substance, moving beyond the limitations of death. It becomes the core symbol of the Gospel. All the other symbols are symbolic precisely because of that core: they too reflect divine glory in their "flesh" because the Logos has become flesh. This is especially true of human beings, who, in becoming children of God, regain their symbolic potential to radiate the glory of God; it is also true of symbols such as bread, with its strongly eucharistic overtones, which now reaches new heights in symbolizing—that is to say, conveying and making present—the incarnate, glorified Christ.

The fusion that occurs between flesh and Spirit to create the basic symbolism signifies a change in the nature of both: the glory of God in human form means the glorification of all created reality. Divine revelation and material reality come together in this symbolic portrayal without loss of identity, neither being devoured nor rendered obsolete by the other. On the contrary, divine glory is now revealed in the symbol of flesh with transfiguring power:

> Oh the new mingling! Oh the blend contrary to all expectation! The one who is, becomes. The uncreated is created. The uncontainable is contained through a thinking soul, mediating between godhead and the thickness of flesh. The one who enriches becomes a beggar; for he begs for my own flesh, so that I might become rich in his divinity. The one who is full becomes empty; for he empties himself of his glory for a little time so that I might share in his fullness . . . I received the image [*eikōn*] and I did not protect it; he received a share in my flesh so that he might even save the image and make deathless the flesh. (Gregory of Nazianzus, *On the Holy Passover* 45.633–36)

Gregory of Nazianzus captures well the Johannine understanding of the divine entering the material world with transforming power, yet also permitting itself to be shaped by flesh. This dual dynamic has its origins in the language of the Prologue. Birth in the Spirit is the restoration of the creaturely world (1:10–14), as we have already seen. The one who lies in the Father's embrace (1:18) is gathered into flesh; God takes shape in human form, created from clay, subject to death, mortal, vulnerable—radiant with deity, yes, but radiant also with the promise of flesh renewed, refined, immortal.

The notion of the restoration of the divine image (*eikōn*) is central to this understanding of the incarnation.[102] The renewal of human nature is the purpose of Christ's coming, a renewal made possible in the Fourth Gospel only by the divine Logos. Irenaeus understands this when he argues that the Logos of God in becoming flesh "became Himself what was His own image" (*Proof of the Apostolic Preaching* 22, p. 61). Likewise, for Athanasius, humankind, already made in the image of the Logos, can be restored only by the advent of the One who is the definitive Image of the Father: "therefore the Word of God came through himself, in order that, being the Image of the Father, he might re-create humanity according to the image" (*On the Incarnation* 13.7). That too is how Athanasius interprets Jesus' requirement of Nicodemus that he be born "from above": it refers to the re-created soul born in the image of God (*On the Incarnation* 14).

In this way, John's theology portrays the Logos becoming flesh (incarnation) yet also the flesh becoming divine (glorification).[103] While these are not equivalent inversions, there is a vital link between them. In the Johannine worldview, both are eschatological and both are related to the flesh. There is no explicit narrative of the Transfiguration in this Gospel (cf. Mark 9:2–13 pars.), perhaps because there is no single, isolated moment in which Jesus' glory breaks through, although 1:14 suggests a parallel. The glory is there from the beginning, at the moment of Jesus' human "becoming,"[104] as a symbol or icon that communicates the eternal through matter. There is a uniqueness to this event in the Gospel: "the only Son, God" who abides "in the embrace of the Father" (1:18) is alone capable of crossing over from Spirit to flesh. The effect of this journey is to bring about the transformation of all things—the corresponding crossing over from flesh to Spirit. The incarnation has to do with flesh transformed by divinity. Glorification is the destiny of those who believe (1:13).

John's use of the language of flesh illustrates, moreover, that the revelation of divine sovereignty in this Gospel is not enacted by force or coercion. The Johannine symbolism implies fragility and finitude, limitation, and susceptibility to pain, sorrow, grief, rejection, oppression, and death. By becoming flesh, God enters the world in the thin garb of mortality, entering the darkness of creation clad only in the armor of skin and vein, sinew and bone: mortal, vulnerable, naked. Tertullian speaks of this flesh [*caro*] as "suffused with blood, structured with bones, woven with sinews, intertwined with veins, which can be born and die, without doubt human as born from a human being [*homo*]" (*Incarnation* 5.28–31). It is a poignant note at the crucifixion where, even with all the rich cultic and sacramental significance of the pierced side, the legs remain unbroken. It is not in the terror of might and conquest, but in feeble flesh that God confronts "his own," revealing and transforming through a substance that is at one with theirs. God reveals and redeems from within: in the flesh, at the feet, through the darkness—in a glory that will not escape the loss and death that are the lot of all creation. The new order of fleshly existence envisaged in the symbolic universe of the Fourth Gospel comes from within, transfigured by the habitation of divine glory in mortal flesh. The enfleshment of the Sophia-Word raises "all flesh" to the level of divine glory.[105]

THE FLESH AND THE EARTHLY JESUS

John's theology of the flesh raises several further issues not indicated directly in the text but arising as implications of its unique perspective. In the first place, we may ask what the relationship is between the flesh of Jesus as depicted in the Fourth Gospel and the earthly Jesus of Nazareth. Not for a moment does the Gospel deny the genuine nature of Jesus' humanity;[106] John's symbolic Christology cannot work without it. At the same time, that humanity is interpreted symbolically through the dual lens of Jesus' divine origins and destiny.[107] The flesh is seen from beginning to end from the perspective of glory, which, for the evangelist, radiates through Jesus' human selfhood, a selfhood shaped by a divine identity, as Word and Son, that precedes and postdates the earthly life. Johannine eschatology interprets the glorious coming of the Son of Man, located in the Synoptics at the end of time (e.g., Mark 8:38 pars.; 13:26 pars.), as already realized in the incarnation. Like the other evangelists, John also writes from the vantage point of the resurrection. The flesh on which/whom believers feed is the risen, transformed body and blood of Christ, not that of a lifeless corpse: the celebration of a "real presence," not the mournful memorial of a dead absence. The resurrection narratives are not visionary but manifestations of a reality that is bodily, of the flesh—apparent in the sight and touch of the wounds still imprinted on the risen body (20:20a, 25–27). The Fourth Gospel regards Jesus with a kind of stereoscopic vision that holds together incarnation (1:14) and exaltation (2:21; 3:14; 12:34; 13:31–32; 17:1; 20:17). The "flesh" of which John speaks presupposes a preexistent and eschatological identity; it assumes the resurrection from the dead; it bespeaks a divine sovereignty over life and death that embraces yet also transcends the human.

Does this mean that the claims about the flesh of the Johannine Jesus cannot be made of the historical Jesus? The relationship between the two is more subtle than the question suggests. On the one hand, it is arguable that there is a real sense of continuity between the Jesus of history and the Jesus of the Fourth Gospel, without assuming that they are identical. Sandra Schneiders sees a vital connection between them, distinguishing between the earthly Jesus as the natural symbol of God and the Johannine Jesus as the literary symbol, the latter possessing a transcendent quality beyond the particularities of the former. Both in her view are "true symbolic expressions of the same person, the Word of the Father."[108] Thus, for example, the "I am" sayings of the Gospel—Jesus as the light of the world, the bread from heaven, the true shepherd—attach an attribute of God to the human person of Jesus, assigning a role and an identity to him that, in metaphorical terms, represent the fusion of two unlike elements: divine (tenor) and human (vehicle). In the symbolism that emerges, the one coalesces with the other: the identity of God is fused in a unique way to the person of Jesus, not just to his teaching and ministry but to his flesh, his humanity. The welding together of the two changes both: humanity in Johannine theology is now part of the being of God; the transformation of flesh means that, without loss of identity, it is now inconceivable to imagine humanity without the presence of Spirit/glory. The flesh of Jesus in the Fourth Gospel represents such a metamorphosis. In the sense in which Schneiders understands it, the humanity of the earthly Jesus—albeit in a different way—is necessary for the divine glory to become manifest.

At the same time, the Johannine claims represent far more than can be established of the historical Jesus by the methods of historical criticism. Flesh takes on added meaning throughout the Gospel, being viewed from the perspective of Jesus' origins and destiny and his sacramental presence in the community, giving it a universal quality beyond the specificities of the historical context. We are not speaking here of the humanity of Jesus as historians might understand it. These are Christian claims about Jesus that are dependent, at least in part, on faith; indeed, the Fourth Gospel was written with the explicit purpose of creating and/or sustaining faith in Jesus as "the Christ, the Son of God" (20:31). As we have seen, the interpretative key for John's portrayal of the flesh of Jesus is the incarnation, with all that it implies. The notion of *sarx* means Jesus' humanity but, more than that, it signifies *the humanity of the divine Word*. This is the perspective from which Jesus' human life is viewed. At each point, those incidents which betray his humanity point, for John, to a *divine* humanity that is beyond the scope of the historian or historical criticism.[109]

THE FLESH AND GENDER: FEMINIST CHRISTOLOGY

Second, the symbol of God revealed in human flesh creates a particular set of problems for theology from the viewpoint of gender. This interpretation of flesh in the Fourth Gospel, for instance, is at variance with the views of Alison Jasper in a recent feminist study of the Johannine Prologue and its interpretation through the history of the church.[110] Using a hermeneutic of suspicion, Jasper argues that the Prologue presents a patriarchal myth in which God is self-sufficient and disinterested, condescending to inferior flesh that lacks all autonomy. This mythic structure is exacerbated by the implicit association of "flesh" with the feminine, which is seen as being on a lower level than the spiritual (associated, by implication, with maleness and divinity); flesh, like women and the "feminine," is different and therefore "other." Jasper believes that the Johannine portrayal of flesh lacks consistency, even in the Prologue. Whereas God is in one sense dependent on the flesh in order to enter a relationship with human beings (1:6–7, 14–15; 6:53), in other contexts, flesh is devalued and depicted as irrelevant to salvation (1:13; 6:63).[111] Yet, even at its best, a text such as 1:14 depicts "a divine humiliation and descent, a compassionate divine, masculine downreach towards a feminine humanity."[112] This tension, according to Jasper, remains unresolved so that, for example, in John 6, "the hierarchical symbolism of Spirit over flesh is challenged to the point of offence (Jn 6.60–61) and then, almost directly, reaffirmed (6.63)."[113]

The problem with this reading is that it interprets every reference to "flesh" as implicitly conveying feminine "otherness," a link that Jasper presupposes but never demonstrates within the Johannine text. Even if we could demonstrate that the "feminine" is associated with the (inferior) body in the patriarchal mind-set of the ancient world, it does not follow that every reference to the body implies such a dualism. This is especially so of the biblical world, given that the Old Testament, whatever its deficiencies on the position of women, does not carry such a radical dualistic anthropology. From the perspective of the Fourth Gospel—which is steeped in the Old Testament—Jasper fails to see that in the Prologue "flesh" functions as metonymy for the whole human person, the "bodyself."[114] Moreover, while it is true that, in Johannine theology, human beings are incapable of saving themselves, it does not follow that flesh is irrelevant or devalued. The distinction made by the Fourth Gospel is between *unenlightened flesh and flesh that is renewed by the divine Spirit*, a distinction that is perfectly consistent with its understanding of salvation as the work of God to which human beings are called to respond in faith (e.g., 6:28–29). The Johannine contrast is not between flesh and spirit within the human person, but between humanity (flesh) and divinity (Spirit); it is not an anthropological division but a theological one. To interpret this as a "devaluing" of the flesh is a serious misreading of the Fourth Gospel. Furthermore, it ignores the holistic eschatological destiny, grounded in creation, to which "all flesh" is called in the Johannine worldview.

Yet the questions framed by Jasper raise important theological issues for gender and theology. Because God's incarnate presence is predicated on the maleness of Jesus, the place of femaleness within the theological orbit of the Gospel seems precarious at first glance, even if we reject Jasper's dualistic assumptions about the Johannine text. How can women be the co-equal subjects of divine address when their humanity seems, by implication, to be accorded secondary status? If male bodily existence is secularized in the incarnation, what happens to the female body? Is women's presence in the Johannine worldview contingent and insubstantial, dependent on the prior inclusion of men—in the same way androcentric language works to "include" the invisible female within the visible male? Such questions directed to the ancient text are, in one sense, anachronistic: the evangelist can have no awareness of the problem as we perceive it today. Yet given that meaning is the creation of text and reader together, it is still necessary to ask whether another reading of the text is possible, one that points unambiguously to the transfiguration of *all* humanity and is not addressed primarily to men, and only in a secondary or derivative sense to women.

It is imperative that theology seek to articulate and understand the problem raised by the Johannine understanding of incarnation from this perspective. Luce Irigaray, for example, argues that incarnation is vital for women yet partial where it consists of the glorification of the male while withholding such divinization from women. For her, a further dimension to incarnation that takes seriously female as well as male is essential for women's distinctive identity to emerge.[115]

The issue, from a symbolic point of view, is what can seem to be the *dis*carnate nature of women's existence within the Christian symbolic world, their discon-nection from both the beatitude and the judgment implied in the incarnation, the consequential lack of ontological substance, and an impaired awareness of being created in God's image (John 1:1–4) and destined for glory through Christ (17:22–24). There is a good deal at stake in the question, for men as well as women. Does the Jesus of the Fourth Gospel incorporate the humanity of women as generously as that of men, or is a dual anthropology at work that has one prin-ciple for men and another for women? Behind the anthropological question lies the fundamental theological issue of the dependability and scope of salvation.

None of this is particularly new for feminist theology, which has been wrestling with the issue at least since Rosemary Radford Ruether asked the question, "Can a male savior save women?"[116] Yet the solutions offered are, in a number of respects, considerably less satisfactory from a theological point of view than the defining of the problem. Most feminist theologians agree that "Church and Christianity are secretly, deeply penetrated with the presupposition that Christ is male"[117] and that women in the tradition are not seen as "christomorphic," able to represent Christ.[118] The post-Christian position rejects at the outset that the male, incarnate Christ is an adequate God-figure for women in any shape or form. In different ways, Mary Daly and Daphne Hampson answer Ruether's question in the nega-tive: for Daly, because arguments for male supremacy are based on Jesus as the deification of maleness, the symbol of incarnation being inherently deficient in her view and not just subject to abuse, and because the liberation of women requires the rejection of "Christolatry" and indeed any kind of slavish obedience or imitation.[119] Women need no salvation outside themselves. Hampson has a more nuanced understanding of orthodox Christology but argues that it contains two irredeemable flaws: it is dominated by male imagery, despite the best efforts of theology to sustain an inclusive notion of the incarnation, and it is grounded in Platonic understandings of the priority of the generic over the particular, thus according a universalism to the incarnation that, in her view, can no longer be sus-tained. Hampson's challenge to feminist Christology is powerful and lucid, deriv-ing from a careful understanding of patristic argument and of Christian feminist attempts to resolve the dilemma. In particular, she argues that Christian theology requires, by definition, some kind of Christology. Whether or not it is Chalce-donian in its interpretation of the incarnation, it needs to establish a case for the uniqueness of Jesus, otherwise it ceases to be Christian.[120]

The most widespread Christian feminist response to the problem is to move away from direct focus on the person of Jesus to a corporate understanding of Christology. Sallie McFague is a good example of this approach. She presents a triple metaphor of God as Mother, Lover, Friend, though this is far from being trinitarian in the traditional sense. While she claims that her understanding is closer to John than Paul, McFague makes a crucial theological shift from the

Johannine text: if the world can be understood metaphorically as the "body" of God, as she proposes, then the incarnation relates not merely, or even primarily, to the divine advent in the uniqueness and individuality of Jesus of Nazareth; rather it is a useful metaphor pointing to "God's promise to be with us always in God's body, our world."[121] Incarnation is now a cosmic statement of that which already exists, and indeed (by implication) must always have existed from the beginning. Hence, the theological locus of incarnation has moved from redemption to creation, from the particular humanity of Jesus to the generality of the world. While Jesus is "our historical choice as the premier paradigm of God's love," other human beings can equally be "sacraments or signs of God the lover."[122] Indeed everyone can be involved in the ongoing work of salvation, a salvation that is co-extensive with creation. Nothing is ontologically different about Jesus: there is no place for an incarnate Savior whose advent is unique and cosmic.[123]

Other forms of Christology in this vein prefer to speak of "Christa" rather than Christ, taking as far as possible the historical-critical divide between the historical Jesus and the Christ of faith. "Christa" originated in a sculpture of a crucified woman by Edwina Sandys, displayed amid great controversy in New York Cathedral in 1984.[124] Carter Heyward and Rita Nakashima Brock employ the term symbolically of the community and the spirit it embodies. For Heyward, Christa is linked to the rediscovery of sexuality, which traditional Christian theology has divorced from spirituality. Christa has many dimensions for Heyward, all with erotic overtones: creation, the sacredness of community and friendship, the hope of renewal for the earth, the strength to change the world, the freedom and spiritedness of all creatures, the power of love.[125] For Brock, the concept is more clearly focused on community and symbolizes the connectedness between people.[126] Even more than Heyward, Brock divorces this symbol from the person of Jesus, since she explicitly rejects the myth of the heroic individual who saves other individuals by his courage and daring.[127] Whereas for Heyward Christa is iconoclastic so as to "shatter the maleness of Christ,"[128] Brock is more concerned to move away from Jesus as an individual: "what is truly christological, that is, truly revealing of divine incarnation and salvific power in human life, must reside in connectedness and not in single individuals."[129] Brock rejects classical trinitarian formulations, along with any understanding of Jesus' death as atoning. Although both still speak of "incarnation," they do so in an abstract sense, divorced from the actual embodiment of Jesus as a human being, a "bodyself." While criticizing traditional Christian theology for spiritualizing the incarnation, Heyward nevertheless sees the focus on the singularity of Jesus as the Christ as deeply problematic.[130]

Elisabeth Schüssler Fiorenza's study of Jesus, particularly as it is illustrated in her account of early Synoptic traditions, seems to accord with most of the presuppositions of this kind of feminist theology. Schüssler Fiorenza recognizes the problematic nature of Jesus' maleness and agrees with other feminist theologians that individualistic, revelatory, and heroic readings of Jesus as Son of the Father and divine Lord promulgate the imperialistic framework inherent in ecclesiastical and social structures.[131] She is most exercised by what she perceives to be the dangers of gender essentialism, which she detects in a number of feminist theologians, and by the risk of adopting what she sees as an uncritical stance toward New Testament Christology.[132] In sum, she rejects the uniqueness of Jesus and sees him as standing in a line of prophetic figures, messengers of Sophia, as depicted in Q traditions.[133] For her, the center of Christian faith lies in Jesus' message of the reign of God, with its fundamental critique of sociopolitical structures of oppression at every level.[134] Christology has become a subset of ethics.

Ruether's answer to her own question is that the maleness of Jesus "has no ultimate significance";[135] she rejects any Christology that "elevates Jesus' human maleness to ontologically necessary significance" because it fails to include women.[136] Yet her explication of this is curiously ambiguous in terms of the uniqueness of Jesus. On the one hand, she seems to argue that the center lies not in the person of Jesus but in his liberating, prophetic message as lived out in his praxis, a message that stands in continuity with the prophets of the Old Testament. This reading she claims to derive from the Synoptic Gospels, to which layers of patriarchal meaning have been added, both in and beyond the New Testament. On the other hand, although critical of Chalcedonian understandings as idolatrous, Ruether is reluctant to reject outright the notion of Jesus as Redeemer. Having discarded the masculine mythology of Jesus as Messiah and incarnate Son, Ruether nevertheless wants to hold to the notion that Jesus is somehow unique: yet she does not explain how he can function as "the representative of liberated humanity" and the one whose manifestation signifies "the kenosis of patriarchy."[137] If anything, this capacity seems to reside primarily in Jesus' message.[138] It is as if questions of identity are illegitimate and thus require no answer.[139]

These feminist understandings of Jesus are theologically problematic in a number of respects. Apart from anything else, there are hermeneutical problems with the way in which the New Testament is read. In trying to hold together the Johannine symbol of incarnation with the supposedly "low" Christology of the Synoptic Gospels, with their presumed disinterest in the person of Jesus in favor of focus on his liberating message, feminist theologians speak of the Gospels at times in an almost uncritical way. At least in practice, the historical Jesus who proclaims the message of the reign of God seems to be confused with the Jesus of the Gospels. As a result, we have something that is dangerously like a polarization between the Synoptic Gospels as conveyers of the simple message of Jesus (without a developed Christology) and the Fourth Gospel as a reservoir of theological symbols and concepts that can be used at will (and without historical foundation). It is significant that Schüssler Fiorenza, who makes no such mistake, has to uncover *primitive* traditions in the New Testament as a basis for feminist Christology, rejecting as "kyriarchal" the Christologies of the New Testament writings in their final, canonical form (including that of the Gospels).[140] Yet, despite her efforts to unearth early Christologies that are free from ideological taint—that is, which predate the notion of incarnation—what she presents is not fundamentally the Jesus of the Gospels, nor of the New Testament as a whole, but rather a reconstruction of early traditions that is driven and directed by her own ideological agenda. Not only the Fourth Gospel but also the Synoptic Gospels (not to mention the apostle Paul) refuse for good reason to separate the message of the reign of God from the person of the messenger, since he bears the message in a way *that is radically dependent on his mysterious identity and his bodily reality*. There is no message divorced from his identity: for him, in a radical way, "the medium is the message." The New Testament writings interpret Jesus' ministry theologically from the lens of his death on the cross and bodily resurrection, and within the context of the defining question of his identity.

It is hard to perceive, moreover, in what way such theologies are distinctly Christian, and in what sense they can claim to be christological, except by stretching the common store of theological language almost beyond recognition. The rejection of the uniqueness of Jesus, along with the widening of "incarnation" to mean little more than the presence of God within creation and/or movements for liberation, raises sharply Hampson's critique: How do such perspectives differ from that of a humanist who respects the teaching and example of Jesus? Most feminist theology offers not a Christology but a "Jesus-ology" that has more problems than it solves. Despite the well-articulated need for radical change in social structure, what such feminism ends up with is little more than pedagogical: if there is any role for Jesus at all, it is as a model whose praxis is to be imitated and as a teacher whose teaching is to be followed. There is no transformation in this "Christology" except for what can be achieved at our own hands. It is hard to see how this can claim to be genuinely radical, given that it lacks any understanding of salvation as the gracious gift of God established in divine self-giving. What is absent, theologically speaking, is the very grounds for transformation, whether that transformation be social, political, or personal. In the end, salvation is something to be achieved for ourselves in the common struggle against injustice. Such a vision is alarmingly minimalist and ultimately without hope, particularly in the face of the kind of evil that feminists (and others) have so clearly and rightly delineated.

If the bodily reality of Jesus is not taken seriously, the concept of incarnation is so weakened as to become negligible. It is obvious to feminist theology that "incarnation" is a powerful vehicle in deconstructing a theology that ignores or downplays the body and material existence. It is also clear to many feminists that the erotic needs to be incorporated into theology in a positive and constructive way. It is ironic, however, as Janet Martin Soskice points out, that these "incarnational" concerns are countermanded by the desire of a number of feminist theologians to distance themselves from the incarnation embodied in Jesus himself, ending up with "a featureless and disembodied Christ."[141] The seeming advantage of side-stepping his maleness is won at the cost of his actual embodiment. What is lost is the foundation stone for a nondualistic theology: the very source for developing a holistic understanding that brings together the diversity of human experience, in all its richness and breadth, body and soul, spiritual and physical, erotic and political, is cut off. The cost, in terms of theology, is too high. Such a pruning is so savage as to kill the plant from which a renewed Christian theology can grow. Men as well as women are the losers in this.

At the same time, it is problematic to argue that the body of Jesus, even if male has relevance only for men. What we have seen of that bodily reality suggests that it has the capacity to be transposed across differences of gender (as well as other kinds of difference). To deny this and imply that salvation is confined exclusively to gender—a male Savior for men and a female Savior for women—is in serious danger of imprisoning the human person within biological gender, a perspective that feminism has strenuously resisted in other respects. Such a view too quickly ends up in idolatry: the absolutizing of gender by projecting it onto the being of God. In effect, this means "redemption via anatomical identification" in which we have succeeded in confusing ourselves with God through a "narcissistically projected divine."[142] Whatever else we may want to say of the incarnation, we need to beware of a form of gender fundamentalism that confines male to male and female to female. Human identification is infinitely more complex.

Those theologians who have taken the feminist question seriously yet remain within the tradition that affirms the uniqueness of Jesus within the divine schema of salvation have found the least problem with the maleness of Jesus.[143] From a Johannine perspective, their discussion of the issues is theologically more coherent than those who have attempted another route: the Logos assumes a humanity in Jesus Christ that is "in solidarity with the whole suffering human race."[144] John, in particular, uses the language of *sarx*, *sōma*, and *anthrōpos* to express the humanity of Jesus rather than the narrower *anēr*—signifying a male—within the overall theological context of the manifestation of divine glory. It is this *divine-humanity* that is definitive for salvation, not the maleness of the historical Jesus, a perspective that is confirmed by the tradition itself.[145] After all, if Jesus is a man and no more, theology has a much more serious problem when it comes to gender. If the identity of Jesus is confined to the human sphere—if he stands merely in a line of prophetic figures from Moses and Miriam through to Mary and Peter, as Schüssler Fiorenza and others have claimed—and if gender issues are taken seriously, then women indeed have a problem. Why should women look definitively and uniquely to a man for salvation? Why should the paradigm figure of liberation be male? "Will the rediscovery, the repristination, of the human Jesus be enough?" is the critical question.[146] If, however, we can also speak of Jesus possessing contiguity with God (in a unique sense), as well with human beings (in a cosmic sense)—

without having to resort to unhelpful and misleading categories such as "hero"—
then the problem is of a different order.

Within such a framework, it is important to understand theologically how the
incarnation—the transfiguration of God in human form—relates to the specificities of human life in space and time: gender, race, class, culture, and so on. If God
becomes incarnate as a male Jew in the first century C.E., living in relative poverty
and obscurity in Palestine, and outside the great events of the day both historically
and politically, then we are left with the question of how the divine humanity is
contiguous with that vast array of human beings outside these narrow bounds.
Moreover, the question now is whether the Johannine understanding of the incarnation, interpreted anew, has the possibility not only for including women but
also for healing those divisions that have dogged parts of the Western tradition,
exacerbated in the Enlightenment and critically highlighted by feminism: the
dualistic split between body and soul, matter and spirit, nature and history, sexuality and spirituality, the political and personal, masculine and feminine. This
bifurcation has had evil consequences for men as well as for women, although it
has been particularly damaging for women, identified in each case with the "lesser"
element.

The perspective of John's Gospel has a vital contribution to make in elucidating such a theology. Although liberation feminists, as we have noted, tend to prefer what they interpret as the Synoptic understanding of Jesus, the Fourth Gospel
has at least an equal claim to be taken seriously in exploring issues of Christology
and gender. It becomes clear that the "flesh" of Jesus in the Fourth Gospel, in its
ability to transpose itself beyond mortal limits, holds as much significance for
women as it has for men. The effect of John's incarnational language in the Fourth
Gospel is to forge an inclusive conception of divine enfleshment that expands
beyond the limitations of male humanity. The presence of women as central characters and exemplary disciples in the Fourth Gospel is important but not as consequential as the way in which Jesus' flesh is depicted. It is not just a question of
how inclusive John's Gospel is in its portrayal of women, nor how women function as disciples and leaders in relation to men. More fundamental is the way in
which the incarnation is portrayed, because on this the question of salvation
hinges: "what he did not take up, he did not heal."

The language of "flesh" is decisive for John, a language that does not accord
idolatrous significance to gender difference, even though such differences are part
of human finitude. Because the Christ of this Gospel in his divine humanity is the
eternal Word of God, preexistent and risen from the dead, his complex identity
includes but is not defined or limited by the particularities of his humanity: "while
Jesus was anatomically male, the representation of the gendering of Jesus is never
a straightforward matter. It is capable of numerous configurations."[147] It is not
that the male Jesus is "deified" at some point in his earthly life—such an adop-

tionist Christology is much more problematic for feminism. Rather, the eternal Word becomes flesh in the human person of Jesus of Nazareth. We are not speaking of the deification of male humanity but, in a more radical inversion, *the divine enfleshment of God* within the bounds of a human life. Those who attempt to make too much of the maleness of Jesus, whether post-Christian or fundamentalist Christian, accord it a cosmic status that it does not receive at the hands of the fourth evangelist. In the opening chapters of Genesis, male and female equally share the image in creation and are equally responsible for its disfigurement. Only the advent of the Logos, who first formed it, can remake that image: "male and female" as at the beginning. The "children of God" who gaze upon the glory in the flesh—in the incarnation and the "signs" ministry, on the cross and in the risen body—see in outline the shape of their own salvation. Only flesh restores flesh. As Augustine, using the image of the eye blinded by sin (cf. John 9) puts it, "by dust you were blinded, by dust you are healed: thus flesh [*caro*] had wounded you, flesh heals you" (*In Joannis Evangelium* 2.16). Only God's humanity heals humanity. In that vision, all manifold human divisions are healed.

There is an obvious objection to this theology, and it concerns the male language used both of God and of Christ throughout the Fourth Gospel, which may seem to belie its inclusive Christology. The resolution to the problem—insofar as it can be resolved—lies partly in the wider connotations of the Johannine imagery and partly in the symbolic nature of the language itself. Alongside masculine categories, Wisdom language uses implicitly feminine imagery of God throughout the Fourth Gospel.[148] The issue here is why Logos (which is masculine in gender) is used in the Prologue rather than Sophia (which is feminine). Although the preference for Logos could be related to the maleness of Jesus, it is more likely that it is preferred by the Johannine evangelist because it retains vital links with the proclamation of the early church.[149] Feminists disagree on whether the fact that Jesus is presented as Wisdom incarnate means that the female icon is swamped by the maleness of Jesus or includes both masculine and feminine.[150] If we take seriously the connotations of language, as well as its strict denotation (its "literal" meaning), the Wisdom overtones unsettle, at the very least, the masculine imagery of the Gospel and point to the inclusive character of the divine flesh beyond distinctions of male and female.

Because the Fourth Gospel is clear that the being of God is beyond human categories and imagery, symbol becomes the most appropriate language for revelation. It does not attempt to exhaust or imprison the divine being. The Father-Son imagery of the Gospel is a way of speaking of the relationship between the Word who becomes flesh and the God whose life he shares. We are not given in this Gospel a photograph of onto-reality, but rather core symbols of faith that possess divine truth and beauty while also reflecting the limitations of human speech. There is an "is not" dimension to the Johannine symbolic language. When the Nicene Creed describes Jesus as "begotten not made," it is doing the same thing, showing where the symbolism begins and ends: the Logos is not begotten of God in a literal, physiological sense. Similarly, we need to confirm—perhaps more clearly today than in the past—that the Word, the preexistent Son of the Father, is not male. His maleness is part of the metaphorical "is not," even though many throughout the history of the church have tried to make it part of the metaphorical "is," marginalizing women in the process. God's triune being is not open to our inspection or control in that way; it utterly transcends our creaturely lives, whether male or female. That is what makes the embodiment of God in the Fourth Gospel so extraordinary.

FURTHER IMPLICATIONS

A further issue arising from Johannine Christology relates to the wider scope of the term "flesh" beyond the human realm. The question may be asked whether the incarnation is in some sense contiguous with the rest of creation, now more than ever "groaning in travail" and in need of redemption. We have already seen that "all flesh" in 17:2, although it is primarily concerned with human beings, need not be confined to human reality. John's terminology suggests a broader sphere that encompasses creation within the orbit of the incarnation. Theology in the Western tradition, at least since the Enlightenment, has tended to be anthropocentric, with little concern to develop a cosmic Christology that addresses the entirety of God's creation. We need not lapse here into a "creation theology" with its tendency to downplay sin and the saving role of Jesus Christ. Other routes are possible that do not foreclose on redemption or revelation. Johannine Christology, in particular, begins with creation as the rightful domain of the Logos (1:3–4, 10–11). The term "flesh," although its primary reference is to human beings, has a more encompassing range of meanings that extends to all creation. We can argue, by extension, that in becoming human, the divine Word expresses solidarity not only with humankind but also with the rest of creation. The Fourth Gospel itself never makes the link that Paul does between fallen human nature and creation (Rom. 5:2; 8:19–22). However, the imagery that encloses the passion narrative (and is uniquely Johannine) may be significant in this respect. Since the arrest and burial both take place in a garden, as does the meeting of the risen Christ with Mary Magdalene (*kēpos*, 18:1; 19:14; cf. 20:15), it is possible that there are symbolic suggestions of paradise restored.[151] In any case, that creation is destined for salvation seems a reasonable inference to be drawn from John's understanding of the Logos as the agent of creation, as entering the sphere that is "his own," as the Savior of the world (4:42) and as possessing authority over "all flesh." In this sense, we can speak of a *creation Christology* arising from the Johannine understanding of the centrality of the divine Word in forming and transforming the world. This perspective has the potential for healing the bifurcation between creation and redemption, and between nature and human life. The phrase "all flesh" enlarges our understanding of the incarnation to include all that is formed by the generative and regenerative power of the Logos.

Linked to the same issue, it is important also to ask whether John's Christology can help in overcoming the body–soul dualism that has pervaded more recent parts, at least, of the Western theological tradition.[152] That the Fourth Gospel presupposes no such bifurcation is clear. More than that, Johannine theology has the capacity for constructively healing the rift, particularly as it relates to the erotic, where the disconnection has been most pronounced. This takes us beyond the literal Johannine text, but is a legitimate inference to be drawn from its theological and symbolic perspective. Words such as "fleshly," "carnal," and "sensual" have distinctly negative connotations in English, in part under the influence of Pauline usage, but also as a result of the fear of bodily intimacy that an overspiritualized theology engenders. Once more this is a question of drawing out the theological implications of the Fourth Gospel rather than pointing to specific proof texts. In the evangelist's understanding of flesh, in the radical embodiment of divine revelation in the person of Jesus Christ, there is a distinctive confirmation of the erotic and the fleshly: desire for the other in a rich and palpable sense, and flesh as the locus of ecstatic and mutual self-giving. The incarnation is itself "erotic" in the divine longing for union with the world which underlies the mission of the Johannine Jesus. Redemption encompasses body and soul, not merely in a moral sense, but in a way that releases human beings from the constraints of a disembodied spirituality that fears, controls, or denigrates the articulation of bodily love. In opening the doors to a nondualistic theology, the Fourth Gospel weaves together need, desire, intimacy, and love, allowing for their rich and varied manifestation in erotic affinity.[153] This kind of theology is grounded not in ethereal principles or political manifestos but in a palpable apprehension of the Word-made-flesh.

CONCLUSION

We can summarize the meaning and significance of flesh in the Fourth Gospel for understanding both Christology and anthropology in the following points:

1. Johannine usage of this word cluster does not permit a dualistic anthropology that divorces spirit and flesh, soul and body. Flesh has its origin in God's creative word and stands in contrast not to the soul but to God's own self. Flesh indicates the full person, the "bodyself." The contrast John draws is along theological rather than anthropological lines. The Fourth Gospel retains its sense of the world as God's creation and the object of divine love.

2. The central symbol of glory in the Fourth Gospel is flesh. In Tillich's terms, it bears something of the reality to which it points. The image of Jesus' flesh becomes the "vehicle" of the metaphor, which points to and conveys the

"tenor"—divine glory. The meaning is primarily christological: "the incarnation is not the loss but the making visible of the *doxa* of Jesus."[154]

3. The christological symbol of flesh is an expanding symbol. Looked at in metaphorical terms, the "tenor" or external referent is not the historical Jesus—still less his bodily existence. As the narrative progresses, the symbol of the flesh of Jesus stretches to incorporate Jesus' incarnation, ministry, death, resurrection, and risen presence with the community in its sacramental life: in each case, symbolizing—that is to say, making present—the divine *doxa*.

4. The juxtaposition of flesh in the Gospel—flesh as good and needful, yet flesh as incapacitated and fragile—is paradoxical but not contradictory, expressing the vital inter-connection of Christology and anthropology. The distinction between flesh (mortal existence) and Spirit forms a contrast between flesh enlivened by the Spirit and flesh that is closed against it. Creaturely flesh can only find salvation through divine enfleshment; believers come to share in the divine nature just as—and indeed solely because—the Logos comes to share in human nature. In patristic terms, the Logos who is himself the true Image (*eikōn*) rebuilds the image in human beings by becoming flesh, so that they become "children of God," symbols resplendent with divine glory (1:12). The coming of the Logos, the agent of creation, has as its purpose the restoration of human beings to the divine image.

5. John's understanding of the incarnation implies also a wider significance: "When it stands by itself, *sarx* is not just another way of saying 'man.'"[155] The Johannine language is inclusive of female and male, transposing itself beyond the limits of Jesus' own historical maleness. In crossing the abyss between heaven and earth, "above" and "below," the flesh of Jesus, enlivened with divine glory, crosses also the rift between human beings, including that between men and women. It is significant that even a writer such as Irigaray, outside the formal bounds of theology, takes seriously the possibility of an embodied humanity in Jesus that speaks powerfully across gender barriers, for all her stress on essential difference. Irigaray speaks of the dying body of Jesus (in language that reflects the Synoptic Gospels as well as John) as redemptive for the woman as well as the man:

> And if "God" who thus re-proved the fact of her non-value still loves her, this means that she exists all the same, beyond what anyone may think of her. It means that love conquers everything that has already been said. And that one man has understood her so well that he died in the most awful suffering. That most female of men, the Son.
>
> And she never ceases to look upon his nakedness, open for all to see, upon the gashes in his virgin flesh, at the wounds from the nails that pierce his body as he hangs there, in his passion and abandonment. And she is

overwhelmed with love of him/herself. In his crucifixion he opens up a
path of redemption to her in her fallen state.[156]

In other words, women as well as men are able to perceive themselves and
their own embodied experience within the iconic portrayal of the divine
flesh in the Johannine Jesus. The transposition of flesh thus opens the gospel
to those outside the narrow bounds of identification with the male, historical Jesus.

6. The Fourth Gospel suggests also the possibility of a connection between the
   incarnate Logos and the rest of creation. Imaged as the restoration of paradise (cf. *kēpos*, 18:1; 19:41), redemption thus moves beyond the human
   realm to that which is created by the divine Logos. This incorporation
   extends to the material world in its variety and complexity—"all things" created at the beginning (1:3) and "all things" enlightened by the revelation of
   divine glory in the flesh.

The main point of the incarnation, in Johannine theology, lies in the symbol of
"flesh," which expands throughout the Gospel to reveal the divine glory by both
encompassing and transcending the particularities of Jesus' human life. In Johannine Christology, flesh signifies the humanity of Jesus, his "bodyself," mortal yet
risen from the dead, absent after his glorification yet present through the Spirit-
Paraclete and the sacramental life of the church. The flesh of Jesus is the core
Johannine symbol of divine glory and spirituality. Only there is the full radiance
of God revealed: "the Logos, as Son of the Father, is truly, in his humanity as such,
the revelatory symbol in which the Father enunciates himself, in this Son, to the
world—revelatory, because the symbol renders present what is revealed."[157]
Because God has entered the fallen world in such a form, the world itself is transformed, the image restored, the darkness overcome, death extinguished. For the
evangelist, incarnation signifies the divine, saving beatitude on all fleshly existence
and its transformation by the Spirit: male and female, erotic and spiritual, humanity and nature. The maleness of Jesus is not of ultimate significance in this vision.
He is the divine *anthrōpos* whose flesh is transposed symbolically and sacramentally beyond the limitations of human finitude: "truly in Christ there is no male
and female, only the reciprocation of bodies; beautiful parodies of the trinitarian
donation."[158] The symbolism of divine embodiment articulates the reunification
of flesh and spirit and the restoring of divine glory to the created world.

CHAPTER 3

Quenching Thirst:
The Symbol of Living Water

When the woman of everlasting memory
came to the well,
She found you, the water of wisdom.
Because of her deep faith,
You satisfied her completely, O Lord,
And you bestowed on her
The kingdom that lasts forever.[1]

THE IMAGE OF WATER is given considerable prominence in the Fourth Gospel. Indeed it is one of the core, impersonal symbols of the Gospel, which enlarges in meaning and significance throughout the narrative.[2] Water is employed in three main physical senses: for quenching physical thirst, for cleansing the body, and as part of childbirth. Perhaps the most prominent Johannine story involving water is Jesus' encounter with the Samaritan woman, where the image gains symbolic significance in the context of the well, raising a number of issues important for gender (4:1–42). The story of Nicodemus introduces the birth image (3:1–21), while the footwashing develops the theme of cultic cleansing. In the piercing of Jesus' side (19:31–37), the three dimensions are implicitly present as these have developed through the Gospel narrative. Thus, although the usage is diverse, with different dimensions shifting from one scene to another, the evangelist succeeds in giving an overarching unity to the imagery of water. In the end, it becomes a sacramental symbol of new life, given through the purifying and life-giving Spirit. More than other symbols in this Gospel, water reveals the multivalence of symbolism and its capacity to move freely across different fields of reference.

EARLY IMAGES OF WATER:
JOHN THE BAPTIST, CANA, AND NICODEMUS

The first reference to water occurs in the opening scene of the Gospel (*hydōr,* 1:19–34), where John the Baptist is interrogated by the authorities for his baptizing and for the identity he claims as the basis of his ministry (1:25–26, 28, 31, 33). Although John's baptizing in water is the result of divine imperative, it is given no particular significance at this point except as a dramatic contrast to the One to whom John testifies (1:7, 15, 26–27, 29–34, 36). John the Baptizer-in-water bears witness to Jesus as the Lamb of God (1:29, 36), Son of God (1:34), and Bearer of the Spirit (1:32) who will baptize with the Holy Spirit (1:33)—an allusion that the reader does not yet comprehend. Nothing more than the contrast is drawn, however, John's role being that of the temporal voice testifying to the eternal Word (1:23). The imagery here relates presumably to water as cleansing and purifying, although nothing explicit is said of its symbolic import. The comparison between Jesus and the Baptist—including the fact that each in some sense baptizes—indicates that John's use of water will become symbolic in the narrative of the Gospel. That John the Baptist's baptizing is linked to the Holy Spirit suggests that water is in some way connected to the Spirit's rejuvenating and cleansing power.[3]

The second reference to water occurs in the first of the Johannine "signs" at the wedding at Cana (2:1–11). The "signs" of the Fourth Gospel, in technical terms, are symbols rather than signs: their meaning is christological and they exemplify the pattern of 1:14 in which flesh becomes symbolic of divine glory. The action of Jesus, despite being "supernatural," operates primarily at the material or physical level—changing water into wine, healing physical disability, feeding a hungry crowd, raising the dead—but its true meaning is to be found at the figurative or spiritual level. Each event reveals Jesus' true identity, and becomes symbolic of the gift of eschatological salvation offered in the here and now, a gift that incorporates yet transforms the nature of fleshly life. Much of the struggle of the central characters in these narratives concerns the movement from one level, the literal, to the other, the figurative—in some instances leading to true, Johannine faith and thus eternal life, in other cases, leading to darkness, violence, and rejection. Remaining at the literal level, no matter how religious it appears, means ultimately death for the evangelist.

In the first "sign," the wedding at Cana, the evangelist introduces the ministry of Jesus after the gathering of the first disciples through the witness and baptizing of John the Baptist (1:19–51). The event will not only launch the ministry of Jesus; it will also reveal the true significance of Jesus' coming and lead the first group of disciples to faith, through the witness of the mother of Jesus. The sumptuousness of the imagery evokes the messianic banquet in the Old Testament—the final, eschatological banquet of the reign of God (e.g., Isa. 25:6; cf. Matt. 22:1–14 par.). At the same time, there is a newness to this event: a transformation of, as well as continuity with, what has gone before. This whole section of the Gospel, framed by the two Cana "signs," will deal with the advent of the new (2:1–4:54) and the means of entry into the "new thing" which Jesus embodies,[4] through a series of contrasting examples: the mother of Jesus, the disciples, "the Jews," Nicodemus,

John the Baptist, the Samaritan woman and villagers, and the (presumably Gentile) royal official. In the context of the first sign at Cana, the narrator employs two uses of water, for drinking and washing, combined in an unusual way. The water in the stone water jars (*hydriai*) represents the purification rites of "the Jews," as the narrator makes plain (2:6), the significance continuous with the opening scene where John the Baptist uses water for a similar purpose. Yet the Baptist, as we have seen, implies that water is itself but a signal for something greater. It functions in a typological way that is characteristic of early Christian interpretation of the Old Testament. At Cana, the water possesses cultic overtones and therefore already speaks of a purification that is more than the cleanliness of the body. Yet its ritual use for washing changes dramatically in the Johannine narrative. Now, at a celebratory event that itself has overtones of fecundity and new life, its use is for drinking rather than purification, and the water transformed into wine supplies a drink that does more than quench thirst. Water is now on the way to becoming a symbol, but it does not yet function in its own right: strictly speaking, the symbolism that emerges is the wine, miraculously transformed.[5] The coming together of different symbolic associations has a christological focus, with elements of both typology and allegory. The presence of the Word-made-flesh is the antitype to which the symbols point, the fulfillment of what is promised in the Old Testament: in its rites and rituals, as well as its hopes and dreams. Jesus himself, allegorically speaking, is the "good wine," which is left till last (2:10): it is his glory that radiates through the story from beginning to end, the force of its revelatory meaning. The miraculous transformation at a figurative level signifies that, in the person of Christ, new life has come, a new relationship is forged, the final celebration of God's divine reign has begun—and the one through whom the new arrives, the guest at the banquet, becomes the host, the giver, the divine self-gift.

In formal terms, the use of the image of water, pointing to what John sees (in terms of typology) as the lesser rites of Judaism—part of the literal level of the story—seems inconsistent with its later development as a core Johannine symbol. Metaphors, however, are not subject to this kind of linear logic. Within different literary spheres, the use of divergent imagery need only be internally consistent. In the Cana narrative, the context is a wedding at which not water but wine is required. The conversion of one to the other works at a symbolic level: the evangelist portrays both continuity and discontinuity between the rituals of Judaism and the advent of Jesus. Wine is the symbol needed for the present narrative with its associations of joy and celebration, symbolizing the fecundity of a new relationship with all the promise of new life. As in the first instance with John the Baptist, there is also a contrast present, though the images are handled differently: whereas the earlier contrast lies between two different kinds of baptism, here it is between water and wine. Yet at a deeper level, the contrast is not so very different. In both cases there is literal and figurative meaning, linked to the old faith and the new. The transformation at Cana suggests that the old functions typologically and symbolically to reveal the new. It is not discarded but rather elevated to a new level of meaning.[6] Later in the Gospel, wine will again be used symbolically with eucharistic overtones, both in relation to blood and the fruit of the vine (6:53–56; 15:1–8; 19:34).

The next reference to water is found in the following chapter, in the dialogue between Jesus and Nicodemus. The basic image is that of birth—at least in the opening sequence—the overarching theme, as we have already seen, being entry into the new life offered by Jesus. In response to Nicodemus's approach, Jesus makes two solemn statements in parallel concerning the need to be born "from above" in order to embrace the new (3:3, 5):

> I tell you solemnly, unless one is born from above,
> one cannot see the reign/realm [*basileia*] of God. ... (3:3)

> I tell you solemnly, unless one is born of water and spirit,
> one cannot enter the reign/realm of God. (3:5)

The second is a restatement and clarification of the first, resulting from Nicodemus's misunderstanding (3:4): he assumes a literal rather than metaphorical meaning and expresses his incredulity at Jesus' demand. Jesus' restatement of the solemn *amēn* saying replaces the adverbial "from above" with the expanded and clarifying phrase "of water and spirit" (*ex hydatos kai pneumatos*) and changes seeing the *basileia* of God to the synonymous image of entering it. Water in this dialogue now becomes a symbol in its own right. Yet the nature of tenor and vehicle are difficult to determine. As we have seen in the previous chapter, it is not immediately obvious (at least to the modern reader) what the phrase "water and spirit" means.[7]

There are three possible meanings that seek to make sense of what John is saying here. The first explanation sees "water and Spirit" as referring to two contrasting elements, the one physical and the other spiritual. Jesus' explanation in 3:5, according to this view, clarifies that by "spirit" we are speaking of the divine Spirit (3:6, 8). Within its context, the second *amēn*-saying represents Jesus' attempt to clarify Nicodemus's misinterpretation of *anōthen*, with its double meaning of "from above" or "again." Whereas Jesus is speaking of the Spirit and a metaphorical new "birth" (3:3), Nicodemus assumes physical rebirth, as is evident in his use of the adverbial "a second time" (*deuteron*, 3:4).[8] The restatement in 3:5, in this explanation, would need to be read as a contrast between physical birth and birth "from above," as in 3:6:

> that which is born of the flesh is flesh,
> and that which is born of the Spirit is Spirit.

In 3:8 a similar contrast is drawn in the form of a simile, this time between the wind and the Spirit, the physical and the spiritual:

> the wind (*pneuma*) breathes where it wills and you hear its voice,
> but you do not know where it comes from and where it goes to;
> so is everyone born of the Spirit (*pneuma*).

In each case, according to the argument, there is both a likeness and a contrast present. In the first (3:6), the likeness is contained in the image of birth, present in both parts of the statement; in the second (3:8), the simile of the wind suggests an even closer correspondence between wind and Spirit—a correspondence that, while maintaining the distinction between "above" and "below," sees the divine Spirit as the source of *all* life, physical and spiritual.[9] From the perspective of these contrasting parallels, water and Spirit are read as contrasting elements in 3:5, the first referring to the natural phenomenon and the second to its spiritual parallel. Physical birth (water) and spiritual birth (Spirit) are both required for entry into the *basileia* of God.[10] In this argument, however, the first element ("of water") seems superfluous.[11]

The second explanation is that water and spirit refer to one and the same thing. The single use of the preposition *ek* (meaning, literally, "out of") suggests that we are dealing with one entity, not two. Larry Jones argues along these lines, but goes further in interpreting the "and" of "water and Spirit" as explanatory: "the water of Spirit."[12] Water, in his view, seems to function only as a marker of the Spirit and not as a vehicle drawn from the human processes of birth. However, if a sense of the literal meaning is retained, and if *pneuma* is not too quickly read as the divine Spirit, the interpretation could be modified: at the first level, for birth to be successful, the infant must pass through the *waters* of childbirth and breathe into its nostrils the *breath* of life (cf. Gen. 2:7). This reading would mean, at the metaphorical level, that the passage of birth and the breaking of the waters *both* refer symbolically to entry into a new kind of "life" that John designates as the *basileia* of God. Thus "water represents the transformation required for entrance into the realm of God."[13] Just as new life at a biological level requires the release of the amniotic fluid, the passage down the birth canal, and the infant's first breath, so entry into eternal life requires a similar process, at a spiritual level. In this interpretation, human birth—water and breath—is the vehicle, and the tenor is entry into the reign/realm of God. The "labor" to enter life, in either case, is difficult and painful, and the outcome uncertain, as Nicodemus's own story indicates.[14]

The third explanation connects the water to baptism as a rite of cleansing and initiation. That baptism is not far from the mind of the narrator is apparent in the last section of John 3 after the dialogue with Nicodemus. Now we find Jesus baptizing (3:22; cf. 4:2) and also John the Baptist (3:23), the context being a dispute with "a Jew" over purification (*katharismos*) (3:25). The passage provides an important link with the opening sequence of the Gospel, where John the Baptist's baptism represents purification. This factor forms a link also with the wedding at Cana, where the wine is miraculously created in stone water jars set apart for purification (2:6). This time, in John 3, the contrast is between John the Baptist's baptizing and that of Jesus, the one witnessing to the superiority of the other. The best man, who gives way before the bridegroom—note the recurrence of the wedding imagery—recognizes the need to decrease in order that the bridegroom may increase (3:29–30); being "of the earth," he gives way before the One who is "from above"/"from heaven" (3:31).[15] In this view, the phrase "water and Spirit" signifies the rite of initiation, at which, by means of water, the purifying Spirit is imparted to the newborn person—an interpretation that is suggestive not just for the Gospel narrative but also for the baptismal practices of the Johannine community.[16]

It is not easy to decide between these interpretations, since each attempts to understand the text within its literary context. Least helpful is any interpretation that loses the sense of "water" as having its origins in the physical reality of birth, whether the phrase is interpreted as "water that is Spirit" or is seen as baptismal.[17] In the first two explanations, where water is allowed to stand in some sense as a vehicle for the figurative meaning, there is no misunderstanding: it is clear that, at the literal level, the image of water signifies the processes of childbirth.[18] For Sandra Schneiders, who takes this view, water in the ancient world can often refer "to the processes of human reproduction and particularly to the actual coming forth from the womb after the breaking of the mother's water" (e.g., Prov. 5:15–18; Cant. 4:12–15; 1QH iii 7–10; 4 Ezra 8:8).[19] Ben Witherington argues along similar lines, drawing on material from the Old Testament and Judaism, and concluding that "water" here and in 1 John 5:6–8 encompasses "various facets of procreation, child-bearing, and child birth."[20] It might include the seed, the nurture in the womb, the rupture of the amniotic sac as the signal for birth, and even the washing and care of the infant once it is born. Thus "of water and spirit" signifies the experience of childbirth, probably as a literal reference at a first-level reading and metaphorical at the second level, rather than each element of the phrase referring to the two separate spheres. The difference between the first two explanations is not ultimately of great significance, however, provided that the imagery of birth is not lost sight of. In any event, the phrase "of water and Spirit" parallels metaphorically Jesus' earlier statement (3:3) in the light of Nicodemus's misunderstanding in 3:4. Two very different kinds of births are required, not a repeat of one: *physical birth becomes a symbol of spiritual birth*.

Taking the text as it stands, we are still left with a choice between water as a symbol of birth and water as a reference to baptism. Yet is the choice really necessary? Baptism is an important secondary theme within the opening chapters of the Fourth Gospel: indeed John the Baptist and Nicodemus are contrasting figures in John 3, both in some sense representing Judaism—the one able to make the transition from the new to the old, the other unable to decide. For the early church, the rite of baptism already had overtones of birth, the baptismal font being an image of the womb as well as the tomb. Thus, at baptism the catechumen journeyed from the darkness of "death" into the light of life, just as physiologically birth is the movement from the dark womb to the light of day (cf. 3:19–21). While little can be deduced of the baptismal practices of the Johannine community, the text suggests a broad rather than narrow metaphorical range. It is likely that water, as a symbol, evokes *both* birth and baptism in this passage, the text making no attempt to delimit the symbolic meaning. While Christian baptism is not the primary focus of the dialogue, John's symbolism is evocative in a number of directions and suggests a wider field of meaning.

What is established in John 3 is the link between water and Spirit, already hinted at in the first occurrence of the image. In its second occurrence, as we saw, water is linked symbolically to the transfiguration of Judaism with the advent of Jesus, the Word-made-flesh, even though it is the wine that takes on symbolic meaning. Now in its third appearance, water becomes a symbol in its own right, pointing to and communicating the Spirit, who makes possible entry into eternal life. In this case, the symbolism refers not to purification or to the quenching of thirst (which is not, in any case, the major focus of 2:1–11), but rather to the amniotic waters, whose rupture heralds birth. In symbolic terms, water in John 3 represents the Spirit of God "laboring" to admit believers into the reign/realm of God. The same imagery of birth—though without direct reference to water—is found toward the end of the Farewell Discourse, where it is used metaphorically of the community living in the painful place between the absence and promised return of Jesus (16:16–22). Once more, the Spirit is the cause of that "birth" for which the disciples long, the source of their joy and consolation, leading them into the fullness of truth and life (16:12–15).[21]

THE WATER OF THE WELL: THE SAMARITAN WOMAN

The next appearance of water (after a passing reference to the wedding at Cana at 4:46a) is one of the most highly developed and significant in the Gospel: the story of the Samaritan woman's encounter with Jesus at Jacob's well (John 4:1–42). The narrative is carefully linked to the previous sequence by a number of common themes (3:1–36): in particular, water, baptism, and the Spirit, but also themes of witness, the world, and the overtones of betrothal (3:5–8, 16, 22–30).[22] There is a striking contrast between the character of Nicodemus and that of the woman. The male, "orthodox" Pharisaic teacher and theologian, who has name and status within the text (3:1), stands over against the female, heterodox Samaritan, who is without name or status.[23] The irony is that, while Nicodemus as representative of the Pharisees hesitates on the horns of a dilemma and cannot (at least at this stage of the Gospel) make a decision for faith (3:9), the woman as representative of her people not only achieves understanding for herself but brings an entire village to Jesus.

John 4:1–42 falls into three scenes, with a narrative introduction at the beginning. Scene 2 is an *inclusio* in which the woman responds to Jesus' request in v. 16 by returning not with one man but with a village (4:30):

Setting	Jesus comes to a Samaritan well (4:1–6)
Scene 1	Jesus' dialogue with a Samaritan woman at the well (4:7–15)
Scene 2	Jesus' dialogue reaches a climax and the woman returns to the village to proclaim her discovery and bring back the villagers (4:16–30)
Scene 3	Jesus' dialogue with the disciples on the meaning of his mission and with the Samaritan villagers, who proclaim his identity (4:30–42)

Each of the three scenes centers on an image: "living water" (*hydōr zōn*) in the first scene, "sacred site" (*topos*) in the second, and "food/harvest" (*brōsis/brōma, therismos*) in the third. The dominant image is that of the well, which, from the point of view of the drama and its stage "props," holds the narrative together even where it seems to shift direction, being visually present in each scene. The journey of Jesus through Samaria focuses the narrative on the well as the dramatic centerpiece, right from the beginning, emphasizing also its religious origins in the wider traditions of Judaism.[24] At the same time, we confront the weariness and thirst of Jesus after the long journey in the heat of the day (4:4–6) and without the company of the disciples, who have gone to buy food from the village (4:8). In this context the Samaritan woman approaches with her water jar: the one who draws water and the one who is thirsty meet each other as strangers beside the well.

In one sense, it is perfectly comprehensible that Jesus requests a drink of the woman (4:7): she possesses access to the well that he needs and lacks. In another sense, by doing so, Jesus transgresses cultural and religious boundaries between Jews and Samaritans—boundaries that, from the Jewish side at least, narrowly define the scope of salvation. Ironically it is the woman who points out the *faux pas*, reminding Jesus of the barriers between them on racial grounds and wondering aloud why the Jewish man before her seems so impervious to them (4:9). Yet, as will later emerge in the narrative, the gender barrier is at least as strong (4:27): that male and female are in dialogue about living water is as significant for the narrative—and as remarkable—as the differences in religion and culture. These barriers are not pursued for the moment, at least not overtly. Instead the narrative unexpectedly changes direction. Ignoring the obstacles and the woman's objection, Jesus reverses the roles of giver and receiver, presenting himself as the watergiver and the woman the one who is thirsty and lacking the means of slaking her thirst (4:10). His invitation, though the woman does not yet know it, is a metaphor structured in three parts: the giver of water ("he would have given you"), the gift of water ("living water," *hydōr zōn*) and the one who is thirsty for water ("you would have asked him"). At this stage the woman, through no fault of her own, fails to grasp the symbolic import: she recognizes neither the identity of the Giver, the nature of the gift, nor indeed her own need.

Note, however, the importance of the incarnation for the dialogue. Although the woman does not yet perceive it, the divine glory is already radiant in the flesh, particularly the "fleshly" level of Jesus' thirst. From a narrative point of view, the mention of his thirst—along with the absence of the disciples—is a literary ploy by the narrator to engage Jesus in conversation with the woman. Yet it is too fundamental to the narrative to be merely a conversation starter. The theme of thirst continues through the narrative, at first explicitly and later implicitly, paralleled in the latter part of the narrative by that of hunger (4:31–34). Although the evangelist does not inform us whether Jesus actually drinks the water (or, later, whether he eats the food the disciples have brought), Jesus' physical need is nevertheless of great significance. It establishes a human bond between himself and the woman beyond other differences, by virtue of their common humanity—a bond that is itself symbolic of a deeper correlation in the longing and need for God. Nevertheless, the deeper level can be reached only by way of Jesus' flesh, through which the divine glory shines. Once the roles are reversed, the only way forward for the woman is to move beyond the literal level and uncover the symbolic meaning. The glory which signifies the figurative meaning is progressively revealed in the ensuing dialogue, in Jesus' words about the Father and the Spirit and his own unfolding self-revelation. The symbolic pattern that emerges as water becomes a symbol of eternal life is grounded in the incarnation: in the revelation of divine glory through the flesh of Jesus. Augustine in his homily on this passage interprets the journey to Samaria allegorically, along with Jesus' weariness and thirst, as symbolic of the incarnation itself, establishing a dynamic between the *power* of the divine Word in creation and the *weakness* of the incarnate Word in redemption:

> It was for you that Jesus was wearied from the journey. We find a strong Jesus and we find a weak Jesus. . . . The strength of Christ created you; the weakness of Christ recreated you. The strength of Christ caused what-was-not to be; the weakness of Christ caused what-was to perish not. He produced us in strength; he sought us in his weakness. (*In Joannis Evangelium* 4.6.2)

In the meantime, the woman's understanding is impeded by the ambiguity of the phrase "living water." Of the two possible senses of the participle "living" (*zōn*), she chooses the literal meaning, "flowing water," as opposed to the still water of Jacob's well. As with Nicodemus, the choice is comprehensible. She has not yet come to perceive the symbolic reality of "life-giving water" as that which gives eternal life.[25] Unlike material water that is a daily physical necessity, the water that is the gift of the Johannine Jesus ultimately slakes all thirst. It becomes an internal well of water that, in Bultmann's words, "quenches in a radical way the thirst for life."[26] Physical thirst is used as a metaphor for spiritual thirst, signifying the need and longing for God. This symbolic sense is already present in the Old Testament, based on the physical experience of the children of Israel in the wilderness, where Moses strikes the rock at Meribah and water comes forth (Num. 20). The Psalms, moreover, speak of the longing for God as like thirst in the desert or a time of drought:

> As a deer longs for flowing streams,
> so my soul longs for you, O God.
> My soul thirsts for God, for the living God. (Ps. 42:1–2a)

> O God, you are my God, I seek you, my soul thirsts for you;
> my flesh faints for you,
> as in a dry and weary land where there is no water. (Ps. 63:1)

> I stretch out my hands to you;
> my soul thirsts for you like a parched land. (Ps. 143:6)

Amos also speaks metaphorically of a thirst (or famine) that will come upon the people of Israel, not for water but for "hearing the words of the Lord" (Amos 8:11). In terms of the two levels of metaphor, Jesus thus invites the woman to understand the same spiritual reality (*pneuma*) within the structures of the flesh (*sarx*). What is different is not that thirst is understood symbolically, but rather that the woman is face-to-face with the one who uniquely embodies the union of flesh and spirit. She is invited to see the material water of the well as a symbol of eternal life. At this stage, however, the woman remains on a literal level, even when she asks for the gift of water, having decided that Jesus is indeed a miraculous water giver in the tradition of Jacob (4:15)—though, like Nicodemus, she does perceive something of the absurdity of Jesus' claim: "Lord, you do not have a bucket and the well is deep; from where do you have living/flowing water?" (4:11). Her struggle to understand the true meaning is transparent in the way she responds and in the seriousness with which Jesus engages her.[27]

The imagery now moves from water to that of sacred site (4:16–26), though the new image is dependent on the primary image of the well. As Bultmann points out, Jesus perceives the woman's longing for "living water" and raises the issue of her husband (4:16) and marital status (4:18) in order to locate, in the restlessness of her relationships, her "thirst" for life.[28] As we will see in a later chapter, these verses function not to expose moral guilt but to uncover the pain of the woman's life in her intimate relationships (4:16–19).[29] Through the woman's developing self-knowledge, Jesus reveals himself as the source of life, the giver of living water. Her spirituality moves appropriately from the self-knowledge she has gained in dialogue with Jesus to the knowledge and worship of God.[30] The woman's understanding thus increases with each step of the dialogue. The disciples' patent disapproval upon their return (4:27) reveals that gender is a barrier in this story as well as race and culture—a barrier to which Jesus is impervious. Finally the woman returns to the village, forsaking her water jar,[31] and proclaims her faith in seemingly tentative terms,[32] encouraging the villagers to meet Jesus for themselves (4:28–30):

> the woman at once believed, and appeared wiser than Nicodemus; indeed, not only wiser, but even stronger. For though he heard countless things of this kind, he neither summoned any other person to Christ, nor did he himself speak freely of him; while she engaged in apostolic work, spreading the good news to all, and calling them to Jesus, drawing to him a whole city from outside the faith. (John Chrysostom, *Homily on John* 32)

In the final meeting between Jesus and the Samaritans, the cosmic identity of Jesus is confirmed: he is truly "the Savior of the world" (4:39–42).

One of the most striking features of 4:1–42 is the way in which the evangelist, by bringing together literary technique and theological context, has created new meaning. In this reading, the woman moves from a literal and material level of understanding to a metaphorical and symbolic one. By the end of the narrative, a new christological vision of humanity is attained. The story is told in such a way that the reader participates in the narrative and shares the revelation as it unfolds.[33] In the end, he or she is challenged by its spirituality and by the self-discovery it evokes. The reader enters the text as an outsider, an eavesdropper, and by identifying with the central character comes face-to-face with Jesus, the Savior of the world. The struggle to move through misunderstanding to understanding becomes the reader's own faith story.

Within this process, the symbolic meaning of the images is of key importance for John's literary and theological outlook—particularly, as we have seen, the image of water. As symbols arising out of the narrative, the images function in a theological as well as literary way. They give expression to John's understanding of the incarnation and its implications for human existence. John's worldview is, in the broadest sense, a sacramental one—not so much in the sense that it deals with individual sacraments as in that it is tied to the incarnation in the closest possible way. Such an outlook does not mean that all reality is absolutized; rather, material reality has the capacity to symbolize the divine, attaining its highest destiny in realizing its potential. In Johannine terminology, all that is encompassed by flesh (*sarx*) finds its true, creative fulfillment in revealing divine glory (*doxa*, cf. 1:14).[34] The fusion of meaning within metaphor, creating a new semantic structure, is paralleled by the theological fusion of matter and spirit, flesh and glory.[35]

The narrative of the Samaritan woman reveals the way in which, for the evangelist, the material world finds its true destiny as symbolic of the divine. For human beings, this means being remade in the image of God and becoming children of God, born of the divine Spirit (1:12–13). Here the reader discovers a new symbolic identity as child of God—the evangelical purpose of the narrative (20:31). In the struggle for faith, the reader breaks through divisive barriers to find "living water" in encounter with Jesus, the Savior of the world, and discovers in the process the existential dynamic between self-knowledge and the knowledge of God. This conversion occurs through a symbolic reading of the text, engaging the reader at the affective as well as the cognitive levels. It means the self-discovery of thirst, the breaking down of barriers, and the finding of living water in relationship with God. Through the narrative, the woman's longing, needs, and struggle are taken seriously; hidden in her daily experience, they become translucent to the divine Word, who sees into the heart and offers living water.

What is the significance of water in this story? There are two important referents to the symbol as it unfolds through the narrative. In the first place, the symbol of water relates to the theme of wisdom (*sophia*) underlying the narrative of 4:1–42, although it is never made explicit.[36] Throughout this and other Johannine narratives (e.g., 2:1–11; 6:1–72), Jesus speaks with the voice of divine Wisdom, who nourishes those who are hungry and thirsty, giving them food and drink to satisfy their need. In Proverbs, Sophia is the hostess who invites those seeking wisdom to her banquet (Prov. 9:1–5), while in Sirach, God gives the gift of Wisdom to the one who desires it: "She will feed him with the bread of learning, and give him the water of wisdom to drink" (Sir. 15:3). Later in Sirach, Sophia's gifts of food and drink are so delectable that the seeker after wisdom never tires of desiring them (Sir. 24:21).[37] Wisdom in these texts is closely linked to the theme of revelation. Just as Sophia gives insight and knowledge, so too the Johannine Jesus offers understanding. The revelation, as the narrative before us suggests, is two-sided: what Jesus offers the woman—as with Nathanael (1:47)—is revelation into her own identity as well as revelation of Jesus' identity. It is this double understanding that the woman takes back to the villagers: "Come, see a man who told me everything I ever did; this couldn't be the Christ, could it?" (4:29). For the evangelist, the knowledge of God and the knowledge of the self are interlinked: both are part of the revelation of Jesus, the Wisdom of God.[38]

Second, the story of the Samaritan woman confirms the link with the Spirit, already indicated in earlier references (especially 3:5).[39] The conversation about sacred place and the nature of true worship, far from being an attempt by the woman to sidetrack the conversation, is precisely what the imagery is about: the indwelling Spirit is the internal well of living water "springing up to life eternal" (4:14). The Spirit is also the inspiration and source of true worship—in which the woman herself is included[40]—assuming that the phrase "in spirit and truth" (*en pneumati kai alētheia*, 4:23) effectively means "the Spirit of truth" (cf. 14:17). The new "sacred site" is the Johannine Jesus, who gives the priceless gift of the Spirit to those who thirst for life, women as well as men, a gift that issues in divine worship in the eschatological now of the incarnation. Water has thus become a full symbol by the end of the narrative. It signifies both the Spirit and the word/revelation/wisdom which Jesus embodies in his own person and gives to those who are thirsty.[41] What the woman seeks and finds is the water of wisdom flowing from the well of the Spirit, implanted in the heart by Jesus. No barrier of race or gender can stand in the way of such a gift.

This interpretation (setting aside, for the moment, the healing of the disabled man in 5:1–9) is confirmed in the next significant reference to water in the Gospel, linked to the Feast of Tabernacles (7:37–39). Water again is used for quenching thirst. Jesus issues a call to discipleship that is closely tied to the imagery and wording of 4:1–42: "If anyone thirsts let him [her] come to me and drink!" (7:37b).[42] The same gift once offered to the Samaritan woman is now offered to the people of Jerusalem and thus, by extension, to the reader of the Gospel. The feast provides part of the foundational imagery, particularly the daily ritual of taking water from the Pool of Siloam, emphasizing the eschatological theme of salvation (e.g., Ezek. 47:1–5; Zech. 14:8).[43] In this context, water is the gift of the glorified Jesus, this time explicitly linked to the Spirit (4:39): "he said this concerning the Spirit which those believing in him were about to receive; for the Spirit was not yet present, because Jesus was not yet glorified" (7:39). The gift first offered to the Samaritan woman is now offered to all at the Feast of Tabernacles, in the once-sacred place, Jerusalem, which is no longer in this Gospel the embodiment and center of Israel's faith. The feast itself and its rituals are typological symbols of the Johannine Jesus.[44] The allusion to the flow of water points back to Jesus' words to the Samaritan woman (4:14) and forward to the piercing of the side (19:34). Although the reference could be to the believer in whose heart a well of water will spring up, the language is primarily christological: believers only find life through the death of Jesus, which itself issues in the giving of the Spirit (16:7; cf. 19:30). The link between thirst/water and the Spirit is already indicated in the Old Testament: "I will pour *water* on the thirsty land, and streams on the dry ground; I will pour my *spirit* upon your descendants, and my blessing on your offspring" (Isa. 44:3). The gift is not individualistic even though its origins are interior: as a spring of living water, it overflows into the community, offering life to others.

WATER AS CLEANSING: HEALING AND FOOTWASHING

There are further references to water in the Fourth Gospel that move in a direction different from the imagery of thirst. Two of these relate to a pool of water that has a symbolic, healing function. In John 5 and 9, water is linked to cleansing, with suggestions also of birth (new life). In the first case, the healing of the paralyzed man takes places near the Pool of Bethzatha in Jerusalem. The man's disability prevents him from reaching the healing waters, the place of new life (5:7), yet Jesus bypasses the water altogether and heals the man directly, without external assistance. By contrast, in the story of the man born blind (9:1–41), Jesus anoints the man's eyes with earth and spittle, instructing him to wash the paste from his eyes in the Pool of Siloam for his sight to be granted (9:6–7, 11, 15). Interestingly, the contrast parallels the difference in outlook between the two disabled men—the one never reaching Johannine faith while maintaining his link with the authorities (5:10–13), the other becoming a supporter of his healer and an opponent of the authorities who are out to destroy Jesus (9:24–38). As Jones notes, in the former narrative, water is used to contrast what the evangelist sees as the limitations of Judaism, in and of itself, with the ministry of Jesus.[45] The link to Tabernacles from the previous discourse is still present in the symbolic significance of the pool and its waters in Jewish eschatological thought. Specifically, for the evangelist, the Pool of Siloam, unlike that of Bethzatha, is a christological pointer to Jesus, the "Sent One" (9:7).[46] Although the Pool of Siloam is not generally associated with healing (unlike the Pool in John 5), the christological significance for John gives it cleansing and healing power. The main symbol for Jesus in this narrative is light (9:5; cf. 8:12)—the other great symbol of Tabernacles, complementing that of water—yet the image of the pool and the ritual washing are important secondary symbols. It is no accident that the early church considered this narrative baptismal in its associations: particularly the journey it depicts from blindness to sight, darkness to light, disability to healing, ignorance to knowledge. The main symbolic function of water is thus in relation to cleansing, healing, and new life. Already the reader is aware of the link with the Spirit and the revelation of Jesus' identity. What is unmistakable in these chapters is that, in John's Christology, "Jesus both acknowledges and transcends Jewish tradition"—partly, at least, through the gift of the Spirit, whose advent will correspond to his departure.[47]

Similar themes of Christology and purification are present in the footwashing, which develops the cleansing motif most fully. Here, at the beginning of the second major section of the Gospel, Jesus washes the feet of his disciples at the Last Supper prior to his death (13:1–20). The action is essentially a symbol by which (in Johannine terms) the literal level discloses figurative and spiritual meaning. The imagery suggests a different constellation from that of the Samaritan woman or Jesus' call to the thirsty in 7:37–39; nevertheless, there are important links with what has gone before. Although we are not speaking of water to drink, nor of internal springs within the believer, water has a similar symbolic power. It operates as a symbol of purification, as it already has in several previous instances. Yet the key verses are surprisingly often ignored, most readers moving quickly to the exhortation that Christians should wash the feet of others (13:12–17).[48] The symbolic action is carefully introduced by the evangelist, an introduction that serves as a kind of "mini-Prologue" to the passion and resurrection narratives, as well as a prelude to the Farewell Discourse, where, along with Jesus' Great Prayer, it forms the frame for Jesus' long discourse.[49] The opening verses (13:1–3) reveal that the footwashing is to be interpreted in relation to the following themes and motifs:

1. The Feast of Passover (the third in the Gospel; 2:13; 6:4; 13:1), where the paschal lamb is offered as a sacrifice of commemoration for redemption, for

the renewal of the covenant, and, in the extended meaning given by John the Baptist, for taking away the world's sin (1:29). The feast is also linked in the Fourth Gospel to the divine self-giving of Jesus who is the manna/Bread of Life, through his incarnation, death, and Eucharist (John 6).

2. The "hour" (*hōra*) of Jesus' return to the Father, through his exaltation on the cross, which is the climax of revelation, salvation, and glorification in this Gospel (cf. 2:4; 4:23; 12:23).

3. Jesus' love for "his own" (*hoi idioi*)—that is, for the children of God, born of the divine Spirit (1:11–13)—which is the purpose of his incarnation and death, and is a radical and self-giving love, complete in every sense as only divine love can be (*eis telos ēgapēsen autous*, "he loved them to the end").

4. The meal at which Jesus is present with his disciples, an unspecified group that need not be interpreted as restricted only to the Twelve.[50] There are Wisdom overtones in the hospitality of the meal (Prov. 9:1–6), a meal that includes also the presence of the betrayer, Judas Iscariot, who is a tool of the devil—the small circle of intimacy tragically penetrated by darkness and evil (13:2, 30). There may be eucharistic implications in the shared meal (cf. 12:1–8), as also later in the giving of the morsel to Judas (13:21–30).[51]

5. The relationship between Father and Son, in which Jesus is given authority over "all things" (*panta*). Jesus' origins and destiny are one and the same, disclosing his identity as divine (13:3). It is this cosmic authority that enables him to perform the action that is about to take place (the footwashing, the cross). What he is given is the power to give life and make judgment as eschatological Son of Man (5:17–30).

The symbolic event of footwashing is performed with a simplicity that, in its brevity and dignity, suggests liturgical action: Jesus rises from table, lays aside his clothes, wraps himself in a towel, pours water, begins to wash the feet, dries them with the towel (13:4–5). In so doing, Jesus performs the role of both host and slave, acting on his own initiative to offer hospitality to the disciples. Not surprisingly, the symbolism is misunderstood and, when he comes to Simon Peter, Jesus' action is first questioned—"are *you* [emphatic] washing *my* feet?" (13:6)—then refused: "you will *never ever* wash my feet" (13:8a). Yet John makes clear that the meaning of the event can be understood only "after these things"—that is, in the light of the cross (13:7). Simon Peter's objection serves an important function, revealing the radical nature of what Jesus does and the love from which it springs, and it enables Jesus to clarify the symbolic meaning. Interpreting the footwashing as an act of servility for physical cleansing, therefore, is inadequate: it means remaining only at the first level without progressing to the second.[52] The symbolic significance is that Jesus "cleanses" the disciples in a symbolic sense in order that they may remain in union with him: "Unless I wash you, you have no share with me" (*ouk echeis meros met' emou*, 13:8). This declaration lies at the heart of the footwashing but is often overlooked, particularly in popular understanding. Simon Peter's further misunderstanding and Jesus' response—both complicated by textual uncertainty—enable the meaning to be elucidated, strengthening the significance of the event as ritual purification (13:10–11). Just as guests may bathe before they leave home for a banquet yet their feet are washed upon arrival,[53] so the disciples have already been "cleansed" by Jesus and need only a small, symbolic act of cleansing to maintain their "purity."[54] That such a cleansing involves Jesus in an act of radical condescension and hospitality is unquestionable: the divine accommodation to human frailty and need points symbolically to the incarnation and the cross, where the Father's self-giving love is revealed. The sense is different from that of washing the feet of the needy as an act of humble service. Rather it points to a ritual cleansing, based in the divine hospitality and grounded in the incarnate love of Jesus that forms, re-forms and purifies the relationship between the Father and the disciples.[55] At its heart is the Fourth Gospel's christological understanding of Jesus' death as the perfect articulation of divine love and hospitality. Even in its further implications (13:12–15), where the footwashing functions as a paradigm of loving relations within the community, the primary focus is on love and unity rather than humble service. That too is indicated in the ritual action. Christology and ecclesiology lie at the heart of this narrative.

Whether or not footwashing was practiced as a "sacramental" act in the Johannine community, the ritual overtones are markedly present in this narrative. John uses water as symbolic of purification and cleansing—a theme that in the Old Testament is linked to the covenant and its ritual renewal, as well as the hope of eschatological salvation (see Gen. 49:10; Amos 9:13; Joel 3:18; Hos. 2:18–23; *1 Enoch* 10:18; *2 Apoc. Bar.* 29:5). There is an important parallel in Ezekiel that is illuminating for this passage, particularly given the proximity of the footwashing to the passion. In a promise of covenant renewal for the house of Israel, God speaks of restoring the holy name which has been profaned by the people of God, despite their covenant obligations:

> I will sanctify my great name, which has been profaned among the nations, and which you have profaned among them; and the nations shall know that I am the Lord, says the Lord God, when through you I display my holiness before their eyes. I will take you from the nations, and gather you from all the countries, and bring you into your own land. *I will sprinkle clean water upon you, and you shall be clean from all your uncleannesses, and from all your idols I will cleanse you.* A new heart I will give you, and a new spirit I will put within you; and I will remove from your body the heart of stone and give you a heart of flesh. I will put my spirit within you, and make you follow my statutes and be careful to observe my ordinances. Then you shall live in the land that I gave to your ancestors and you shall be my people, and I will be your God. (Ezek. 36:23–28)

There are several distinctive themes present in this text that relate not just to the footwashing but also to the Farewell Discourse as a whole (13:1–17:26): the sanctification and exaltation of the divine name (glorification), the ingathering of "his own," the revelation of God's holiness within the community, the cleansing in water and the transformation it effects, the giving of the Spirit, the keeping of God's ordinances, and the restoration of the covenant. Even the blessing of the land can be linked to the Johannine Jesus as the "sacred site" (*topos*, 4:20–24) in whom/which the Father dwells. Later in the passion narrative, the concern of "the Jews" who are clamoring for Jesus' death to maintain ritual purity before eating the Passover (18:28)—which, for the evangelist, is deeply ironic, given that Jesus *is* the Lamb of God (1:29, 36)—reinforces the importance of the purification theme as a major focus of the footwashing, explicitly set within the context of Passover. Temple imagery is also implicit in the footwashing, reinforcing the ritual theme. According to Philo, entering the inner court of the temple required first the cleansing of feet: "one should not enter with unwashed feet on the pavement of the temple of God" (cf. Exod. 40:30–32).[56]

In the Fourth Gospel, the footwashing thus expresses ritually and symbolically the intimacy of union with Christ, in whom the dwelling of God's glory abides, an intimacy effected through the death of Jesus as an act of self-giving, self-emptying love that cleanses and makes whole. Previous references to water as cleansing indicate a link with baptism; indeed, J. C. Thomas argues that what John has in mind, in terms of the Johannine community, is the ritual cleansing of postbaptismal sin (see 1 John 5:16–18), using symbols associated with baptism.[57] The expansion of water, moreover, as symbolic of the Spirit is also of significance. While there is no explicit mention of the Spirit in the footwashing narrative, the symbolic associations of water and spirit are too well established in the Gospel to be bypassed. Later in the Farewell Discourse, the Johannine Jesus will introduce the Paraclete as an important dimension of the Holy Spirit, who, while not linked in these chapters to cleansing and purification, has the role of sustaining union with Jesus and the Father (14:16–17, 26; 15:26–27; 16:7b–11, 13–15). The purifying role of the Spirit is indicated elsewhere in the Gospel: in the baptismal theme, as we have seen, and also in the resurrection narrative, where the Holy Spirit is breathed on the disciples by the risen Christ, enabling them to forgive sins (20:22–23).

WATER IN THE PASSION NARRATIVE

There are two further references to water, both linked to the passion narrative, one implicit and the other explicit. On the cross, just before his death and final declaration, Jesus utters the one word, "I thirst" (*dipsō*, 19:28), in response to which the soldiers pass him sour wine on a sprig of hyssop. There are several indications that this statement is to be taken metaphorically. At the literal level, Jesus' utterance signals the raging thirst immediately prior to death, and the soldiers' response, while it may be mocking, is more likely to be a rough gesture of sympathy.[58] Yet the reference to Jesus fulfilling the Scriptures (Ps. 69:21) and the fact that hyssop is not a large or strong enough plant to hold a sponge soaked in fluid, point to a deeper, symbolic meaning.[59] This is the second time in the Gospel that Jesus has indicated his thirst, and the second time John has given it symbolic meaning. Since Jesus' response to the disciples who bring food from the village is to declare that his food is "to do the will of the One who sent me and to accomplish his work" (4:34), and given that Jesus' final utterance on the cross consists of "it is accomplished" (*tetelestai*, 19:30), it follows that Jesus' thirst on the cross expresses the desire not just for physical water but for the will of God.[60]

The final reference to water is at the crucifixion, in the piercing of Jesus' side (19:34). This occurrence represents a different metaphorical constellation, yet with continuity to what has gone before. At one level, the pouring forth of water and blood reveals that Jesus is truly dead, obviating the necessity for his legs to be broken. Ironically, given the piety of "the Jews" in this scene, who wish not to defile the Sabbath/Passover, Jesus is portrayed as the paschal Lamb, whose body is whole and undefiled as an offering to God. Yet the symbolism goes further. The flow of water and blood from Jesus' side signifies that life comes through his death. As J. P. Heil points out, this moment represents the climax of the theme of living water in the Gospel.[61] The two elements, water and blood, are symbols of eternal life throughout the Gospel (cf. 1 John 5:6–8), the one relating to purification and healing, with suggestions of baptism and footwashing (water), the other related to the eucharistic flesh and blood, symbolized in the wine of Cana and the vine of the Farewell Discourse (15:1–11). The reader is well aware by now that the water is "living water," symbolic of the Holy Spirit, which purifies by washing and gives life by drinking. Together with the blood, the two elements indicate that life issues from the side of the crucified Jesus; in such proximity, the two images reveal the divine glory radiant in the flesh. Thus the presence of these Johannine symbols forms a double yet unified icon of sacramental life.[62] The true life-giving and loving nature of God is disclosed in this event, and thus both Jesus and the Father are glorified: a glorification to which the final witness testifies (19:35).

There is a further aspect to this symbolism. In John 3, Jesus speaks to Nicodemus of the necessity of being born "from above," a new birth effected by the Spirit of God. In particular, as we have seen, the reference to water in 3:5 is suggestive of childbirth. It is arguable that the water and blood are also symbols of birth at this point in the Gospel, reinforcing the imagery of new life issuing from the body of Jesus. The connection between the flow of blood and water and childbirth is not one that is generally made by commentators—perhaps because of an inability to perceive the transpositions of Jesus' bodily reality as John portrays it.[63] Yet, with an understanding of the flexible nature of Jesus' flesh as it is symbolically presented in the Fourth Gospel, and its capacity to take on cosmic significance, the imagery makes perfect sense—of the elements themselves (birth being an experience that brings together blood and water) and the significance of the crucifixion as life-giving. The imagery also coheres with what has gone before, where water is symbolic of cleansing, drinking, and also birth. This interpretation has all kinds of implications for understanding the body of Jesus, some of which we have already examined and more of which will be explored in a later chapter.[64] Suffice it to say at this point that it is not insignificant that Nicodemus will soon reappear in the Gospel narrative, once more in the context of birth—and this time without doubt of his allegiance (19:39).

IMAGES OF THE SEA

John's narrative also contains two further stories that may be mentioned briefly, although they are only loosely connected to the symbol of water: Jesus' walking on the sea and revealing his identity to the disciples (6:16–21), and the miraculous catch of fish after the resurrection (21:1–14). These stories both have symbolic elements but are different from the image of water for washing, drinking, or giving birth as it is used throughout the Gospel. In the first episode, set in the middle of the Bread of Life narrative, the sea signifies chaos and the threat of destruction, as in the Synoptic accounts (Mark 4:35–41 pars.; 6:47–52 par.), a theme that is common in the Old Testament (e.g., Pss. 107:23–30; 124:4–5). Jesus' miraculous presence on the sea and his majestic self-disclosure ("It is I; do not be afraid," 6:20), bringing the boat suddenly to land, reinforces his authority over the natural (and by implication supernatural) elements. Whereas the sea is symbolic of threatening chaos and death, Jesus reveals that he holds divine authority over all such powers, as already witnessed in the multiplication of the loaves. These frightening powers do not threaten or detract from the manifestation of his glory. In the second story, probably an appendix to the original Gospel (although using Johannine material),[65] the sea is an ambiguous symbol. On the one hand, it provides food and sustenance for life, yet at the same time it resists human attempts to control it, threatening the livelihood of those whose subsistence depends on it. Once again, the narrative implies Jesus' sovereignty over the sea in his supernatural knowledge of its ways (cf. Luke 5:1–11). This story may well build upon John 6 and its assumptions of Jesus' divine authority, but it is given a particularly strong focus in the light of the resurrection. Whatever the precise meaning, the symbol of the sea occupies a rather different metaphorical constellation in this Gospel from that of water and is really a separate symbol.[66]

SALVATION AND GENDER

By the end of the Gospel, the evangelist has presented Jesus as Savior of the world (4:42) and giver of the Spirit through the revelation of glory in his life, death, and resurrection. The symbol of living water, as it develops across the narrative, is central for what salvation means in the Fourth Gospel. We can summarize what we have observed so far:

1. Salvation in Jesus gathers up yet also transcends the rites and images of Judaism: indeed, the old points typologically to the new. Judaism is not discarded but is given new symbolic significance in relation to the Johannine Jesus. This transformation is symbolized in the way water functions to disclose that which is greater: the baptism of John the Baptist, the water jars at Cana, the Pool of Siloam.

2. Salvation, for John, signifies initiation into a new life that gives human beings a new identity as children of God. Only the Spirit is able to bring to birth this new life. Water symbolizes the laboring and life-giving Spirit of God, and the painful birthing which brings into being the family of God. The symbolism has baptismal overtones: baptism for John means entry into a new community—an inclusive sociality created by the Spirit and born of the revelation of Jesus.

3. Salvation in John's Gospel fills the yearning for life and for God. The symbol of water as thirst-quenching points to the capacity of Jesus to respond to that deep longing, in his self-revelation as the Wisdom of God and his giving of the Spirit. The gift is symbolized as an interior well or spring of water that flows over to others, refreshing and watering them as dry land after drought. The story of the Samaritan woman embodies the longing and its fulfillment. Yet the same invitation to the female Samaritan is also issued at large to the people of Jerusalem. Living water is for all.

4. Salvation is also, in this Gospel, concerned with cleansing, purification, and forgiveness. The new life that Jesus brings and the thirst he quenches have to do with a new relationship of love and intimacy. Entering that relationship, and maintaining its covenant form, requires a cleansing of the heart, a growth toward purity, integrity, and wholeness. Living water, the inner gift of the Spirit, provides cleansing power. It is part of the baptismal significance of the Gospel, yet in the story of the footwashing it also enables a continuing growth in holiness. It is not individualistic: the footwashing creates union with Jesus but also functions sacramentally to bind the community together in self-giving love.

5. Salvation, for John, is not confined to the original people of God but opens up to include others: Samaritans and Gentiles. Only when "the world has gone after him" and the "Greeks" (Gentiles) ask to see him does Jesus recognize the advent of the "hour" (12:19–23). The living water which Jesus offers the Samaritan woman and the people of Jerusalem is a universal offer, without exclusion.

The last point concerning John's universalism has particular significance for issues of gender.[67] The evangelist is aware that the gift of living water which Jesus offers is only available with the overcoming of divisions. There is an important relationship between the christological affirmations of the Gospel and the theme of barriers dissolving, linked to the symbolism of water. What makes the image of water so powerful a symbol in the narrative is its cosmic appeal. Regardless of the barriers that separate human beings, water is a part of everyday life: in the birthing of children, in quenching thirst, and in cleansing and washing. Water is necessary for survival and unites human beings in a common need for authentic life, for salvation, for God. The christological themes of Jesus as giver of living water, Savior of the world, and breaker of barriers are profoundly linked to the symbolism of living water.

At the same time, for the evangelist, the universality that derives from the symbolism does not deny Jewish priority in God's salvation nor its historical particularity (4:22b).[68] The narrative of the Samaritan woman contains a subtle tension between the Jewishness and, for that matter, the maleness of Jesus and his universal appeal. In the same way, the Samaritan woman's own religious experience is taken seriously in the narrative,[69] along with the challenge to move to a more adequate understanding of God and a more authentic mode of worship (4:22a). Alongside the motif of bringing down barriers is also the Johannine conviction of the definitive nature of revelation in Jesus. In the Fourth Gospel it is only Jesus who gives the living water to quench the universal longing for life; only Jesus whose life, as John presents it, is so divine and self-transcending that it is able to cross such barriers. The exclusiveness of the christological claim in focusing on an individual ("Savior of the world") is intimately linked to the universality of the message ("living water"); the one stands as guarantor of the other. Similarly, within Jesus himself, the specifics of his Jewishness and maleness are joined to a divine identity that knows no such limitation. Together the two dimensions express the universalism and the particularity of John's understanding of salvation. This dual dynamic makes the encounter between Jesus and the woman more than the engagement between male and female.[70] To be faithful to Johannine Christology, and particularly the Prologue, the encounter needs also—indeed, primarily—to be read as the meeting between divine and human, God and humankind. Indeed, union within Jesus makes possible the profound sense of connection and understanding that emerges in the dialogue.

John uses this "daughter of Samaria" to exemplify a common human need, a thirst, a longing beyond differences of religion, culture, and gender. The Samaritan woman, as we have seen, plays a critical role in establishing the image of water as a key Johannine symbol. In her we encounter not a disembodied theme but a powerful symbol at work in human experience. This is a story of transfiguration and life. The openness with which the woman engages Jesus and the symbols he presents lead her to find in him the water of wisdom. On this basis, the woman's role is important for gender as well as race. It is true that Christianity—like Judaism—is not a religion that excludes women from the blessings of salvation or the covenant. Yet that inclusiveness, despite rhetoric to the contrary, is often qualified. Where females are less visible in language and imagery, in liturgy and theology, they are less present, whatever may be said to the contrary. In this context, the story of the Samaritan woman is particularly important for establishing female presence at the core of faith. Although the Johannine Jesus asks that the woman's husband (*anēr*) be present at the conversation, this is clearly a rhetorical device enabling him to uncover the truth of her life—not in a shaming or judgmental spirit, but in order to disclose her spiritual need. The woman's struggle to understand, her theological opinions, her traditions, her growing insight, and later her witness to the villagers are all taken seriously by the Johannine Jesus—to the dismay of the returning disciples. Though her gender, like her race, is enough to stop the conversation before it ever begins, the narrator places her at the center of the narrative, so that her human experience, her longings, and her growing theological insight elicit the revelation of living water.

This is not, for John, a solitary narrative about Jesus' openness to an individual woman. Characters in the Fourth Gospel have a representative function, standing usually for a group they represent.[71] As the closing verses of the narrative indicate, the woman's reception of faith is communicated effectively to the other villagers, who acknowledge her role in bringing them to faith (4:39–42). In the dialogue between Jesus and the woman, she stands for the Samaritan people, evident in her use of "we," "our," and "us": "*our* father Jacob who gave us the well" (4:12); "*our* fathers worshiped on this mountain" (4:20); "I know that Messiah is coming who is called Christ; when he comes, he will explain everything to *us*" (4:25). Jesus responds in kind, addressing her sometimes with the plural "you": "the hour is coming when neither on this mountain nor in Jerusalem will you [pl.] worship the Father" (4:21); "you [pl.] worship what you [pl.] do not know" (4:22). This is not a narrative only for women, in whatever circles it may have originated. The male reader is invited, as much as the female, to identify with the woman in her faith development. Her representative role embraces the reader as much as it does the other Samaritan characters of the text, as with other representative characters in the Fourth Gospel. Females are genuinely included when they are able to function not just as the alien "other" to what is generic but in a representative and collective role: representing males as well as females. Only in this sense can we speak of the restoration of the image in females as well as males. The woman is drawn into the orbit of salvation and given living water, becoming a reborn child of God— not indirectly but directly. This implies that the implanted image of God is restored in her, independent of her relationship to men. This independence in dialogue with Jesus enables the woman paradoxically to play a symbolic role for the community of faith. Having her own identity, her own knowledge of faith and understanding of living water, she can play a public role: she can become an over-flowing spring, a deep, inner well that waters the land surrounding it.[72]

From this glance across the Johannine narrative, water can be seen as a dynamic and multivalent symbol in the Fourth Gospel. Despite the different ways in which the imagery is employed throughout the Gospel—including the seeming opposition at the wedding at Cana—there is no real contradiction. Each symbol points to and conveys the one transfiguring reality: the life-giving Spirit, given by Jesus the Wisdom of God, which restores the image and draws human beings into a divine community that cleanses and makes whole, and that satisfies the yearning for life and love. Water functions as a symbol of cleansing, healing, and renewal; it expresses the new birth for which the Johannine Jesus calls; it quenches in a radical way the thirst for life. In all these ways, the symbol of living water points to and conveys the presence within the community of the divine Spirit, whose presence makes real the vibrant life and love of God.

CHAPTER 4

Abiding on the Vine:
Symbols of Love and Friendship

Lo now Thy banner over me is love,
All heaven flies open to me at Thy nod:
For Thou has lit Thy flame in me a clod,
Made me a nest for dwelling of Thy Dove.
What wilt Thou call me in our home above,
Who now has called me friend? how will it be
When Thou dost bid me come and sup with Thee,
Now Thou dost make me lean upon Thy breast:
How will it be with me in time of love?[1]

IMAGES OF LOVE AND FRIENDSHIP are particularly important for a symbolic reading of the Fourth Gospel. The Johannine symbolism forms a dynamic picture of the deep attachment that is the origin and goal of the incarnation. These images are echoed in contemporary theological concerns to reassert the primacy of relational categories in theological thinking. In John's understanding, the love of Father and Son ripples out from the divine being to embrace human beings and indeed all creation in a relationship of abiding. Resting in that love is the meaning of salvation for John: it denotes the life of heaven and draws the community of earth into its orbit. Becoming children of God in this Gospel—being restored to the divine image—means returning to that primordial love and resting-place which is the ground of creation. The image of abiding is vital in this context as it expands throughout the Johannine narrative; by the Farewell Discourse its symbolic center unfolds in the symbol of the vine and images of friendship. Abiding in love and friendship becomes a key Johannine symbol that challenges individualism and abusive forms of relationship, offering a new way of being in affinity with God and others. It is another instance of the divine glory manifesting itself within the structures of the flesh.

THE IMAGE OF ABIDING

The word "to abide" (*menein*) is scattered throughout John's Gospel, occurring some forty times, with a significant number of instances clustered around the

Farewell Discourse.[2] "Abiding" is an important Johannine theological term, often occurring in the formula "to abide in/on" (*menein en*), but it is also used in the colloquial sense of "stay" or "remain."[3] In some instances it is difficult to determine whether the literal or the symbolic meaning is required.[4] In its theological sense the word *menein* overlaps with other Johannine conceptions such as unity, oneness, love, and indwelling. In particular, it is related to the Johannine understanding of disciples as "friends" of Jesus (*philoi*)—an image that, like abiding, relates to the symbolism of the vine.

The verb "to abide" first appears in the opening chapter of the Gospel. In the context of the witness of John the Baptist, who testifies to Jesus' identity and sets in motion the gathering of the first disciples, "abiding" is used in two contexts. Its first occurrence describes the Spirit's presence with Jesus. John the Baptist does not baptize Jesus in this Gospel, as in the Synoptics, although they too make mention of the descent of the Spirit "like a dove" (Mark 1:9–10 pars.). The Baptist's primary Johannine role of witness is evoked in the vision he has of the Spirit's descent on Jesus:

> I saw the Spirit descending as a dove from heaven and it remained [lit. "abode"] on
> him. And I did not recognize him, but the one who sent me to baptism with water,
> he said to me, "The one on whom you see the Spirit descending and remaining [lit.
> 'abiding'], this is the one baptizing with the Holy Spirit." And I myself have seen and
> borne witness that this is the Son of God. (1:32–33)

The identity of Jesus as the Son of God—the climax of the Baptist's testimony here—is interlinked with the descent and abiding presence of the Spirit on Jesus.[5] (Note that, in the Synoptics, the declaration of the divine sonship of Jesus comes not from John the Baptist but from the divine voice [Mark 1:11 pars.]) The first sense of abiding occurs in the context of the relationship between Jesus and the Spirit, the sign of Jesus' heavenly identity. Abiding belongs fundamentally to the divine realm. The second occurrence flows from the first, linked by the testimony of John the Baptist. As a result of the recognition of Jesus as the Lamb of God (1:35; cf. 1:29), two of the Baptist's disciples follow Jesus (*akolouthein*, 1:37). The ensuing dialogue operates on two levels, the literal and the symbolic. In response to the searching question, "What do you seek?" the two disciples of the Baptist respond with another question, equally evocative: "Rabbi . . . where do you abide?" (*pou meneis*, 1:38).[6] At Jesus' invitation to "come and see," evoking Johannine images of discipleship (1:50–51; 3:3; 12:21; 20:8), the narrative concludes with the granting of their request: "they saw where he stayed [lit. 'abode'] and remained [lit. 'abode'] with him that day" (1:39). This brief narrative makes sense at the literal level—the disciples remain in Jesus' house for the day—but there is also an intimation that their visit to Jesus is of greater significance: the language is carefully and theologically nuanced in the light of later, symbolic usage; "Nothing is more important than to know where Jesus abides and may be found."[7] Although both John and the Synoptics describe discipleship through images of following (cf.

Mark 1:16–20; 8:34; 10:32; John 1:37, 43; 8:12; 10:4, 27; 12:26; 21:19–22), the Fourth Gospel sees discipleship also in terms of abiding. The two disciples begin a relationship with Jesus that will develop throughout the Gospel. Yet it is dependent on Christology: Jesus is the abode of the Spirit and discipleship means abiding where he himself abides; Jesus' own abiding place is linked to the Spirit, who "stays" (abides) on him and to the disciples with whom, as the later narrative reveals, he abides forever through the Spirit-Paraclete (14:17).

As the Gospel narrative progresses, the symbolic meaning of abiding unfolds. In terms that recall the gathering of the first disciples—where the initial two disciples "abide with" Jesus—Jesus "stays" (abides) with the Samaritan villagers for two days (4:40). Once again, this can be read simply on the literal level: Jesus accepts the hospitality of the Samaritans, breaking his journey from Judea to Galilee. At a symbolic level, however, the evangelist intimates a deeper meaning. Through the testimony of the Samaritan woman (4:29, 39)—paralleling the testimony of John the Baptist in 1:29ff.—the Samaritan villagers come to faith in Jesus. Indeed, the mutual exchange of "hospitality" is one way of viewing the entire narrative, on a symbolic as well as a literal level: Jesus invites the woman's hospitality (4:7) and offers his own "hospitality" in its place (4:10); his divine hospitality crosses boundaries to reach both her and the villagers who later arrive at the well; finally, recognizing him as "the Savior of the world" (4:42), they extend their hospitality to Jesus, both literally and symbolically, and he accepts. Though effectively Gentiles, at least in Jewish eyes (4:9), they too enter a relationship of "abiding" with Jesus, this time in his abiding with them.[8] Once more, this is an evocative and symbolic narrative about discipleship. Yet the imagery of abiding and its symbolic power are still somewhat concealed within the text. The full symbolic import will be disclosed more fully later in the narrative.

The next occurrence of the verb *menein* sees it becoming more overt in its symbolic meaning. The context is the Bread of Life, and the necessity of eating and drinking the "flesh and blood" in order to gain eternal life (6:53–58). Abiding, in this context, now has distinctly sacramental overtones: the "Son of Man" both *gives* and *is* the food that "abides to eternal life," in contrast to mortal food that perishes (6:27). The Eucharist is a dramatic representation of the reciprocal abiding between Jesus and believers: "The one eating my flesh and drinking my blood abides in me and I also in him [her]" (6:56). The colloquial, literal sense is not adequate to translate the verb here. Already it has taken on a heightened, symbolic meaning, just as the bread does throughout the narrative of John 6: from the miraculous feeding at the beginning to the overtones of manna in the discourse and finally to the revelation of the eucharistic "feeding" by faith on the bread from heaven. It becomes clear that abiding is the source of life. Just as in 6:56 the one eating the flesh of Jesus abides, so in the next verse the one eating the flesh will "have life."[9] Abiding is symbolic of a new relationship with Jesus that is life-giving, transcending the power of death. The relationship between Jesus and disciples has overtones of Sophia, who likewise draws followers and companions to her table and, in the intimacy of abiding, feeds them with her wisdom.[10]

From now on, the symbolic significance of abiding expands through the narrative. In the Tabernacles Discourse (7:1–8:59),[11] many of his interlocutors come to believe in Jesus but their faith, it transpires, is a superficial one (8:30), and soon enough they are attacking Jesus, both verbally and physically (8:48, 52, 59). In this context, Jesus reveals that true discipleship means more than an immediate response of attraction; rather it signifies abiding in Jesus' word and entering an enduring covenant relationship with God through Jesus (8:31; see 1 John 2:14, 24), moving beyond a superficial faith that sees the outer "signs" but fails to perceive their symbolic meaning. As with the bread, where Jesus as Wisdom is both the giver and the gift, so he is both the Word spoken and the speaker of that life-giving word. Later in his final public address, Jesus reiterates the symbol of light and speaks of abiding as dwelling not in darkness but in light (12:46; see 1 John 2:10). In both cases, the different images of abiding in Jesus' *word* and abiding in *light* express a similar symbolic reality: fidelity to the relationship with Jesus is where true life and the knowledge of God are to be found.

In the Farewell Discourse, John employs the noun form of "abiding," *monē*—meaning "abode" or "abiding place"—as well as the verbal form. The symbol of abiding is about the realization of discipleship as a present reality, yet also with a future dimension: "in my Father's house are many abiding places" (*monai*, 14:2).[12] The concrete imagery of place (*topos*, 14:3) correlates with the "I am" saying a few verses later: "I am the way (*hodos*) and the truth and the life" (14:6; cf. 14:4). As we have already seen in John 4:20–24, the language of "place" is essentially christological: Jesus is the "sacred site" where salvation and life reside, the true home of believers. Behind the language of place and home lies the Johannine God, the eschatological "home" of the community. The language is that of connection and affinity. What is now made clear is that the affinity is with the Father through Jesus, and that to live within its eschatological orbit gives a defining future horizon to present existence. So the symbolism of place is that of believers journeying on a pathway that is Jesus himself (compare the symbol of the door at 10:7–10), the destination of which is the Father. Abiding in Jesus takes believers to the Father as the eschatological abode of faith.

Later in the same chapter, the evangelist inverts the imagery. In response to the question of Judas-not-Iscariot concerning the scope of Jesus' self-revelation (14:22), Jesus responds in a characteristically Johannine way that seems at first to bypass the question: "If anyone loves me, he [she] will keep my word, and my Father will love him [her] and we will come to him [her] and will make an abiding place [*monēn*] with him [her]" (14:23). Now it is not the believer who makes the journey—via Jesus—to the Father, but the opposite: the journey of Father and Son into the heart and life of the believer, the basis of this visitation being the believer's love for Jesus and keeping of his "word." Abiding becomes a symbol of the indwelling Father and Son who together make a resting place or home within the believer. The contradiction is purely formal; in the end it does not matter who journeys toward whom. The point is the final meeting place and the sense of divine initiative in bridging the gulf between above and below.

As Jesus has already indicated, abiding is actualized in the community after his glorification, through the presence of the "other Paraclete," the Spirit of truth, who "abides with you and will be in [among?] you" (14:17). Later in John 14, the connection is reinforced: Jesus' abiding will continue through the Paraclete, who will be the teacher and reminder of Jesus' word once Jesus has departed: "These things I have spoken to you while abiding with you (*menōn*); but the Paraclete, the Holy Spirit, which the Father will send in my name, will teach you everything and remind you of everything which I have told you" (14:25–26). Jesus' abiding will continue even in his absence—indeed especially in his absence (16:7)—but this time through the presence of the Spirit-Paraclete, the channel of the abiding-in-love of the Father and Son.[13]

As a symbol of discipleship, abiding is most explicitly enunciated in the extended metaphor of the vine and the branches (15:1–17).[14] According to Wayne Brouwer, 15:1–17 forms the center of a "macro-chiasm" that embraces John 13–17.[15] On this basis he argues that the center and controlling theme of the Farewell Discourse is "Abide in me!"—a theme that is indicated in the footwashing and Great Prayer, which provide the outer frame of the chiasmus (13:1–35; 17:1–26). The image of the vine and branches is the theological and literary heart of these chapters, "the climax around which the rest of the discourse turns."[16] The language of abiding multiplies in this passage, being used eleven times, converging on the core symbolism of the vine, which, it now appears, underlies the theological usage of the word in earlier chapters of the Gospel. Yet, as Moloney points out, while commentators focus almost exclusively on the imagery of the vine, it really "serves to articulate the importance of abiding."[17] The passage falls into two sections, closely linked by the motif of abiding and by interweaving images of love, fruit-bearing, keeping of the love command and friendship:

15:1–8   Parable: Union with Jesus the True Vine
- "I am the true vine": vinedresser, vine, and branches (1–4)
- "I am the vine": bearing fruit (5–8)
- abiding in love (9–10)

15:11–17   Joy, Friendship and Mutual Love
- fullness of joy (11)
- love command: love of others (12–14)
- friendship with Jesus (15–16)
- love command: love of others (17)[18]

   The vine functions in this passage as a kind of Johannine parable with allegorical elements, each identified by the evangelist:[19] the Father is the vinedresser, Jesus is the vine, disciples are the branches, and purification is the pruning of the branches (15:1–2). The background of the imagery is found in Old Testament references to Israel as the vine (e.g., Ps. 80:9–16; Isa. 5:1–7; Jer. 2:21; Ezek. 15:1–8; 19:10–14). These passages all have overtones of failure and/or judgment, because of Israel's inability to produce fruit: "Yet I planted you as a choice vine, from the purest stock. How then did you turn degenerate and become a wild vine?" (Jer. 2:21). The initial picture of cultivated beauty and fecundity gives way before images of burning, disintegration, neglect, barrenness, and despoliation. The imagery is paralleled in the Old Testament by that of the sheep, shepherd, and the sheepfold, another powerful symbol of Israel—a parallelism that is present also in the similarities of structure between John 10:1–17 and 15:1–17.[20] John draws much of the pungency of the imagery not just from the symbolism but also from the narrative of failure and rejection with which both images are associated in the Old Testament. This vineyard will no longer fall into disrepair or be uprooted (just as the flock will not be ultimately scattered or destroyed). Other Old Testament imagery, however, gives the image of the vine a more positive focus and is just as important for John's symbolism. In the Song of Songs, for example, the beloved is symbolized as a vineyard (Cant. 8:11–12), emphasizing the theme of loving and self-giving union. Sophia also speaks of herself as a fertile vine:

> Like a terebinth I have extended my branches,
> and my branches are branches of glory and grace.
> *Like a vine I have budded forth beauty*
> *and my blossoms are the fruit of glory and riches.*
> Come to me, those who desire me,
> and from my fruits be filled.
> For the memory of me is sweeter than honey,
> and my inheritance is sweeter than the honeycomb.
> Those who eat of me will still hunger,
> and those who drink of me will still thirst. (Sir. 14:16–21)

The description of Wisdom as a blossoming vine is followed immediately by the invitation to come to her vineyard: to be saturated by her fruit and still yearn for more. Here Wisdom is fecund, enticing, and desirable. Once again, she is herself the owner/giver of the fruit as well as the vine from which it grows.

   From these Old Testament connotations, we can ask how the image of the vine in John 15 contributes to our understanding of abiding in the Fourth Gospel. In the first place, drawing on the Wisdom tradition, Jesus is now presented as the vine itself rather than Israel.[21] The symbolism highlights in vivid color the desirability of connection to Jesus, a theme that is integral to the Fourth Gospel. The evangelist emphasizes abiding as an image of the relationship between disciples and Jesus, stressing that it is vital for survival; without such abiding, discipleship will die. Disciples are dependent on Jesus as the source of life, just as branches "abide on" the vine in order to have life (*menein en*, 15:1–8). The imagery works in a way similar to the bond between mother and child: the infant in the womb is dependent for its very life on being connected to the umbilical cord, and after it is born, to the maternal breast. In a similar way, the attachment between Jesus and the disciples is not something optional or occasional; for John, it stands at the center of their relationship with God. In the understanding of the evangelist, affinity with Jesus means affinity with the divine source of life. The livelihood of the community of faith is dependent on such affiliation. Disciples cannot be disciples except to the extent that they abide in union with Jesus. Christology lies at the center of John's understanding of relationship.

Second, the symbol of the vine produces paradoxically both rest and joy for those who abide. It is restful because abiding is something to be achieved not by human effort (1:12–13) but by the faithful work of the vinedresser who cares for and cultivates the plant in order that it might flourish and bear fruit:

> For we cultivate God, and God cultivates us. But we do not cultivate God in such a way as to make him better for our cultivating. For we cultivate him in adoring, not in ploughing. But he cultivates us as a farmer the fields. Because therefore he cultivates us, he makes us better. (Augustine, *Sermon* 87.1)

This perspective takes from disciples the burden of having to manufacture their own salvation (compare the image of Jesus-Sophia offering the restful yoke [Matt. 11:28–30]). It is also restful because, being fundamentally relational, it forges a deep intimacy with God that takes away fear and anxiety, replacing it with a sense of well-being and peace, even in the midst of trouble (14:1, 27; 16:33). Yet abiding is also joyful. The eucharistic overtones of the vine imagery recall the Wedding at Cana and the transformation of water into wine, expressing a sense of *jouissance* (joy and ecstasy) that comes from a self-transcending experience of union—a union that is fecund and life-giving (15:11; 16:20–22).[22] In his commentary on John, commenting on Christ as the true vine, Origen links this Johannine symbol allegorically to Ps. 104:15, which speaks of God providing "wine to gladden the human heart":

> For if ... that which rejoices [the heart] is the most drinkable Word, taking us away from human affairs and making us inspired (*enthousiąn*) and drunk with an intoxication not irrational but divine, ... it is clear that the one who brings wine which rejoices the human heart is the true vine. (Origen, *Commentary on S. John's Gospel* 1.30)

The symbol of the vine contains a distinct note of joy and celebration. It is not surprising that what the disciples experience when they first encounter the risen Christ behind the closed doors of their fear is a sense of intoxicating joy and peace:

the continuation of that abiding relationship, on the other side of death, which they assume they have lost (20:19–23).

The symbol of the vine reveals that abiding is not static, but dynamic and vital. The image of fruit-bearing is an important part of this dynamic, although John does not make explicit the external referent. According to Witherington, the language is mission-oriented, showing that the image of the vine is not concerned only with the connection to Jesus or relations with other believers.[23] Yet, while the Fourth Gospel does have an outgoing missionary focus (4:1–42; 20:21), it is hard to see how the imagery of sending into the world has primacy here. Fruit-bearing is concerned with growth in *love*, a growth that draws the community closer to the Father, who is the source of love. This is not without implications for mission: it is precisely the community's love that will reveal to all people "that you are my disciples" (13:35) and that will bring glory to the Father (15:8). In any case, however we interpret fruit-bearing, it confirms the point that the symbolism of abiding on the vine is not passive but active. The vine is a vibrant image of fecundity and growth, the flourishing of human life in relationship with God.

Third, the image of the vine is essentially a symbol of community. Although ecclesiology is not the primary focus of the passage, being subsidiary to the overarching theme of revelation,[24] it does play an important role, offering a parallel to the Pauline image of the church as the body of Christ (1 Cor. 12:12–27).[25] The vine, with its Old Testament reference to Israel, does not present an individualistic vision of discipleship, but sets disciples within the life of the community of faith, in its collective as well as personal relationship to Jesus:

> Individuals in the community will prosper only insofar as they recognize themselves as members of an organic unit. No individual is a free agent, but is one branch of an encircling and intertwining vine whose fruitfulness depends on abiding with Jesus.[26]

The vine is thus a powerful expression of the mutuality of relations within the believing community, as well as the love between believers and Jesus—a theme that becomes explicit in the verses that follow with the double reference to keeping the commandments (15:12, 17). Such language in John 13–17 refers to the love command, directed both to God and to one's fellow members within the community and centered in the love of Christ: "love one another as I have loved you" (13:12–17, 34–35). The concern with ecclesiology is manifest in the eucharistic implications of the imagery; the vine "has an inherent affinity with the eucharistic symbol of the wine" which "reflects and evokes" the union of the community with Christ.[27] The sacramental overtones link the theme of abiding with the eucharistic sense it bears at 6:56, where those who eat the flesh and drink the blood "abide in me and I in them." The Wisdom overtones are vibrant in this eucharistic sense: the fruit of the vine is plentiful and desirable, creating in those who taste it the longing for more, yet also paradoxically satisfying fully the desire for life (4:14).

Finally, John extends the meaning of abiding to include the theme of judgment, through the imagery of pruning. The verb for pruning, *kathairein*, can also mean "cleanse" and John exploits both meanings here. In the footwashing, Jesus has already spoken of the disciples being "cleansed" (*katharos*, 13:10). Pruning is another image for "cleansing," the process of removing what is dead and useless in order that the plant may flourish; it parallels the imagery of washing away impurity that the self may be whole and without blemish. It is not immediately clear, however, what is meant allegorically by the pruning and burning of dead branches. Are the branches to be cut off the vine certain individuals—such as the unbelieving "Jews" of the Gospel or those superficial and apostate believers whose faith is quickly stimulated and soon dies (e.g., those in 2:23 or 8:30), or those who, like Judas Iscariot (13:30), betray the very one to whom they are attached?[28] John does not specify which group or individuals he has in mind: what is important is the grim note of judgment against those who fail to abide. For the evangelist, abiding is a matter of life and death; in the next section of the Farewell Discourse, it distinguishes the community from the *kosmos*, which is characterized by hatred and rejection (15:18–16:4a). For such people, there is a simple choice: "One of the two the branch must be united with, either the vine, or the fire: if it is not on the vine, it will be in the fire: so that therefore it may not be in the fire, it must be on the vine" (Augustine, *In Joannis Evangelium* 81.3).

Yet there is also a sense in which pruning is necessary for *all* disciples. Brodie speaks of the necessity of "purifying or separating" for all disciples: "breaking free from the world [*kosmos*] with all its enslaving habits, values, and relationships."[29] While in 15:6 Jesus speaks of apostate Christians being cut off the vine—"if anyone does not abide in me, he [or she] is thrown out like the branch and is withered and they gather them and toss them into the fire and they are burnt"[30] —earlier in 15:2 Jesus speaks not only of dead branches being "taken away" (*airei*) but also of healthy branches being pruned: "every branch bearing fruit he [the vinedresser] prunes in order that it may bear more fruit." All branches are cut back, even if not all are cut off the vine; such pruning is necessary to promote new growth in healthy plants. Thus the symbolism of pruning and burning (15:6)—in the light of Old Testament images of burning associated with the vine—is used of judgment in a constructive sense, whether in relation to individual believers or the community as a whole. The cultivation of the plant makes necessary cutting off what is dead in order to make way for new life. Such "purification" is the work of the vinedresser, and it takes place in union with Jesus, its purpose being to lead disciples to a deeper knowledge of love (15:9–10). As a result of the vinedresser's pruning, the fruit produced by abiding on the vine is that of love.

The pruning of the branches by the vinedresser is thus a metaphor of the interplay between suffering and growth, both of which are vital for the community to thrive. Without adherence to the vine and careful tending by the vinedresser, the branches wither and die; their only use is as firewood. In the mutual abiding formula—where the imagery of the vine begins to break down, or rather break open into further symbolism[31]—true disciples are those who abide in Jesus as the source of life and in whom Jesus himself reciprocally abides (see also 1 John 3:24; 4:13, 15–16). The language coheres with that of the giving of the beloved disciple and the mother of Jesus to each other at the foot of the cross (19:25–27). In the context of the passion, suffering and dying are seen to be a kind of pruning or cleansing that brings life and growth (cf. 12:24). The discipleship of abiding has as its heart the symbolic reality of the cross.

Not only disciples but also Jesus himself shares in the mutuality of abiding; indeed this dimension of abiding has theological priority. Jesus' place in the divine "household" as Son is an abiding one, as distinct from the place of the household slave: "The slave does not abide in the house forever, the Son abides forever" (8:35). While his opponents question whether Jesus is the Christ who "abides forever" on account of his death (12:34), it is clear that Jesus' death does not negate this abiding with the Father, but on the contrary confirms it through his glorification on the cross (cf. 17:1). In the Farewell Discourse, the theological dimension is strengthened. There it is revealed that the Father abides in Jesus—this abiding is the source of the intimacy and union between them (14:10); and Jesus abides with the disciples only because the Father abides in him (15:9–10). The unity he shares with the Father is the ground of this abiding, which is a relation of "mutual or reciprocal immanence" (see 3:35; 6:57; 10:30, 38b; 14:9–11, 20; 17:20–23).[32] Moreover, the works of Jesus are the concrete manifestation of this indwelling, which is not static but dynamic, expressing the shared life of Father and Son (see 5:17–30).[33] In this sense, abiding has a vertical dimension that is theologically prior to the horizontal, though the two are finally inseparable. The mutual abiding of Father and Son is the source and archetype of the abiding of believers, the foundation of the abiding-in-love of the community. This divine abiding creates a centripetal force that draws human beings out of isolation into community. What disciples are drawn into, in other words, is a preexisting union and communion within the divine being. They do not manufacture their own abiding but are gathered into that which already exists, already flourishes, is already redolent with love and life. Disciples are to abide within that love (3:16; see 1 John 3:17; 4:12)— an abiding that, as we have seen, is dependent wholly on Jesus (14:1–11) and on his relationship with the Father.

The particular form of this reciprocity is expressed in the Great Prayer, in terms that are synonymous with the language of abiding. Disciples are gathered into the "I in you and you in me" of Jesus' affinity with the Father, so that it now embraces disciples in the same exchange of love: "I in them" and "they in us" and "I in them and you in me" (17:23; see 6:56; 15:5). Jesus is the Symbol or Icon of both dimensions of abiding, the divine and the human, since in his own flesh he is the abiding place of God among people (1:14), the one who establishes an I–Thou union of persons, the embodiment of divine indwelling. In his abiding with the Father, he is able to bridge the estrangement and alienation between the divine and the human, gathering all that is human—like the scraps at the feeding of the multitude (6:12–13) or the bringing in of the sheep "not of this fold" (10:16)—into the divine love which precedes and undergirds all creation. This is the theological core of the Johannine imagery of abiding.

John also uses the verb *menein* in an ironic sense where it expresses the opposite of the trinitarian abiding into which disciples are drawn. In particular, it can be used of the sense of judgment against those who continue to abide in death and darkness, despite the offer of life. In this sense, God's anger can be said to "abide" on those who reject the Son and knowingly choose death over life (3:36); while this is the expression of divine judgment, it is also the result of a person's own choice (cf. 3:19). In usage that coheres with the positive concept of abiding as the expression of discipleship, Jesus says that God's word *fails to abide* with the religious authorities in Jerusalem, even though they think otherwise ("you do not have [God's] word abiding in you," 5:38). By implication, therefore, God's judgment remains on them. The sin of the Pharisees *abides* upon them in the story of the man born blind (9:41) because of their illusion of sight—because they believe they alone have access to the light and can decide who is and is not a sinner; and because, on the basis of false judgment, they persecute those who, like the man himself, dare to challenge their authority. The seed that will not submit to "death and burial" is unable to bear fruit; it is said to *abide alone*, solitary and infertile (12:24). Whereas abiding means openness to light and life, the failure to abide means being closed against the light; in terms of the symbolism of the vine, this closure signifies disconnection and death (15:6). To reject true abiding is to condemn oneself to isolation and detachment—everything that is the opposite of life, affiliation, community. This is nothing but the rejection of the divine Logos, who, having come to "his own domain" (*ta idia*, 1:11), is tragically rejected by "his own people" (*hoi idioi*). Those who reject life find instead an ironic "abiding," an acute sense of separation, a solitary descent into darkness, a languishing in sin and death (cf. 1 John 3:14–15).

There is also a further ironic sense in which the abiding of the community gives rise to hostility and opposition. In literary terms, the central text for abiding, the image of the vine (15:1–17), is immediately followed by the hatred of the "world" (*kosmos*, 15:18–16:4a).[34] In these verses we encounter the other face of abiding, or rather the consequences of failing to abide. Images of friendship, union, love are now replaced by the language of hatred, rejection, and persecution.[35] The community that abides within the divine love is the same community that is hated by the "world" and that suffers because of its identity, its belonging to the light.[36] The *kosmos* opposes the community that abides; it is hostile to everything for which believers stand. Yet the community's sense of abiding is not crushed by such hostility. On the contrary, persecution intensifies the symbolic perception of belonging and abode. For John, the solidarity of believers, while in one way cutting across the boundaries of community ("they will make you excluded from the syna-gogue," *aposynagōgos*, 16:2), in another way is strengthened: the believing com-munity shares the rejection of Jesus and his Father. Opposition is a catalyst for abiding: for the evangelist, it creates ironically the very parameters within which love and intimacy thrive.[37]

Abiding is primarily a quality of the divine realm, an aspect of eternal life that in John's Gospel is offered to all human beings. As a heavenly quality, it expresses the intimacy and reciprocity that lie at the heart of the universe. The relationship between Father and Son is the archetypal symbol of this understanding of abid-ing. Discipleship is not a self-generating relationship with God and others but rather entry into a divine, preexisting relationship through the Spirit-Paraclete. To be a disciple means to be in union with Jesus, and through Jesus with the triune God—a union that is reciprocal and oriented toward community, the antithesis of isolation and seclusion: "one has the sense of the divine Community working together to bring the faithful branches into vital and healthy relationship to the vine, as they are pruned to produce more fruit."[38] Abiding is not grounded in human achievement or action, but derives from an interior divine source, a well-spring, a mystical indwelling that is intimate and personal. The symbolism of the vine signifies growth and fecundity, mutuality and homecoming, friendship and self-giving. Yet abiding, as a force for life, does not bypass suffering and death: the vinedresser prunes, the world pours scorn, the seed "dies," the Son buds forth community with his dying breath.

LOVE AND FRIENDSHIP

It is impossible to explore the Johannine symbol of abiding without coming up against the closely related notion of friendship. The Johannine vocabulary of friendship and love spans two basic word groups, *agap-* and *phil-*, used synony-mously in the Gospel and often interchangeably, though the latter word cluster (*philein*, "to love," and *philos*, "friend, lover, beloved") occurs less frequently than the former (*agapan*, "to love," *agapē*, "love," and *agapētos*, "beloved").[39] Friendship was a popular theme among ancient writers, and in the Greco-Roman world highly prized. Although in principle the term "friendship" (*philia, amicitia*) could apply to all kinds of relationship—allies, homosexual lovers, followers of political leaders, members of philosophical groups, or the relationship between wealthy patrons and their clients[40]—personal friendship is particularly extolled, where it is to be grounded in virtue and integrity, equality (despite any actual differences in social status), maturity, intimacy, love and affection, honesty, constancy, reci-procity and self-sacrifice.[41] Friends are seen as part of one's household (*oikos*).[42] "Without friends," says Aristotle, "no-one would choose to live, even possessing all the other good things of life" (*Nicomachean Ethics* 8.1). The Old Testament prefers the covenant language of neighbors and kin, yet it contains outstanding examples of friendship, even across social and racial boundaries: Ruth and Naomi, for example, or David and Jonathan (cf. Ruth 1:14–18; 4:15; 1 Sam. 18:1; 2 Sam. 1:17–27). Philo, who is influenced by Greco-Roman as well as Jewish understandings of friendship, uses the common proverb "the possessions of friends are held in common" (*koina ta philōn*) to speak not only of human friendship (especially with fellow Israelites) but also of friendship with God (*philia*), a friendship based on monotheistic worship and a deep sense of affinity (*oikeiotēs*).[43] Figures such as Abraham and Moses are portrayed as friends of God in the Old Testament, able to discourse with God face-to-face and even able to change God's mind (e.g., Gen. 18:1–33; Exod. 32:7–14; 33:11). Friendship and love are also associated with Wisdom, a significant influence on John's understanding. Despite rejection (Bar. 3:9–31), Sophia gathers around herself a community of friends, bound together in mutual love (Prov. 8:17; Sir. 4:12; Wis. 6:12); those whom she loves are loved by God (Sir. 4:14; Wis. 7:28). As the image of divine light and goodness, she descends to earth, renewing and restoring all things and seeking out friends:

> Being one, she is capable of all things
> and abiding [*menousa*] in herself she renews all things,
> and down through the generations, crossing over into holy souls,
> she makes them friends of God [*philous theou*] and prophets.
> For God loves nothing
> except for the one living together with Wisdom. (Wis. 7:27–28)[44]

John's Gospel is heir to this rich tradition and influenced by its understanding of love and friendship.[45] Sharon Ringe speaks of "the intertwining images of divine Wisdom and friendship" as a major theme running through the Fourth Gospel. Love, like friendship, "sounds a persistent beat from the beginning to the end of the narrative,"[46] commencing with the programmatic announcement of divine love for the world in 3:16: "For God loved the world in this way (*houtōs*), that he gave his only Son. . . ." This love is the reason for the sending and dying of the Son: it is an act of self-giving love by the Father, whose will draws the world to its eschatological destiny, manifest in the restoration of the divine image. The language of love intensifies at the Last Supper, where it undergirds the meaning of the footwashing (13:1), the significance of Jesus' death and the vibrant center of the believing community (13:34–35). It congregates in the explanation of the vine (15:9–17), as we have seen, which is a major symbol of the connection between the personhood of God, the advent of Jesus, and the formation of the church. The same love that God has for the world, and in particular the believing community, is the fundamental basis of the relationship between Father and Son. Love is associated with a number of other Johannine conceptions such as unity (17:23–24) and homecoming (1:11; 19:27).

Love, moreover, is a feature of community that can also be used of individual disciples, most notably, the beloved disciple.[47] The role of the beloved disciple is "both individual and representational" in the Fourth Gospel.[48] It is likely that he was a historical figure outside the circle of the Twelve,[49] the source of the Johannine tradition, who now plays a symbolic role in the Gospel, particularly the second half, where he figures as the apostolic witness of the Gospel's unique tradition and the exemplar of the love of Christ for the disciples. His place of honor at the Last Supper, reclining on the breast of Jesus (13:23), is emblematic of the church, which resides in the same place, enjoying the same intimacy with Jesus. This is symbolic of the love that has its source in the loving union Jesus shares with the Father. As the beloved disciple reclines "on the breast of Jesus" (*kolpos*, 13:23), so the Word, being "turned toward" the Father (1:1–2), exists "in the bosom of the Father" (*kolpos*, 1:18).[50]

Jesus' relationship with the beloved disciple is "embedded in a wider love relationship" between Jesus and the wider group of his followers.[51] "Jesus' inviolable intimacy with God transforms his followers with the gift of a parallel relationship."[52] So other disciples share a similar intimacy with Jesus, reflecting also the love between Father and Son. Simon Peter, in the postscript of the Gospel, is rehabilitated for his denial with a threefold challenge to love Jesus above all things, even to the point of death (21:15–19; cf. 15:13).[53] The group of "beloved disciples" decidedly includes women. The mother of Jesus, for example, holds a privileged position in the Johannine community, intimately associated with the beginning of Jesus' ministry and the revelation of his glory (2:1–12). It is the union of love between her and the beloved disciple, through the indwelling Paraclete, which forms the basis of the post-Easter community. The acceptance of her into the "home" of the beloved disciple (*eis ta idia*, 19:25–27), in language that is synonymous with friendship, gives her such a status in the Johannine community. The same could be argued of the Samaritan woman in the openness and honesty of her dialogue with Jesus; and even more so of Mary Magdalene, present at the foot of the cross, who mourns and searches for the body of Jesus as a grief-stricken friend, recognizing his presence when her name is spoken and greeting his risen presence with love and joy (19:25; 20:1–18). The most overt mention of friendship and love between Jesus and women, however, is in the story of the raising of Lazarus, where the narrator makes explicit the love Jesus has for the Bethany family: "And Jesus loved [*ēgapa*, imperfect tense, implying an ongoing state] Martha and her sister and Lazarus" (11:5; cf. 11:3). This love is confirmed in the story of the anointing, where the friendship Jesus shares with the two sisters and their brother is mirrored in the feast they provide for him and the extravagant anointing of his feet (12:1–8). Moreover, as we have already noted, the Fourth Gospel (unlike the Synoptics) does not explicitly confine the Farewell Discourse to the Twelve, but seems to imply a wider group gathered together as Jesus' "friends" (cf. Mark 14:17 pars.). There is no reason to think, from a dramatic viewpoint, that women would not be present, in some way, at such a Johannine gathering.[54]

In the Fourth Gospel, the language of friendship is vital within the semantic field of abiding and love. The noun "friend" (*philos*) occurs in several contexts, the first in reference to John the Baptist, who identifies himself as "the friend of the bridegroom" (3:29), the best man at the nuptial celebration. His role is secondary to that of the bridegroom, yet the closeness between the two is signified by the friend's capacity to wait for the other, to listen for his voice with joy and to withdraw when the time is right (3:30). The language of friendship is clearest in the story of Lazarus, where, as we have seen, Jesus identifies Lazarus as "our friend" (*ho philos hēmōn*, 11:11). There is a certain irony to this designation, given that Jesus does not attend his friend until four days after burial (11:17); yet the love in Johannine terms is real and evidenced in Jesus' presence and actions at the tomb (11:38–44). Whatever is lost of friendship by the delay—note the reproachful words of both sisters when they approach Jesus (11:21, 32)—is restored in the banquet that follows (12:1–2). Jesus proves his friendship for this family with the authoritative voice which draws Lazarus from the tomb and frees him from the trappings of death (11:38–44). So radical is this friendship that, as the narrative implies, the consequence of Jesus' action in raising Lazarus is the laying down of his own life for his friends (cf. 15:13).

The language of friendship, as it arises from the symbol of the vine, unfolds its significance in terms of love and intimacy.[55] Once again, this begins in the Father's love for the Son (15:9) and becomes the central "command" of the believing community's life: "love one another as I have loved you" (15:12; cf. 13:34–35). In an astonishing revision of the master–slave paradigm—imagery that is common in the New Testament[56]—the Johannine Jesus prefers the language of friendship as the appropriate model of relationship between Jesus and disciples (15:15): "No longer do I call you slaves [*douloi*], because the slave does not know what his lord is doing; but you I have called friends [*philoi*], because everything which I heard from the Father I have made known to you." Here the voice of Wisdom speaks, making those who have come in response to her invitation the "friends of God." The language is not primarily about power relations among believers—though it has ecclesial implications—but rather is about the sharing of knowledge within a theological and christological framework. This is a significant feature of friendship within the ancient world: the mutuality that shares knowledge, plans, and secrets among friends, a friendship based on understanding, affection, and trust. Yet the friendship out of which it comes is essentially divine. It is the love and friendship—the intimate knowing—between Father and Son which is flung open to the community of faith, giving disciples access to an experiential knowledge of the life of God. Friendship begins in the divine love for the community of disciples revealed in Jesus. Chrysostom enlarges on this aspect in his homily on the passage:

> Do you not perceive in how many ways He showed His love? By disclosing secrets; by taking the initiative in seeking eagerly for their friendship; by bestowing great benefits upon them; by enduring the sufferings which he then experienced for their

sake. And after this He indicated that He would remain always with those who were going to produce fruit. (*Homilies on John* 70)

This divine ingathering of the believing community into the friendship within the godhead is closely related to the incarnation. As Wisdom travels around seeking out friends for God and graciously inviting them to eat and drink the fruits of her table, so the Word enters into "flesh" and seeks out friends for God, inviting them into table fellowship at which he is both the host and the repast. The fruits that he gives his "friends" at this table are his flesh and blood, given in self-giving love through incarnation, death, and Eucharist. Jesus acts as the true friend, revealing that "greater love" through his self-giving death on behalf of his friends (15:13). The language here—like the structure—parallels that of the Good Shepherd who knows his sheep by name (10:3), offers life and protects them from adversity (10:9–10), shares mutual knowledge with them (10:14), and lays down his life for them (10:15–17). In both sets of imagery—the vineyard and the sheepfold—the relationship between believers and Jesus (the Shepherd, the Vine) is a deep, abiding friendship that signifies intimacy, personal knowledge, and self-sacrificing love. The qualities of the ideal friend are embodied in Jesus' relationship with the company of disciples.

At the same time, although deconstructive of the master–slave paradigm, the language of friendship does not deny divine sovereignty nor revoke the compliance of the community to the divine will.[57] The imagery becomes stretched beyond the normal categories of intimacy. Friendship as a symbol of divine–human relations has profound similarities to personal friendship at a human level, but there are also differences. There is a paradox, if not an outright contradiction, in the idea of friends rendering obedience to one another: "You are my friends if you do the things which I command you" (15:14). It could be argued in purely human terms that the two aspects, friendship and obedience, exist simultaneously only with considerable difficulty: that friendship cancels out any sense of deference and that the language of obedience belongs within a world of ranked social ordering that has no place in friendship. Or is the Fourth Gospel employing the language of patronage, where "friendship" is one way of denoting the mutual obligations between clients and their patrons? Yet this is not the understanding of friendship found in the Fourth Gospel. John uses the language of personal friendship, overturning servile models of relationship. At the same time, the evangelist retains the notion of obedience, which belongs to servanthood rather than friendship. Strictly speaking, the verb "obey" does not occur at all: the Johannine Jesus speaks instead of "keeping my word" (8:51–52, 55; 14:23–24; 17:6) and "keeping my commands" (14:15, 21; 15:10, 20; cf. 9:16; 17:11–12, 15). The verb "keep" (*tērein*) is perhaps more evocative than "obey" (*hypakouein*) because it suggests guarding or holding that which is precious and life-giving (cf. 12:50), rather than acting with unquestioning subservience. It is not a servile obedience that is called for; the language of love draws disciples into a divine sovereignty that offers them knowledge, freedom, and love, while still demanding their allegiance and commitment. The form of obedience is not that of the fearful slave who has no understanding of or involvement in the decisions made. Augustine distinguishes between a servitude based on fear (the opposite of love) and a servitude without such fear, although the latter retains a sense of "holy fear" that is perfectly compatible with love (*In Joannis Evangelium* 85.2). The friendship which Jesus offers across the abyss between "above" and "below" does not dissolve the distinctions. In a similar vein, Ringe speaks of the paradox between "intimacy and tenderness," on the one hand, and the "majesty" of Christ, on the other. The tension is not collapsed here. Friendship is an astonishing symbol of the relationship between God and humanity, but as a symbol it cannot be equated in a simplistic way with human friendship. Disciples are friends of Jesus, but they remain disciples, followers of the one who is the *Kyrios*, and who directs that their love for each other be as radical and self-giving as his for them.

There is also an ironic element to the portrait of friends in the Fourth Gospel, this time with a sharp political edge. In the trial before Pilate, which is the centerpiece of the Johannine trial narrative, the authorities manipulate Pilate into condemning Jesus to death, playing on his fear, ambition, and sense of political expediency. In the last of the seven scenes, which takes place inside the Praetorium (19:12–16a),[58] Pilate once more determines to release Jesus but "the Jews" accuse him of being "no friend of Caesar" if he fails to condemn Jesus (*ouk ei philos tou Kaisaros*, 19:12). The irony is that friendship has its source in the divine realm and is offered to all, including Pilate, yet Pilate will choose friendship with Caesar over friendship with God through Jesus. Pilate will allow the *basileia* ("sovereignty") of the human to have precedence over the divine *basileia* which Jesus embodies (18:36–37). Faced with so ultimate a choice, Pilate makes judgment against the true King, in a parody of loyal and life-giving friendship, and condemns Jesus to death (19:13–16a).

The friends of God are those who abide on the living vine, those in whom the image is restored, those who have become adult children within the household of faith. Though obedience is asked of them, it is an obedience that arises from love and is directed toward love. They are not kept in the dark nor treated as servile or childish, but are given understanding and knowledge, so that the obedience they render is intelligent and knowing. Yet the only command they are called to obey is the love command, drawing them deeper into the Father's love for the Son, and thus closer to one another. This ecclesial vision is far from legalism or servility. The friends are commanded simply to be friends: in the first place, to the God whose friendship goes as far as it possibly can—to the end (*eis telos*, 13:1) and the laying down of life—and to those others in the community who are drawn into the same divine circle of love.

IMPLICATIONS: ABIDING, LOVE, AND GENDER

What are the implications of the Johannine symbolism of love and abiding for discipleship? This is a pertinent question in view of feminist theological concerns to recapture friendship as a model of Christian community. The way in which women are perceived in relation to men becomes a case study in a broader picture of disruption and alienation within the created world. In an essay entitled "The Fecundity of the Caress," Luce Irigaray speaks of the way in which woman in relationship to man is often reduced to the status of object, thus "remaining passive within the field of activity of a subject who wills himself to be the sole master of desire." Irigaray sees this objectification in the distinction between woman as beloved and woman as lover, in which the woman in relation to the man is "[n]ecessarily an object, not a subject with a relation like his, to time."[59] Conceived as the beloved, woman is reduced to "animality, perversity or a kind of pseudo-childhood" where her subjectivity is diminished.[60] Irigaray is offering a critique of the distortion of subject–object relations fostered by the Enlightenment preoccupation with strict objectivity, as a consequence of which women have been abused and marginalized in the masculine "voyage toward an autistic transcendence."[61] This has been accompanied by a dualism and ranking in which "masculinity" is polarized from "femininity," exalting independence, autonomy, and detachment above intimacy and attachment. Feminist philosopher of science Evelyn Fox Keller sees this duality in terms of separation and distance against subjectivity and connection, affecting perceptions not just of women but also nature:

> the division between objective fact and subjective feeling is sustained by the association of objectivity with power and masculinity, and its remove from the world of women and love. In turn, the disjunction of male from female is sustained by the association of masculinity with power and objectivity, and its disjunction from subjectivity and love.[62]

The cultural paradigm of subject–object lies at the heart of Enlightenment thinking, with implications beyond that of gender relations. The result, across a wide spectrum, is the "severance of subject from object," the illusion of a neutral and disconnected objectivity,[63] and the objectification and thus domination of some human beings by others.

Writing in more general terms and from a different perspective—that of Eastern Orthodox theology—John Zizioulas argues that such objectification, in whatever guise, is the result of the sinful denial of communion. Such a denial, exacerbated in the Enlightenment, is a manifestation of the Fall, in which "the created world tends to posit its being ultimately with reference to itself and not to an uncreated being [i.e., God]."[64] The separation of being from communion, in this sense, leads to individualism and objectivism: our relationship to God becomes secondary or derivative rather than prior and intrinsic. We are divorced from that divine communion which constitutes our very being, and are thus cut off from communion with one another and the created world. In theological terms, this disjunction discloses the need for salvation, beginning with the severed connection between Creator and creation. For Zizioulas, such a renewal is ecclesial and eucharistic, grounded in the Christian experience of baptism that signifies entry into a restored communion of persons.[65] Relationship and mutuality are fundamental to such a vision of salvation. Communion is intrinsic to personhood, and redemption signifies "participation not in the nature or substance of God, but in His personal existence"—an existence that is intrinsically loving, since God's own being is "identical with an act of communion."[66]

Viewed from this perspective, the Johannine symbolism of abiding and friendship as the paradigm of redemption is of particular relevance. First and foremost, abiding-in-love dissolves the subject–object relation between divine and human. This dissolution begins within the divine realm, which, as we have seen, is the archetype of all relations in the Johannine worldview. Abiding is an expression of the divine life, revealed in the Johannine Jesus, who lives in profound union with the One who is the source of all being and whose nature is revealed as relational and immanent. The trinitarian shape of revelation is not self-sufficient and isolating, but the source of intimacy. Into this abiding-in-love, human beings are drawn not as objects but as subjects. The mutuality of the language of abiding-in-friendship is important. The divine is not presented in this Gospel as paternalistic and condescending. As we will see in the next chapter, the Father's love for the world is vulnerable and self-giving (1:11–12; 3:16), calling disciples not to slavish servitude or childish obedience but to an obedience that is based on intimacy, knowledge, and friendship. Through the divine indwelling of the Spirit, human beings stand before God as subject to subject. The divine "I am" stands in personal relation to human becoming, so that human beings find within themselves a subjective "I am,"[67] a sense of selfhood that is the gift of the incarnate God. Abiding defines the divine–human relationship as one of immanence: subject to subject, face-to-face, I–Thou, redeeming the world from the terror of objectification, the fear of alterity, the dread of intimacy.

In the second place, by dissolving the subject–object relation between divine and human, John's theological understanding of abiding and friendship extends to the relationship between human beings. Abiding in the love of God is never an abiding in isolation. Separation and autonomy are overcome in the vision of an ecclesial communion that encompasses heaven and earth. Being drawn into friendship with God, human beings become friends to one another; they meet as subject to subject. To abide in love with others is to live together in a community that works to overcome alienation and isolation, individualism and the ranking of human life.[68] It is mutual rather than condescending, cooperative rather than competitive, self-giving rather than status-ridden. The community may be called

to live as a persecuted and prophetic minority in an objectivist world, nevertheless, if abiding means kinship with God, it means simultaneously kinship with
others who share similar yearnings, even though they may be sheep "not of this
fold" (10:16). As Mary Grey has argued, right relationship lies at the heart of
redemption; we need to recover "those deeper patterns of affiliation and mutuality" which are, in her judgment, part of the very fabric of the world.[69]

In an important study of community, Elizabeth Johnson has argued that theology needs to recover a renewed sense of the communion of saints (*communio
sanctorum*), a concept that has been largely forsaken in contemporary, industrial-
ized society with its denial of death and sense of reality as limited to the perceptible and immediate. Johnson sees the communion of saints as consisting of the
"friends of God and prophets" of Wisdom 7:27, who are "freely connected in a reciprocal relationship characterized by deep affection, joy, trust, support in adversity, and sharing life."[70] This *communio*, which is central to the New Testament, is
based on baptism and "shows an inclusive equality" of all the baptized.[71] It is
essentially a companionship of friends, gender inclusive and nonhierarchical, as
opposed to the Roman patronage system, which developed by medieval times into
the widespread practice of invocation of the saints.[72] The medieval model, in
Johnson's view, tended to create a two-tiered model of discipleship, focused on
superior individuals invoked for help rather than a companionable sense of "the
saints" as a corporate body, beyond the perceptible yet everywhere present. Johnson describes the biblical model as "an interlocking community of equal companions in grace that extends across the world and beyond death."[73] This communion
of "friends and prophets" derives, at least in part, from the Johannine understanding of friendship in which the divine image is restored and the believing
community abides in loving relation to God and one another. It contrasts with the
master–slave model and presents instead an experience of "persons connected to
one another in virtue of being connected to the sacred mystery at the heart of the
world."[74] Johannine symbols of friendship and abiding support the feminist concern to develop a sense of inclusive community, equally critical of individualistic
segregation and isolation, on the one hand, and institutional exclusion, privilege,
and hierarchy, on the other. Neither is permitted in the Johannine understanding
that friendship lies at the core of divine as well as human identity.

This is a further dimension to this, which takes us somewhat beyond the Johannine text but not against its spirit. In an earlier chapter, we saw that the symbol of
"flesh" points beyond the male humanity of Jesus to include both female humanity and creation in a wider sense.[75] Abiding and friendship can be extended to
imply kinship with a bruised and battered creation, exploited by the individualism and anthropocentrism often associated with technological advancement. The
Johannine symbolism of friendship belongs in a cosmic vision in which human
beings learn to befriend the nonhuman world to which they belong and which
they have exploited. This is not primarily a moral but a christological statement.

The world is sacred by virtue of its Creator by whom all things are made, by virtue of the incarnation in which matter is transformed, and by virtue of its eschatological destiny in God. Grey argues that creation itself is part of redemption and that relationship extends to all living things: "The theological meaning of Easter night, the night of redemption, symbolizes the renewal of the cosmos, with every aspect of creation drawn into the mystery of the resurrection."[76] Similarly, Johnson argues that the communion of saints embraces the oppression of nature as well as human beings.[77] The love/friendship symbolism of the Fourth Gospel has the potential to overcome alienation and objectification, revealing "the way out from the fall,"[78] the path from isolation and dissipation to union and empathy with all created things.

Third, the symbol of abiding has its roots in interiority rather than in external achievement; cooperative "being" rather than competitive "doing." John emphasizes the relational rather than the work-oriented aspects of discipleship, and the miracle of grace from which it arises (1:17). The dichotomy between doing and being is misleading: we have seen that abiding is not static but, as the imagery of the vine indicates, fecund and creative; to bear fruit in love is essential to abiding. This means that action is resourced from an interior well of water springing up to eternal life (4:14). It also means that the development of the self within a spiritual and ecclesial framework is not antithetical to the evangelical message of the Gospel. There is a befriending of the self needed where it has been damaged by alienation and discord. A relational understanding of love and friendship requires a distinctive sense of identity that can be very different from egoism or individualism. Such authentic selfhood, derived from Christian anthropology (which is essentially christological), facilitates authentic relations with others; it represents an "abiding in the self" within the communion of saints (see Wis. 7:27), a mystical friendship in the Spirit that heals the inner wound, restoring the divine image in women as well as men.

The symbolism of friendship and abiding signifies freedom not only from isolation but also, in the other direction, from inauthentic self-denial. The Johannine symbolism makes possible the selfhood necessary for companionship and reciprocity. By overcoming the subject–object relation between men and women, the model of friendship provides the freedom for human beings to become their true selves in Christ, undoing the effects of paternalistic deprivation and partiality. To abide in this sense means to move through suffering, to accept the reality that life and fecundity come through pain and death, through pruning and the pierced side (7:38; 19:34). In the struggle between giving and withholding, self-loving and self-bestowing, women in friendship with men find within themselves a divine enclosure that does not imprison, an envelope opening onto the world,[79] an abiding place that sets them free for others. Keller speaks of this as a "dynamic autonomy" that, being distinct from either dependence or neutral distance, reflects a sense of self . . . as both differentiated from and related to others, and a sense of others as subjects with whom one shares enough to allow for a recognition of their independent interest and feelings—in short for a recognition of them as other subjects.[80]

As a symbol, abiding is thus not individualistic but deeply personal, requiring a deepening awareness of one's true abode in communion with others. Such friendship is costly and demanding, as well as liberating, as the image of the vine illustrates. The divine abode as mutual indwelling is located in the interplay between selfhood and community, singularity and welcome, "self-possessing and . . . self-giving."[81] The language and imagery of the Fourth Gospel present a challenge to Enlightenment polarities, offering, in place of a rationalistic and objectivist view of the world, an icon of wholeness and intimacy. It gives hope of an abiding place where women can belong as subjects in communion with men, and in harmony with creation. The Johannine symbolism of abiding and friendship opens the way to a new sense of personhood, grounded in the love of the Spirit. It signifies participating in the trinitarian life of God and in the communion of saints, both within and beyond the visible world.

CHAPTER 5

Authoring Life:
The Symbol of God as Father

Holy God, loving Father, of the word everlasting,
Grant me to have of Thee this living prayer:
Lighten my understanding, kindle my will, begin my doing,
Incite my love, strengthen my weakness, enfold my desire.

Cleanse my heart, make holy my soul, confirm my faith,
Keep safe my mind and compass my body about;
As I utter my prayer from my mouth,
In mine own heart may I feel Thy presence.

And grant Thou to me, Father beloved,
From Whom each thing that is freely flows,
That no tie over-strict, no tie over-dear
May be between myself and this world below.[1]

T HE PRIMARY SYMBOL for God within the Johannine narrative is that of
Father. The symbol of divine fatherhood functions as the core personal
description of the God who sends Jesus into the world and with whose glorification Jesus above all else is concerned. The Johannine portrait of God as
Father confirms the divine love for the world, the dependence of the world on God
and the destiny of human beings to become children of God. The title is linked in
the first place to Jesus, who is portrayed as the eternal Son, the true Image, the one
whose being has its source in the life of God. Only in a secondary sense does the
Gospel speak of divine fatherhood in relation to human beings and the community of faith.[2] While some forms of feminist theology believe that male symbolism
for God is implicitly oppressive and illegitimate, the presentation of the Father in
this Gospel is far from the distant, all-controlling father deity of popular supposi-
tion or cultural conditioning.[3] It is set within the context of the holy otherness and
mystery of God in which God's self-communication (*logos*) accommodates itself
to human experience (*sarx*).

FATHERHOOD IN THE JOHANNINE NARRATIVE

As with other Johannine symbols, John's understanding of divine fatherhood is not isolated in its usage but belongs, as a religious symbol, within a complex field of reference. In the Hellenistic context—which is of indirect rather than direct influence on the Fourth Gospel—the religious occurrence of Father is widespread. A common epithet for Zeus in Homer is "the father of gods and men" (*patēr andrōn te theōn*), depicting an all-controlling deity who presides on Mount Olympus, with authority over the world of mortals and immortals.[4] His authority has often to be reasserted over the unruly members of his cosmic "household," including within the divine court itself. The concept of an all-wise, beneficent, and all-ruling father corresponds to the domestic household, where, in Roman civil law, the father exercises *patria potestas*, "fatherly power" over life and death;[5] he is responsible for the well-being of the domestic world in every aspect of its life, including the spiritual and moral, and requires total submission from all members of the household. While affection and love are by no means absent from this conception, there is a strong focus on the responsible yet absolute sacral power of the father over his family, reflecting understandings of divine fatherhood in both state and cultic religion.[6] In Greek philosophy, the ethical dimension is foremost: in Plato, for example, the divine Father is the supreme moral source and "corresponds to . . . the idea of the good,"[7] as well as being "the Maker and Father of this Universe" (*poiētēn kai patera toude tou pantos*);[8] in Stoicism, the true sage lives in the confident awareness of his relatedness to God as Father, sharing the divine *logos* and knowledge which give him dignity and freedom.[9]

According to Marianne Meye Thompson, the real source and significance of fatherhood in the New Testament are to be found primarily within Judaism and its sacred writings. In the Old Testament, Father, though not a common title for God, is vital in denoting God's paternal relationship to Israel, which is portrayed as God's firstborn son and heir, inheriting the Promised Land (e.g., Exod. 4:22–23; Deut. 32:4–6; Ps. 103:13–14; Isa. 63:15–16; 64:8–9; Jer. 3:19; 31:9; Hos. 11:1; cf. also 1QH 9:35–36). In Second Temple Judaism, the covenant understanding of divine fatherhood is likewise important (e.g., Tobit 13:4; 1QH 9:35), sometimes being presented in very personal terms (e.g., "my Father and my God," 4Q372 1.16), but it extends also to a cosmic conception of God as universal Father-Creator under the influence of Hellenistic thought, particularly in Philo and Josephus (e.g., "God and Father and Maker of everything" [Philo, *De decalogo* 51]; "Father and Source of the whole universe" [Josephus, *Antiquities* 7.380]).[10] In this sense, the title of Father is not a distinctly Christian mode of address for God but is grounded in those Jewish traditions from which Christian faith arises. Broadly speaking, according to Thompson, the image of divine fatherhood in the Old Testament has three dimensions, all related to Israel:[11]

- It signifies God as the author and source of Israel's life and presents Israel as God's true heir.

- It connotes the special fatherly care and providence of God toward Israel, God's covenant people.[12]

- It depicts the divine authority to which Israel is to submit in loving obedience, giving honor to Israel's God.

Although the primary force of the language is corporate, individual forms of the same pattern are also found within the Old Testament—for example, where the king is depicted as "son" of God (2 Sam. 7:14; Pss. 2:7; 89:26) or in the experience of the individual Israelite (e.g., Ps. 27:10).

This Old Testament presentation of God's fatherhood has profoundly shaped Jesus' own self-understanding. While much has been made of the historical Jesus and his unique sense of relationship to God as *abba*,[13] it is important to set this alongside the recognition of Jewish influence on Jesus' sense of identity. Both the Old Testament and Jesus' own self-awareness are significant for New Testament theological understandings of divine fatherhood: all three Old Testament dimensions are present in different ways, and with significant modification, in the Synoptics, the Pauline Epistles (where Israel is extended to include the Gentiles among God's heirs), and the Fourth Gospel. Both individual and corporate lines flow in tandem throughout the New Testament, as through the Old. John is unique, however, in focusing divine fatherhood not directly on the community of God's people but rather on Jesus.[14] As a title for God, therefore, Father is not the creative invention of the Fourth Gospel, but is continuous with Old Testament and Jewish understandings, including that of the historical Jesus.

God is referred to as Father in the Fourth Gospel more often than anywhere else in the New Testament. It is the main title used for God—occurring well over a hundred times—and "God" (*theos*) and "Father" (*patēr*) are often employed interchangeably throughout the Gospel,[15] although *theos* is also used of Jesus (e.g., 1:1, 18; 5:17–18; 20:28). "Father" is found mainly on the lips of Jesus himself, who speaks frequently of God in absolute terms as "the Father,"[16] and often as "my Father."[17] In prayers, the Johannine Jesus addresses God as "Father,"[18] sometimes with an epithet: "holy Father" (17:11) or "righteous Father" (17:25). An important expression by which Jesus refers to his sense of mission and unity with God is "the Father who sent me."[19] Most often, the title denotes the relationship between God and Jesus: "according to this Gospel it is the prerogative of Jesus to address God as Father and to speak of God in these terms."[20] By extension, the title can refer to the relationship between God and the disciples, who are said to be loved by "the Father" in and through Jesus (14:21, 23; 16:27); yet only once does the Johannine Jesus speak explicitly of disciples having God as "your Father" (20:17). Fatherhood is used by the evangelist himself, with the same christological focus, in a few editorial comments (1:18; 13:1, 3), and in one context only it is used in relation to "the Jews," whose relationship with God as Father is called into question by the Johannine Jesus (8:41–42; cf. 8:19).[21]

Although the imagery is so extensive that it is impossible to cover every instance, it is important to begin with the Prologue, where the imagery of God as Father originates—as with so many other Johannine themes.[22] In both cases, the primary import is in relation to Jesus as Son (*monogenēs*, 1:14, 18[23]), a usage that represents a radical, christological reformulation of the Old Testament picture of God as Father to Israel. This signifies the basic parting of the ways between John and the Judaism of his day, despite the distinct continuity between John's theological understanding and the Old Testament. The one who in the Old Testament is Father to Israel is now interpreted primarily as the Father of the Johannine Son; indeed, in the Fourth Gospel, "God's relationship to Jesus is constitutive of God's Fatherhood."[24] Father appears first as a simile (1:14) and then as a formal designation for God (1:18). In the first instance, the definite article is missing, which may or may not have significance (the noun *theos* also lacks the definite article in 1:1c, 18a); the phrase could be translated either "glory as of a father's only son" or "glory as of the only Son from the Father."[25] In either case, the simile operates metaphorically, unfolding the intimacy of relationship between the two, which, at the beginning, is captured in the phrase "turned toward God" (*pros ton theon*, 1:1).[26] The paternal metaphor is used to explicate the relationship that each has to "glory" (*doxa*): the Word radiates the glory of God just as, in human terms, a son reflects the nature of his father, who is the source and origin of his existence.

It is significant that the central theological theme of the Gospel is unfolded at the point of incarnation, the coming of the Word in mortal flesh. Only now is the imagery of Father-Son introduced, although later in the Gospel Jesus will pray as the Son of the Father from all eternity (17:5). Nevertheless there is a sense of the incarnation in 1:14 as the self-disclosure of the Name, especially the divine correlation of Father and Son—just as in Exodus 3 God reveals the Name to Moses at the burning bush. This is the first usage of the symbolism in the Fourth Gospel, yet the language is not novel: Jesus clearly does not become Son at the point of incarnation, any more than God suddenly becomes Father. As Janet Martin Soskice points out in discussing Exodus 3, given that the name of YHWH is already known in earlier Israelite traditions, the moment of revelation is not literally new, nor does it operate within the strict bounds of chronological time. Similarly, as symbolic of the profound relationship between "God" (*ho theos*) and "the Word" (*ho logos*), the Father–Son relationship manifests itself as the movement from the center outward, forming the originating "we" of the believing community in 1:14, just as YHWH in Exodus is to be read "not as from its first occurrence in Genesis and then cumulatively but rather outwards from the middle—from the burning bush and from Sinai as Israel's defining moment."[27] The point is reinforced by the language of revelation and glory in 1:14, which, along with the imagery of Father-

Son, parallels the Transfiguration elsewhere in the New Testament (cf. Mark 9:2–8 pars.; 2 Pet. 1:16–17).[28]

The imagery of 1:14 begins to take on a more obviously symbolic quality in its second occurrence at the end of the Prologue (1:18). The two aspects of the divine nature are present in this final verse, linked together in a striking way that reflects the characteristic dynamic of symbolism. In the terms of Schneiders's definition of religious (Johannine) symbol, both the "transcendent mystery" and the "sensible reality" coalesce, creating a tension that the Johannine text thereafter never loses.[29] On the one hand, God is declared to be beyond human sight or vision and thus transcendent: "no one has ever seen God" (1:18a);[30] on the other hand, God is freely and willingly made manifest. The particular form of this gracious self-revelation is perceptible in the imagery of Father and Son: "the only Son, God, who is in the bosom of the Father, he has revealed God" (1:18b). The sense of oneness yet differentiation between *theos* and *logos* at the beginning of the Prologue gives way to the symbolism of *patēr* and *monogenēs*—the former now possessing the definite article—expressing a dynamic between union and distinction in the language of kinship:

> The relationship of father and son assumes at one and the same time an indissoluble unity and a clear separateness: for while a son is not his father, no other human relationship connects people in quite the same way as does the relationship of a parent to a child, for this is a relationship in which the very being of the one comes from the other, and in which neither has an identity as "Father" or "son," "parent" or "child," without the other.[31]

This intimacy is articulated in the metaphor that describes the Son, in vivid terms, as lying "in the bosom/breast of the Father" (*eis ton kolpon tou Patros*), thus making him more than qualified to reveal the Father: both in the status of sonship itself and in the radically intimate form it assumes.[32] Fatherhood in the Prologue emerges in symbolic form, demonstrating that its force is linked inextricably to the personhood of the Son. It is significant also that, in both uses of this imagery in the Prologue, there is a vital connection to the human apprehension of God. The two verbs, *etheasametha* ("we have seen," 1:14) and *exegēsato* ("he has revealed," 1:18), convey the powerful link between the Father-Son symbolism and themes of revelation and believing that are central to the Fourth Gospel. The imperceptible divine is made perceptible through the incarnation and through the subsequent unfolding of symbols that convey a sense of God's loving selfhood and costly self-giving. The "flesh" which the Gospel reveals to the believing gaze is that of the Son in the glory of his relationship to the Father.

The first use of Father outside the Prologue occurs in the cleansing of the temple (2:13–22). In line with the Prologue, Jesus' objection to the buying and selling in the temple is based on his apprehension of God as "*my* Father": to the sellers of doves, he commands, "Do not continue making the house of my Father a house of trade" (2:16; cf. Zech. 14:21). In the end what is controversial in this story is not

Jesus' depiction of God as his Father, but rather his reference to destroying and rebuilding the temple of his "body," of which the earthly temple is a symbol (2:18–21). Nevertheless, the absolute use of "my Father," without any allusion either to the authorities or other worshipers in the temple, becomes significant and controversial later in the Gospel (cf. 5:17–18).[33] The Johannine Jesus declares, right from the beginning, a unique relationship with God that entitles him to call God not "our Father" (Matt. 6:9 par.) but "my Father" (cf. Luke 2:49; also Matt. 26:39). The christological significance of this declaration occurring in the Jerusalem temple does not become apparent until John 5–10. For now, the evangelist indicates what will become dominant later in the Gospel: that Jesus' possessive mode of address for God is decisive for his identity and ministry, and the basis and justification for his "works."

Father imagery is implicitly present in the discourse with Nicodemus, although the title "Father" does not appear until the end of the chapter. Jesus here is designated as "Son" in language that recalls the Prologue: God's sending of the Son derives from self-giving love and calls for a response of faith (3:16). Note that John is emphatic in his view that judgment in the sense of condemnation is the purpose neither of Jesus' coming nor of God's sending: God's purpose throughout is life-giving, not judgmental: "God did not send the Son into the world in order that he might judge [i.e., condemn] the world, but in order that the world might be saved through him" (3:17). Yet the response called for already represents a kind of "judgment": those who fail to believe "in the name of the only Son of God" (*to onoma tou monogenous huiou tou theou*, 3:18) have already, in a sense, judged themselves.[34] Hence John reiterates the closest possible connection between "God" and the "only Son," while at the same time revealing that such intimacy is definitive for salvation and judgment. A person's attitude to God is defined now in terms of his or her response to Jesus as the self-revelation of divine life and love. The paternal imagery and the intricate relationship of Father and Son become explicit later in the discourse, where Jesus declares that "the Father loves the Son and has given everything into his hand" (3:35). This brief utterance reinforces theologically the earlier Johannine theme that vindication and judgment are based on people's reaction to Jesus (3:36): because he is Son, their reaction to him reveals their eschatological stance in the here and now.

Although John's focus, as we have seen, is largely on the relationship between God and Jesus, the language of fatherhood is introduced into the dialogue with the Samaritan woman in a more general sense. This is the first place in the Fourth Gospel where it is indicated that divine fatherhood embraces not just Jesus but also others:

> Jesus uses the term "Father" [in this passage], not just because it is his usual way of speaking of God in the fourth Gospel, but because he is describing the new relationship of the true adorer to God. The Johannine Jesus often speaks of "God," but here he is inviting men who seek God to an unheard-of intimacy with the "Father."[35]

Whereas the woman refers to "our father Jacob" (4:12) and "our fathers" worship-
ing on Mount Gerizim (4:20), Jesus responds by speaking of worship of *the Father*
in a new dimension, no longer tied in the old way to sacred place (4:21–23), except
as that is revealed in the "flesh" of Jesus himself. It is the woman's worship of the
Father that is the issue here—the woman and those Samaritan villagers whom she
represents. Yet, while Jesus' identity is crucial for the revelation to the Samaritans,
it does not overtly draw on the imagery of divine sonship, despite the presence of
father imagery. The language of fatherhood as Jesus uses it in this context anticipates postresurrection language, where the believing community will be invited to
share with the risen Christ a similar (though not identical) experience of God as
Father (20:17).

Only in the next chapter of the Gospel does the Father-Son imagery become
expansive and develop the symbolic meaning indicated in the Prologue. Characteristically, John sets the explication of the Father symbol within a distinctive narrative context, the healing of the disabled man at the Pool (John 5). Yet this
signifies also a turn in the broader narrative of the Gospel where the plot moves
to more overt conflict with "the Jews," leading to attempts on Jesus' life—a conflict
that occurs mainly, though not exclusively, in Jerusalem and in the context of a
series of Jewish feasts (John 5–10).[36] In this section, the evangelist presents Jesus
as the one who fulfills the rituals associated with the temple: "Embodied in the
incarnate Son of God the reader finds the perfection of what was done in the Jewish Temple in signs and shadows."[37] The story of the healing of the lame man is
the first in this series—indicated by the unnamed feast in 5:1—and begins with
the Sabbath. In a sense the narrative leaves much to be desired in terms of the
man's faith (in marked contrast to the man born blind in John 9),[38] yet the Christology that flows from the "sign" through Jesus' dispute with the authorities is of
critical importance. The context is that of unbelief and hostility on the part of "the
Jews" (5:16–18), the man aligning himself with their authority over against that of
Jesus, despite his healing (5:15)—which may account for the otherwise inexplicable word of judgment in Jesus' response (5:14).[39]

The discourse that follows the "sign" is the most consequential in the Fourth
Gospel for understanding the Father–Son relationship (5:19–30).[40] There are two
supporting symbols that draw out the significance of the core imagery. In the first
place, John unfolds the typological significance of the feast: "now it was a Sabbath
on that day" (5:9b, 16). The discourse turns on Jesus' justification for working on
the Sabbath, a justification that revolves around the central statement that "the
Father is working until now and I too am working" (5:17). This seemingly innocu-
ous utterance is one of the most astonishing statements of Johannine Christology
in the Gospel—very different from the kind of justification of Jesus' Sabbath work
to be found in the Synoptics (cf. Mark 2:23–3:6 pars.). Jewish thinkers were exercised by the contradiction implicit in Gen. 2:2–3: How could God literally rest on
the Sabbath without creation grinding to a halt? How was it that, if God did rest,

infants could be born and people die on the Sabbath? With various kinds of justification, the conclusion was drawn that God's quintessential work of giving life
and judging continued, in some sense, on the Sabbath even while God, in another
sense, rested. Such a proviso or exemption belonged, however, only to God, whose
providential work never ceased even in the midst of Sabbath rest. Philo, for example, speaks of God's rest as perpetual but not inactive (*De cherubim* 87), while
some of the rabbis see the divine exemption lying in the fact that creation is God's
dwelling (*Genesis Rabbah* 11.10; *Exodus Rabbah* 30.9).[41] Whatever the particular
rationale, the Johannine Jesus is seen to share uniquely in the divine exemption
from the Sabbath because the work he does is not his own—indeed is not strictly
speaking a human task—but rather is the uniquely divine work of giving life and
judging. The Sabbath, like the other feasts, becomes a symbol of Jesus' identity and
mission.

Second, John makes it clear that Jesus shares the divine exemption and the
divine work precisely as Son of the Father. C. H. Dodd has argued that the underlying parable or proverb beneath the Father–Son relationship in this text is that of
a son apprenticed to his father.[42] The context is that of the family trade passed
down through the generations from father to son—the commonest form of
employment in the ancient world.[43] Both father and son are at work in the workshop on the same task: "He [Jesus] answered and said, 'The Father is working and
I too am working'" (5:17). The son is learning the trade from his father, who owns
the workshop and the family business and thus supervises his work: "the Son is
able to do nothing of himself, except what he sees the Father doing" (5:19b). The
son watches his father at work and learns by imitating him: "for that which he
does, the Son likewise does also" (5:19c). The work which the son does is not his
own but his father's work: "For the Father loves the Son and shows him everything
that he does" (5:20). This metaphor of divine apprenticeship encompasses not
only redemption but also creation (1:3–4, 10): it is grounded in the life-giving
nature and sovereignty of God spanning all aspects of existence.

The same imagery expands to include the idea of "sending," taking the image
of an apprentice relationship in a somewhat different direction: "the one not honoring the Son does not honor the Father who sent him" (*ton patera ton pempsanta
auton*, 5:23). Although this is not the first reference in the Gospel to Jesus being
sent (cf. 3:17, 34; 4:34), it is the first occurrence of "Father" in relation to sending,
using the characteristic Johannine phrase which means literally "the having-sent-
me Father" (see 6:44; 8:18; 12:49; 14:24). Apart from this context (cf. 5:36, 38),
there are further references to the Father (or God) sending Jesus in the Fourth
Gospel (e.g., 6:57; 8:16; 10:36).[44] Behind John's sending language seems to lie the
Old Testament eschatological promise of a prophet-like-Moses (Deut. 18:15–22),
a messenger who will alone speak the word of the Lord entrusted to him by God
and whose faithful word will be vindicated by its effectiveness and power.[45] The
promise is given to Moses by God, who in turn reports it to the people of Israel: "I

will raise up for them a prophet like you from among their own people; I will put my words in the mouth of the prophet, who shall speak to them everything that I command" (Deut. 18:18). As with the Moses-like messenger, the one who is sent is given along with the message both the authority and something of the identity of the sender. Jesus in the Fourth Gospel is the messenger par excellence, who, as the divine Word, alone speaks faithfully the word of God and whose word is authenticated by its witness (5:31–40). Sending language is associated with Jesus' true origins and destiny (e.g., 7:28, 33) and relates not just to his mission but also to his fundamental identity as Son of the Father.

At the same time, underlying the imagery of a shared task and common work between Father and Son is the conviction that the Son shares the Father's very life—in a way that is not true of the believing community which is given life but does not possess divine authority over it: "for just as the Father has life within himself, so also he has granted it to the Son to have life in himself" (5:26). For Thompson, "the formulation assumes the unity of the life-giving *work* of Father and Son, but also predicates a remarkable status of the Son, one which is not made of any other creature or entity. The Son 'has life in himself.'"[46] This is the basis on which the "signs" of Jesus' ministry are to be understood, while revealing the inner, christological meaning of the feasts and rituals of Judaism. The evangelist interprets both the Jewish traditions he inherits and also the traditions of Jesus' ministry within the symbolic framework of the Father–Son relationship: the power to heal, the sovereignty over life and death, and the covenantal life-giving love disclosed in ritual and festival. Each is articulated within the central symbol of divine fatherhood, expressing the one creative and redemptive life into which human beings are drawn, reformed and renewed to become the people of God.

The theme of the Father as the source of life is reinforced in the Bread of Life narrative, drawing out the nurturing and providential aspects of that life. That the Father is the source of Jesus' ministry is emphasized in the symbolism of Jesus as the Bread from heaven (6:33–35, 41, 48, 51), whose origins from his human parents are symbolic of his divine origins "from above" (6:42). As a result, those who are drawn to Jesus for salvation and life are drawn there by the Father, the two being in this respect identical (6:37), since the Father is the sender of Jesus (6:39). The focus later in the discourse is on the second of Thompson's categories, the Old Testament apprehension of God's fatherly care for Israel. Once again, that life-giving source points in the direction of the Son who lives uniquely in and through the Father—"just as the living Father [*ho zōn patēr*] sent me, and I live on account of the Father" (6:57)—with the result that life flows in a single stream from Father to Son. The Father is also the source of Israel's life, creating a sense of continuity between past and present. Even the manna was not the gift of Moses but of the Father and is thus, by implication, a type of the Son, who, like Sophia, is both host and food: "not Moses gave you the bread from heaven, but *my Father gives* you the true bread from heaven" (6:32).[47] The nurturing life of the Father flows through the Son to the believing community, symbolized in the eucharistic flesh and blood of the Son of Man (6:53). It is a life in continuity with, yet superior to, the life received by "the fathers" who ate the manna and yet died (6:49, 58). The perfection of divine life is given through God's fatherly and self-giving love, in the incarnation, death, and sacramental presence of the Son, thus overpowering death itself.

In the Tabernacles Discourse, a new note of controversy is sounded, joined to the symbol of divine fatherhood. The conflict is a kind of tug-of-war over the person of the Father, whose covenant relationship with Israel is celebrated at the Feast of Tabernacles (cf. 8:20).[48] Does the Father belong to "the Jews" who claim no illegitimacy as freeborn children of Abraham (8:33, 39–40), yet fail to realize that Jesus "was speaking to them about the Father" (8:27)? Or does the Father belong to Jesus, who claims a unique status and knowledge as the Son sent "from above" (8:18, 23)? As the dialogue progresses beyond the semblance of faith to hostility,[49] the discord becomes a skirmish—as John constructs it—between Jesus and his Father, on the one hand, and the apostate "Jews" and their "father," on the other. Despite the filial kinship "the Jews" claim to possess with God (8:41–42), as well as with Abraham, John reveals that their real father is the devil and not God or Abraham (8:44). This judgment is based, in Johannine terms, entirely on the response of the authorities to Jesus, the Son sent from the Father: "If you knew me, you would know also my Father" (8:19); "If God was your Father, you would love me, for I came from God" (8:42). By contrast, Jesus' connection both with Abraham and with God is so substantial that it radically transcends space and time. Both opponents are vindicated (in Johannine terms) in the final scene, each revealing his true father. The solemn self-disclosure of Jesus' identity links him directly with the divine life and being, as true Son to the Father: "I tell you solemnly, before Abraham was, I am" (8:58). Whereas the authorities, whose hatred has escalated to physical violence, finally attempt to stone Jesus (8:59)—the penalty for blasphemy—disclosing thereby their true affiliation to their father the devil, who "was a murderer from the beginning" (8:44). As Augustine aptly concludes, "As a human being [Jesus] flees from the stones; but woe to those from whose hearts of stone God flees!" (*In Joannis Evangelium* 43:18).[50]

The theme of conflict continues in the following chapters, leading up to the formal plot to put Jesus to death as the one who claims to be the Son of the Father (11:47–53). The imagery of the shepherd and sheepfold, within a polemical context, reveals the Father in all three dimensions: as source of life, as carer and provider, and as sovereign. The theme is expanded by explicit reference to Jesus' death and resurrection, where the divine sovereignty over life which Jesus receives from and shares with the Father is to be displayed in the concrete history of the crucifixion (10:17–18). The laying down of life—the giving over of life by the one who possesses divine authority over life—is linked to the love which flows from Father to Son, spilling out in self-sacrificing and self-giving love to the sheep in the sheepfold. The debate that follows (and, in a sense, continues) the Shepherd Discourse is set within the context of the Feast of Dedication in the temple (10:22–23).[51] This time it is the oneness of Father and Son that provokes the violence of the authorities (10:30–31). Jesus' claim to filial oneness with God elicits the charge of blasphemy (10:33)—a correct deduction if, in Johannine terms, Jesus is not the divine Son—to which Jesus responds by pointing to "the works" (*ta erga*) as witnesses to his identity (10:37–38). They bear witness to the divine sabbatical work (*ergon*) which Jesus performs as Son on behalf of the Father.

References to God as Father are frequent throughout the Farewell Discourse. In these chapters, we are given the fullest treatment of the interrelationship between the Father, Jesus, and the community of disciples. Theology and ecclesiology cohere in a perfect union of intimacy and love: the disciples "had to be made to understand Jesus' going away and the new communion that it gave with him, from Easter onwards."[52] The circle is complete with the introduction of the Paraclete, who is sent directly from the Father or from the Father by Jesus (14:16, 26; 15:26): in any event, as with the Son, the Father is the source of the Paraclete's life. In the portrait of the Paraclete, and also the figure of the vine (15:1–8), the evangelist completes our understanding of that life and love which originate in the Father and bring into being the community of faith. As we have seen, the Father's love manifests itself in the life of the community through abiding and indwelling (14:21; 17:21).[53] Yet the Farewell Discourse, more than elsewhere in the Gospel, makes it vibrantly clear that there is no other access to God except through Jesus. That is the significance of the image of the Way (14:2–11)—no sight or touch, no hearing or knowing, no love or knowledge of the one except in and through the person of the other. Although the language is still that of Father and Son, behind it is the iconic significance of Jesus as the Word made flesh: Jesus as the definitive Symbol of the Father, the true Image, the visible manifestation of divine glory in fleshly form. As Witherington observes, "the point is not that Jesus *is* the Father but that he is the perfect likeness and exegesis of the Father as his unique Son, as God's Wisdom, the expression of the very mind and character of God."[54] Here we see both the strength and the limitations of the Father-Son symbolism. The imagery emphasizes that to have one means to have the other; on the one hand, it is impossible to have fatherhood without sonship (and vice versa), the identity of the one being dependent, in every sense, on the other. At the same time, we begin to make out the ragged edges of the symbolism: no human child could claim to be the visible manifestation of the parent except in a limited and specific sense. The Father, in this Gospel, cannot be "seen," in any case. The *visio Dei* ("vision of God") is perfected in beholding the glory of the Johannine Jesus (1:14)—implying also the advent of the Paraclete who mirrors his life, and the birth of the believing community, which receives the realization of his risen life.

Thus the core of John's symbolism in these chapters lies in the identity of Jesus as Son, the one whose origins and destiny lie in and with the Father (13:1, 3; 14:12;

16:28). Jesus' relationship with God, as Son to the Father, is characterized by the language of love (14:31; 15:9), knowledge (17:25), and union (14:10; 16:32; 17:11, 21). Yet there is a peculiar dynamic operative in the relationship between Father and Son which begins, in these chapters, to expand the metaphor. On the one hand, Jesus' mode of address is profoundly reverent and compliant with the divine will. The Father's authority is everywhere acknowledged: Jesus will glorify God and give honor to the Father (14:13); Jesus is conscious of being sent by the Father (14:24) and of receiving all things from the Father's hands, the Father being the source of his life (16:15; 17:24); he accepts the Father's commands and keeps them (14:31; 15:10); he acknowledges the Father as greater than himself (14:28). At the same time, there is a reciprocity to this relationship that stretches the symbolism. Thompson's three criteria are all present in the Farewell Discourse in the Father-Son dynamic—the Father as source of life, the Father's love for the Son, the Son's recognition of the Father's sovereignty—yet these begin to shimmer in the vibrant sense of mutuality and oneness with which the Son responds. Not only does the Son glorify the Father, but the Father also glorifies the Son; indeed, Jesus confidently expects such glorification (13:31–32; 17:5); the love of the Father for the Son is mirrored perfectly by the Son's love for the Father (14:31). The sense of oneness and intimacy is beyond anything we might imagine of a parent–child relationship, moving closer to the language of sexual intimacy. While therefore the Father is the source of the Son's life, loves the Son and receives glory from the Son's obedience to the Father's will, there is another sense in which the profound union that is expressed, particularly in the Great Prayer, extends the language and symbolism almost to breaking point.

In many respects the Father-Son imagery reaches its climax in the Great Prayer, which, along with the Prologue and the discourse of John 5, represents the most significant presence of this particular symbolism in the Fourth Gospel. The language here is performative: the prayer is a visualization, an enactment, a "performance" of the perichoretic relationship between Father and Son. John 17 partakes of an ascent of the Son to the Father, as we have already seen,[55] where Jesus enacts the exaltation of his life before God, already acting out, in prayer, the shape and direction of the crucifixion—just as it has been the shape and direction of his ministry. Here, above all, Jesus is the divine Son, dwelling "in the bosom of the Father" (1:18) and sent by the Father's love into the world. The prayer not only speaks of glory; it also enacts that mutual glorification which encapsulates the identity and mission of Father and Son. Within the prayer itself, however, that relationship can also be depicted not only in the imagery of ascent but also as a continuous circle of intimacy in which each flows into and out of the other, without beginning or end. The Father-Son symbolism in this prayer thus represents the imprint of the divine, internal relationship within human history in archetypal ways that are definitive for human identity as much as divine. Commenting on Jesus' Sonship, Dodd concludes:

> The relation of Father and Son is an eternal relation, not attained in time, nor ceas-
> ing with this life, or with the history of this world. The human career of Jesus is, as
> it were, a projection of this eternal relation (which is the divine *agapē*) upon the field
> of time. It is such, not as a mere reflection, or representation, of the reality, but in the
> sense that the love which the Father bore the Son "before the foundation of the
> world," and which He perpetually returns, is actively at work in the whole historical
> life of Jesus. . . . The love of God, thus released in history, brings men into the same
> unity of which the relation of Father and Son is the eternal archetype.[56]

In the end, the radical shape of the symbolism enacted in the Great Prayer dis-
mantles a hierarchical understanding of the dynamic between Father and Son,
with consequential implications for the life of the Christian community.[57] After
this prayer, Christology and ecclesiology now partake of the same reality, belong
within the same perichoresis, sharing the same eternal source and projected outward onto the world in a procession of sendings.

There are few references to divine fatherhood in the final chapters of the
Gospel. In a sense, the symbolism is replete. All that is to happen in Jesus' death
and resurrection is interpreted beforehand in the light of the Father-Son imagery:
Jesus' death is his return to the Father, his glorifying of the Father and glorification by the Father, the manifesting of the Father's love for "his own" and forming
of them into a life-giving community. Two further references remain, however, to
complete the picture in terms of the Gospel's ecclesiology. The words of Jesus to
Mary Magdalene, after the resurrection, when she receives the commission to the
disciples, signify the moment at which the believing community enters fully into
its own relationship with the Father. The language is strongly covenantal, yet
maintains a delicate distinction between Jesus' relationship with God as Son of the
Father, and the disciples' relationship with the Father: "I am ascending to *my
Father* and *your Father, my* God and *your* God" (20:17c).[58] As we have already seen,
the fatherhood of God relates primarily to Jesus as "Son" and only in a secondary
and derivative sense to the community of faith. God is never referred to as "our
Father" in this Gospel: the distinction is maintained between the eternal Son
(*huios*) and the reborn children of God (*tekna*).[59] The covenant with Israel as
God's children/people is renewed with the God who is Father of Israel, but it possesses a radically new dimension in the person of the Son, whose relationship is
both contiguous with, yet in another sense distinct from, the sons and daughters
of the Father.[60]

The final reference to the Father is on Easter Sunday, when Jesus appears to the
disciples and gives them the gift of the Holy Spirit (20:19–23; cf. 19:30). The parallelism of the relationship between the Father and Jesus, and Jesus and the disciples is very obvious in this passage. Jesus, in this Gospel, is designated as the one
sent by the Father. Now, in turn, as a consequence of Easter, the Sent One (cf. 9:7)
becomes the Sender, commissioning the disciples and sending them forth: "Just as
the Father sent me, so I send you" (20:21; cf. 4:38; 13:20). Like Jesus, they too are

to speak the prophetic words of God as faithful messengers and their word will likewise be determinative (in this case, the words of forgiveness, 20:23). They are empowered with the Spirit, who is breathed on them by Jesus for the task of mission (20:22), the Paraclete also having been "sent" from the divine realm (14:26; 15:26; 16:7). The ultimate source of all this sending is the Father, whose love for the world provides the motivation and shape of the mission. Once again, as in the Farewell Discourse, the circle is complete, though in the real and vital context of Easter: the Father sends the Son, who sends the believing community sustained and animated by the presence of the Spirit-Paraclete.

JOHANNINE FATHERHOOD AND PATRIARCHY

A preliminary reading of the Fourth Gospel may give rise to the impression that God as Father reflects Roman-Hellenistic understandings of fatherhood, built on a pyramidal set of social relationships that places the father of the family (*paterfamilias*) at the top and female slaves at the bottom. In this view, the powerful father who possesses *patria potestas*—both in the domestic economy and in the political economy of the state—exercises the authority of life and death over all the other lesser members of the household.[61] Christian feminism has critiqued such a ranking of persons as oppressive and degrading to women and other "lesser" beings (including slaves and children), arguing that such imaging of the divine limits women's access both to God and to their own identity as children of God.[62] Feminism extends the critique to contemporary theories of fatherhood that condone the domination of the father within the family, including his absenteeism, arguing that this kind of model leads in the end to violence and sexual assault.[63] From this perspective, it may seem at first glance that, in the Fourth Gospel, we are looking at a symbol for God that confirms the divine image in males but denies or reduces it in females.

Such a reading of John's Gospel does not accord with a closer inspection of the Johannine text. As with other issues, however, we need to remember that the questions we ask of the text are not necessarily questions with which the text is overtly concerned. At the same time, texts such as the Fourth Gospel have a life that extends beyond their immediate context: Johannine symbols have the power to speak across diverse cultural contexts. Moreover, the interpretation of symbolism requires the distinctive voice of the interpreter, whose own subjectivity is not absent. While that is not a license to read into texts whatever we want to find there, it does mean that new questions can be addressed to ancient texts, and new interpretations woven from the fabric of the past. From this perspective, it can be argued that the fatherhood of God in the Fourth Gospel cannot be used to support domineering and authoritarian constructions of power, but rather challenges all human pretensions to power and status.

This reformulation of divine fatherhood happens in the Fourth Gospel in two ways. In the first place, the Johannine Father symbol occurs in contexts that are concerned with *the surrender or giving away of power*. An example of this is the Johannine language of "sending," focused on mission, which clusters around the Father-Son imagery. As we have seen, God is "the Father who sent me," and Jesus, as Son, is the one who is "sent." At one level, this language reads as classic, paternalistic imagery: the male sovereign of the divine court confers authority on his son and heir, sending him into the world with the seal of his authority (see 6:27c). Bearing the tokens of the sender gives the messenger a borrowed identity and protects him from harm. The sender also remains secure; after all, what does it cost the monarch to send the messenger armed with the badges of his authority? Yet, in John's Gospel imagery of dominion and mastery is overturned: the sending of the Son by the Father does *not* protect either from harm. On the contrary, the sending—motivated by love for the world—costs the Johannine Father everything. The Son is sent into the world to confront human mortality (e.g., 3:14–17; 12:27), while the Father is prepared to risk exposure to hurt and rejection (1:11; cf. Mark 12:1–12 pars.). For John, the Son represents the Father's gift to the world: the gift is God's own self (cf. 1:1), and it is a costly and vulnerable sending, given through death (12:24).

Similarly, John speaks of the Father giving everything over to the Son (3:35; 5:22; 13:3; 16:15).[64] This giving over refers in particular to the dual authority, as we have seen, of giving life and judging, associated with the Sabbath (5:16–17, 21–27).[65] The symbolism might seem to derive from the Greco-Roman patriarchal household and the authority of the *paterfamilias*. Johannine fatherhood undoubtedly includes sovereignty and power: as Thompson has demonstrated, the paternal symbol involves an authority that calls for obedience and honor.[66] But in John's Gospel, the divine power of the Father is constantly being handed over, or given away: to the Son, who exercises it on God's behalf (5:21–22), and to the believing community, who, as God's beloved friends, are given access to the divine mysteries (15:15; 16:25–27). Authority is not held onto in the Fourth Gospel. The Father of the Johannine Jesus does not scheme to retain and increase power; on the contrary, it is given away again and again. Fatherhood becomes a symbol of divine, costly self-giving for the empowering and capacitating of others. The basic function of divine power in the Gospel is thus not oppressive but life-giving:[67] Jesus' ministry exercised on God's behalf creates healing and wholeness, enabling people to resist the powers of darkness. The authority that Jesus exercises on behalf of the Father contrasts markedly, in this respect, with the religious and secular authorities. Whereas they harass and destroy those without power (9:22–23, 34; 10:10a; 19:6–7, 15a) and succumb to political expediency (11:47–50; 19:8, 13–16a), Jesus, who exercises the true sovereignty of the Father, empowers those who are weak and stands up for truth, no matter how costly (19:14–18).[68] Here again Jesus' words and actions demonstrate that the symbol of divine fatherhood in the Fourth Gospel is concerned not with dominance and suppression but, on the contrary, with freedom and life.

Divine sovereignty is associated also with judgment, a judgment that the Father hands over to the Son. The Fourth Gospel displays a complex attitude to judgment. On the one hand, it is intrinsic to the divine being. The word of judgment in the Fourth Gospel blazes out against those who misuse power, who hurt and destroy, who try to quench the light, who knowingly turn away from the source of life (1:5; 3:19–20; 5:39–40; 8:39–41; 9:39–41; 10:31–39; 11:46–53). This theme reaches its climax in the passion and resurrection narratives, where the judgment of the *kosmos* against Jesus is turned on its head and becomes the divine judgment against, and overpowering of, the darkness (16:8–11, 33). Even here, however, John is insistent that the purpose of Jesus' mission is not that of judgment but salvation (3:17). That is why Jesus can assert both that he does not judge and that he exercises divine judgment (8:15–16). There is a kind of tentativeness about the language of judgment in the Fourth Gospel. Responsibility for judgment is handed over not just to the Son but also to human beings in general in their response to the life that Jesus brings: the light of the world shines and illuminates people's true selves, inviting their response (3:19–21; 8:12). The Johannine God is far from being a stern, judgmental father figure who is demanding, punitive, and vindictive. Even so grave a task as judgment is not held onto in this Gospel.

Although John's Gospel pictures the crucifixion as ascent and glorification rather than powerlessness and suffering (cf. Mark 15:34 par.; 1 Cor. 1:18–25), the meaning of power is still found ultimately in relation to the cross. The power that the Johannine Jesus is given by the Father is the authority (*exousia*), as we have seen, "to lay down my life in order than I might take it up again" (10:17). It is not given for self-aggrandizement but rather is the authority of self-surrender and self-giving, standing paradoxically alongside the picture of divine vulnerability in the incarnation and crucifixion. Texts such as the Shepherd Discourse (10:14–18) and the trial before Pilate (18:36–37) reveal the way in which Jesus' divine authority discloses the paradoxical "glory" of the cross. Similarly, the Johannine vocabulary of "glory" and "glorify" is not concerned with the increase of divine status, but represents through the Gospel narrative the unfolding manifestation and handing on of the Father's love.[69] The cross is the climax of the theme of glorification because, by implication, the Father's true nature and life-giving glory are unveiled (cf. 6:51c; 12:32).[70] The radical giving of God's self is, for John, the source of life and salvation (3:16), and the very heart of the symbol of God as Father.

The second indication that divine fatherhood, according to John, represents a challenge to domineering structures is *the quality of intimacy that exists between the Father and the Son*. The basis of the relationship between the Father and the Son is the love each bears the other (3:35; 5:20; 10:17; 14:31; 15:9; 17:23–24, 26). It is a love that is expressed in affectionate rather than dutiful terms, suggesting the most profound attachment and the deepest unity of will and heart. This intimacy, however, does not exist merely in and for itself. As we have already observed in more than one context, the relationship of Father and Son is the archetypal pattern of relationality which both models and determines every other relationship within the believing community; indeed, it defines the meaning of personhood.[71] Setting love at the heart of relationship is not of itself enough to disentangle authoritarianism—a form of "love patriarchy" can continue to thrive (cf. Eph. 5:21–33)[72]—but when it is defined in terms of intimacy and self-giving, an intimacy that sets free and empowers the other, then it enters an entirely different framework that seriously destabilizes paternalistic models.

As a result, the relationship of Father and Son in John's theological framework is inclusive and embracing of others.[73] This is part of the way intimacy operates in the Fourth Gospel around the symbol of fatherhood. In the Roman-Hellenistic pyramid of family and society, patronage relations are exclusive and selective, and keep others on an inferior level.[74] In John's symbolism, however, believers are drawn into the relationship between Father and Son; the intimacy that exists within the being of God opens itself to others. All are invited in this Gospel to share the same love, the same "filiation" that Jesus himself possesses with the Father.[75] The divine circle of intimacy presents itself as an expanding horizon, a point illustrated by the dramatic movement of Jesus' Great Prayer, which begins in the inter-relationship of Father and Son (17:1–5), moves to include present believers (17:6–19), and finally incorporates future believers (17:20–26).[76] The language of "abiding," as we have already seen, is part of the same framework: the community of faith is drawn into the "abiding-in-love" of Father and Son (14:10), and Father and Son, through the Spirit-Paraclete (14:17), take up their "abiding-in-love" within the believing community and the hearts of believers (6:56; 8:31; 14:23; 15:1–17). Unlike kinship patterns, those outside the immediate family (cf. 4:1–42; 12:20–26) are drawn into the immanence of Father and Son. The symbolism is the very opposite of remoteness, detachment, and indifference.

In John's symbolic presentation of divine fatherhood, there is thus a two-way movement that establishes the basic pattern of the Gospel, the first outward and the second inward. Both movements are closely related. God's fatherhood reveals itself, on the one hand, through the giving away of power. Although unlike Paul, John does not explicitly use the language of *kenosis* (self-emptying; see Phil. 2:6–8), a parallel conception is found in the divine surrender of selfhood, autonomy, and power that is implied in the incarnation. This self-giving is apparent in the relationship between Father and Son, and the connection between the divine interrelationship and the world that is dependent on it. On the other hand, God's fatherhood operates in the Gospel by drawing others into the filial relationship between God and Jesus, so that it becomes symbolic of God's relationship to the world. Both movements, the inner and the outer, challenge the autocratic desire to retain power and maintain exclusive relationships. The father language of this Gospel reveals a fundamentally relational theology and anthropology.[77]

The Johannine Father-Son symbolism comes to have a powerful influence on subsequent Christian thinking—in Athanasius, in particular, who is the first to explore and develop the symbol of divine fatherhood in a systematic way.[78] According to Peter Widdicombe, in the Alexandrian tradition (with the exception of Arius) there are clear elements that are recognizably Johannine—particularly in Athanasius who stresses the reciprocity of the Father–Son relationship and the centrality of the incarnation. Both Origen and Athanasius emphasize the distinction in the relationship between God as Father of Jesus and God as Father of the believing community. For Origen, the distinction is between the Father's eternal generation of the Son and the adoption of the children of God by grace;[79] for Athanasius, father-son language describes first "relations internal to the divine being" because on these salvation depends.[80] Athanasius in particular defends the relational character of God whose personhood begins in the "plurality and mutuality" of the divine being, with its source in the Father and its eternal emanation in the life of the Son and the Spirit, a relation that extends to the community of faith (and, ultimately, to all creation).[81]

As Catherine LaCugna has pointed out, the trinitarian theology of the Cappadocian fathers, influenced by Athanasius, belongs within the same tradition. It is profoundly relational, emphasizing not a solitary monarchy but a dynamic and personal relationship within the threefold being of God, which, at least in its essence, does not involve subordination of any kind (unlike in Origen).[82] Following Rahner, LaCugna argues against later attempts to cut off the inner, relational being of God from the economy of salvation, without denying divine mystery.[83] There is "an essential unity though not a strict identity between divine essence and divine energies" in salvation.[84] A renewed understanding of the divine being, within such a trinitarian framework, must therefore be conceived of as the mutual outpouring of divine love in creation and salvation. As a consequence, for LaCugna, any understanding of divine rule contains an implicit critique of all forms of subordinationism—even where the church fails to perceive the radical consequences of its own dogma. The implications of such a relational theology, for LaCugna, are pervasive:

> The *archē* [rule] of God, understood from within a properly trinitarian theology, excludes every kind of subordination among persons, every kind of predetermined role, every kind of reduction of persons to uniformity. . . . A reconceived doctrine of the Trinity affirms what Jesus Christ reveals: that love and communion among persons is the truth of existence, the meaning of our salvation, the overcoming of sin, and the means by which God is praised. *Therefore any theological justification for a hierarchy among persons also vitiates the truth of our salvation through Christ.*[85]

The picture of divine fatherhood that emerges from the Fourth Gospel—and develops in the Eastern Church of the fourth century—is essentially relational and personal. The Johannine understanding of the cherished solidarity of Father and Son is seen from within the drama of salvation and is constitutive of reality at its core. It is far from being remote and inaccessible. The symbol of divine fatherhood is not presented in a dictatorial or subjugating way; on the contrary, authority is seen within the context of intimacy and love, and divine sovereignty is presented, within a relational setting, as life-giving, liberating, and inclusive. The tenderness and compassion of the Father are far from the gender stereotyping that associates fatherhood with discipline and authority. The symbolism opens up a sense of affiliation and connection that is expressive of authentic life, and it is this divine communion to which the community of faith is joined.

Although the church of the fourth and fifth centuries develops this language much further, it is nonetheless following a trajectory that has its origins in the Fourth Gospel. The argument against subordination reflects the Johannine understanding of the reciprocity of the Father–Son relation and the consequent Johannine vision of a community of "friends," joined together in mutual love. The language and imagery run counter to the subordinationist strand in much Christian theology, which leads, all too quickly, from the subordination of Christ to God to that of women to men, emotion to reason, and spirit to flesh.[86] Such a limited Christian anthropology distorts also the Christology and theology on which authentic personhood, for women as well as men, is built. On this basis, feminist theology need not reject the father-title for God, but on the contrary may find that its expression provides precisely what is needed to dismantle the "principalities and powers" that demean and abuse women, subordinating their humanity and denying, in effect, the presence and possibility of the divine image.[87]

FATHERHOOD AND THE GENDER OF GOD

It could be argued that the Johannine symbol of God as Father still fails to deconstruct patriarchal authoritarianism adequately because it remains a masculine symbol—despite its immanence and inclusiveness. The question is whether women's redemptive status as daughters and friends of God is damaged by the maleness of this symbol for the divine being. What underlies the question is whether the price of entry is higher for women than for men, and whether such entry requires a loss, rather than a transformation and restitution, of their identity. For many feminists, this kind of symbolism has become not a window on the eternal but a barrier that excludes and alienates. LaCugna's vision of what a revitalized trinitarian theology can mean for persons-in-communion, male and female, is lost in what seems, to many, a confirmation of female invisibility and inferiority at the heart of the Christian tradition.

To answer such questions in relation to the fatherhood of God—inasmuch as they are answerable—requires the inclusion into the discussion of other symbols in the Fourth Gospel, such as Wisdom themes and motherhood images, as we will see in the next chapter. Even so, the tradition influenced by the Fourth Gospel reflects some degree of accommodation to the androcentric presuppositions of the ancient world. Athanasius's language demonstrates this dynamic, which is to some extent inevitable when it comes to speaking of—or representing pictorially—the divine. Athanasius describes the work of the Trinity in creation as deriving from a unified energy. God is present to creation in three ways: "above all things" (*epi pantōn*) as Father, "through all things" (*dia pantōn*) as the Word, and "in all things" (*en pasi*) as the Holy Spirit (*Letter to Serapion* 596). What is significant here is that, in expressing so succinctly the communion and solidarity within the trinitarian life of God and its profound, diverse relatedness to all creation, Athanasius nevertheless links the imagery of divine fatherhood to God's role as "principle and source" of all life, divine and human (*archē kai pēgē*; Latin: *principium et fons*). This accords with Aristotelian embryology, which sees the biological father as literally the "principle and source" of life—an understanding that, according to Adele Reinhartz, may well have influenced the Fourth Gospel's understanding of divine fatherhood.[88] Once again, we are observing that theological language, even at its most profound, is but "to stammer at infinity."

Cultural accommodation, however, is a small part of the story. It is as mistaken to underestimate the coherence that holds together both symbol and theology in countercultural ways as it is to ignore the contingent nature of theological symbolism.[89] The God of the Fourth Gospel is portrayed as transcendent, unable to be confined in human definitions despite the weight of iconic representation: "no one has ever seen God" (1:18); "not that anyone has seen the Father except for the one who is from God" (6:46). As Thompson points out, even though God is designated "Father" in this Gospel, "the Johannine God has no name."[90] Some feminist rhetoric notwithstanding, the Christian tradition is well aware that God is not male, even while using masculine symbolism. The early church in many respects took a stand against the culture of its day, insisting that the being of God, as a first principle, is "ingenerate, eternal, and incorporeal" and thus beyond biological classification.[91] Even though emerging from a patriarchal culture where "the male was assumed to be the active principle in begetting," the Cappadocians "denied any comparisons between divine and human begetting" and "challenged the Christian imagination to renounce biological, cultural, and commonsense notions of fatherhood, including the patriarchal idea of the self-sufficient father."[92] Thus Gregory of Nyssa, although using masculine language and imagery for God, notes that either mother or father can be used to name God, since essentially "there is neither male nor female in the divine" (*oute arrēn, oute thēlu to theion esti*). No human category can adhere to the innermost being of God, including that of gender:

> (For how could anything of such a kind be apprehended to the godhead, when even for us humans, this [aspect of our humanity] does not continuously endure; but when we all become one in Christ, we are divested of the signs of this destruction, together with our old humanity?) For this reason, every name which is found is of

> equal power in manifesting the [divine] incorruptible nature: neither female nor
> male defiling the significance of God's undefiled nature. (Gregory of Nyssa, *In Canticum Canticorum: Homilia* VII.3.11)

In his *Against Eunomius*, Gregory acknowledges implicitly the necessity of symbolic language for God because ultimately God is transcendent: "The uncreated Nature alone, which we acknowledge in the Father, and in the Son, and the Holy Spirit, surpasses all significance of names" (*Refutatio Confessionis Eunomii* 15).[93] As often in patristic thought, Gregory seems to speak of Father and Son as the actual names of God[94]—partly in defense against the subordinationism of the Arians—although even here in understanding fatherhood as expressive of divine essence, he defines that fatherhood carefully, denying its corporeality and thus by implication its masculinity.

A number of contemporary theologians have maintained the view that "Father" is the literal and revealed name for God—though it could be argued without Gregory's nuanced understanding of the way religious symbolism works.[95] In their view, fatherhood expresses the divine essence disclosed in the incarnation, without gender overtones and without being a symbol. Father encapsulates accurately God's true name and nature, originating in the experience of Jesus and developed in the New Testament (especially the Gospel of John) and the ecumenical creeds of the early church. Karl Barth, for example, asserts that divine fatherhood is unconnected to human understandings of fatherhood, the former in no sense dependent on the latter; on the contrary, God as Father is the one "from whom every family [*patria*] in heaven and on earth is named" (Eph. 3:14–15).[96] Barth's views have been reinforced in a collection of essays on feminism and Trinity edited by Alvin Kimel, arguing in some cases not just for Father as the revealed name but also for masculine language and imagery in general as more appropriate to the divine being, since—unlike feminine language—it is supposedly more successful in avoiding the dangers of Gnosticism and pantheism.[97]

Barth's argument concerning the otherness of divine fatherhood, it must be admitted, has a distinctive force that needs to be taken seriously. Widdicombe points out that the early church does not explicitly draw on contemporary cultural understandings or discussions of human fatherhood in order to understand the fatherhood of God.[98] The being of God as Father, for Barth and other theologians in the same tradition, transcends human life at every point. Thompson, who has some sympathy for this perspective (though not an uncritical one), points out that, in the biblical world,

> the understanding of God as Father does not explicitly serve to legitimate masculine identity or behaviors, nor does scripture draw specific "lessons" from God's Fatherhood for human fathers. . . . Nor do fathers image God more fully or completely than mothers do simply by virtue of being male or being a father to one's children.[99]

There is a vital dimension to this view that is consistent with the Johannine presentation of divine fatherhood and must not be lost. As Gregory himself observes, "there is a similarity of names between things human and things divine, revealing nevertheless underneath this sameness a wide difference of meanings" (*Contra Eunomium* I.622).[100]

Yet there can be problems with this perspective, especially when it overstates divine transcendence, associates that otherness with divine fatherhood in a one-sided way or demands the exclusive use of fatherhood in Christian worship. While it is true that Christian theology needs to resist becoming anthropology and to critique all human projections onto God, an extreme Barthian position denies the "flesh" any place in the revelation of divine glory. Human beings are passive recipients, the effects of the Fall pervasive, the image defaced beyond recognition, and the significance of divine enfleshment limited. It is hard to see, moreover, how "Father" is not a masculine word (as is claimed) unless we admit, to some extent, the limitability of human language in the face of the divine. Otherwise, the argument for gender neutrality can only work by conceding universalism to masculine language, which reduces the female to the specific and "other," while the male is regarded as universal and normative. Furthermore, so uncompromising a position seems to ignore the intuitive dimensions of theological symbolism, assuming that it is enough to know rationally that God is not male—that the title "Father" is gender-free—while ignoring its affective power. "There is no doubt that the use of only masculine images and metaphors in worship and in theology *creates the impression that God is male* [emphasis added]."[101]

Finally, and most significantly, the Barthian view is based on an inadequate understanding of symbolism, particularly as it operates in the Fourth Gospel.[102] Symbol and metaphor, as we have seen, are not employed to decorate the plain truth, but rather bear within them the transcendent reality to which they point. In Tillich's terms, as we have already seen, a religious symbol such as divine fatherhood is "the expression of a true revelation."[103] The pitting of symbol against truth, and the assumption that metaphor and symbolism are somehow less substantial than "plain prose"—particularly in dogmatic formulations—and thereby captive to a postmodern relativity, reduce metaphor and symbol to decoration and fail to see that symbolism can itself be the vehicle of revelation as it accommodates itself to human reality. In this sense, we can speak of theological symbolism as rooted in human experience, even while it is also the product of divine revelation: it is part of the meaning of the incarnation that God deigns to be clothed in the garments of our flesh and blood. What this means for the symbol of divine fatherhood in the Fourth Gospel is that, as verbal icon, it is neither an optional picture of God to be arbitrarily discarded, nor a photograph of ontic reality unsullied by human hands. In a Johannine framework, it is indeed "not an exchangeable metaphor,"[104] but not because it is the literal and exclusive name for God as the fountain and source of life. Rather it is a core metaphor of faith that cannot be ejected without seriously compromising the truth of Christian faith: "If metaphors are uniquely informative—if they enable insights that are unobtainable from any other source—then changing religious metaphors means changing religions."[105] This viewpoint need not be argued in a literalistic way that gives insufficient weight to the symbolism of the Fourth Gospel or its narrative flow. As a core symbol in the Gospel, fatherhood can be seen to be both divinely revealed yet also accommodated to human life.

An understanding of the Father symbol in the Fourth Gospel needs to locate itself, therefore, between two paradoxical theological poles. On the one hand, we need to begin with the mystery and incomprehensibility of the Johannine God, a theme we have already observed in the Gospel. As Gregory of Nyssa remarks, "the infinity of God exceeds all the significance and comprehension that names can furnish" (*Contra Eunomium* III.1.110).[106] Though not separable from the processes of salvation, the divine being is ineffable even in the act of self-communication: "for as the hollow of one's hand is to the whole deep, so is all the power of language in comparison with that Nature which is unspeakable and incomprehensible [*aphraston kai aperilēpton*]" (*Contra Eunomium* III.5.55).[107] Similarly, writing from an Orthodox perspective, Thomas Hopko, while arguing that the formulation "Father, Son, and Holy Spirit" is irreplaceable, affirms also that "God's *essence* cannot be identified with fatherhood or sonship or spirithood" or with "any of the metaphors applied to it from creaturely existence . . . because Divinity in itself is beyond them all."[108]

At the same time, paradoxically, we need to maintain that in the incarnation God chooses to be revealed within the flesh. Revelation is made within the language and structures of human life. The symbol of divine fatherhood is a concrete symbol that is familiar to human life, regardless of the irregularities of people's individual experience. As noted in earlier chapters, symbols articulate this paradox in a way that discursive language cannot, holding together the separability yet fusion of divine and human, spiritual and material, sacred and profane, mystery and openness, glory and flesh. The core symbols of the faith—those which have the capacity to continue speaking across generations and cultures—are not arbitrary or simply the product of human invention; they contain something vital of that divine reality to which they point. Divine fatherhood is not a symbol that can be dismissed: it is too firmly embedded in the tradition, too vital in understanding the complex interrelationship between God and Jesus, too vivid an expression of divine love. To say this is not to deny that other images and symbols have something to offer in understanding God, or that the church is constrained and limited to this language as the sole expression of its trinitarian life.

CONCLUSION: THE POWER OF THE SYMBOL

God's fatherhood, so vividly portrayed in the Fourth Gospel, is a critically important symbol of the foundational relationship between God and the Word-made-flesh. As a Johannine symbol it articulates the three dimensions of divine father-hood which emerge from the Old Testament. Its fundamental significance is chris-tological and can be expressed as follows:

- God is the ongoing source of Jesus' life—or, in other Johannine terms, God represents Jesus' origins and destiny.

- God's love for Jesus is total, radical, and self-giving.

- God's divine sovereignty and glory are acknowledged in Jesus' human obedi-ence and in his glorification of God through incarnation, ministry, death, and resurrection.

The Johannine symbol of Father extends also to the community of faith, which participates in Jesus' divine sonship through the narrative events of the Gospel. In this sense, we can reformulate the three dimensions of the symbol in relation to believers and the community of faith. This time, however, we do not speak of the Father alone but include the Son, who shares the divine life in each respect. The word "God" (*theos*) is thereby enlarged to include the Son, as well as the Father—as Thomas's confession makes plain (20:28; cf. 14:9)—and also, by implication, the Paraclete who makes present that divine life to the community in the absence of Jesus. Thus we can reframe the three dimensions to include the Father and Son, and also by extension the Spirit-Paraclete:

- God is the source of the believing community's life, its final origins and des-tiny.

- God loves the disciples "to the end": in living and dying, in rising, in loving and becoming present through the sacramental life of the church.

- God's authority is the basis of the community's life; its love and mission, its freedom, joy, union, and peace, all express its ultimate goal to glorify God in all things and keep God's commandments.

Note that this last point leads back full circle to the first. The recognition of divine sovereignty and the glorification of the Father and Son will result in the glorifica-tion (or deification) of believers who already receive, and will in the future receive once more, the gift of eternal life beyond all power of death.

As an icon of divine and human identity, the fatherhood of God enables us to grasp, with stereoscopic vision, the intimate union of Creator and creation envis-aged by the Fourth Gospel, and symbolized above all in the centripetal relation-ship of Father and Son. This symbolism offers a challenge to paternalistic and domineering ways of thinking and acting, and rightly holds a secure place within the tradition. Yet even the most fundamental of religious symbols are always to an extent limited, always ambiguous in some respect, always yearning beyond them-selves in the struggle to articulate the ineffable. The only adequate "speech" is the divine Word, a word not of our making but clothed nonetheless in our human frame. Only the Word reveals God in the Fourth Gospel, yet that Word paradoxically is bone of our bones and flesh of our flesh. Divine revelation and human experience meet harmoniously in this dynamic. God's self-emptying means that, though Self-naming, God is also divulged in symbol, metaphor, and speech. Human beings have a part to play in shaping a language fit for the Father who renames our humanity in the Son.

CHAPTER 6

Giving Birth to Believers:
Symbols of Motherhood

Alleluia! light
burst from your untouched
womb like a flower
on the farther side
of death. The world-tree
is blossoming. Two
realms become one.[1]

FATHERHOOD, AS WE HAVE SEEN, is a prominent symbol in the Fourth Gospel, with frequent usage and a discernible pattern. It conveys a sense of God as the author of life, in relation to both Jesus and the believing community. The same clear delineation cannot be drawn from the symbol of motherhood. Although it is possible to locate maternal symbols in the Johannine text, their presence is not as visible and their focus more diversified. Yet divine allusions to motherhood are present, even if more implicit than explicit, while the mother of Jesus is generally recognized as playing some kind of symbolic role in relation to the community of faith. We are thus in different terrain than when speaking of fatherhood imagery—more tenuous and heuristic, probing beneath the outer skin of the text. Once it emerges from the shadows, we discover in this variegated Johannine symbol of motherhood two distinct and overlapping meanings that form a trajectory of considerable power.

SOURCES OF MOTHERHOOD IMAGERY

In the ancient world, mothers were generally believed to play a lesser role than fathers, the latter being seen as responsible for the generation of offspring and thus the biological source of their children's lives. In Aristotelian terms, the mother's body was an incubator for the male seed, and her role, from beginning to end, was that of nurturer. As a result, mothers were associated with compassion and tenderness, whereas fathers were responsible for authority and discipline.[2] Roles, spheres, character traits, and virtues were clearly delineated for men and women

—associated with public and private, honor and shame—each gender having a specific place and corresponding values within complex kinship patterns.[3] The understanding of the household, with its mutual obligations and ties, was essentially a pyramid in which the mother had a distinct place, though significantly below paternal authority. This picture has an impact on the later epistles of the New Testament, particularly the Household Codes, where Christian wives are instructed to render obedience to their husbands in return for love and consideration (e.g., Col. 3:18–19; Eph. 4:2–33; 1 Pet. 3:1–7). While there are traditions in the ancient world of motherhood possessing authority and sovereignty—especially in cultic rites—these are strictly delimited by the overriding masculinity of political and domestic life, not to mention state religion.

In ancient Israel, mothers received honor and respect, though subject to the authority of their husbands.[4] Parents were seen as a gift of God and worthy of honor; the Mosaic commandment is accompanied by the promise of long life as a reward for honoring father and mother (Exod. 20:12; Deut. 5:16; cf. Mark 7:8–13 par.; Eph. 6:1–3).[5] The mother belonged within the *bêt-ʾāb*, the "father's house," where she lived in an extended family consisting of three generations, "all the descendants of a living ancestor," who is the *rōʾš-bêt-ʾāb* ("head of the father's house"); she was subservient to his authority. The family included married sons and grandsons, unmarried children, and various dependents.[6] Mothers are not present in Old Testament genealogies (cf. Matt. 1:1–18), only fathers passing on the genealogical line, just as inheritance passed from father to son. Nevertheless, there are strong maternal figures within the Old Testament, often in relation to powerful and important offspring:[7] Eve, the "mother of all living" (Gen. 3:20); Sarah, the mother of Isaac; Rebekah, the mother of Esau and Jacob; Naomi and Ruth, great-great-grandmother and great-grandmother respectively of King David; Hannah, the mother of Samuel; and the heroic mother of the seven sons in 4 Maccabees 8–12. Deborah, given the honorary title of "a mother in Israel" (Judg. 5:7), is exceptional in being not a biological mother but rather a judge, prophet, and warrior. After surveying the background of motherhood in the Bible, W. Michaelis concludes his sparse discussion of maternal patterns in the biblical world with this comment:

> If the position of the mother . . . is free from emotional exaggeration, mythological excess, or elevation to a religious symbol, there is a sense of the significance of the mother and what she stands for, and of her place in God's creation.[8]

Yet there is more to motherhood in the world of the Bible than Michaelis grudgingly concedes. There are signs of a feminine face to the God of Israel, whether in terms of a female consort (Asherah) or maternal imagery used of YHWH. While there is resistance to pagan cults and religious syncretism in the developing monotheism of the Old Testament, particularly in the postexilic context, "there exist . . . enough indications that ancient Israel and Judah have worshipped motherly aspects of their God."[9] J. Massyngbaerde Ford's survey of the Old Testament material concludes that God as Redeemer is presented in a (small) number of key texts as mother and midwife and that redemption itself can be pictured as childbirth.[10] This imagery is visible in the Song of Moses, in the portrait of the mother bird with her offspring:

> He [God] sustained him [Israel] in a desert land,
> in a howling wilderness waste;
> he shielded him, cared for him,
> guarded him as the apple of his eye.
> As an eagle stirs up its nest,
> and hovers over its young;
> as it spreads its wings, takes them up,
> and bears them aloft on its pinions,
> the Lord alone guided him;
> no foreign god was with him.
> He set him upon the heights of the land,
> and fed him with produce of the field;
> he nursed him with honey from the crags,
> with oil from flinty rock;
> curds from the herd, and milk from the flock. . . .
> You were unmindful of the Rock that bore you;
> you forgot the God who gave you birth. (Deut. 32:10–14, 18)

Although the pronouns are masculine, the imagery expressing God's protective care—guiding the people through the wilderness to the Promised Land and feeding them with bounty—is distinctly maternal (see also Exod. 19:4). Maternal imagery is especially striking in Isaiah 40–66, where there are four distinct references to motherhood (Isa. 42:14; 45:9; 49:15; 66:10–13; cf. Num. 11:2).[11] The most overt symbol of motherhood in these chapters is found in images of the mother breast-feeding, carrying, and comforting her infant:[12]

> Rejoice with Jerusalem, and be glad for her,
> all you who love her;
> rejoice with her in joy,
> all you who mourn over her—
> that you may nurse and be satisfied
> from her consoling breast;
> that you may drink deeply with delight
> from her glorious bosom.
>
> For thus says the Lord:
> I will extend prosperity to her like a river,
> and the wealth of the nations like an overflowing stream;
> and you shall nurse and be carried on her arm,
> and dandled on her knees.

> As a mother comforts her child,
> so will I comfort you;
> you shall be comforted in Jerusalem. (Isa. 66:10–13)

The primary focus of the symbolism is on Jerusalem as mother, nourishing, protecting, and comforting her children, the inhabitants of the city. It blends with other biblical imagery that depicts the city in female terms (e.g., Isa. 47; 52; Apoc. 18; 21) and parallels the Roman-Hellenistic custom of associating female deities with cities (Athene, Roma). As the final statement of the prophecy reveals, behind the maternal role of Jerusalem is that of the God whose motherly comfort Jerusalem provides: it is *God* who is the real comforter of Israel, *God's* nourishment that feeds and restores, *God's* protective love that gives safety and joy. The symbol of Jerusalem as mother thus opens up images for God in maternal terms: God is "the Mother of Israel" who actively gives birth, who has compassion, and who does not abandon Zion.[13]

J. Massyngbaerde Ford points out that Wisdom motifs are also significant for this kind of symbolism, overlapping with maternal images. Of particular importance is the portrait of Sophia as nourisher who feeds her people/children with the bread and wine of wisdom.[14] Maternal overtones are present, for example, in the poem on Wisdom in Sirach, a poem worth quoting in full for the motherly images that emerge in the second stanza and the richness of its related imagery:

> I. Blessed is the man who will meditate on Wisdom
>   and who will in his mind converse with her,
>   who considers her ways in his heart
>   and on her secrets will reflect.
>   He goes out after her as a hunter
>   and lies in wait on her paths.
>   Who stoops to look in her windows
>   and listens at her doorways,
>   who lodges near her house
>   and stakes his tent-peg against her walls,
>   who will set up his tent near her hands
>   and lodge in a dwelling-place full of good things,
>   who will place his children in her shade
>   and under her boughs will encamp,
>   who will be sheltered by her from the heat
>   and in her glory will find lodging.
>
> II. The one who fears the Lord will do it,
>   and the one trained in the Law will accept her.
>   She will go out to meet him as a mother
>   and as a bride will welcome him.
>   She will feed him with the bread of understanding,
>   and the water of wisdom she will give him to drink.
>   He will be supported by her and will not fall over,

and to her he will hold fast and not be put to shame.
She will exalt him above his neighbor
and in the midst of the assembly he will open his mouth.
Joy and a crown of gladness will he find
and a name for ever will he inherit.
People without understanding will never accept her
and sinful men will never see her.
She is far from arrogance
and lying men will never call her to mind. (Sir. 14:20–15:8)

This portrayal of Sophia moves from one loosely connected image to another: she is an interior companion, a hunted animal, a substantial and well-built house, a large and leafy tree, a loving mother, a welcoming bride, one who will nourish with food and drink, a source of status and good repute in the community, a means of joy and lasting memory. Correspondingly, the seeker is presented in the first stanza as needing her presence for advice and friendship, for food, lodging, and shelter from the sun (14:20–27). In the second stanza, because of his true piety, the seeker receives what he seeks and so finds in Wisdom, metaphorically speaking, motherhood and marriage, nourishment, a reliable moral and spiritual foundation, dignity, and reputation (15:1–8).[15] Much of what the seeker desires from Wisdom is parental, if not actually maternal: home, shelter, food, drink, welcome, education, guidance—all producing an adult who will live an honorable life within the community. As the hostess of Proverbs 9:1–6, who nourishes her guests with sumptuous food and drink, and the same figure in Sirach 24:19–21, who invites people to taste the sweetness of her fruits (*apo tōn genēmatōn mou emplēsthēte*, 24:19b), Sophia as giver and gift are one and the same.[16] Wisdom feeds her children/guests with her own self. As we will see, this metaphorical field of reference—mother, hostess, cook, nourisher—has its symbolic origins in the experience of infancy, where the infant is fed from the mother's body.

It is always difficult to specify the sources from which the Fourth Gospel, both knowingly and unknowingly, has drawn. We have already encountered the Wisdom influence in this Gospel, especially where Sophia is presented, through images of eating and drinking, as hostess and nurturer of the hungry and thirsty (John 2:1–11; 4:7–15; 7:37–39). Whether there is direct influence from Hellenistic cultic understandings is another question: the portrayal of Sophia in the later Wisdom writings of Israel seems already to have drawn on imagery from the Egyptian-Hellenistic cult of Isis before Sophia reaches the New Testament.[17] Apuleius's *Metamorphoses*, for example, has perhaps the most famous portrait of Isis. At the end of the narrative, the goddess responds to Lucius's cry for help, revealing herself in his need as the source of all life, divine and natural:

Behold I have come, moved, Lucius, by your prayers, Mother [*parens*] of the universe, Mistress of all the elements, first Progeny of the ages, highest of Divinities, Queen of the dead, first of Heavenly Beings, single Manifestation of gods and goddesses, I who rule with my signs the bright heights of the sky, the health-giving breezes of the sea, the awful silences of the underworld. (11.5)

Isis appears as a figure of divine sovereignty, uniting all deity within herself, maternal and authoritative, possessing dominion over the whole creation including the powers of life and death. While this figure may have something in common with Greek (and earlier) earth goddesses—particularly the Great Mother—there is a transcendent quality in Apuleius's description that makes of Isis more than a personification of Mother Earth.[18] It is plausible that this imagery has had an indirect affect on the Fourth Gospel via the Wisdom traditions; certainly it seems to have influenced the imagery of the Heavenly Woman in Revelation 12.[19] Yet it is also likely that other Old Testament maternal images have influenced the Fourth Gospel, associated particularly with Jerusalem, in the self-understanding of the community of faith. What is not present in this Gospel is the use of explicit mother symbolism to explicate the relationship between God and Jesus, although Sophia is an image that unites yet differentiates both God and Jesus.

MOTHERHOOD AND BIRTH IN THE FOURTH GOSPEL

The word "mother" (*mētēr*) occurs eleven times in the Fourth Gospel, mostly in reference to the mother of Jesus: at the wedding of Cana in Galilee (2:1, 3, 5, 12), in the Bread of Life narrative (6:42), and at the foot of the cross (19:25 [twice], 26 [twice], 27). Twice there is reference to Jesus' human father, though only once in partnership with his mother (1:45; 6:42). There is a reference to entering the womb of the "mother" in the dialogue with Nicodemus where birth becomes a symbol of eternal life (3:4), an image that derives from the Prologue (1:12–13). There is the possibility that *koilia* means "womb" in 7:38 (as in 3:4). In the Farewell Discourse, explicit imagery of motherhood also appears in the description of childbirth, though without employing the word "mother" (16:21). It is also possible that the self-justification of the authorities in the Tabernacles Discourse echoes accusations against Jesus regarding his irregular birth: "we were not born from sexual immorality [*porneia*]" (8:41). Finally, there is the crucifixion itself, with suggestions of birth imagery in the flow of water and blood from the crucified Christ (19:34). This material is best examined within the narrative flow of the Gospel, even though its range is diverse and not easily gathered into a single thread.

Birth in the Prologue

The image of birth occurs early in the Fourth Gospel: indeed, the fact that it occurs within the Prologue indicates that it is a theme of some importance. Unlike the *kosmos*, which rejects the light, believers welcome it and in so doing open themselves to the gift of new birth (*hoi . . . egennēthēsan*, 1:13), a birth that is impossible from human origins but possible through the creative power of God.[20] This birth springs from acceptance of the Logos and the recognition of him as the source of creation, the one to whom all things belong (1:12). Of that divine power, human generativity is but a pale reflection. Those who recognize the Word as Creator make up the company of those whom the evangelist calls "we" for the first time in 1:14, who share a common identity as children of God, born of divine love. The contrast is between human devising and effort, including the "labor" of childbirth, on the one hand, and divine generativity, on the other. The antithesis is expressed in overlapping phrases (1:13), which vividly depict—albeit in somewhat ponderous phraseology[21]—the ineffectiveness of human effort, and the extraordinary simplicity of that which is divinely wrought. The contrast is emphasized by the attenuation of the wording and the succinctness of the phrase "from God" (*ek theou*). The original word order is "who, not from blood, nor from the will of flesh nor from the will of a man, but from God were born." In exploring the significance of Jesus' flesh, we already observed something of the force of each phrase.[22] These are difficult to pin down especially in their chronology,[23] but together they include the entire process of procreation and birth, with male and female elements:

- "*not from blood*": In parts of the ancient world, including Judaism, it was assumed that conception was caused by the mingling of blood between male and female, semen being regarded in some quarters as the foam of blood.[24] There is probably also a reference to the blood of childbirth. Far more than modern biology, blood was seen as the main element (in various forms) in the producing and nurturing of children.

- "*nor by will of flesh*": It is not easy to know the precise meaning of this phrase, particularly in relation to the other two. Does it summarize all three or is there a distinctive meaning? While it describes in part sexual desire, it also probably refers to the human decision to conceive and bring forth a child. Once more, this would refer to both parents.

- "*nor from [the] will of a man*": The word "man" is not the generic *anthrōpos* but the word for male or husband (*anēr*). The phrase refers to the male initiating role in generating a child, which encompasses both the seed as the source of life and also the need for heirs.[25]

The language is metaphorical and does not evince a dualistic anthropology. Flesh, as we have seen, does not contrast with the human soul or spirit. Rather, what is contrasted are *human generativity and divine generativity:* the one unable to effect new birth (any more than it can create the world), and the other which can and does bring about transformation and new life, just as it produced creation at the beginning. This portrait of flesh presupposes the darkness and the gulf between human and divine, evidenced in the (ironic) lack of recognition of the light (1:5, 10). Somehow, somewhere, the *kosmos* created by the Logos has become alienated from him.[26]

The irony is apparent in the next verse. Whereas God bypasses human generation and birth in forming the community of believers, God does not bypass flesh in sending the Son: on the contrary, God becomes flesh and in so doing transforms it. To "become flesh" means, in effect, to be born; it describes "the inauguration of the incarnation."[27] Although, unlike Matthew and Luke, John narrates no birth narrative and makes no mention of Jesus' mother, Jesus' enfleshment is dependent on human birth—just as the fact of believers becoming children of God is dependent on celestial birth. Jesus' identity is that of the eternal Son of the Father, who becomes the son of his human parents, not yet alluded to. Similarly, the destiny of believers (who have already experienced human birth) is to become children of God by spiritual birth. The identity of both is changed, and the change is indicated through the metaphor of birth/becoming. John's theology indicates how the eternal God enters the temporality of time and submits to the processes of human generation and birth.

Raymond Brown argues that the imagery in 1:13 (and also in John 3) refers exclusively to the paternal role and that the verb *gennan* means "beget," not "give birth."[28] His objection is circular: John could not use a birth image because he never refers to the Spirit in maternal terms.[29] We have already seen that the later association with water makes the birth imagery overt (3:5). Yet the imagery of birth does not negate the divine begetting; in giving birth to believers, God also begets them (cf. 1 John 2:29–3:2; 3:9–10; 4:7; 5:1, 6–7). At this stage in the Prologue, the Spirit has not been mentioned, nor has the role of Jesus in bringing human beings to faith. All we can see for the moment is an implicitly maternal dimension in the reference to being "born of God." The use of maternal symbols to signify the relationship between God and believers contrasts with the imagery for the relationship between God and the Logos, which is largely paternal, even with the Wisdom overtones. In another sense, however, there is a firm connection between the filiation of Jesus and that of believers, making them all "offspring" (though in a very different way) of God. How God gives birth to believers is not indicated at this stage. While there is no overt reference to motherhood, it is implied in the birth imagery of 1:13 and will be developed later in the Gospel. What matters for the moment is the inadequacy of human birth to generate children of God. Only the miracle of the incarnation, the divine entry into human life, can bring about the miracle of new birth.

Motherhood in Jesus' Ministry

The second reference to motherhood is the appearance of the mother of Jesus, the only overtly named maternal figure in the Fourth Gospel. Her appearance follows reference to Joseph, Jesus' human father, in 1:45. Although the Prologue has made no direct mention of Jesus' human parents, they are introduced by name or designation early in Jesus' ministry. His mother is never named or described in any detail, but is referred to as "the mother of Jesus," "his mother," or, in relation to the beloved disciple, "your mother." She appears in company with Jesus' disciples and also with his *adelphoi* (brothers [and sisters]).[30] The Johannine portrayal of the mother of Jesus, introduced without name or description in Jesus' adult life, contrasts with that of Luke, who describes Mary's response to the annunciation, emphasizes her faith and courage, presents the honor she receives from Elizabeth in her pregnancy, puts an inspired song in her mouth, narrates the birth of Jesus, and hints at Mary's own struggle for faith in the unfolding story of her son (Luke 1:26–56; 2:34–35). In this respect, the mother of Jesus in the Fourth Gospel is similar to the beloved disciple, who is likewise unnamed and introduced with minimal description (13:23; cf. 1:25?).

The mother of Jesus makes only two appearances in the Gospel of John (2:1–12; 19:25–27), although she is also referred to in 6:42. In contrast to the Lukan narrative, she has little to say: on the first occasion only two terse utterances, and on the second occasion nothing at all. More important is her *presence* in two narratives of defining importance in John's theological vision at the beginning and end of Jesus' ministry. Though she speaks little and little is said overtly of her faith, her role on both occasions is of considerable importance. In some sense, she seems connected with beginnings: the beginning of Jesus' "signs" ministry and the beginning of the community's life. On both occasions she "stands near," as it were, the revelation of divine glory. However we might define it, her role creates an *inclusio* that frames the intervening narrative of Jesus' ministry. The fundamental issue, for our purpose, is the significance to be attached to her designation as mother. Is it to be read only on the literal level or does it possess symbolic force?

The place to begin is the wedding of Cana, which immediately follows the gathering of the first disciples (1:19–51) and has, as its purpose, the leading of the disciples to faith through the revelation of divine glory (2:11). The opening exchange between Jesus and his mother is notoriously puzzling and difficult. The mother of Jesus initiates Jesus' ministry with her implicit request for a miracle: "they have no wine" (2:3). Jesus' response is surprising. While seeming to dismiss her request as unwarrantable interference in his affairs (2:4; cf. Luke 2:49), he nonetheless accedes to her request (2:7). This is one of the most disputed passages in the Fourth Gospel. Part of the difficulty is deliberate; the text has several "prolepses," anticipatory references that can only be understood later in the Gospel. Yet not everything is made clear in retrospect. The question is why Jesus seems to distance himself from her in so abrupt a way: "What have I to do with you?" or possibly "What is that to me and to you?" (*ti emoi kai soi*, 2:4).[31] Culpepper argues that we should not make efforts to tone down these words: "Jesus's sharp response to his mother is not to be glossed over in a misguided effort to rescue Jesus' civility."[32] It is of vital importance, moreover, that we do not import modern psychological categories into this transaction. The Johannine narrative, here as elsewhere, is highly stylized.

If we interpret the rebuff as a Johannine literary and stylistic device, therefore, rather than a rude exchange between a young adult son and his interfering mother, we can detect at least three elements operating in the evangelist's theological understanding. These need not be seen as rivals but rather as complementary evocations of the story's symbolic meaning. In the first place, Jesus' own explanation for distancing his mother—"my hour has not yet come" (2:4b)[33]—introduces a critically important (even if baffling) motif into the Johannine narrative. The effect of the rebuff is, at least in part, to direct the reader's attention to the mysterious "hour" (*hōra*) which, as we will later discover, signifies Jesus' exaltation on the cross (7:30; 8:20; 12:23, 27; 16:32; 17:1; 19:27). The "hour" is recognized only with the coming of the Greeks (12:23), yet is linked also to the eschatological "now" of Jesus' ministry: "the hour is coming *and now is*" (4:23; 5:25). It is the hour of glorification, accomplished climactically on the cross but anticipated in the words and works of Jesus' ministry (2:11). In literary terms the reference functions as a prolepsis, an anticipation of the narrative of Jesus' ministry, pointing to the cross, where significantly the mother of Jesus will have a role to play:[34] there the question *ti emoi kai soi* will not be asked.[35] More immediately, as John McHugh points out, Jesus' response to his mother is part of a general Johannine device to alert the reader to the *symbolic* significance of what is about to take place in the revelation of divine glory.[36]

Second, in a narrative that is concerned with the development of the disciples' faith, it is possible that the rebuff acts as a test of faith (cf. Gen. 22). There is an important parallel in the feeding narrative, where, although no miracle is requested, Jesus challenges Philip to ask for one (6:5). The narrator carefully points out that the question functions to test Philip's faith, since Jesus "already knew what he was about to do" (6:6). Jesus' supernatural knowledge in the Fourth Gospel (already seen by the reader in 1:47–48; cf. 2:22–25) prevents the assumption that the mother of Jesus draws him reluctantly into performing a miracle. If Jesus knows that he is about to change the water into wine, his rebuff takes on a different character from what a psychological reading might suggest. The story of the royal official, in the second "sign" at Cana (4:46–54), parallels the wedding at Cana—creating the outer frame of a composition cycle ("Cana to Cana," 2:1–4:54)[37]—and is helpful in understanding the rebuff. Jesus' response to the man is also abrupt and awkward. After the official's request for healing, Jesus seems to turn on him (though addressing him in the plural) with the rebuke, "Unless you [pl.] see signs and wonders, you [pl.] will not believe" (4:48). The royal official is not discouraged by Jesus' response but repeats the request for healing (4:49): his faith, like that of the mother of Jesus, has been tested and proved. In both cases, therefore, the rebuff has the effect not of discouraging but of stimulating faith. With "unconditional trust in the efficacy of his word," the mother of Jesus directs the waiters (*diakonoi*) to follow Jesus' instructions, whatever these might be: "Do whatever he tells you" (2:5).[38] To this word his mother draws attention, anticipating the hour of glory and making it possible for the newly gathered disciples to see the glory in the flesh. The Cana story is concerned with the divine power of Jesus' word, its revelatory and dynamic quality and capacity to transform through faith.[39]

Third, John makes the theological point that Jesus works at his own timing, which is divinely ordered and therefore different from that of human beings. Elsewhere in the Gospel, Jesus seems to be waiting for a directive that is not identical to human priorities and needs, distancing himself somewhat from human initiative (e.g., 7:3–10; 11:3–15); yet sooner or later he does what is asked of him.[40] In the case of the illness and death of Lazarus, while Jesus utters no harsh words, his absence from Lazarus's sickbed, after the sisters' distress call, is equally difficult to comprehend. Jesus finally does accede to the needs of others. He responds to those who seek (as it were) to anticipate the hour, particularly in the case of those who, like the mother of Jesus and Martha and Mary of Bethany, are people of faith. Yet he also distances himself from their requests or demands, even when these seem, to our understanding, perfectly reasonable. Although this motif in the actual narrative seems rather clumsy from a literary perspective, it expresses, for the evangelist, the conviction that the Father's will takes precedence over human initiative.[41] The gap between request and response establishes the divine will as the ultimate source of all Jesus' works. This need not be seen as contradicting other themes in the Cana story, particularly that of faith. The mother of Jesus acts as an example of faith, even while Jesus expands that faith—in relation both to the symbolic significance of the "signs" and to the divine initiative to which he responds.

There is another element that some have detected in the Cana story—that Jesus is distancing himself from his mother's physical motherhood. Supporting this view is the unusual use of *gynai* as a mode of address, not unusual in addressing women in general (since it is perfectly polite) but unusual from a son to his mother (2:4). Later in the Gospel, Jesus will address both the Samaritan woman and Mary Magdalene in the same way (4:21; 20:13, 15), including his mother once more at the foot of the cross (19:26). According to Witherington, for example, this disengagement refers to her maternal authority: "Jesus responds in a way that distances him from Mary's authority, but does not reject the need."[42] In this case, we would have a Johannine parallel to Luke's story of the youthful Jesus in the temple, where he too distances himself from family obligations to his parents in order "to be concerned with the affairs of my Father" (Luke 2:49). The problem with this view is that the Johannine Jesus does *not* dissociate himself either from his mother's request or from her motherhood.[43] On the contrary, she is not in the least perturbed by the rebuke,[44] nor does Jesus perform the miracle in a grudging or reluctant spirit: it is spectacular, in both the quantity and the quality of the wine produced (2:10). She continues to remain in relationship with him and to be his mother (2:12).

Arguing that the function of the mother of Jesus in the Fourth Gospel is precisely to establish his humanity, Beverly Gaventa takes issue with the view that Jesus is separating himself from family ties: "The Logos is not a disembodied spirit, after all, but has family and location just as does any other flesh-and-blood human being." The motherhood of Mary plays a vital role in confirming the humanity of Jesus. Far from severing Jesus from his family connections, the Cana narrative and the preceding story of the gathering of the first disciples "*invest* Jesus with a human mother and father and brothers and home."[45] Gaventa makes a vitally important point, emphasizing the literal level and its importance in confirming the genuine nature of the *sarx* of Jesus. It challenges any view that might diminish the flesh of Jesus in this Gospel. Yet Gaventa's interpretation need not rule out figurative significance for the mother of Jesus, whether as "mother" or "woman."[46] Nor need it contradict the view that the Johannine Jesus—whose full humanity is indicated in his family connections—might want to test the faith of those who are connected to him, either by friendship or kinship. It is undeniable that Mary's maternal role cannot fully define his identity, and her relationship to him cannot be determined by family obligations alone. The issue is whether her implicit request in 2:3 derives from maternal authority, based on biology, or from personal faith in Jesus. If there is a testing element in the narrative, what 2:5 suggests is that she is operating primarily from faith and that any maternal significance is metaphorical rather than literal. In many respects the Prologue plays a role similar to the birth narratives of Matthew and Luke, which establish Jesus' identity, both human and divine. Yet the Prologue lacks any reference to Jesus' human parents, and in particular his mother.[47] In this sense, the wedding at Cana parallels the birth narratives in disclosing the faith of Jesus' mother at the beginning not of his earthly life but of his ministry. It is perfectly possible to argue, therefore, that the presence of the mother of Jesus functions to establish the humanity of the incarnate Logos, but also has further significance. Her presence and faith also function to reveal something of Jesus' divine identity. In a symbolic reading of the Fourth Gospel, the flesh of Jesus discloses divine glory.

We may note, in passing, that in the next appearance of Jesus' *adelphoi*, their lack of faith becomes apparent (7:5). Neither the mother of Jesus nor the disciples are present with them (7:2–10). If it is her faithful *presence* that is of real importance in the Johannine narrative, then we may ask whether her *absence* possesses a corresponding significance. Is there the suggestion of her dissociation (and that of the disciples) from those whose physical proximity to Jesus remains opaque and never moves beyond the material realm? Although encouraging Jesus' ministry (at one level), the *adelphoi* also express doubt and lack any understanding of the purpose of the "signs" (7:4b).[48] Here they contrast with the mother of Jesus, who belongs with those who, like John the Baptist, the royal official, and the Samaritan woman, reveal faith in the word of Jesus.

In many respects, the wedding at Cana raises more problems than it solves. If anything, it tantalizes the reader into pushing further into the narrative as it unfolds, in hope of elucidation. The Cana narrative teases the imagination, in part because its function is largely proleptic. "Most of what is needed in order to understand the story is *not* said."[49] The narrative presents the mother of Jesus as establishing Jesus' humanity but it also indicates that her role is *not* limited to the physical or biological sphere, important though that undoubtedly is. What that "more" is, and whether it relates symbolically to motherhood, is not yet uncovered. Her faith in the "word" of Jesus is nevertheless important for what will follow: it is precisely such faith that reveals the true identity of the "children of God," placing them among the "we" who behold the divine glory. Both the mother of Jesus (in 2:5) and the disciples (in 2:11) perceive something of the true, divine origins of Jesus in the Cana story: advertently or inadvertently, her role has helped to deepen and nurture the disciples' faith. Only the coming of the "hour" will disclose the full meaning of the glory and of her place within it.

Birth imagery is developed further in Jesus' dialogue with Nicodemus (3:1–11). In an earlier chapter, we saw that the reference to water in 3:5 refers primarily to childbirth (and, in a secondary sense, baptism).[50] The birth imagery is introduced by Jesus in his retort to Nicodemus's opening conversational gambit (3:2). Jesus explains that biological birth is symbolic of spiritual birth (3:3–8). The Spirit, being "from above," is the One who gives birth to believers (*gennan*), enabling them to see and enter the reign/realm (*basileia*) of God. This is not a metaphor for the human struggle to believe, even though "initiation into life" is the overarching theme of John 2–4.[51] It is not the struggle of the infant to be born that counts but the labor of the mother pushing the child into life. Likewise, it is not the struggle of Nicodemus or any other human being that is definitive, although without faith no such movement is possible. It is the Spirit whose "labor" gives birth to believers (3:6, 8c). The same birthing imagery remains in the background throughout the rest of the discourse. References to eternal life (3:16–18) and the symbol of light (3:19–21) are consonant with the imagery of birth and probably derive from it. To enter life is to move from the darkness of the womb into the light of the visible world, a process beset with pain, difficulty, and danger. The same is true of entry into eternal life. Through birth that is divine in origin—that is to say, through the Spirit—believers discover a source of identity, a destiny, a new life. In being born as children of God, they experience the divine image renewed and restored (1:13). Motherhood is part of the birth symbolism implied in the role of the Spirit who gives birth to believers, enabling them to enter the *basileia* of God and experience eternal life. This represents an expansion of the phrase *ek theou* ("from God") in the Prologue. The Spirit is depicted here in more obviously maternal terms.

Images of motherhood are suggested also in the imagery of John 6, though they take a rather different direction. The first is in relation to the mother of Jesus, once more alluded to (though not actually present) in the dialogue between Jesus and "the Jews." Jesus' identity is complex and paradoxical, as is apparent from the beginning of the Gospel. As the Logos, his origins and thus identity are "from above"; as the Bread of Life, he is "the one who descends from heaven" (*ho katabainōn [ho katabas] ek tou ouranou*, 6:33, 41–42, 50–51). At the same time, the Logos "became flesh," so that integral now to his identity and origins are his ordinary human birth and parentage: "Is not this Jesus the son of Joseph whose father and mother we ourselves know?" (*hou hēmeis oidamen ton patera kai tēn mētera*, 6:42). In the escalating conflict of this narrative, the reference to Jesus' parents is dismissive of his divine origins. What "the Jews" imply is that Jesus' human origins are enough to define his selfhood; for them, no further disclosure of identity is needed. This at once excludes his identity "from above" and, in Johannine terms, totally undoes the effects of the feeding. Yet these two defining statements of identity are not presented as either-or in the Fourth Gospel. Jesus encompasses both. He has a divine Father *and* two perfectly ordinary human parents, both—though in different ways—the source of his life and identity,[52] just as the bread of the feeding is ordinary barley bread yet also the "flesh of the Son of Man." The same paradoxical and symbolic dynamic is operative in both.

Second, the portrayal of Jesus in John 6 as the one who nourishes the community of believers with his own "flesh and blood" suggests the presence of maternal imagery in the background. Scandalous though it seems to "the Jews," now increasingly alienated from Jesus' self-revelation, such feeding is necessary for the community of faith to find life (6:53). This divine food and drink are "true" (*alēthēs*), because, unlike ordinary fare—including even the manna in the desert—they prove ultimately lasting and give life to those nourished by them, a life that transcends death (6:27a, 54–56). The particular nature of this imagery, inspired by Wisdom, is not revealed in the narrative of John 6 until late in the dialogue between Jesus and the crowds/"Jews."[53] At first the focus is on the feeding (6:1–15), which leads into discussion of the manna and the true meaning of the bread (6:26–33). Gradually, through the conversation, Jesus is revealed as the true bread from heaven, a revelation that culminates in the "I am" saying of 6:35 (echoing the self-revelation of Jesus at 6:20): "I am the bread of life; the one who comes to me will never hunger and the one who believes in me will never thirst." Only toward the end of the dialogue, as the conversation becomes more hostile and uncomprehending on the part of his interlocutors (see 6:41, 52), does Jesus reveal in full the meaning of the original "sign"—that he is himself both the host at the table and the food itself. This is not disclosed until the last and most detailed of the "I am" sayings in the narrative (see 6:48): "I am the bread of life who has come down from heaven; if anyone eats of this bread he [she] will live for ever, and the bread which I will give is my flesh for the life of the world" (6:51).[54]

By this stage of the narrative, the symbolism in John 6 has become eucharistic, with Jesus as "host" at the table and his flesh and blood as nourishment. Yet the sacramental symbolism does not rule out the human experience from which it symbolically derives. The dread of cannibalism is presumably the basis of the mis-understanding of "the Jews" in 6:52, yet it makes no sense, since Jesus is speaking of feeding on a living person. The literal meaning gives way before the metaphor-ical. In the terms of the metaphor—and even allowing for the Wisdom origins of the language, which, as we have seen, already has distinctly maternal overtones— *there is no context in which the nourisher both gives and is the nourishment except that of the mother feeding her child with her own body.* In those parts of the world where lactation was (and is) the only source of infant nourishment, the child would literally die without it, just as believers will die without being sustained and nourished by the Bread of Life. The maternal background is reinforced by the addition of blood (6:53), which, while pointing to the Eucharist in a secondary sense, is linked to breast-feeding. In the ancient world, breast milk was regarded as processed menstrual blood (for understandable reasons, given that lactation tends to suppress ovulation).[55] The Johannine Jesus is speaking as more than a host hos-pitably inviting guests to his banquet. In effect, he speaks as a mother to her chil-dren, feeding them with the "milk" (which is itself both food and drink) of his own body. The symbolism is implicit and suggestive rather than explicit, yet it takes the maternal imagery in a new direction. Both the Spirit and Jesus can now be depicted in terms that are suggestive of motherhood.

In the light of this maternal imagery, it is appropriate to ask whether "womb" might be an appropriate translation for *koilia* in the Tabernacles Discourse (7:38).[56] As we saw in an earlier chapter, the christological reading of this passage is preferable. The "rivers of living water" are to flow not primarily from the disci-ple but rather from Christ, who promises to quench the thirst of all who come to him.[57] This is probably a proleptic reference to the flow of blood and water from the side of the crucified Jesus (19:34), which, as we will see, is suggestive of a "womb" giving life. Although *koilia* rarely means "womb" in classical Greek, it is more common in the Greek Old Testament: the same word, which refers literally to the hollow of the body or abdomen, is used for the womb, the belly or digestive system, the male genitals, and (metaphorically) the innermost recesses of the heart.[58] In the sense of "womb," for example, *koilia* is used in relation to Rebekah's twin sons (Gen. 25:24), in the blessings of the covenant which bring fertility ("the fruit of the womb," Deut. 28:4, 11), and of Naomi's infertility (Ruth 1:11). The meaning "womb" is found also in the New Testament to translate *koilia* (e.g., Matt. 19:12; Luke 11:27; 23:29; Gal. 1:15). In a similar way in the Fourth Gospel, *koilia* is used in 3:4 to mean "womb": "How can a person be born, being old? Can one enter into the womb of the mother [*tēn koilian tēs mētros*] a second time and be born?" In each of these examples, it is clear that the reference is to the womb ("the mother's womb" being the most common phrase), whereas it is not as clear that

7:38 refers to the mother's *koilia*. Massyngbaerde Ford is one who takes seriously the possibility that 7:38–39 is "a feminine text that complements the eucharistic text in John 6."[59] In the light of the transposition of Jesus' flesh throughout the Fourth Gospel, the translation "womb" cannot be ruled out, particularly in the light of the flow of blood and water. At this stage, it is still a small piece in a jigsaw from which a maternal image of the Johannine Jesus begins to emerge.

Mother Imagery in the Farewell Discourse and Passion Narrative

The second half of the Gospel has four references to motherhood—relating, as in the first half, to the Spirit, Jesus, and the mother of Jesus. In the Farewell Discourse, Jesus comforts the grieving disciples using maternal imagery. Immediately following the first prediction of the Paraclete, Jesus assures the disciples that he will not abandon them but will console them with his love and presence:

> I will not leave you as orphans, I am coming to you.
> A little while and the world no longer sees me,
> but you yourselves see me; because I live so you live.
> In that day you yourselves will know that I am in my Father
> and you are in me and I in you.
> The one holding my commandments and keeping them
> is the one who loves me;
> and the one loving me will be loved by my Father,
> and I will love him [her] and will reveal myself to him [her]. (14:18–21)

These verses are important in elucidating the significance of the Spirit in relation to Jesus' absence. The Spirit continues Jesus' presence after his departure, returning to the community as "another Paraclete" (14:16). In this sense, "[t]he departure and the return coalesce."[60] The consolation of this passage derives not primarily from the final return of Jesus but more immediately from the arrival of the Paraclete, who will make present the absent Jesus and therefore also the Father. The reference to orphans points to the love of the Father (4:21), in line with Old Testament concerns for the widow and orphan (Exod. 22:22; Lam. 5:3; Mal. 3:5; cf. Jas. 1:27), yet Jesus speaks also of himself, and therefore the Spirit, in the same maternal terms.[61] The passage recalls Isaiah 49:15: "Can a woman forget her nursing-child, or show no compassion for the child of her womb?" (cf. Ps. 27:10; Hos. 14:3). In the light of what we have seen already in the Fourth Gospel, it is likely that what we have here is an extension of the maternal imagery for Jesus. The Jesus who has nourished, comforted, counseled, and guided the disciples with his presence will not abandon the disciples on his departure; as well as friend, Lord, and brother, he will also continue the role of mother.[62] The same maternal role will be passed on to the Paraclete. Once again, the imagery is implicit rather than explicit.

The second maternal reference in the Farewell Discourse is explicit, and at some variance with the usage we have examined so far. Toward the end of the Farewell Discourse, just before the Great Prayer, Jesus again offers words of reassurance and comfort to the disciples in the context of his departure. The small section is a "sustained metaphor,"[63] a kind of parable, with a loose quasi-narrative progression and allegorical elements:

> I tell you solemnly, you will mourn and wail, but the world will rejoice. You will be grief-stricken but your grief will turn to joy. The woman [*hē gynē*] when she labors has pain, because her hour [*hē hōra autēs*] has come. But when she gives birth to the child [*gennēsę̄*], she no longer remembers her distress on account of the joy, because a human being [*anthrōpos*] has been born into the world. You too therefore have grief, but soon I will see you and your heart will rejoice and no one will take your joy from you. (16:20–21)

In terms of the metaphor, the "vehicle" is that of childbirth in which the mother endures agonies of pain during the birthing—exacerbated in the ancient world by the ever-present threat of death and the lack of pain relief—but afterwards is filled with joy at the birth of the child. There is a vividness to the metaphorical language that accords with many women's experience: the escalating pain of the contractions, yet the happiness at the successful birth, which comes quickly to blot out the memory of pain, as the mother holds the living child in her arms. The focus of the parable is thus on the *movement* from one to the other, from the suffering to the joy, a transition that is far more significant than the mere cessation of pain: "Then He shews that sorrow brings forth joy, short sorrow infinite joy" (John Chrysostom, *Homily on John* 79).

The "tenor" of the metaphor is made explicit by the Johannine Jesus, but it is a curious one: just as mothers move from sorrow to joy in giving birth, so too the disciples will move from sorrow to joy at Jesus' departure and return. His death will be for them like the pain of childbirth, whereas his return, through the Spirit, will be like the birth of a child after pain and struggle. What makes the metaphor curious is that the disciples, unlike the laboring mother, are passive in this enterprise. John is speaking not of their mission to the world but rather of their immediate response to his death, a response that will be short-lived. The "little while" that seems to puzzle the disciples refers to the period of labor (16:18)—that is, the period between Good Friday and Easter Sunday.[64] The disciples' distress would seem closer, in some respects, to the experience of a child that loses its mother than of a mother who gives birth to a child. Nevertheless, John is drawing on Old Testament images of Zion in labor, a labor that turns from anguish to hope and joy:

> Writhe and groan, O daughter Zion,
> like a woman in labor;
> for now you shall go forth from the city
> and camp in the open country;
> you shall go to Babylon.

There you shall be rescued,
there the Lord will redeem you
from the hands of your enemies. (Mic. 4:10; cf. Isa. 66:7–9)

In a similar way, John uses childbirth as a powerful image of suffering and hope within the believing community—in this context, in its struggle to come to terms with the death and resurrection of Jesus.

There are other curious features to this small parable. The laboring mother is not referred to as "mother" but as "the woman" (*hē gynē*, 16:21), the period of labor is called "her hour" and the infant is not called "child" but "human being" (*anthrōpos*). Similarly, the phrase "into the world" echoes one of the most significant epithets for Jesus in the Fourth Gospel.[65] There are, in other words, deliberate echoes of other Johannine passages associated with the "hour" of Jesus' own glorification. Hoskyns sees the Old Testament background of sorrow and joy in childbirth as pointing to the messianic age and the promise of the resurrection from the dead, which he relates to the resurrection of Jesus himself.[66] Similarly, Massyngbaerde Ford argues that, although it refers primarily to the experience of the disciples, the symbolism can also be accommodated to Jesus' own sufferings, because of the resonance with the "hour" of Jesus' death and resurrection.[67] There is an interesting parallel in the *Thanksgiving Hymns* from Qumran, which depict the suffering of the Messiah in terms of labor pains (1QH 3:7–11).[68] Thus, although the reference to the suffering of "the woman" in her "hour" is metaphorical of the community of believers, there are overtones that are suggestive of Jesus' own suffering, death, and resurrection: his own transition from pain to joy.[69] This helps to prepare the reader for what is to come in the narrative of the passion.

As we have come to expect of motherhood symbolism in the Fourth Gospel, its usage in the passion narrative is ambiguous and diverse, spanning the divine and human realms. There are two further maternal allusions in this part of the Gospel, both in relation to the crucifixion. Clearly the "hour" has arrived, the hour of both suffering and exaltation, in which the divine glory will be manifested fully in the flesh of Jesus on the cross. Here we encounter the mother of Jesus for the second and last time in the Gospel. She is present "near the cross" in company with three (two?) other women—her sister, Mary of Clopas, and Mary Magdalene[70]—and also the beloved disciple.[71] This small group of disciples witnesses the events of Jesus' crucifixion and testifies to their significance (19:35). The scene has a number of echoes with the wedding at Cana. Once more, we are dealing with a text that has provoked debate and disagreement—not all of it on predictable denominational lines. Once more, the center of debate concerns the symbolic significance, if any, to be accorded the mother of Jesus.

We begin with the literal meaning to discover whether something "more" is required of our interpretation. Jesus, observing his mother and beloved disciple declares to the one, "Woman, behold your son," and to the other, "Behold your mother"—at which point the beloved disciple takes the mother of Jesus "into his own" (*eis ta idia*, 19:26–27). The mother of Jesus is no longer needed at this point to ensure the humanity of Jesus; in the context of his death, that is hardly in dispute.[72] A more common view that restricts itself to the "literal" level is the preferred Protestant interpretation that regards Jesus' words as indicative of his filial piety, an interpretation that goes back to Augustine. But this view—termed by Gaventa the "emotional interpretation"[73]—makes little sense at the level of Johannine theology. If Jesus' words at Cana are, at least in part, a testing of her faith, then her significance goes beyond (though without contradicting) her human motherhood. In neither scene is John concerned to present Jesus as a model of filial devotion, carrying out his obligations to his mother, regardless of what we may want to claim of the historical Jesus. A more attractive form of the "literal" view is Gaventa's suggestion that what Jesus does on the cross is to divest himself of all that is associated with his earthly life: "Just as he is stripped of his clothing, he divests himself of his mother and his beloved disciple. The human family that is ascribed to him early in the Gospel, and especially at Cana, here is removed at the 'hour' of his return to the Father."[74] This is an imaginative attempt to dispense with the need for further symbolic interpretations, but in the end it is not convincing. The stress on Jesus' humiliation and *kenosis* (self-emptying) does not resonate with John's understanding of Jesus' death as an experience of glorification and exaltation. Moreover, given that Jesus promises all through the Farewell Discourse to continue his presence with the disciples beyond his departure, why would he now "abandon" the beloved disciple and hand him over to someone else? Is that not, in effect, leaving him "orphaned"?

At the literal level, the scene is difficult to understand. The question is why Jesus would instigate a kind of adoption ceremony to provide his mother with a son when the Johannine text has made it perfectly plain that Jesus already has *adelphoi* capable of taking responsibility for their mother.[75] If the giving of Jesus' mother and beloved disciple to one another as mother and son does not make sense at a literal level, then a second-level metaphorical and symbolic meaning can and must be sought. The symbolic level is hard to avoid, even if it means stepping into a whirlpool of conflicting interpretations. The minimal symbolic view is that the scene represents Jesus' love for his disciples. That Jesus cares for "his own" and loves them "to the end" is certainly a Johannine theme, evidenced at the arrest where Jesus asks for the release of the disciples (18:8–9; cf. 6:39; 13:1; 17:12); indeed, his death is itself the supreme symbol of the radical love he has for his "friends" (15:13). Yet is this interpretation enough to make sense of the solemn conferral of mother to son and son to mother? Presumably something simpler would be adequate to indicate Jesus' love for the disciples, if anything explicit is needed at this point.

A more developed version of the love interpretation is that Jesus' words are performative, bringing into being the community of faith. Part of the symbolic meaning of the crucifixion is that life issues from the death of Jesus. The mother of Jesus and the beloved disciple, in this view, form the nucleus of the new community. This community is visualized in terms of a family, as the mother-son language shows. As Culpepper observes, the numinous moment is ecclesiological, signifying the birth of the Christian community:

> Now, at the cross, when Jesus' hour has come, Jesus employs a revelatory formula ("Behold") and performative language. Like a marriage declaration, his pronouncement actually accomplishes or effects the new relationship that it declares. By his declaration, Jesus constitutes a new family, mother and son.... The formation of this new family at the cross provides a nucleus for the community of believers.... More than a theory of atonement, John has an underlying ecclesiology of the cross.[76]

The clue to the symbolism of family comes after the resurrection, when the *adelphoi* of Jesus refer no longer to the members of Jesus' physical family, as they have in the first half of the Gospel, but rather to his disciples (20:17; cf. 21:23). In other words, already at the foot of the cross the literal language of family begins to give way before the metaphorical: kinship imagery is now used of the community of faith. It is not that Jesus divests himself of kith and kin, but rather that the kinship bonds are transformed to become symbolic of a whole new understanding of "family." Just as those who believe are born "from above" in a symbolic way and become, metaphorically speaking, "children of God," so the "brothers and sisters" of Jesus are no longer those who belong to his human family—unless they are themselves believers—but rather those who have entered the celestial family through birth in the Spirit, passing into the filial relationship of the Son to the Father. Jesus' care for "his own" extends to the new family in which the love command, and thus his own presence through the Spirit-Paraclete, can flourish. The mother of Jesus exemplifies the transformation: her motherhood shifts from Jesus to the beloved disciple, who now becomes symbolically her "son" and thus part of the new "family." In this respect, the scene is not dissimilar to the Markan episode in which Jesus declares his disciples, sitting around him, to be his true "family," sharing the same passion for the will of God (Mark 3:31–35 pars.). However, unlike Mark, for John (as for Luke), the mother of Jesus belongs within both families: the earthly and the heavenly. Indeed, in this scene she functions in some sense as the bridge between the old and the new, taking the reader symbolically from one to the other, just as Jesus' patent humanity on the cross reveals his true, divine origins.[77]

Nevertheless, it is surprising, in the light of the birth of the community, that the mother and beloved disciple are *not* given to one another as brother and sister and that the other women present at the cross are not directly incorporated into this event. The language of *adelphoi*, in the context of the Easter proclamation (20:17), as we have seen, is now the appropriate language in which to describe the Christian community. The mother of Jesus' own relationship to Jesus undergoes a significant transformation; she is given to the beloved disciple, not as his sister in faith but as his mother, and he is given to her not as a brother but as a son. There is another element at play, therefore, in the symbolic language. The ecclesiology presupposes a distinctly christological shape to the community, based on the theological significance of Jesus' departure. The mother of Jesus is to *replace the absent Jesus* in the heart of the beloved disciple, to be the "mother" he is about to lose, just as she will regain, in the beloved disciple, the son she is about to lose. But why does the beloved disciple need a maternal replacement? If the mother of Jesus is about to lose and find a son, who is the mother the beloved disciple is about to lose? The only conclusion is that Jesus' solemn words imply that *Jesus himself in his earthly ministry has been the "mother" of the beloved disciple.* The symbolism becomes more forceful if the beloved disciple is seen as a representative figure, here and elsewhere in the Gospel. The one who reclines on the breast of Jesus at the Last Supper (just as the Son reclines on the breast of the Father, 1:18; 13:23, 25), and stands in the place of honor with the holy women at the foot of the cross, is emblematic of the stance of the community of faith. Jesus' words imply that the new family, with God as its Father (20:17), requires concrete symbols of motherhood, already supplied in the earthly presence of Jesus. If the beloved disciple's "sonship" symbolizes the filiation of the new family of God, then motherhood also shifts: not just from the literal to the symbolic but from the period of Jesus' earthly sojourn to the period of his glorified and risen presence. Whatever else we may want to say, the maternity needed in the new family has its origins in Jesus himself. It is Jesus who is the "mother" the beloved disciple is to lose and yet also, in a symbolic sense, regain.

If motherhood has its location within Jesus himself, what does that mean for the mother of Jesus and the role she plays within the new family? Is there more to be said about her significance in this scene? At this point, above all others, "it is very difficult to be certain of the limits of Johannine symbolism."[78] There are at least four possible ways of understanding her symbolic significance, which can only be entertained while acknowledging the difficulties of determining the scope of John's meaning. The least compelling is the view that the mother of Jesus represents Jewish Christianity, while the beloved disciple represents Gentile Christianity.[79] The problem with this reading is that, while it makes sense of the mother of Jesus, nowhere in the Fourth Gospel is the beloved disciple identified as a Gentile Christian or associated with Gentile Christianity. Yet, as we will see, the association of the mother of Jesus with Israel is not as problematic, particularly given the symbolism arising from Judaism in the wedding at Cana.

The second view is that the mother of Jesus becomes the mother of the Christian, with the beloved disciple representing the new community of faith. It seems odd, however, that of the two unnamed figures one is a representative character while the other is not. This view may be adjusted to recognize *both* figures as representative and yields a third possible interpretation: that the mother of Jesus points symbolically to Zion-Jerusalem, the mother-city who consoles her children/inhabitants with her maternal care.[80] The symbolism works in tandem with the beloved disciple, who represents the community of believers, reclining on the breast of Jesus, gazing upon his crucified flesh and witnessing to his true identity. Both figures, in this interpretation, symbolize different dimensions of the believing community, the mother of Jesus signifying its motherly capacity, inherited from Jesus himself, and the beloved disciple epitomizing its filiation, likewise having its origins in Jesus. This view need not deny the individual status of each figure, however: the mother of Jesus is also "a mother in Israel" for the beloved disciple, and the beloved disciple—the source of the Johannine tradition—is given the singular honor of standing with the holy women at the cross and receiving the mother of Jesus. Indeed, both individual and communal elements come into play, shifting between one and the other. In the iconography of the scene, the mother of Jesus functions both as a maternal figure within the new family and as representative of the community's motherhood, bequeathed by the dying Jesus, pointing the reader to Old Testament imagery of Jerusalem as mother. In this view, the two representative figures become the founding figures of the community, in association with the other women at the cross, but their mother–son relationship—rather than brother–sister—symbolizes the maternal and filial nature of the community itself. In one sense this is not so far from the interpretation that sees the mother of Jesus representing Jewish Christianity.

There is one problem with this reading that might otherwise make sense of the Johannine symbolism in relation to earlier maternal imagery. The question is why the beloved disciple, by taking the mother of Jesus into his own home, seems to be caring for her, rather than the other way around. (Note that this objection also applies to the second explanation). This implies a literal reading of the narrative, however, that ignores the fact that each is the recipient in this transaction. The imagery of "home" is evocative and symbolic in the Fourth Gospel, reflecting a number of themes in Johannine Christology, symbolized in the two representative figures:

> Where she is the one who literally embodied the divine word, he is the one who embodies the love commandment that Jesus has given so emphatically to his disciples. . . . The mother will now dwell with her new son, just as Jesus dwelt among humankind, just as the Paraclete will dwell among the disciples.[81]

The language is symbolic of embodiment, relationship, and abiding—symbolism that is christological before it is extended to the community of faith. That the beloved disciple receives the mother of Jesus into the domain of "his own" (cf. 1:11) reveals the founding of the new family, based not on kinship ties, but rather on relationship to the Father through Jesus, grounded in the identity of Jesus as both Son and Word-made-flesh.

A fourth explanation takes further the same symbolism, arguing that the mother of Jesus represents the new Eve, undoing the effects of the Fall in Genesis 2–3.[82] This view can be read as an extension of the second interpretation, which sees Mary as the mother of the Christian: just as Eve is "the mother of all living," so the mother of Jesus becomes the mother of all believers, all who have gained eternal life.[83] More generally, the Eve typology could relate to the birth of the church. It is perhaps significant that the word for "rib" in the Greek Old Testament is *pleura* (Gen. 2:21–22 LXX), which is the same word used for "side" in 19:34. The imagery is not identical: although in the case of Adam a *pleura* is removed and Eve created from it, in the second, the *pleura* of Jesus is pierced. This possible parallel, however, is more relevant to the piercing of the side than the words of Jesus to his mother and beloved disciple. Although the link with Eve is an ancient interpretation (Ephrem, Ambrose), and attractive for its emphasis on the parallelism between creation and redemption, it is hard to be certain of its presence in the Johannine text at this point.[84] Moreover, it seems to go against the Christology of the Fourth Gospel, which presents Jesus not as a new Adam but as the Savior of the world (4:42), as relevant in his flesh for women as well as for men.

There is no interpretation entirely free of problems. The primary focus of the passage is on the new community, formed by the dying Christ, shaped in the pattern of his life and death. That community is the new family, containing within itself both filiation and maternity, in relationship to God as Father. The focus of this scene is not primarily mariological but christological and, in a secondary sense, ecclesiological. It advances our understanding of motherhood in the Fourth Gospel by symbolically portraying the motherhood of Jesus as it is passed on to the community at the foot of the cross, through the giving of the Spirit-Paraclete (as his death reveals). In this context, we can see that the motherhood of the community has symbolic connections with Israel-Jerusalem and its maternal role.[85] This is a view that accords with the Heavenly Woman of the Apocalypse (Apoc. 12) who gives birth to the messianic community, symbolized by the child who is snatched up into heaven. While this passage cannot be used to support any interpretation of the mother of Jesus in John's Gospel, it does suggest the prevalence of the symbolism of Israel-Zion as mother. The Johannine transposition of the mother-son relation implies that, with Jesus' departure, the "motherhood" of Jesus is now located *within the community of faith itself*. This resonates with the Zion imagery, where Jerusalem is the mother consoling her inhabitants, as infants at the breast (Isa. 66:7–14). The motherhood of the community is disclosed at the moment of glorification, when Jesus "gives birth" to the community.[86] As in Isaiah 66, "Mother Zion" is a symbol of *God's* maternal consolation: behind the mother of Jesus is the divine motherhood evinced in Jesus himself and the role of the Spirit, released from Jesus' crucified flesh.[87]

There is a further dimension to the symbolism at the foot of the cross. The revelation of the glory has transformed the relationships around the cross. This transformation, however, embraces also the other women at the foot of the cross, Jesus' mother's sister, Mary of Clopas, and especially Mary Magdalene. As Lieu points out, it is not the mother of Jesus who meets the risen Christ in the garden, as we might expect, but Mary Magdalene (20:1–18).[88] Just as Jesus' mother becomes mother to the beloved disciple, and thus the community of faith at the moment of "birth," so in the following chapter, Mary Magdalene will witness the empty tomb and the reborn presence of the Risen One, a presence that will lead to the giving of the Spirit and the sending forth of the faith community.[89] The story of the woman at the cross is not complete without the woman at the tomb. The role of the mother of Jesus as "woman" is complemented by the role of Mary Magdalene as "woman," and cannot be isolated from it. The experience of the disciples at the absence yet presence of Jesus is symbolized in the experience of the two women at the cross and the empty tomb, the mother of Jesus and Mary Magdalene. The painful yet joyful experience of birth becomes a paradigm of salvation, grounded in John's christological understanding and extended to the life of the community. Suffering takes on a new guise with this symbolism: no longer meaningless and destructive, it is the divine means by which the world is made new, reborn in the image of the maternal Christ through the work of God the Father. In this symbolism, both the mother of Jesus and Mary Magdalene play a vital role: together they signify the birth of the community through the three-day journey of Easter from death to life.

One further maternal image is to be found in the Fourth Gospel. After his death, Jesus' side is pierced with a sword and blood and water pour forth; this replaces the breaking of his legs by the soldiers, normally performed to hasten death. The scene is followed by reference to the witness of the one who sees these things, whose testimony is declared to be "true," in part because it is grounded in Scripture (19:31–37). This is the climax of the passion narrative. We have already examined the flow of blood and water and have seen that it confirms the humanity of Jesus: part of the *sarx* which Jesus embraces.[90] Yet the question, for our purpose, is how we are to understand the glory that exudes from this scene. The Gospel has already presented both water and blood as symbols of life, with secondary sacramental meaning. Yet, as we argued in the discussion of water and its symbolic significance throughout the Gospel, birth is one aspect of its complex symbolism, as seen particularly in the dialogue with Nicodemus (3:5). The mingling of water and blood is particularly evocative of childbirth, in which both elements flow: the amniotic fluid, the breaking of which signals the onset of labor, the blood in which the newborn child is covered, and the continual flow from the mother after labor is complete.[91]

At a literal level, however, the birth allusion in the blood and the water makes no sense: Jesus is not literally a mother giving birth. The reader is compelled to seek a symbolic meaning to make sense of the imagery.[92] The maternal overtones in previous scenes open the possibility of a feminine, metaphorical reading of the scene. As with the image of feeding, the meaning that makes most sense, particularly in the light of 7:38–39, is that it expresses a maternal dimension to the flesh of Jesus.[93] In accord with the imagery of the Farewell Discourse and earlier suggestions in the Johannine text, Jesus' death is presented as the sorrowful labor that brings forth the joy of life (16:21); his wounded side is also the *koilia*, womb, that produces life.[94] The symbolic overtones of this event are suggested also by what follows. Just as the "we" of 1:14 refers to the reborn "children of God" who gaze upon the glory in the flesh, so here at the cross, the one who testifies to this event—presumably the beloved disciple[95]—gazes upon "the one whom they pierced" (19:37),[96] revealing himself to be a child of God, born of divine love, and the labor of Jesus and the Spirit. Moreover, it is consonant with the symbolism that, in the ensuing narrative, Nicodemus, who cannot comprehend the symbol of birth in John 3, moves now into the light of day in his final appearance in the Gospel (cf. 7:45–52). In the burial scene (19:38–42), he comes into the open about his faith and risks participating in the embalming and burying of Jesus, along with Joseph of Arimathæa (cf. Mark 15:42–47 pars.). His conversion occurs immediately following the flow of blood and water: he is born "from above" out of the death of Jesus.[97] This symbolic "birth" occurs in the immediate context of the giving of the Spirit (19:30).

MOTHERHOOD AS A TRAJECTORY IN THE TRADITION

Motherhood is a somewhat limited symbol—or series of symbols—in the Fourth Gospel. Unlike fatherhood, it rarely becomes explicit, particularly in relation to God. Maternal imagery is present, however, in a number of different ways, intrinsic to the familial symbolism of the Gospel in its diversity. When taken as a whole, the symbolism of motherhood establishes a recognizable overlap between the maleness of Jesus and the femaleness of the one who gives birth, not only to his physical life but also to his ministry, and whose role is to mother the community that he has formed. In the latter sense, motherhood arises from the maternal role played by Jesus in the Gospel narrative and by the Spirit who succeeds him. The role of the mother of Jesus is itself symbolic of the Paraclete, who, paralleling Jesus, comes to the disciples to comfort, guide, and defend them (14:16–18, 26; 15:26; 16:7, 13).

There is a further dimension to the expansion of this symbol in the presentation of the Johannine Jesus. This aspect has to do with symbols of motherhood and their implicit christological meaning. In the Gospel's iconography, Jesus' flesh, though unquestionably male, bears something of the characteristics of the female body. We have already noted the closeness between the Johannine Jesus and the women of the Fourth Gospel, creating a bridge between the maleness of Jesus and the experience of women in the Johannine text. That bridge is widened as aspects of Jesus' bodily life reflect distinctively feminine qualities: in particular, giving birth and lactating. Historically this may seem awkward or absurd, but in the stylized iconography of the Fourth Gospel, it is no more inconsistent than other forms of biblical imagery that may seem, to modern eyes, grotesque or illog-ical.[98] Such symbols possess an inner "logic" that defies conformity to external standards of consistency or the imitation of nature. The portrayal of Jesus' flesh with female characteristics—breasts, womb, vagina—has a similar quality. The christological symbolism is part of the transposition of Jesus' flesh throughout the Fourth Gospel. It is effective theologically in drawing women as well as men into the divine glory manifest in the incarnation.

Previous generations, beginning with the early fathers, had no problem inter-preting this kind of symbolism in maternal terms. Clement of Alexandria, for example, in discussing what it means to be children of God, speaks of being fed by the milk of Christ, which, for him, is directly related to the blood of Christ. Clement shares the widespread view that breast milk is processed menstrual blood which feeds the infant *in utero* and then, at its birth, is cut off and moves upwards in the mother's body, filling the hollows of her breasts with milk (*Paedagogus* 1.6.39). Thus the blood of Christ, poured out on the cross, is linked to the nour-ishment with which he feeds his people—the milk of the Word—through a bio-logical analogy in which blood has primacy, in the human body and the processes of birth, and also in the spiritual realm: in the faith and sacramental life of the church. The imagery is used primarily of Christ feeding his people with his own flesh, particularly in relation to John 6, and it relates also to the Father and Holy Spirit:

> The flesh represents [*allēgorei*] to us the Holy Spirit; for the flesh was created by him. The blood points out to us the Word, for as rich blood the Word has been infused into life; and the mingling of both is the Lord, the food of the infants, the Lord who is Spirit and Word. The food—that is, the Lord Jesus—that is, the Word of God, Spirit made flesh, the sanctified heavenly flesh. The food is the milk of the Father, by which alone we infants are nourished. The Word himself, then, the "beloved One," and our nourisher, has shed His own blood for us, saving humanity; and through him, we, believing in God, flee to the "care-soothing breast" of the Father, the Word. And he alone, as is befitting, provides us infants with the milk of love, and these alone are truly blessed who suck this breast. (*Paedagogus* 1.6.34)

At different points, Clement quotes from John 6 to substantiate his argument, linking blood and milk particularly in relation to the Eucharist, and showing that breast milk serves "both for drink and food [*poton . . . kai trophēn*]" (*Paedagogus* 1.6.45). Jesus not only feeds his people but has also given birth to them. Quoting John 6:53–54 in the context of regeneration, Clement speaks of

> the body of Christ, which nourishes the young brood with the Word, which the Lord himself brought forth in fleshly birth-pangs [*ōdini sarkikē*], which the Lord himself swathed in his precious blood. O holy child-birth! O holy swaddling clothes! The Word is all things to the infant, both father and mother, and instructor [*paidagōgos*] and nurse. (*Paedagogus* 1.6.42)

Similar imagery is used also of Mary, who, representing the church, feeds her "children" by nursing them with the "holy milk" of the Word (cf. 2:5) (*Paedagogus* 1.6.42). As in John's Gospel, motherhood symbolism spans the divine and human: the Father, Christ, and the Spirit; the church and the mother of Jesus.

The same symbolism is found in the poems and other writings of Ephrem the Syrian. Feminine imagery for God is not uncommon in the Syriac fathers. For example, Aphrahat speaks of the one who "loves and reveres God his Father and the Holy Spirit his Mother" (*Demonstration* 18.10).[99] Sebastian Brock shows how important feminine imagery is in Ephrem's writings also.[100] Strikingly, Ephrem interprets John 1:18 to refer to the "womb" of the Father which "gives birth" to the Son:

> The Word of the Father came from His womb,
> and put on a body in another womb:
> the Word proceeded from one womb to another. (*Resurrection Hymns* 1.7)[101]

There is a sense here that Christ, the "Firstborn," experiences two births, the one eternal and divine, and the other human and temporal. This parallels the need for human beings also to experience two births:

> The Firstborn, who was begotten according to His nature, underwent yet another birth outside His nature, so that we too would understand that after our natural birth, we must undergo another (birth) outside our nature. As a spiritual being, He was unable to become physical until the time of physical birth. And so too physical beings, unless they undergo another birth, cannot become spiritual. The Son, whose birth is beyond investigation, underwent another birth which can be investigated. (*Homily on Our Lord* 4)[102]

God is compared to a wet-nurse, knowing how and when to nourish the infant in order that it may grow and flourish. There is also maternal imagery used of Christ: Ephrem perceives the paradox in Jesus, who suckles at his mother's breast to find nourishment and life, yet is himself the source of the world's sustenance:

> Though Most High, yet He sucked the milk of Mary,
> and of His goodness all creatures suck!
> He is the Breast of Life and the Breath of Life;
> the dead suck from His life and revive.
> ....
> When He sucked the milk of Mary,
> He was suckling all with life.
> While He was lying on His Mother's bosom,
> in His bosom were all men lying. (*Hymns on the Nativity* 3)

The birth of Christ, for Ephrem, implies also the giving birth by Christ to all humanity:

> Yes, O Lord, Thy Birth has become mother of all creatures;
> for it travailed anew and gave birth to mankind which gave birth to Thee.

Thou wast born of it bodily; it was born of thee spiritually.—
All that Thou camest for to birth, was that man might be born in Thy Likeness.—
Thy Birth became the author of birth to all. (*Hymns on the Nativity* 3)

Similarly, baptism in Ephrem's theology is seen primarily in terms of birth, drawing on Johannine symbolism for its understanding of the new life that is given in baptism.[103] The wounded side is seen in later Syriac writing as a symbol of birth. Jacob of Serugh, for example, compares Adam's side with that of Christ, the creation of Eve being a type of the birth of the church from the wounded side:

He slept on the cross as Adam had slept his deep sleep,
his side was pierced and from it there came forth the Daughter of Light,
water and blood as an image of divine children
to be heirs to the Father who loves his Only-begotten.[104]

Maternal imagery, and feminine imagery in general, seem prominent in the Syriac tradition—more so than in the West. The Syriac tradition, with its sensitivity to typology and symbolism, draws from symbols within the biblical text in its inter-textuality, detecting fields of reference and symbolic patterns across the biblical books. The Gospel of John is particularly important within a maternal field of reference, from which later tradition draws images for Christ, the Spirit, and the church.

This tradition of feminine imagery is revived in the Middle Ages, where it develops in the twelfth century, particularly among Cistercian monks, in relation to Christology and also to male leadership in the church.[105] According to Caroline Walker Bynum, the symbolism of Christ as mother arises both from a spirituality that stresses the affective and also from the feminizing of religious language in this period, among men as well as women. Christ is seen as an approachable figure, to be understood in terms of human relationships and homely images. The imagery is based on an admittedly stereotyped picture of women, in which mothers are portrayed as generative, sacrificial, loving, gentle, and nurturing. As in the ancient world, breast milk is viewed as processed blood—like the symbol of the pelican, sometimes used of Christ, who tears open her own side in order to feed her offspring with her blood. Thus blood and milk are interchangeable, and the mother, like the pelican, feeds her infants with her own blood, in self-giving tenderness and love—imagery that links the fleshly nature of Christ and the nursing mother.[106] Blood is linked also to purging and cleansing, which are associated with "female bleeding and the motherhood of Christ."[107] Thus maternal language is seen as "appropriate to a theological emphasis on an accessible and tender God, a God who bleeds and suffers less as a sacrifice or restoration of cosmic order than as a stimulus to human love."[108]

In the *Shewings* of the fourteenth-century anchorite Julian of Norwich, this symbolism becomes a rich theological mine for Christology. Indeed, for Julian, motherhood is so much a part of Christ's nature that it is women who are like

Christ in this respect, not the other way around: maternity is a divine attribute in which women are privileged to share.[109] Julian herself derives this imagery from that of Wisdom: "and our essence is in our Mother, God all Wisdom."[110] Christ is mother in both nature and grace, creating and redeeming God's children. As a mother, Christ labors to give birth to the church:

> Thus He carries us within Himself in love, and labours until full term
> so that He could suffer the sharpest throes
> and the hardest pains that ever were
> or ever shall be,
> and die at the last.
> And when He had finished, and so given us birth to bliss, not even all
> this could satisfy His wondrous love.

As mother, Christ feeds believers with milk from the breast in the Eucharist:

> The mother can give her child suck from her milk,
> but our precious Mother Jesus can feed us with Himself;
> and He does it most graciously and most tenderly
> with the Blessed Sacrament which is the Precious Food of true life . . .
> The mother can lay the child tenderly on her breast,
> but our tender Mother Jesus can more intimately lead us *into* His
> blessed Breast by His sweet open Side,
> and show therein part of the Godhead
> and part of the joys of heaven
> with spiritual certainty of eternal bliss.[111]

The mother in Julian's writings protects, loves, disciplines, understands, and encourages the child to grow to maturity. It is a picture consonant with Anselm of Canterbury's earlier *Prayer to St. Paul,* where Christ again is mother, this time in the image of the protective mother bird:

> And you, Jesus, are you not also a mother?
> Are you not the mother who, like a hen,
> gathers her chickens under her wings?
> Truly, Lord, you are a mother
> for both they who are in labour
> and they who are brought forth
> are accepted by you.
> You have died more than they, that they may labour to bear.[112]

Anselm sees Jesus as the heroic mother who dies giving life to her infant—a common enough phenomenon in the medieval (and ancient) world. Medieval religious art could also treat Jesus' body, especially in relation to the church, as female and thus equally important in that guise for men and women; his "humanation," body and soul, is often personified in images of motherhood.[113] Even in the Protestant Reformation the same metaphorical conception of Jesus is found in the writings of the Strasbourg Reformer Katharina Schütz Zell: "he has given birth to us in such cruel pain, has nourished us and given us life, breast-fed us with water and blood from his side, like a mother stilling her child."[114] Although the imagery is influenced by other passages in Scripture, such as Jesus' lament over Jerusalem (Matt. 23:37–39 par.), its primary source would appear to be the Fourth Gospel and the symbolism of birth and lactation.

Clearly the force of maternal symbolism in the Johannine text seemed more patent and less troublesome to earlier generations than to the modern world. (One twentieth-century commentator described the spirituality of the mother-hood of Christ in the Middle Ages as "a devotion that makes theologians wince."[115]) The fact that feminine symbolism was used of the male Christ was not problematic for generations who had a greater awareness of how symbols operate, both their iconic power and also their limitability. The knowledge that God exists beyond language and symbol also gives an imaginative freedom to the text in its composition and interpretation; there is a limit to what is being claimed and thus a license not to be confined by the limits of linear logic. This intertextual connec-tion certainly cannot be used as an argument to prove maternal imagery for Jesus in the Fourth Gospel, but it can raise the question of whether we more squeamish moderns have neglected symbols that to earlier generations seemed obvious and untroubling. If so, we have lost sight of a vital dimension of Johannine Christol-ogy and a feminine iconography that is needed to restore a full, theological vision to our understanding of God's love and presence.

CONCLUSION

The symbol of motherhood is a complex one in the narrative of the Fourth Gospel, articulating the birthing and nourishing of believers as children of God. On the one hand, it can be seen as complementing the more dominant father imagery, which is used primarily in relation to God and Jesus. Yet the maternal imagery, though not predominant in this Gospel, is nevertheless palpable and offers a complementary set of images to that of divine fatherhood, images that do not readily fit the paternal role, no matter how radically loving and self-giving in this Gospel. Massyngbaerde Ford expresses the difference well:

> The paternal model evokes the image of one whose semen gushes forth from his body, who projects his empathy outwards, "outside" his body. He must seek beyond himself for resources, nourishment, shelter, protection, and help for the foetus. He does not have the luxury, privilege, the startling intimacy of feeling the created being within him. He is not confronted with death before the imminence of the birth of the child. No suckling nourishment exudes from him, and the child is fully aware of this.[116]

The same intimacy of birth and lactation is present symbolically in the Fourth Gospel's understanding of Jesus and the believing community. Mother symbols in this Gospel cross boundaries, following the imagery of Isaiah 66, drawing together the roles played by Jesus, the Spirit, and the mother of Jesus. This is a symbolic concept that, unlike fatherhood, crosses the divide between divine and human: it is shared by representatives of both realms, whereas fatherhood as a symbol accrues only to God as the fountain-source of life. In this respect, the mother of the community, symbolized in the mother of Jesus, parallels the work of Jesus and the Paraclete by restoring and nurturing the divine image through birth and lactation.[117] It is both transcendent and yet profoundly immanent. A moment's reflection, however, shows that the difference is consistent. Whereas fatherhood belongs to the first person of the Trinity, motherhood is a symbolic characteristic of the divine Son and thus, by extension, of the Spirit. Jesus the Word-made-flesh crosses the divide between divine and human: his nurturing maternal role, while emerging from the divine realm can also be predicated of the human. As the bridge between heaven and earth, Jesus makes possible the crossover so that symbols that belong to God now become part of human reality. There is thus a kind of gradation in the Fourth Gospel's understanding of motherhood. The motherhood of the community is dependent on that of Christ and the Spirit. The mother of Jesus continues, in one sense, the maternal role of Jesus in relation to the beloved disciple and the community as a whole; in another sense, this reflects the presence of the Spirit leading and guiding the church into all truth.

In the end, the three aspects of motherhood, though disparate, flow together into one christological and ecclesial symbol of nourishment and life. In the symbolic framework of the Fourth Gospel, feminine symbols overlap and complement masculine symbols in ways that the tradition can develop in its theology and iconography. Much of that symbolism is implied rather than overtly named. Nevertheless, tradition is a dynamic reality opening itself to new ways of understanding the ancient gospel. This perspective is a particularly Johannine one: the Spirit-Paraclete is the vibrant companion on the church's journey, leading and guiding the community of disciples "into all the truth" (16:13). Maternal symbols are one aspect of this Gospel that need to be discovered afresh. From the shadows of the text, as well as from the illuminated center, we draw forth symbols of new life that promise a transformed community, a new apprehension of the love of God that is both mysteriously holy yet intimately present. We rediscover an ancient theology that embraces men and women alike: the portrait of a deity whose life-giving presence transcends all symbols yet who graciously stoops to be revealed within the contours of our flesh and blood.

CHAPTER 7

Walking in Darkness:
Symbols of Sin and Evil

He watched, and they were drowning in the river;
faces like sodden flowers in the river—
faces of children moving in the river;
and all the while, he knew there was no river.[1]

I T MAY SEEM STRANGE to include the subject of sin and evil in a study of Johannine symbolism. Because the symbols of the Gospel are images of eternal life, it is hard to imagine symbols that articulate the opposite. Yet such images also belong within the rich symbolic framework of the Fourth Gospel: they are part of its literary and rhetorical dualism. Symbols of light and dark, sight and blindness, freedom and slavery, truth and falsehood belong to the Gospel's bipolar vision of reality, which is essentially eschatological. This dualistic perspective is not the only way symbols are presented in the Gospel. Some forms of symbolism have no strictly corresponding opposite—not at least in moral terms—except as expressions of human need (e.g., water and thirst). Other forms of symbol gather one element into another, as with the dynamic between flesh and *doxa*. In regard to sin, which is part of the evangelist's spiritual and moral dualism, there are a number of symbols to depict its power in human life. In this chapter, we explore some of these Johannine symbols, relating them to the characters who appear as "sinners" in the Gospel and setting these symbols within contemporary discussion about sin and gender.[2]

JOHANNINE SYMBOLS OF SIN AND EVIL

For the most part, the Fourth Gospel is more concerned with "sin" in the singular than "sins" in the plural. The evangelist uses the singular some thirteen times (*hamartia*, 1:29; 8:21, 34 [twice], 46; 9:41 [twice]; 15:22 [twice], 24; 16:8, 9; 19:11) and the plural only four times (*hamartiai*, 8:24 [twice]; 9:34; 20:23), as well as the cognates "to sin" (*hamartanein*, 4:14; [8:11]; 9:2, 3) and "sinner" (*hamartōlos*, 9:16, 24, 25, 31). John also uses synonymous terms throughout the Gospel such as "evil" (*ponēros*, 3:19; 7:7; 17:15; *phaulos*, 3:20; 5:29; *kakos*, 18:23, 30), "falsehood" (*pseu-*

dos, 8:44), "liar" (*pseustēs*, 8:44, 55), "slave" and the verb "to enslave" (*doulos* and *douleuein*, 8:33–35). The devil is also referred to (8:44; 13:2) including by different names: "the Satan" (13:27), the "evil one" (or "evil," 17:15), and "the ruler of this world" whom Jesus has overthrown (*ho archōn tou kosmou [toutou]*, 12:31; 14:30; 16:11); Judas Iscariot is described as "a devil" (*diabolos*, 6:70).[3] Jesus himself is accused of sin (5:16; 9:14–16, 24–33; 18:23, 30; 19:7) and of being possessed by a demon (8:48–49, 52).

Perhaps the definitive statement of the Johannine preference for "sin" over "sins" occurs in the witness of John the Baptist, pointing to the ministry and especially the crucifixion of Jesus: "Behold the Lamb of God who takes away the sin of the world" (*tēn hamartian tou kosmou*, 1:29; cf. 1:36). The image of the lamb is difficult to locate, its Old Testament background linked either to the Passover lamb as the symbol of exodus and freedom (Exod. 12; cf. Apoc. 5:6), the Suffering Servant of Second Isaiah (42:1–9; 49:1–6; 50:4–11; 52:13–53:12),[4] or a triumphant, apocalyptic figure associated with final judgment (*Testament of Joseph* 19:8–9; Apoc. 7:17; 17:14).[5] Whatever its precise location, the wording here is particularly Johannine: the symbol of the lamb who takes away the world's sin is not found directly in such a form anywhere in the Old Testament. The closest is the paschal lamb, which, though not linked directly to sin, appears to possess a later association with sacrifice and the temple cult.[6] In the passion narrative, the Passover theme is exploited not at the Last Supper (as in the Synoptics, where it is a Passover meal [Mark 14:12–26 pars.]), but in the crucifixion, where Jesus dies at the time of the slaughter of the paschal lambs.[7] This theme is reflected ironically in the concern of the authorities for ritual cleanliness so as to be able to eat the Passover (18:28; 19:31).[8] Although John nowhere offers an abstract definition of sin, the Baptist's testimony to Jesus' identity as the Lamb of God, a testimony that derives from God (1:32–34), makes clear that the removal of sin is the purpose of Jesus' coming.[9] It also shows that, for the evangelist, sin has a core, or a core set of symbols, and is not simply a list of wrongdoings: it is "a sinful condition" rather than "sinful acts."[10] Thus at 1:29, sin refers to "the whole collective burden of sin which weighs on mankind."[11] There is a singular force in human life that necessitates the incarnation of the divine Word, a force that stands over against the life created by God and which only God, in human form, can resolve.

Sin and evil are depicted through the narrative in a number of contrasting symbols. The most important of these, introduced in the Prologue, is the polarity of darkness/light, which is a manifestation of death/life and is particularly prominent in the first half of the Gospel: "that which came into being in him was life, and the life was the light of human beings" (1:4). In speaking of the Logos as the agent of creation, the evangelist unfolds the key symbols of light and darkness, imagery that is common in the Old Testament and Judaism to refer to sin, evil, death, and separation from God.[12] Like Torah, Sophia also is associated with the light of divinity, which illuminates the darkness of ignorance and folly (Wis.

7:25–26, 29–30; *2 Bar.* 59:2).[13] Craig Koester interprets the symbolism of darkness in a threefold sense in the Fourth Gospel: first, it symbolizes "the powers that oppose God," namely, sin and evil; second, it signifies the "lethal estrangement from God," which results in death, whether literal or moral (or both); third, it points to human "ignorance and unbelief" in the face of the revelation.[14] At its first introduction in the Fourth Gospel, the darkness that stands over against the light is unable to "grasp" it (1:5), the verb (*katelaben*) possessing a double meaning: the darkness (*skotia*) cannot seize or overpower the light (*phōs*) and is unable to comprehend or understand it. At once it is apparent that John is speaking not only of creation but also of subsequent human history.[15] Darkness is personified as an active force attempting to gain power over the light yet perpetually unable to do so, its efforts directed against God as the source of life (*zōē*).

Later in the Prologue, the meaning of darkness is further explicated in relation to the entry of the light, which enters the world in order to illuminate human beings (1:9). In two parallel statements the evangelist describes the domain that belongs to the Logos by right of creation—the Light who created light—as ignorant of the identity of the Logos and thus unable to welcome him: "the world did not know him" (1:10c); "his own [ones] did not accept him" (1:11b). The reference to "his own" could mean either human beings in general or, more specifically, Israel as God's chosen people; indeed, it is likely that both meanings are present, Israel's rejection being a poignant example of a universal human tragedy.[16] This failure of knowledge, full of tragic irony, is the basis on which Jesus himself will be rejected and finally crucified in the Fourth Gospel. Sin and evil are thus bound up with a failure of recognition, an incomprehensible absence of knowledge: "the fundamental sin is the refusal of the divine light of the Logos."[17] Those who do not accept the Logos are those who fail to recognize their own Creator, the source of life and light, and who fail thereby to know their own identity as God's creatures. They dwell in impenetrable darkness that cannot see the light and cannot receive the revelation. Already it is implied that this dwelling in darkness, the failure to discern the light, and fear and hatred of it, are the very opposite of life: those who reject the light choose not only darkness but also death. They are the living dead whose own darkness they do not perceive.

In the dialogue with Nicodemus, darkness symbolizes the realm of moral and spiritual deadness, a rebellion against God and against goodness. The reference to Nicodemus's coming by night has symbolic overtones, confirmed by Nicodemus's approach to Jesus—his desire to move from darkness to light—yet also by his incomprehension of the invitation to new birth (3:4, 9–10).[18] For the evangelist, it is not whether Nicodemus keeps the law but rather how he responds to the Revealer that determines his place of abode: in the light or in the darkness.[19] As becomes plain in the later part of the discourse (3:16–21), the reluctance to come to the light is itself the manifestation of a spiritual malaise: people prefer to cover the evil of their lives in a cloak of darkness. Indeed, what they fear most is the revelation of the light, because it exposes them: "This is the judgment that the light has come into the world and people have loved the darkness [*skotos*] rather than the light; for their deeds were evil" (3:19). Darkness is a cover for those who cannot face the truth about themselves. It is the symbol of sin and also represents its camouflage. Darkness therefore draws to itself the (reluctant) judgment of God, which is paradoxically a form of self-judgment (3:18). Judgment, in this sense, "is only the dark, reverse side of God's eschatological act of love and redemption."[20] Whereas light is connected in this passage with faith and belief in Jesus as the one sent by God, darkness on the contrary is linked to the rejection of Jesus as the source of life and salvation. Those who act out the truth welcome the light; but those who act out evil (*ponēra, phaula*) avoid the light in dread of its exposure (3:19–21). Similarly, Jesus exposes the illusion in which those who reject the revelation live. The whole passage represents a challenge to Nicodemus—and others like him—who hesitate between faith and unbelief, light and darkness, unable to move one way or the other. For John, the choice is a matter of life and death: people are confronted with the darkness of sin or the light of salvation, the former bringing judgment and the latter giving life.

As a major motif of the Fourth Gospel, the symbol of darkness recurs in the context of the Feasts of Judaism (John 5–10), where Jesus reveals himself as the Light of the world illuminating those who follow him. In the Tabernacles Discourse, Jesus reflects the divine reality associated typologically with the temple in the Old Testament and Judaism: "I am the light of the world; the one who follows me will not walk in the darkness, but will have the light of life" (8:12).[21] Just as Torah is the light that guides and illuminates the people of Israel in its life before God, and just as the flooding of the temple with light in the evening rite of Tabernacles symbolizes the eternal day of God's eschatological kingdom,[22] so the Johannine Jesus represents the fulfillment of that which Judaism seeks to portray. He is the light of the world for his followers, the fullness of reality to which both the law and its feasts symbolically point. As Koester observes, "Jesus does not reject the law and even shows that his claims are consistent with the law; but he tacitly displaces it as the central locus of divine revelation."[23] Darkness in this context suggests both ignorance and danger: walking along a path at night without any source of illumination to show the way. The end result of such a journey is death (8:21, 24).

In the same discourse, darkness is also linked to slavery, falsehood, and untruth. Those who claim to know, to possess light and freedom, are in reality enslaved to darkness and self-deceit unless they open themselves to the shining of the light. Otherwise they belong not to God as they suppose, but to their real father, the devil, who is the author of lies. As a result, they too participate in lies: about themselves and about God (8:44). Enslavement in the Johannine worldview is the inability *not* to participate in sin, imprisonment within a way of being that blinds one to the true nature of the revelation and cuts one off from life itself (8:31–38). Those who are enslaved contrast with those who are free. There is all the difference in the world between the free children of the household and the household slaves, the former exemplified in Jesus himself who is the source and giver of freedom by reason of his status as Son: "The slave does not abide in the house forever, the son abides forever" (8:35). As with other Johannine conceptions of a similar kind, the symbolism is used ironically: "the Jews" who have come to faith in Jesus resent the implication that they lack freedom and are enslaved to sin.[24] Their rejection of the revelation and lack of self-knowledge are the signs of their entrapment in sin. Those who dwell in darkness—who live out of untruth and reject the divine knowledge of the Revealer—come to hate the light, experiencing it as searing and painful, and attempt in every possible way to extinguish it: both the source itself and those who walk by its beams (8:37, 40, 44, 59). For those who dwell in darkness, the light is generally not perceived at all—or, if perceived, is not comprehended. There is a lingering in darkness and an inability to walk toward the light, a self-deceit in knowing about the self and the true nature of God, and an active hostility toward the revelation that derives from hatred. Later in the Gospel, this hatred contrasts with the love that exists within God and, by extension, the community of faith. Jesus' death is the direct result of such hatred, as is the persecution experienced by the community (cf. 15:18–16:4a).

In John 9, the imagery of light/darkness folds over into that of sight/blindness through the symbolic experience of the man born blind: the healing of his eyes, both literally and metaphorically. Once more, with the two main symbols of Tabernacles still present (water, light), Jesus reveals his identity as the one sent from God to illumine the darkness: "It is necessary for us [me?] to do the works of the one who sent me while it is day; night comes when no one can work. When I am in the world, I am light for the world" (9:4–5). The darkness here is the "night" of Jesus' absence, now beginning to loom on the horizon. Those who reject Jesus as the light of the world, falsely setting him over against the light of Torah, are living in a freely chosen darkness exacerbated by the delusion of sight (9:40–41). Here the evangelist reveals that it is not just a question of the darkness enveloping people but also the fundamental defect in their "eyes," the very organs of seeing. It does not matter how much light surrounds people if their eyes remain rebelliously closed. Even worse is the case, therefore, of those who fail to perceive their blindness and are under the illusion that they possess sight. The double symbolism for sin—darkness and blindness—which plays across the characters of the man born blind and the Pharisees, vindicating the one and condemning the others, concerns the kind of willful ignorance that refuses the revelation and rebels against its truthfulness. Self-knowledge and the knowledge of God are closed to such people. In rejecting the light, they reject the divine revelation embodied in Jesus; in the process they reject the man himself (9:34).

In the first scene of the raising of Lazarus (11:1–16), Jesus again makes mention of light and darkness, using the symbolism of day and night. Jesus has finally announced his intention of visiting Judea in order to see Lazarus (now dead,

11:11–14), and the disciples have questioned him about the danger from "the Jews" who have so recently tried to stone him (11:7–8; cf. 10:31). Jesus' response is hardly a direct answer to the disciples' anxious questioning: "Are there not twelve hours in the day? If anyone walks in the day, he [or she] does not stumble, because he [she] has the light of this world to see by. But if anyone walks in the night, he [she] stumbles, because the light is not in him [her]" (11:9–10). The relevance of these words is not immediately clear, yet Jesus is speaking primarily of his mission to the world in the context of those who threaten his life. He has a limited time to do the "works" of the Father and is unafraid of those who menace him. Similarly, for disciples, their only confidence lies in knowing that the light of Christ illumines them. They are therefore free not from persecution and hatred but from the forces of darkness, which cannot cause them ultimately to "stumble." As in 8:12, "walking" is an image of discipleship. Jesus speaks of his own destiny and that of his disciples, for whom the darkness—the sin and evil of the world—is but a seeming threat and from which they are, in an eschatological sense, protected (cf. 17:15).[25]

This message is a particularly powerful one in the context of the Lazarus story, in which a beloved friend of Jesus dies.[26] John certainly makes no direct link between sin and death, but there is no question that Lazarus's death is tragic, even if Jesus' delay seems inexplicable (11:5–6). This is confirmed by the grief of the sisters and the (admittedly, ambiguous) signs of Jesus' own grief and anger (11:21, 32–38). Jesus' authoritative presence at the tomb signifies that divine life which is more powerful than death and before which death gives way (11:38–44). Lazarus emerges from the darkness of the tomb, which signifies death, into the light of day, where the Light of the world stands before him, instructing those around to "unbind him and let him go" (11:44). According to Schneiders, John is struggling with the question of how death can be compatible with the life that Jesus brings: "the problem of death in the community of eternal life." The evangelist's answer is that "human death is brutally real,"[27] yet does not have final victory for disciples— either eschatologically or in the present moment where the light and glory of Jesus' resurrection power illumines even that darkness (11:4).

At the end of Jesus' public ministry, in the summation of the first half of the Gospel, the evangelist again uses the symbolism of light and dark to draw together the narrative threads. Once more, the imagery is that of discipleship as walking along a path; once more, the choice is to walk in the darkness without light or to proceed along a road that is illumined by the one who is the "light of the world." The darkness is a threatening power that will finally "overcome" (*katelabē*) the unwary and misguided pedestrian who imagines such a journey possible without trustworthy illumination: "walk while you have the light, lest the darkness overtake you" (12:35). Again the symbolism of light, representing spiritual and moral guidance, is linked directly to faith (12:36). John finds the source for this symbolism in Isaiah 6:10, where darkness is linked to blindness, a blindness that is far from innocent but knowing and freely chosen (12:40; cf. Mark 4:12 pars.; Acts 28:16; Rom. 11:8).[28] The purpose of Jesus' coming is to illuminate the world and overpower the darkness, drawing people into the light of faith and life: "I myself have come as light into the world, in order that everyone who believes in me may not abide in darkness" (12:46). The true abiding, canceling out the false, deathly one, is the abiding in love and friendship which begins in God and extends to the community of faith.[29] Only with such an abiding-in-love can Jesus' followers become true "children of the light" (12:36).

As the passion narrative reveals, the irony is that those who try to quench the light—and, at a human level, succeed—do so from religious motivation. Out of an apparent love for God and the light of truth, they are driven to smother the hateful rays of light, not knowing—not desiring to know—that their salvation depends on the capacity to face the light. What they fear, according to John, is precisely the self-revelation that exposes the evil of their "deeds" (3:19). Just as the "works" (*erga*) of God to be carried out by believers refer to the one "work" of believing (6:28–29), so the evil deeds (*erga ponēra*) are the polar opposite: the refusal to believe, the rejection of the light, the preference to live without true faith. Yet the evangelist makes no attempt to explain or account for the darkness. It is there at the beginning and active in the world, though never on an equal footing with the light. The entire plot of the Gospel is based on the virulent hostility of the darkness toward the light. Indeed in his ministry, Jesus' actions and teaching represent the divine, eschatological assault against the powers of darkness, against evil and falsehood, and this leads in turn to a series of violent counter-attacks, at first spontaneous and later carefully planned, against Jesus and any with whom he is associated. The darkness acts in a hostile way to choke the light. Finally the one who illuminates the darkness and reveals the liberating truth in love—who embodies the divine light and life, truth and freedom, love and joy—himself enters the darkest shadow, the deepest level of hostility and untruth, and defeats it in the light of Easter morning.

There are several other references in the Fourth Gospel that complete the picture of sin. In the Farewell Discourse, speaking of the hatred of the *kosmos* against Jesus and the believing community (as the mirror image of abiding-in-love within the community, 15:1–17), the Johannine Jesus links the manifestation of sin to his own coming:

> If I had not come and spoken to them, they would have no sin; but now they have no excuse for their sin. The one hating me hates also my Father. If I had not done among them the works which no one else did, they would have no sin; *but now they have both seen and hated both me and my Father.* But [this happened] in order that that which is written in their law might be fulfilled: "They hated me without cause." (15:22–25; cf. Pss. 35:19; 69:4)

The evangelist makes several vital points here concerning sin. First, and most importantly, sin is understood in christological and eschatological terms as the rejection of Jesus as the Revealer, since only the full presence of the revelation leaves people without excuse for their choice of darkness over light. Second, no matter how religious the motivation for such hostility and persecution, hatred of Jesus represents the rejection of God, since God is defined in this Gospel as being "my Father." Third, the law itself speaks prophetically of the eschatological rejection of Father and Son, making clear that, in Johannine theology, the law and Jesus are on the same side and are not pitted against each other; rather, the one points symbolically to the other (cf. 1:17).[30] The rejection of the revelation is thus in Johannine eyes irrational and inexplicable.

The last references to sin and evil in the Fourth Gospel—apart from a reference to Judas Iscariot's sin (19:11)—occur in relation to the Holy Spirit. Later in the Farewell Discourse, in the second to last of the Paraclete passages, the Johannine Jesus assures the community of believers that it will be the task of the Spirit-Paraclete to "convict the world concerning sin and concerning righteousness and concerning judgement" (16:8). The explanation that follows for each of these concepts seems to possess its own logic, though in the first case the connection is reasonably clear. The Spirit will convict of sin on the basis of the rejection of Jesus: "concerning sin, because they do not believe in me" (16:9). Sin, in other words, is linked inextricably with rejecting Jesus; such rejection is the sign indicating the presence of sin and evil. In this sense, the role of the Paraclete parallels that of Jesus in uncovering the sin of the *kosmos*.[31] Furthermore, in a passage that is connected by its emphasis on the Holy Spirit, the resurrection narrative depicts the risen Christ granting the apostolic community the authority to forgive sins: "whoever's sins you forgive are forgiven them; whoever's sins you retain are retained" (20:23). This passage is unusual both for its reference to sins in the plural and its explicit use of the language of forgiveness. The terminology is new for John (especially the contrasting verbs *aphieinai*, "to forgive," and *kratein*, "to hold onto" [i.e., not forgive], 20:23[32]), and may seem surprising at the end of the Gospel. In another sense, the concept of forgiveness is implied in earlier Johannine images of washing and cleansing (13:8–10; 15:2–3; cf. 1 John 1:9), where it is probably not just confined to prebaptismal sin.[33] Here we are moving beyond the usual Johannine understanding of sin, therefore, to something that arises from the post-Easter life of the community, where the forgiveness of sins will become a serious issue for the church (cf. 1 John 1:5–2:2; 3:4–17; 4:10; 5:16–18). From the viewpoint of the Fourth Gospel, the main point is that the community which carries on the mission of Christ in love for the world is given power over sin and evil, a power that has its source in the Holy Spirit.

Although the imagery of darkness recedes in later chapters of the Gospel, its power remains symbolically present; the symbolism is well enough established in the first half of the Gospel for it to carry through into the second. The light begins to hide itself by the end of the first half. After Jesus has spoken of the necessity of believing in the light in order to become "children of light," he withdraws (12:36), hiding from the public domain and retreating to the intimacy of his disciples (13:1). The "night" into which Judas Iscariot walks after the Last Supper (13:30) is the darkness of sin and evil to which Jesus himself, at the will of the Father and the behest of the Scriptures, will submit. It is still night when Jesus is arrested and the arresting party carries "lanterns, torches, and weapons" to guide them to the Light of the world (18:3). Although the Fourth Gospel lacks the apocalyptic signs of the Synoptic tradition—particularly the three hours of darkness (Mark 15:33 pars.)—the symbolism of entering the darkness of sin and evil is nevertheless present: the paschal Lamb is about to take away "the sin of the world," heralding the end of darkness and the overthrow of the "ruler of this world." Nicodemus, who first came furtively by night, now comes openly to request the body of Jesus (19:39); Mary Magdalene comes to the tomb on Easter morning "while it is still dark" and sees only darkness and emptiness (20:1), not realizing that the light has dawned and overcome the night of sin and evil. By the end of the Gospel, darkness is established as a major symbol of unbelief, rejection, and death.

SINNERS IN THE FOURTH GOSPEL

In addition to various symbols of sin and evil, the Fourth Gospel uses the characters of the Gospel as representative figures: not only to depict positive values but also to display symbolically the personal dimensions of falsehood and self-deceit. The evangelist is concerned with sin not in the abstract but in its personal manifestation in human life. The issue here is how John characterizes evil in the lives of those who encounter Jesus. Which characters play such a representative role and how does John use them to symbolize the personal nature of sin? To answer these questions, it is necessary to begin with individual characters in the Johannine narrative—both male and female—who are in some sense associated with sin, whether overtly or by implication. Thereafter we turn to the role of Jesus' opponents, since this group symbolically represents sin in its most vivid manifestation in the Fourth Gospel.

There are a small number of Johannine narratives that make reference to sin, either directly or indirectly, in the lives of individual characters. The story of the Samaritan woman's encounter with Jesus at the well is the first such story (4:1–42), even though the word "sin" does not occur throughout the narrative. The woman's situation is an ambiguous one: she is not explicitly designated as sinful, yet there is at least some irregularity in her marital life, unfolded at the beginning of the second scene of the narrative (4:16–30). It is too easy to assume that she is a woman of considerable sexual immorality, leaving marriage after marriage—shunned by the villagers as a whore and an adulteress and compelled to make solitary visits to the well at midday. This reading has been criticized in feminist circles as based on stereotypes of women's sexuality that are exegetically misleading. Gail O'Day, for example, points out that the text does not describe the woman as five-times divorced (as commentators tend to assume), but five-times married, divorce in the Old Testament being initiated not by wives but husbands.[34] O'Day suggests a possible situation of levirate marriage, where the woman has married consecutive brothers-in-law following the decease of her husband (cf. Mark 12:18–27 pars.).

There is another interpretation entirely, however, of the woman's marital life that bypasses the problem of her sexuality. Jesus' dialogue with the woman has been interpreted as allegorical,[35] representing the idolatry of the Samaritan people in the postexilic period: the woman's current relationship points supposedly to the religious syncretism of the Samaritans (2 Kgs. 17:24–41). In this view, Jesus is the bridegroom summoning the Samaritan woman and her people to a true "marriage" with the God of Israel.[36] This particular allegory, however, does not quite fit: the idols of the Samaritans are worshiped simultaneously, not serially, and there are seven deities referred to in 2 Kings, not five. The literal reading of these verses seems preferable to the allegorical, since the latter does not suit the Samaritan woman's context. Bearing in mind O'Day's warning about reading into the text a past history of sexual immorality, we may draw the conclusion that while the woman's past is unusual and unconventional—Jews believed that three marriages were sufficient in one lifetime—it is not itself sinful, and that the woman is more likely to be the victim of tragedy or divorce. Nevertheless, it is hard to avoid the implications of her current situation. The real sexual problem lies not so much in her past as in her current relationship (4:18b). If the emphasis of Jesus' words is, "the one whom you have is not *your* man/husband," then this is an adulterous union, and her lover is married to someone else. The ancient reader—unfamiliar with the modern Western practice of unattached couples living together outside of formal marriage—would assume that the Samaritan woman (probably in secret, cf. 4:17a) is involved in a sexual liaison with a married man.

We have already seen something of how salvation operates in the woman's story, drawing her into awareness of the need for living water and of the presence of Jesus as the divine water-giver.[37] Jesus perceives the woman's longing for "living water" and raises the issue of her husband (4:16) and marital status (4:18) in order to uncover her "thirst" for life. The unsettled and restless nature of the woman's relationships, regardless of whether she is the victim of misfortune or arbitrary dismissal, is the key issue.[38] Surprisingly, Jesus' response to the woman's partial self-disclosure ("I do not have a man/husband," 4:17) is not moralistic or denunciatory but reveals that he possesses divine insight into her life: "You have spoken truly that you do not have a man/husband. For five men/husbands you have had, and now the one whom you have is not your man/husband; this you have said truthfully" (4:17b–18). Significantly, the woman's reaction to the opening up of her life, both here (4:19)—"Sir [*Kyrie*], I see that you are a prophet" (4:19)—and later when she addresses the villagers—"Come, see a man who told me everything which I have done" (4:29a)—suggests not that she feels ashamed, but rather surprised and even delighted that her life has been miraculously uncovered by this stranger whose own identity is beginning to emerge.[39] Through the woman's developing self-knowledge, Jesus reveals himself as the source of life, the giver of living water. Her spirituality moves from the self-knowledge she has gained in dialogue with Jesus to the knowledge and worship of God.[40]

That Jesus' conduct is unusual is made clear by the disciples' patent disapproval upon their return: "they were amazed [imperfect tense] that he was speaking with a woman; no one, however, said, 'What are you seeking or why are you speaking with her?'" (4:27). Two things are clear from the narrator's description: first, that Jesus' conversation with the woman has suggestions at least of unconventionality, if not scandal; and, second, that Jesus himself is impervious to the gender barrier and its implications. An important element in the narrative is the ironic contrast between the woman as "sinner" and those who represent moral uprightness. The story of the Samaritan woman juxtaposes male-authority-insider and female-"sinner"-outsider. Drawing on Old Testament traditions, the evangelist contrasts the Samaritan woman with the imperceptive disciples and with the indecisive and unknowing Nicodemus in the previous narrative (3:9–10). We have already noted the comparison between the woman and Nicodemus (3:1–10), the Pharisee and "leader of the Jews," who comes to Jesus by night and cannot decide for the light or the darkness.[41] The comparison with the disciples who are shocked by Jesus' sexual impropriety coincides with their later misunderstanding of Jesus' talk of food/harvest, which they interpret on a literal rather than metaphorical level (4:31–34). Unlike the Samaritan woman, they have not participated in the sowing (4:38) and thus have no notion of the harvest.[42] The female "sinner" contrasts, in her faith and insight, with those who possess theological knowledge. The contrast exposes the ineptitude of the disciples at this point in the narrative, as against the perceptiveness of the woman's response to Jesus.

In contrast, the story of the disabled man who is healed by Jesus at the Pool of Bethzatha makes explicit reference to the man in connection with sin (5:14). Yet it is a puzzling reference and seems to come from nowhere; the only question of sin in this story is that of breaking the Sabbath.[43] Although Jesus will later explicitly deny any connection between the man born blind's physical disability and sin (either his own *in utero* or that of his parents), the parallel narrative of John 5 seems at first to imply otherwise. Why does Jesus, after the healing, set out to find the man in the temple and warn him, "See, you have become healthy; no longer sin lest something worse befall you" (5:14)? Is he implying that the man's disability is the product of sin—at least in this case? This explanation seems to have no basis within Johannine theology. An alternative approach is to interpret Jesus' utterances within their literary context. In this reading, Jesus' words (however awkward and clumsy) function as a warning against unbelief;[44] they possess a prophetic quality, confirmed in the following verses, where the man goes immediately to the authorities to inform on his healer (5:15). Somehow, the man's failure to move to a deeper level of "healing"—to perceive the healing in symbolic terms—is itself the sin that leads him, in effect, to reject his healer and turn him over to the authorities. This interpretation belongs within the wider context of Jesus' Sabbath work, symbolic of his uniquely divine authority to give life and make judgment, which he inherits as Son of the Father (5:17). Jesus gives the man life, but also offers him saving judgment—a judgment that, by his subsequent actions, the man refuses. The disabled man accepts the healing (at a physical level) but rejects his healer, collaborating instead with the authorities, in vivid contrast to the man born blind in John 9, who finally sides with his healer over against the religious authorities. In this respect, as a representative figure, the healed man of John 5 symbolizes unbelief in his failure to heed the warning and in his identification with "the Jews"; he remains in sin, a state that leads to death and judgment.[45]

The most explicit story in which sin is viewed as an act of moral wrongdoing is that of the woman caught in adultery (7:53–8:11). The narrative is almost certainly not part of the Johannine text but a later addition, included in the Gospel sometime after its circulation.[46] This conclusion is based on the external manuscript evidence,[47] and also the internal evidence of vocabulary and style, which are non-Johannine and seem, if anything, closer to Luke. However, despite stylistic differences, the location of the narrative at the end of John 7 is an apt placement and not insensitive to the Gospel's narrative and theological structure. If it belongs anywhere in the Fourth Gospel, the Tabernacles Discourse seems the right place. In particular, the story coheres with Jesus' declaration to the authorities later in the discourse: "You yourselves judge according to the flesh; I judge no one" (8:15). Brown comments that, even if the story of the woman caught in adultery is later than the original Gospel, it "does not rule out the possibility that we are dealing with a stray narrative composed in Johannine circles."[48] The story may possibly be "Johannine" in a broader sense and thus worth including (although with appropriate reservations) in a discussion of sin in the Fourth Gospel.

The woman's sin is the focal point of the story: she has committed an act of adultery and is dragged before Jesus in the temple by the authorities for his judgment.[49] Even more than the story of the Samaritan woman, the story is as much about the "scribes and Pharisees" as it is about the woman herself:[50] her role is that of victim, bait to entrap Jesus (cf. Mark 12:13–17).[51] The theological counterpoint around which the narrative turns is present in the interplay between legalists and "sinner," judges and judged. The religious authorities refer the problem of the woman's sin to Jesus, not out of love for the law or concern for the woman but in order to discredit him as a teacher of the law (8:2, 4–6a). If he condemns her, he is exposed as lacking in compassion; if he exonerates her, he is undermining the Mosaic law. Ironically, by the end of the story the authorities are silenced and the tables turned. At Jesus' challenge, the real sinners are exposed and depart in shame

(8:9), while the woman is freed from the burden of condemnation (8:10–11). Those who try to "bring a charge against him" (8:6) are themselves convicted (9:9). The presentation of a leadership that misunderstands, whether willfully or not, thus acts as a foil to the "sinner," who is unimpeded in her access to Jesus and open to his redemptive word.

Though defended by him, the woman caught in adultery remains silent and passive throughout her "trial."[52] In the final scene, when her judges have departed, neither Jesus nor the woman chooses to go away. He sides with the one who has lost honor, risking his own in the terms of his world. In the story of the adulterous woman, judgment belongs to Jesus, who reveals a divine truth and gentleness that comprehends and embraces human frailty (so Augustine, *In Joannis Evangelium* 33). The religious leaders are exposed for being at least as sinful—as failing in their responsibility to love—as the woman herself. The gender aspect is highlighted by the absence of the woman's lover, who according to the law shares the same judgment as the woman (Deut. 22:22). In balancing the scales weighted against sexual sin, Jesus in this story balances the scales set against the woman.[53] The movement from "righteous" to "sinner," which deconstructs moral and religious rank, is made by the one who exercises God's judgment in forgiving sin, whose perspective is not human but divine. Jesus is left vulnerable to scandal and misinterpretation, while the woman stands expectant, awaiting his response. No longer condemned by her accusers (8:10–11a), she lingers to hear what Jesus will say. The sense of expectation is reinforced by her use of *Kyrie* (8:11a, probably "Lord"), which "betrays her reverence for Jesus and her realization that he has still to speak the last word."[54] Jesus' final words assume her receptivity to forgiveness and conversion (8:11b). She is treated with compassionate awareness of her moral dignity. Lost honor is restored before God in the refusal to condemn, in the knowledge that the woman's life is open to transfiguration. It is this attitude toward women and sin that may explain in part the placement of the narrative within the Johannine text. Despite the differences—the more passive role played by the woman and the lack of a witness theme—there is a level of congruence between this story and that of other Johannine narratives, particularly the Samaritan woman.

The next story in which sin is mentioned in regard to an individual is the narrative of the man born blind. In the context of light and darkness, blindness and sight, John 9 is concerned with the identity of the real sinners. For the most part, the question revolves around Jesus and the man born blind, both being designated as "sinners" by the religious authorities, who, like the scribes and Pharisees in the story of the adulterous woman, believe themselves to be free from sin and thus able to discern the sinfulness of others. The story is centered on the issue of sin, which the disciples assume to be the cause of the blind man's disability: "Rabbi, who sinned, this man or his parents, that he was born blind?" (9:2).[55] The question of whether the blind man is a sinner is linked to the question of whether Jesus himself is a sinner, since Jesus heals the man on the Sabbath. In the end, the narrative unequivocally clears both Jesus and the man of sin: indeed, the man himself—using reasons that derive, in Johannine terms, from the discourse of John 5—reaches the conclusion that, since Jesus cannot possibly be a sinner on the basis of his "works," he must therefore be "from God" (9:30–33). Once more, Jesus' Sabbath work reveals his true identity as the divine Son. Yet even from the beginning Jesus has made it clear that the man's disability has nothing to do with sin (9:3; cf. 9:34).

Somewhat more ambiguous is the introduction of the man's parents (9:18–23). The issue turns on the question of the man's identity: Is the one who can now see the same as the one who was born blind? The parents are the obvious people to settle the matter definitively. Yet, when approached, they are reserved in their answers and throw the question back on their son. The main point is the terror induced by the authorities' questioning, with the threat of excommunication for those who confess Christ (*aposynagōgos*, 9:22);[56] the narrator is at pains to point to this fear as the main cause of the parents' refusal to speculate on their son's healer. But is the fear for themselves or for their son? Do they desire to protect him from the accusation of "confessing Christ" or to protect themselves? In distancing themselves from the destructive power of the authorities, are they also distancing themselves from their son? And if so, does the narrator then regard them as sinners?

There are two pertinent issues in the parents' response. In the first place, they freely confirm the man's identity as their son: yes, he is our son; yes, he was born blind; yes, he can now see: "we know that this is our son and that he was born blind" (9:20). From a narrative perspective, the man's parents move forward the plot by confirming unconditionally that there is no question of mistaken identity: the transformation of their son's life is indubitable. Second, having acknowledged his identity as one and the same—before and after the miracle of illumination—they refuse to answer the question of *how* such a miracle has taken place: "but how he now sees we do not know, or who opened his eyes we do not know" (9:21a). They want no part in such questioning and place the responsibility for answering the christological question back on their son: "Ask him, he is of age, he himself will speak for himself" (9:21b). It is hard to avoid the conclusion that timidity and fear are dominating their response, and that their moral courage is limited, to say the least. They make no attempt to rescue their son—if such were possible—and show no desire to identify with him in his growing defense of his healer. On the contrary, they are determined to know nothing of such matters. At the same time, it is also equally difficult to avoid the impression that the narrator is sympathetic to their plight—and can clearly account for it. The overwhelming sense for the reader is of the powerlessness of the man's parents before powers that are much larger than themselves. Although their conduct is less than heroic, the real sin is once more attributed to the powers that be and their capacity to terrorize ordinary folk. As with the Samaritan woman, there is no explicit indication of sin and no moral denunciation.

The most poignant and tragic figure associated with sin is Judas Iscariot. Belonging to the inner core of disciples, he is present throughout the ministry of Jesus and is a witness to the two "Suppers" where Jesus' identity is revealed within the intimate circle of the disciples: the anointing at Bethany (12:1–8) and the Last Supper (13:1–30). Judas is portrayed invariably as the one who betrays Jesus—indeed, "the Betrayer" is virtually a title. Jesus does not hesitate to describe him as a devil (6:70–71); he is a petty thief, greedy and grasping, raiding the common purse of the small band of disciples (12:6). He allies himself with the powers of darkness (13:2), betraying Jesus by stealth, even when he cannot but know that Jesus sees through him (13:21–30). Treacherously he acts the part of the true disciple in various acts of intimacy: present at numinous moments in the Gospel, dipping in the same bowl and receiving from Jesus' hands the morsel at the Last Supper (13:26), leading the arresting party straight to the private place of the disciples' meeting (18:2–3). He is the "son of perdition" (17:12), the one who is ultimately lost, slipping through the net of intimacy and friendship even while he continues to play the part of belonging. His acts of betrayal, both small and great, are profoundly consequential for the small band of friends; he stands over against the loyalty, love, and even naïveté of his companions, who trust him and lack any conception of what he has done or is about to do (13:29). Judas's sin is inexcusable in the Fourth Gospel; he is given over entirely to the darkness. His is a worse sin even than Pilate's betrayal of justice and truth, with which Judas's is compared: "for this reason the one who betrayed me has the greater sin" (19:11).[57] The betrayal of the intimate friend is worse than the "betrayal" of the Roman judge.

There is no overt sympathy for the character of Judas Iscariot in the Fourth Gospel (as there is, for example, in Matthew's account of Judas's suicide, Matt. 27:3–10 [cf. Acts 1:16–20]). The uncompromising moral dualism of John's symbolic universe does not allow any psychological insight into Judas's character nor consideration of perhaps the complex reasons for his betrayal. He is not a figure of tragedy in the sense of Oedipus or Othello, because he is in no way associated with personal greatness or virtue. His betrayal, in the evangelist's editorial hands, is petty, mean, and ugly. Yet, for all that, it is strange that his character evokes no anger in the reader. Judas appears pathetic, meager, unheroic, and for that very reason evokes a sense of pity in the reader, despite his actions. Perhaps this is in part because the destructiveness of his nature is contained within a wider, divine context. In some mysterious sense Judas's actions, however freely chosen, lie within the sovereignty of God: the betrayal, the lostness, the evil—which are the evangelist's final word on his character—are somehow contained in the Johannine theme, prevalent throughout the passion narrative, of the fulfillment of Scripture (17:12). Jesus himself gives Judas a kind of "permission" to do the thing he has chosen to do, knowing that it is already incorporated into the will of God: "what you are doing, do quickly" (13:27). There is nothing appealing or mitigating about Judas or his sinful betrayal of Jesus. Yet it too has its place within the divine schema. The small-mindedness of his character does not prevent the reader from being awed by the appalling lostness of his final condition.

In this respect, Judas Iscariot contrasts with the other disciples in the Fourth Gospel. Unlike him, nowhere are their moments of misunderstanding designated sinful or evil. Like the man born blind, their struggle to understand is engaged sympathetically by Jesus, who draws them from darkness into light. Although they may not immediately understand, they possess an openness of heart to the revelation that results in their illumination. Far from being sinners, they are the heroes of the Gospel—male and female alike—who move toward the light and discover the truth about themselves and God. The exception to this might be the story of Peter's threefold denial (18:15–18, 25–27). Twice Peter uses the words "I am not" (*ouk eimi*) in response to the question of whether he is a disciple of Jesus, contrasting with Jesus' "I am" throughout the Gospel and Jesus' own trial before Annas (18:19–24; cf. Mark 14:53–72). Nevertheless, although John makes no reference to Peter's tears (cf. Mark 14:72), there is sympathy for him within the Johannine text, confirmed later by the threefold confirmation of his love for Jesus after the resurrection and his own calling to martyrdom (21:15–19).[58] Peter's sinful denial of Jesus is motivated by fear rather than treachery or demonic power like Judas Iscariot; his intentions are right but he lacks self-knowledge of his weakness and the courage to confess Christ (13:37–38). It is Judas, not Peter, who is the exception among the group of Jesus' disciples.

The fourth evangelist also presents sin symbolically through groups as well as individuals: in particular, Jesus' opponents. The evangelist calls this group "the Jews" and they, more than anyone else in the narrative, symbolize John's understanding of the real sinners in the Fourth Gospel. Certainly this group is one of the main "characters" in the Gospel and plays an important symbolic role.[59] Yet the concept of "the Jews" is not an easy one to define. It is used in different contexts with different shades of meaning: in the raising of Lazarus, for example, the term *hoi Ioudaioi* to describe the mourners is not pejorative but descriptive of ethnicity (possibly "Judeans"[60]). Sometimes it refers to the Jewish authorities; at other times, it is broader. Often the term refers negatively to Jesus' opponents and raises sharply the question of whether the Fourth Gospel is, if not anti-Semitic, at least anti-Judaic. If so, this may reflect a historical situation of bitterness and hostility between post–70 C.E. Pharisaic groups and the nascent Johannine community, testing its wings against the synagogue as the parent body.[61] A more recent challenge to this widespread view comes from Stephen Motyer, who argues that the polemic of the Fourth Gospel is not anti-Semitic or bitter but rather rhetorical, attempting in the prophetic style to win over the Jewish opponents.[62] It is a "passionate appeal to change direction" rather than a racial and prejudiced denunciation of the Jewish people as a whole.[63] In any event, Culpepper points out that, while interpreters need to be careful in their reading of the Johannine "Jews," the evangelist "says nothing that condemns Jews of subsequent generations."[64]

At the same time, the group characterized as "the Jews" overlaps with the Johannine use of the term "world" (*kosmos*). Even more than "the Jews," the terminology of "the world" is employed in the Fourth Gospel in a variety of ways, sometimes within the same context. Thus, for example, *kosmos* is used in three ways:

- in a positive sense, where the "world" is the object of divine creativity and love, having the capacity to respond to that love;[65]

- in a neutral way that overlaps with the positive usage, where the "world" is the abode of human beings into which the Light comes;[66]

- in a negative sense to refer to the realm of unbelief, where the *kosmos* is under the power of the Evil One, resists the revelation, and stands for all that is oppressive within the structures of the world.[67]

The *kosmos*, in other words, is both "the object of God's love and the entity that hates God."[68] As the Gospel progresses, "the Jews" become interchangeable with the *kosmos* in its hostility toward God: indeed, the latter substitutes for *hoi Ioudaioi* in the Farewell Discourse, where *kosmos*, sin, and the devil seem to be coextensive terms.[69] It is in this distinctive sense that Jesus refuses to pray for the *kosmos* (17:9). While the reader presupposes God's love for the world and the mission of the disciples into the world, nevertheless in the context of John 17 the reader also knows that "to pray for the *kosmos* would be almost an absurdity, since the only hope for the *kosmos* is precisely that it should cease to be the *kosmos*."[70] Through both terms, "Jews" and *kosmos*, John offers a symbolic representation that gives shape to his understanding of sin. Both terms need to be comprehended within their literary context and complexity, since neither is used by John in a monolithic or simplistic way.[71]

Throughout the Gospel, the most obvious characteristic of "the Jews"—and the *kosmos*—is that as Jesus' opponents they reject the revelation from God disclosed in the flesh of Jesus. The theme of rejection runs through a number of narrative stages, across the Gospel as a whole as well as in particular episodes. As Culpepper points out, hostility from "the Jews" escalates in the first half of the Gospel:[72] from the opening scenes with John the Baptist, to the cleansing of the temple (2:13–22), the debate with Nicodemus, the healing of the disabled man (5:1–47), the fiery polemic of the Tabernacles Discourse (John 7–8), the story of the man born blind and his excommunication (9:1–41), the Good Shepherd Discourse (10:1–18), the polemical debate which surrounds the Feast of Dedication (10:19–42), and, as the climax of this theme, the plot of the Sanhedrin to kill Jesus and the warrant for his arrest after the raising of Lazarus (11:45–57). The same hostility is present in the Farewell Discourse in relation to the *kosmos*. It reaches a climax in the passion narrative, where "the Jews" finally reject Jesus as their king (19:15). By the end of the Gospel, the chief characteristic of "the Jews" and "the world" is one and the same: they symbolize all that is hostile to Jesus and to the believing community.

There are also individuals as part of this group who stand out in the Gospel narrative. Their role is exemplified in the character of Caiaphas, who, in religious guise, unwittingly prophesies the meaning of Jesus' death even while plotting to annihilate him (11:45–53). Caiaphas, in league with his father-in-law, Annas (18:19–24, 28), represents the response of "the Jews" in authority who reject Jesus on the basis of the supposed threat to their nation (11:48). Just why the council believes that the faith of Jewish people in Jesus will lead to Roman reprisal is not made clear. What is clear is that the sole concern of the authorities is with what will benefit them: "It is for your [our?] benefit that one person should die on behalf of the people and the whole nation not perish" (11:50). The irony of Caiaphas's statement is drawn out carefully by the evangelist, who sees in it the word of God still active in the high priestly office, despite its corruption: not only is Jesus' death to be "for the [Jewish] people" but also for all "the scattered children of God" (11:51–52).[73] Caiaphas is unintentionally right because he is serving, in spite of himself, the divine will. Yet he is drastically wrong to assume that belief in Jesus will lead the people of God to death; on the contrary, for the evangelist, Jesus is their salvation and life.

Pilate also needs to be included in this characterization (18:28–19:16a), as the Roman counterpart of Caiaphas. Against his own better judgment, Pilate is finally the one who condemns Jesus to death (19:16). It is often argued that Pilate's character is whitewashed by the evangelist on the basis of his resistance to "the Jews" and their accusations against Jesus.[74] Read in another light, Pilate's character seems every bit as negative as that of "the Jews" and his rejection of Jesus as indicative of the rejection of the *kosmos* as theirs.[75] Pilate's attempts to free Jesus from the accusation of "the Jews," in this reading and his conviction of Jesus' innocence throw into relief the unjust judgment he pronounces against Jesus. Unlike "the Jews" who genuinely believe that Jesus is a dangerous figure, both theologically and politically, Pilate is convinced of Jesus' innocence yet still condemns him to death. His motivation springs not from any commitment to truth, but partly from political self-interest and partly from antagonism toward "the Jews" and the desire to thwart and vex them. The trial scene is formed by a triangular relationship in which "the Jews" and Pilate equally pursue their own ends and, despite being opponents to each other, finally collude (along with Judas Iscariot) in using the darkness to quench the light. In the end, Jesus becomes the victim of political power-play, a point that emerges from the chiastic structure of the trial in which Pilate shuttles feebly between Jesus and "the Jews," concerned only with the assertion of his own power against those who might threaten it.[76] Yet in the end Pilate, like all the authorities in the Fourth Gospel, serves the divine will: everything he does, however unwittingly, attests ironically to Jesus' true identity. The reader is not without sympathy for his struggle. Like Caiaphas, Pilate speaks the truth despite himself. Just as Caiaphas stands for the *kosmos* in its determination to quench the light, so Pilate stands for the *kosmos* in its incomprehension of the light and its refusal to follow the path of illumination. The miscarriage of justice which is the human side of Jesus' death is brought about by the political fears, injustice, and blindness of the unbelieving *kosmos*.

As a group, "the Jews" in their hostility to Jesus become prominent in the Tabernacles Discourse, where the issue of sin is first raised explicitly in relation to the authorities. Jesus accuses "the Jews" of not keeping the law—"not one of you does the law" (7:19)—manifest in the murderous desire to kill him. Jesus defends his sabbath work, displaying that "right judgment" which the authorities lack (7:24). Throughout the following internal dispute among the authorities, it is clear that some see themselves in a superior category to that of "the crowd," which is ignorant of the law and therefore, in the authorities' own view, under its curse or judgment (7:49). Yet, for the evangelist, Moses and Jesus are not in opposing camps as the authorities assume, but rather the one acts symbolically and typologically upon the other: the law is on Jesus' side (cf. 7:51). As the dispute continues and the authorities fail to understand Jesus' meaning, Jesus points to his own origins and destiny and warns that his opponents will "die in your sin" (8:21). Their misunderstanding of Jesus' identity represents their failure to comprehend that which is "from above," thus confirming that they belong only "from below" (8:23). Strangely enough, when the Johannine Jesus repeats his earlier warning (twice), "sin" is found in the plural rather than the singular: "you will die in your sins" (8:24; cf. 8:21). Once more, death is the result of rejecting Jesus' heavenly identity. It is clear that, whether in the singular or plural, "sin" or "sins" refer to one and the same thing: the rejection of Jesus and the life he offers.

We have already observed the theme of slavery and freedom in relation to sin that emerges in the next section of the dialogue, where a number of "the Jews" seemingly come to faith in Jesus (8:31–38). This faith is short-lived: within no time they are rejecting Jesus and the truth he proclaims (8:33, 37–38). The problem is their illusions about themselves and their inability to face exposure to the light (8:12). They cannot bear the revelation into their own identity—as slaves to sin—any more than they can bear the revelation into Jesus' true identity. As the remaining section of the discourse proceeds, this enslavement to sin and evil, the drastic failure to guard the very law the authorities think they are maintaining, becomes dramatically exposed in their rejection of Jesus. The more Jesus reveals of his identity, the more "the Jews" resist the truth until finally they attempt to stone him, unveiling their true identity as children of the devil (8:59).

There are two aspects of John's understanding of sin that flow from this depiction of the authorities/*kosmos*. First of all, sin is fundamentally linked to the rejection of Jesus. As Barrett observes, both sin and its remedy are christological in the Fourth Gospel: "[s]ince sin is concentrated into the rejection of Christ it is clear that sin can be removed only by Christ."[77] Similarly, for Bultmann, such rejection is connected to the revelation:

> What the world does is sin, because it turns itself against Jesus, who has shown himself to be the Revealer by his words and his actions. If there were no revelation then there would be no sin either, in the decisive sense of the term.[78]

This rejection is symbolic of a more ultimate rejection. The Johannine Jesus can be scathing of nominal and superficial attachment to his ministry (e.g., 8:30–47). True attachment to Jesus, who has theological and symbolic identity, suggests a deeper relationship of attachment to God. Correspondingly, rejection of Jesus signifies rejection of the Father, who is the source of Jesus' being. In rejecting the Johannine Jesus, the opponents reject God. As a consequence, the opponents of Jesus throughout the Gospel represent the rejection of life. The meaning of "eternal life" (*zōē aiōnios*) is unfolded in a series of related symbols throughout the Gospel: truth, freedom, joy, peace, unity, intimacy, love, friendship. These characterize the richness of life which belongs to the believing community; it is life that thrives in the face of death, and it is embodied in the person of Jesus. In rejecting Jesus, the authorities in John's Gospel reject true life and instead choose death. It is significant that the plot to kill Jesus (after various spontaneous attempts to stone him throughout John 7–10) directly follows the raising of Lazarus: as we will see, Jesus is rejected precisely at the point where he gives life.[79] His life-giving revelation poses such a threat to the authorities that, in an act of political pragmatism, they decide to destroy him.[80] In this sense, they reject life not only for themselves but also on behalf of others.

The narrative of John 9 is a good example of the sinful rejection of life, as is clear from the Good Shepherd Discourse, which acts as a commentary on the experience of the man born blind.[81] As we have already seen, the perplexing theological issue of whether sin is involved in the healing is taken to the religious authorities: they are the experts, the ones who "see," the ones who are by definition without sin. Yet, as with the adulterous woman, by the end of the narrative the tables are turned: both Jesus and the man born blind are vindicated of sin, whereas the authorities are the ones whose "sin remains" (9:41). What is sinful is not any previous act of sin leading to disability, nor the man's ignorance and misunderstanding. Rather, as the Good Shepherd Discourse reveals, sin is symbolized in the way the authorities bully the man, using the law of Moses not to give life but to harass and withhold life. What lies behind such abuse is unbelief, the rejection of Jesus. Thus, the conflict between Jesus and the authorities symbolizes the conflict between the Revealer and the unbelieving world.[82] The opponents of Jesus finally

reject the light and condemn themselves to darkness. For the evangelist, in rejecting Jesus they reject life.

Moreover, in rejecting Jesus and the gift of eternal life, the opponents are
unwittingly engaged in *self*-rejection. Throughout the Gospel narrative, the religious authorities reject more and more of their own traditions: "You are the
teacher of Israel and you do not know these things?" Jesus asks in astonishment of
Nicodemus, a leader of "the Jews" (3:11). In John 5–10 the same group rejects its
own Scriptures and law (John 5), its own heroes (Moses in John 5, Abraham in
John 8), and members of its own nation (John 9:1–10:21). In their last appearance
in the passion narrative, "the Jews" reject their identity as God's people. "We have
no king but Caesar," they exclaim to Pilate in a supreme denial of identity (19:15).
The declaration of adherence to the Roman emperor is a tragic surrender of who
they are and everything for which they stand. As a result, for this writer, the
authorities reject God as their Father and their own identity as God's children; in
Johannine terms, they choose death over life because "their deeds are evil" (3:20).

There is a second characteristic of Jesus' opponents that is not perhaps so obvious. In John 5, Jesus accuses his opponents—unlike himself—of seeking "glory"
(*doxa*) not from God but from one another:

> I do not accept glory from human beings, but I have come to recognize in you that
> you do not have God's love within yourselves. I have come in the name of my Father,
> and you do not accept me; if someone else came in their own name, you would
> accept them. How is it possible for you to believe when you accept glory from one
> another and yet do not seek the glory which comes from the one God? (5:41–44)

Elsewhere, the Johannine Jesus warns against those who seek "their own glory"
(*tēn idian doxan*) as opposed to "the glory of the one who sent" Jesus into the
world (7:18). Similarly, the evangelist pronounces judgment against those who
"loved the glory of human beings rather than the glory of God" (12:43). Jesus
honors not himself but the Father, seeking only God's glory; the Father is the
source and giver of Jesus' glory (8:49–50, 54). In John's Gospel "glory" is the main
theological conception holding together incarnation and salvation. The classical
Greek meaning of the word (used also in Josephus, Philo, and secular Hellenistic
Greek) is "opinion," which comes to mean also "good opinion" or "good repute."
In biblical Greek, the original meaning "opinion" has dropped out; "good opinion" or "good repute" still survives, but has now developed into the *kĕbôd YHWH*,
"the glory of the Lord," translated as *doxa* in the Greek version of the Old Testament. There "glory" is the divine splendor made visible to humankind and associated with the temple.[83] John normally uses the word in the latter sense, as the key
term for describing the divine gift which the Johannine Jesus both embodies and
gives to the believing community. Thus in most occurrences in the Fourth Gospel,
doxa is translated "glory" where it describes the divine love and self-giving,
unveiled in the incarnation and in the "signs" and works of Jesus' ministry,[84] rad-

ically revealed on the cross,[85] and passed on to the believing community through the Spirit-Paraclete.[86]

In John 5, however, the evangelist shifts the focus of the word *doxa* to its other (biblical) meaning of "good opinion," variously translated "praise,"[87] or "honor").[88] The opponents of Jesus represent those who seek approval (*doxa*) from one another rather than seeking glory from God (see also 12:43). They strive to find glory/honor in the wrong place, apart from the revelation of God in Jesus, exposing a spiritual disorientation despite their religiosity—a disorientation based on "misplaced love"[89]—and a loss of identity as children and heirs of Abraham (see 8:39–47). This tragic misdirection stands in direct contrast to Jesus' own spirituality, which is centered on the Father as the only source of glory (7:18; 8:50, 54). The evangelist exploits the ambiguities of the term: while "glory" belongs to the divine realm and is virtually synonymous with "God" (*theos*), it is also given as a gift to human beings. In this sense, the giving of *doxa* in the Fourth Gospel symbolizes the restoration of the image, since humankind's original relationship to God has been ruptured and the divine glory, given in creation, lost.[90] The rabbinic commentary on Genesis 2:3, for example, speaks of the removal of Adam's glory after the Fall: "The glory stayed the night, but at the end of the Sabbath, [God] took the splendor from him and drove him out of the Garden of Eden" (*Genesis Rabbah* IX.5). The same tradition is found in the Gnostic *Apocalypse of Adam*, where Adam, speaking to his son Seth, recounts the story of the Fall: "Then we became two aeons, and the glory in our hearts deserted us, me and your mother Eve. . . . And the glory fled from us" (1:5–6). Although glory in the biblical world is primarily theological—referring to divine reality—there is also a sense in which human beings are drawn into that glory: either through contemplation of the *shekinah* (the rabbinic term for the divine dwelling) or by participation in the life of God. In this sense, we are speaking once more of the divine image in human beings, restored through the incarnation of the one who is himself the true Image of the Father. In the third section of the Great Prayer, Jesus prays for the unity of believers, who have already been given a share in the glory that the Father has bestowed on him:

> The glory that you have given me I myself have given to them,
> so that they may be one just as we are one.
> I in them and you in me, so that they may be fulfilled in unity,
> that the world may know you have sent me and have loved them
> just as you have loved me. (17:22–23)

Note that here, as in John 5, glory is closely linked to love and includes unity as an aspect of love. The believing community is to be the place of divine glory, the place where God's loving, life-giving, and unifying nature is revealed. The goal of human beings is the transfiguration which results from being caught up in the glory of God, signifying the restoration of the divine image.

If glory is a gift imparted by the Word-become-flesh and resides within the community, sustaining life and creating love and union, then it follows that the problem with Jesus' opponents is that they seek love and life in the wrong places. Seeking glory "from one another" in the sense of John 5 means being mistakenly dependent on others to gain ultimate approval: using others, we might say, in order to legitimize identity and ensure self-aggrandizement. While identity in the biblical world is never individualistic but always found in community, bypassing God in this search can lead to a desperate craving for self-promotion, built on self-deception rather than self-knowledge, and on the exploitation of others. Turning toward others for identity and honor implies a simultaneous turning away from the divine destiny of the self, where the Spirit abides as a spring of water welling up to eternal life (4:14). For John, the center of true identity, its focal heart, resides in the love of God; as a divine gift, glory now abides in the heart of the believer who has become the divine abode (14:23). As we have already seen, John shows that the nature of love is not domineering or exploitative, but grounded in mutual love and friendship (15:12–17).[91] Such mutuality flourishes only where each has a legitimate sense of self-worth within the community. To seek selfhood in a relationship to God and in the mutual love of the believing community is the very opposite of the opponents' desire to seek "glory" in one another.

There are several points that emerge from this brief survey of sin in the Fourth Gospel:

1. John does not offer a concise or abstract definition of sin, nor does he attempt to explain the origins of evil. He is more concerned with warning and transformation: "The prophet does not 'reflect' on sin; he 'prophesies' *against*."[92] Moreover, John does not have one word to designate sin, but employs a number of different symbols, including the use of representative figures. The main symbolism for sin is that of darkness, into which are incorporated images of untruth, self-deceit, willful ignorance, slavery, death, and unbelief.

2. With the exception of the woman caught in adultery (in any case, not part of the Johannine text), John is not concerned primarily with sin as a series of discrete acts of moral transgression, but rather with the theological and spiritual root of evil within the human heart. Where human beings reject the light, they enter into league with the forces of darkness, personalized in the devil, who is "the ruler of this world" and the "father of lies." Sin is a fundamental disorientation in relationship to God underlying acts of wrongdoing, that can be removed only by the divine miracle of incarnate love. Because of the loss of the divine image, and the light and love that flow from it—because human beings have forfeited the "glory" of their status as children of God—the Light enters the world in flesh in order to undo the deprivation wrought by sin and darkness.

3. Although sin and evil are pervasive, John does not consider all human beings in the same category as "sinners." There is a kind of innocence in misun-

derstanding and ignorance that Jesus does not condemn. Those who move toward the light, no matter how fumbling and inept their journey, no longer belong to the darkness; they are slowly but surely emerging from its grip. No blame or guilt is to be attached to them for what they have still to learn. On the other hand, those who willfully and knowingly choose the darkness—especially those who imagine themselves to dwell already in the light—are the ones with whom John has least patience. In the end, they are in league with the demonic forces of deceit, treachery, violence, and death, forces that enslave and ensnare human life. Both responses reveal that the overcoming of evil by the divine Word is already realized yet in another sense still awaiting final manifestation.

4. John's understanding of sin is primarily christological: the fundamental issue that decides the nature and reality of sin is the response of people to Jesus. How the characters in the Fourth Gospel respond to him as the Revealer is the only significant determinant in naming sin: "the Revealer uncovers the essence of sin."[93] To belong to the realm of sin and evil, to side with the darkness, is exemplified in the refusal to believe in Jesus as the light of the world, the Wisdom of God, the only Son of the Father who shares the life of God. In the Johannine worldview, it means to reject life itself and, in doing so, to reject both self-knowledge and the knowledge of God. The "sin of the world" which the "Lamb of God" takes away is the sin of unbelief. Sin is to choose death over life, darkness over light, deceit over truth, slavery over freedom, self-delusion over self-knowledge, the "ruler of this world" over the *Kyrios*. In the Fourth Gospel, sin means the unbelieving rejection of life, epitomized through the symbol of darkness which stands over against all that is meant by "God":

> [f]rom a Johannine perspective, walking in darkness means persisting in unbelief, since antipathy toward God and Jesus is the sin at the root of all other sins. Conversely, walking in the light means living by faith in Jesus.[94]

5. Embracing death and darkness means also a turning away from divine glory (*doxa*)—and, in particular, glory as it is unfolded in the incarnate flesh of Jesus. Such a disorientation results in turning to others for good opinion and esteem (*doxa*) rather than to God as the author and giver of life. The loss and restoration of *doxa* are one way of depicting the underlying narrative of the Fourth Gospel, centered in the incarnation of the Logos, who transfigures flesh with divine glory.

6. Religion itself is no proof against sin and evil. On the contrary, there are no more culpable sinners, for the evangelist, than those religious leaders who lack self-knowledge and are filled with self-delusion; who harm those entrusted to their care; who abuse others in order to gain power; who rob and deceive the innocent; who place the demands of goodness and justice beneath their own self-preservation; who close themselves against the very light they claim to radiate. The darkness here is willful, self-conscious, and self-chosen: the most destructive form

of all, leading to alliance with the forces of darkness. Such deliberate rebellion and unbelief are the true manifestation of sin in the Fourth Gospel.

SIN AND GENDER

This brief presentation of sin in the Fourth Gospel has a contribution to make to contemporary questions about sin and gender. In feminist theological discussion, for a number of years, there has been awareness of the problem of whether sin has a gender dimension: whether it is the same for women as for men, particularly as sin has been understood in the Western tradition. Valerie Saiving wrote an article in 1960 in which she suggested that women's sinfulness was of a different character from that of men;[95] and in 1980 Judith Plaskow, a Jewish feminist theologian, published a study of sin and grace in the theologies of Reinhold Niebuhr and Paul Tillich.[96] Plaskow argued that ideas of pride as the cardinal sin and self-sacrificing love as the means of redemption were irrelevant to women's experience and destructive of their lives. For Saiving and Plaskow, women's sin is symbolized not so much in pride—that is, idolatry and worship of the self, "a rebellion of self-assertiveness" whose only solution is "the self-abnegation of total obeisance to God's sovereignty"[97]—but rather its opposite, the lack of selfhood. Plaskow sees sin as "the failure to center the self, the failure to take responsibility for one's own life."[98] Saiving describes women's sin more graphically as:

> triviality, distractibility, and diffusiveness; lack of an organizing center or focus; dependence on others for one's own self-definition; tolerance at the expense of standards of excellence; inability to respect the boundaries of privacy; sentimentality, gossipy sociability, and mistrust of reason—in short, underdevelopment or negation of the self.[99]

Since the publications of Saiving and Plaskow, theological discussion about sin and gender has reflected the liberationist stance of much feminist theology. In the liberation approach, sin is associated with unjust social structures that benefit the privileged minority over against the oppressed majority; redemption is found in the struggle to gain emancipation from these structures. Sin is interpreted primarily in social terms. The socially and politically oppressed are the victims of sinful structures rather than active doers, liberated by the message of the prophets and Jesus of Nazareth. When liberation theology is translated into women's theology, women are seen as the victims of sin at the hands of domineering structures and misogynist attitudes.[100]

Despite the strengths of this kind of theology in broadening Christian understandings of sin, there are also problems, particularly in its translation into feminist categories. In the first place, feminist political theology can too easily settle on the external world as the battleground for sin, while downplaying the internal and spiritual dimensions. Writing on self-esteem, the (political) secular feminist Gloria Steinem makes the point that the political cannot resolve all internal issues in human life. She believes it possible to hold together the two dimensions, turning the early feminist slogan "the personal is political" into its opposite, "the political is personal"—both, in her view, equally true.[102] Steinem's experience suggests that changing political structures is insufficient for the transformation women desire: there is an "enemy within" as much as an "enemy without," and feminist political action is limited largely to the second. What is required is attentiveness to the inward dimensions of transformation as well as the outer, with awareness of the ways in which women's inner lives have been damaged—and perhaps also the extent to which women collude (even if unwittingly) in their own oppression.

Second, from a theological viewpoint there are problems with a feminist hermeneutic that attempts to make women guiltless of sin and merely the passive victims of the sin of others. Writing from a feminist perspective, Angela West exposes the dangers of a feminist dualism of sin in which women are regarded as innocent victims while men are deemed guilty and responsible.[102] According to West, this is an understandable but false response to those who have blamed Eve for sin and made Adam its helpless victim (see 1 Tim. 2:13–14).[103] A genuinely emancipatory theology, in West's view, resists such dualism, holding women and men equally responsible for human sinfulness: "it is not [Eve's] innocence that can confirm our spiritual equality, but precisely her disobedience, her capacity for sin."[104] A traditional concept like the Augustinian view of original sin, for West, holds out more hope than the kind of reactive theology that acquits Eve and proclaims her innocence, because it emphasizes the corporate nature of sin.[105] More importantly, as sinners in partnership with men, women are equally the recipients of divine grace.[106] West also questions Saiving and Plaskow's view of women's sin as self-negation, arguing that such a definition ignores women outside the confines of white, Western, middle-class culture. Equating self-negation with the sin of sloth, West considers it an inappropriate definition of sin for those who have been condemned to lives of hard physical labor in contexts of virtual or actual slavery:[107] to West, this is another misguided attempt to declare Eve innocent.[108] Speaking of the recovery of the female image of Sophia, West concludes:

> the real children of Sophia will recognize that women are quite as capable of being caught up in the mystifications of ideology as men are; that women—even the children of the oppressed—can be adept manipulators and children of Folly. And men—even white middle-class ones—can occasionally possess the milk of human kindness.[109]

West's study is an important challenge to a dualism of sin that simply reverses the patriarchal assessment of one gender as guilty and the other innocent, without questioning the mistaken framework on which it is based.

It is unlikely that the Fourth Gospel understands sin and evil to have a direct gender focus; the question is in any case anachronistic. It is true that the women of the Fourth Gospel are nowhere held solely responsible for evil, nor is their sinfulness seen in starker or harsher terms than that of men. None of the women disciples is guilty of betrayal or denial, and most of the small group present at the foot of the cross are women. Nevertheless, this need not indicate female moral or spiritual superiority in the Johannine symbolic world: also to be taken into account is women's limited access to political power, which makes them, ironically, less vulnerable to charges of sedition. Similarly, while the group designated as "the Jews" is presumably male, the evangelist makes nothing of it in gender terms; it is more likely to be linked to men's superior sources of power. While it is true that women are sympathetically portrayed, the same may be said of many of the male characters. What the Fourth Gospel's presentation of women does is to confirm symbolically the faithfulness and courage of the women disciples—an important witness in a patriarchal world that tends, if anything, to rate women as morally inferior to men. Yet the same women are as affected as their male counterparts by the darkness: equally capable of misunderstanding and unconscious ignorance.

Despite this qualification, in several important respects the Fourth Gospel's symbolic portrayal of sin and darkness is an important voice in contemporary discussion. In the first place, the Johannine understanding of sin does not focus on sexual sin, nor does it create a ranking of sin that places female sexuality high on a list of moral transgression. On the contrary, the Johannine Jesus does not see femaleness as unclean, nor does he regard women as sexually predatory and thus to be feared. In the story of the Samaritan woman, Jesus is indifferent to the disciples' amazement and the risk of possible scandal attached to his dealings with her. He does not condemn or exclaim at her current relationship but seeks rather to reveal the underlying spiritual need. In the story of the adulterous woman, while not condoning her conduct, Jesus refuses to pronounce condemnation and sends the woman away unscathed, overturning the moral superiority of those who take pride in their own self-righteousness and who rank female sexual sin above other sins. Admittedly, the story is more concerned with moral acts of transgression than the Fourth Gospel generally is, with its more theological understanding of sin. Even so, as in the Johannine story of the man born blind, the reader is left with the question of who the real sinners are: in all three stories there is a sense of overturning. The supposed "sinners" are the spiritual heroes whose openness to divine love and revelation brings them closer to God than those whose superior testimonials are betrayed by spiritual obtuseness, self-congratulation, and judgmentalism.

Second, there can be little doubt that the destructive consequences of sin create a dichotomy between perpetrators and victims. To a certain extent, this perspective coheres with feminist emphasis on the way in which women have been the victims of sinful structures and attitudes—though whether it is tied exclusively to gender is another question. The symbolic portrayal of the authorities exposes how abusive authority works against people to deprive them of identity and selfhood, destroying an authentic community of mutuality (cf. 11:50).[110] The narrative of John 9 is an example of this. The text draws the reader to identify with the man in his darkness and ignorance, in the denial of his experience, in the domineering tactics of the authorities who are supposedly responsible for his well-being, and in the pain of his exclusion. The reader is able to identify with the man's experience: his victimization and exclusion, and his sense of illumination and belonging to a new community through encounter with Jesus. John's symbolism here and elsewhere dramatizes the way in which loss and deprivation, where they are challenged by the revelation, can be transformed paradoxically into an experience of enlightenment in communion with others. Because women as well as men act as representative figures, male and female readers need not be confined by gender in entering the dynamics of the text.

Third, if we are to take seriously West's warning of the dangers of replacing the condemnation of Eve by the declaration of her innocence, a further step is required beyond victimhood. It is as important that the reader (female as well as male) recognize not only the experience of marginalization within the Johannine text but also the use and abuse of power. Even within a liberation model, the view that women are to be defined only as the victims of sin can be challenged. Elisabeth Schüssler Fiorenza, for example, speaks against the syndrome of the "white lady," who participates in structural injustice against others on the basis of supposed racial or class superiority.[111] Even in the realm of relationships, where women, though lacking political power, can have a considerable degree of personal power, it is possible to damage others with a love that smothers or manipulates, even on the basis of low self-esteem and unacknowledged need. In any domain where power exists, whether it be political, psychological, moral, or spiritual, there exists also the possibility (whether conscious or unconscious) of abuse. What is lacking in such contexts is self-knowledge. While feminists are right to emphasize the need for women to engage in proper social and political analysis—a vital part of self-knowledge—the personal dimension cannot be neglected. The revelation that leads to life gives dual insight into the true nature of the self and of God. The farther we stand from the revelation, and the more vehemently and knowingly we refuse it, the more complicit we become in the promotion of sin. The misuse of power, whether by domination or manipulation, is in Johannine terms the rejection of authentic life and the deadly embrace of darkness.

Fourth, even allowing for West's critique, the feminist exposure of self-negation as a form of sin is an important insight. As we have seen, the rejection of life in the Fourth Gospel involves an element of self-rejection. Where human life is dominated by timidity and fear, there is also participation in the sinful denial of life. For John, such enslavement means the rejection of identity and freedom, and the ultimate denial of God's revelation in Jesus. All human beings need to recognize the ways in which they are deprived—or deprive themselves—of life. Feminist theologians have drawn an important distinction between self-giving and self-sacrifice, arguing that women traditionally have been required to practice the latter without the former:

> Women are those whose sense of self is not overabundant. More typically, their sense of self is submerged in relationships to others, whose identities, desires and needs displace their own to the extent that one may speak of a loss, dissipation or diffusion of self and of identity: a virtual collapse of self into relationships.[112]

Such is not the theological perspective of the fourth evangelist. The theme of abiding illustrates that disciples, even in their love for one another, need to discover their own friendship with God and the gravity of their own longing for salvation. Those traditions which have least room for mysticism and place little emphasis on growth in personal holiness, emphasizing instead Christian service and self-sacrifice, arc particularly prone to a theological solipsism that in effect denies the development of Christian selfhood. The image of the seed which "dies" to produce fruit (12:24), set in the context of Jesus' death, can be interpreted not just in relation to the need for self-transcendence. As a parallel to the Johannine image of childbirth,[113] it may mean facing the "death" and "labor" of self-negation, whether or not this is a form of darkness that is confined to women. Like self-transcendence, it is a painful "death" to die. Yet both dimensions—the finding of selfhood and the summons to self-giving—paradoxically and together lead to life. According to Regina Coll, salvation comes "in the form of affirmation, respect, and the development of a healthy and holy pride in oneself, not in crucifying the prideful self but in the resurrection of a redeemed self into new life."[114]

Fifth, and arising from this, it is important to recognize the damage and alienation that low self-esteem can generate, a point that West tends to minimize: sloth, after all, is not primarily a physical problem. There may be an element of truth in Daphne Hampson's conviction that female self-negation and low self-esteem should not be termed sinful at all.[115] Nevertheless, there is a form of self-rejection that has destructive consequences both for the self and others. McFadyen argues that, in feminist reinterpretation, the sin of sloth is not just the passive failure to do right. It also refers to "*acts* of omission arising out of a *wilful* indolence or indifference which is culpable because it involves a free choice: one could have done otherwise."[116] Sloth signifies personal involvement in the "diminution of selfhood" and also an "active inaction,"[117] which is at the same time "a disorientation and sequestration of the power of personal involvement."[118] Self-rejection is symbolic of the rejection of God as Creator and Redeemer: the One who creates the world in its goodness and restores it in Christ. Beverly Gaventa, commenting on Paul's understanding of sin in Romans as rebellion against the Creator, takes the gender debate into account when she suggests:

> What Romans offers women is an opportunity to reflect on the ways in which they participate in the human condition of rebellion against God. In some instances that rebellion may take the form of pride, perhaps a religious pride that presumes to

know God's will and God's favor. In other instances, rebellion may take the form of low self-esteem, even a self-negation that implicitly denies that the creature in fact derives from God. Contrasts drawn in very generalized terms about the principal sin of men as pride and the principal sin of women as self-negation fail to perceive the depth of the situation Paul portrays. Such analyses—whether or not they are accurate—limit sin to the sphere of human relations. Paul would insist that whatever form sin takes, it arises from a common human rebellion against God.[119]

Gaventa's helpful comments reveal how important it is to move away from an understanding of sin that is primarily moral to a theological apprehension. In many respects, a moralistic reading of sin can lead, in West's terms, to letting women off the hook. If we stand with our "first parents" in their ejection from paradise, mutually guilty and responsible for the tragedy of sin, we face the disfigurement of our relationship with God as the core of sin and the loss of the divine image/glory. For the Fourth Gospel, sin is the willful choice of death over life, darkness over light, evil over goodness, and the even more tragic inability to distinguish between them. John describes this kind of mistaken apprehension—the confusion between mask and reality, illusion and truth—as part of the great lie, perpetuated by the devil: the self-deceit which is the product of the one who is "a liar and the father of lies." While we cannot deduce from the Fourth Gospel the answer to the question of whether women's sin differs fundamentally from that of men, we can locate a more comprehensive understanding that delineates sin and evil theologically as willful separation from the divine Source of life, the rejection of the Son who comes from the Father's love, the tragic choice of illusion over reality. As Ricoeur points out, discussing in general various conceptions of sin, "missing the mark, deviation, rebellion, straying from the path do not so much signify a harmful substance as a violated relation. . . . The symbolism of sin . . . suggests the idea of a relation broken off."[120]

Lastly, such a perspective means that a theology of sin needs to heed the Johannine warning of the danger of seeking glory from one another rather than from God. The warning needs to be read in the context of the Fourth Gospel's emphasis on relationship and interdependence, a theme expressed powerfully in the symbol of abiding.[121] Nevertheless, there is also concern for discipleship, witnessed in Johannine narratives that stress growth in faith. At least in Western culture, according to Coll, women to a greater extent than men have been socialized to please and placate, to find approval in submissiveness and service of others, leading to a shifting sense of selfhood that adapts itself readily to the demands and expectations of others.[122] What the Fourth Gospel challenges is the center of the self located solely in either self-preoccupation or relationship with others. The Johannine Gospel sees the source of true identity—in a theological rather than psychological sense—as friendship with God: an interior meeting of heart to heart that becomes an abiding-place, a strong and stable locus for self-knowledge and self-giving love within the context of the community of faith. Ultimately *doxa*, whether in the sense of glory, honor, or good opinion, begins in relationship to God through Jesus: in the transformation of selfhood, bodily existence, and sociality that is implied in the incarnation. Not only the powerful but also the powerless need to heed this message. The Johannine view of salvation from sin and darkness is focused around the restoration of the image—rebirth "from above"—as the ultimate determinant of identity.

The Fourth Gospel offers a more complex understanding of sin and evil than the Western overemphasis on pride as the paradigmatic form of sin. John unfolds a symbolic theology that enables the reader to recognize the complexity and complicity of sin: in structures as well as attitudes, in taking responsibility as well as recognizing victimhood. The core symbol of sin is that of darkness, which signifies self-delusion, falsehood, hatred, and enslavement. Sin begins in the disconnection from the divine Source of life, yet is only confirmed—and only takes shape—where the Revealer and the revelation are knowingly discarded. Such a rebuff means the rejection of life, and the seeking of identity in anything other than the God of Jesus Christ, leaving the self dangerously insubstantial and the community without a center. Johannine symbolism for sin evinces both truth and gentleness in the conduct of Jesus toward those who are open to the revelation. These Johannine symbols function not to moralize but in order that, illuminated by the light and fullness of grace, the reader of the Gospel—whether male or female—may discover freedom from the darkness and treachery of sin.

CHAPTER 8

Costly Self-Giving:
The Symbol of Anointing

*And I shall sing all the day long. I shall fill the air with
the joy of you in me, of me in you. Guarding you and
guarding me in that incantation. Sonorous home in
which I shelter you. Which protects me from the violence of the day. Childhood's cradle, where any rapture
is given free play. An attentive hymn. Which does not
falter and is not interrupted. And whose tender
fragility is never breached by fixed duration.*[1]

MARY OF BETHANY's action in anointing Jesus after the raising of her brother
from the dead is an important symbol in the Fourth Gospel, both in its
own right and on account of its position in the Gospel narrative. The
anointing functions as a symbol of discipleship, particularly in its relationship to
Christology. Mary responds to Jesus' love with her own love; in this sense she and
the action she performs play a symbolic role. There is a kind of mirror reflection
between Jesus and Mary that encapsulates the intimacy between disciples and the
one who, in this Gospel, is friend, lover, Lord, and Savior. Mary's action reveals
also a multilayered contrast: between the tomb of Lazarus, signifying death, and
the banquet, which symbolizes life;[2] between the living ones (especially Lazarus)
and the one who is soon to die on their behalf; between the exemplary disciple,
who loves totally, and the false disciple who is thief and betrayer; between the one
who anoints the feet with oil and the one who will later wash the feet with water.

The story of the anointing has a number of links with similar narratives in the
Synoptic Gospels. In the first place, there are two different Synoptic traditions in
which Jesus is "anointed" by a woman, yet with significant differences from the
Johannine account. The first, in Mark's Gospel, and followed fairly closely by
Matthew, depicts an unnamed woman who, at the beginning of the Passion narrative, prophetically anoints Jesus' head with oil as a symbol both of his kingship
and of the death he is about to die; the anointing is set within the house of Simon
the leper and framed by the story of Judas's betrayal (Mark 14:3–9; Matt. 26:5–13).
The second tradition is the Lukan narrative of the sinful woman—also unnamed
—who washes Jesus' feet with oil and tears as an act of contrition, gratitude, and
hospitality in contrast to the frugality and self-righteousness of Jesus' host, Simon

the Pharisee; there is no link in this story with Jesus' passion (Luke 6:36–50). In contrast to Luke, John's account is set in the broader context of the passion yet, unlike Mark and Matthew, it is an anointing of the feet rather than the head—with oil, not tears. In contrast to the Synoptic accounts, the Johannine anointing is performed as an act of faith by a known and named disciple, Mary of Bethany. While there are obvious links between these traditions, the differences are even more striking, and it is important (whatever their historical origins) not to harmonize them, as early generations tended to do.[3] It is also important not to import the name of Mary Magdalene into the stories, since in none of the Gospels is she connected to the anointing in any way.[4]

Second, there is a further Synoptic parallel with the Johannine narrative in the Lukan story of Martha and Mary of Bethany, though the overlap is rather different (Luke 10:38–42). The Lukan Jesus visits the sisters during his ministry—a visit that gives rise to conflict between the two women over their relationship with him. Once again, there are similarities in the two narratives: the names of the sisters, the impression of Martha as the elder sister, the sisters' hospitality to Jesus and sense of friendship between them and Jesus, Martha's role in serving the meal, the possible overtones of ministry in her work (*diakonia/diakonein*, Luke 10:40; John 12:2),[5] and the physical posture of Mary at Jesus' feet in the context of a meal (Luke 10:39; John 12:3; cf. 11:32).[6] The differences are equally noteworthy: Luke makes no reference to a brother, Lazarus,[7] giving instead the impression that Martha is the head of household; the Lukan village is presumably in Galilee (on Jesus' journey to Jerusalem), not Judea; the context is earlier in the ministry of Jesus; and the narrative of conflict between the sisters is very different from the more harmonious Johannine account of their relationship. Here too it is important to keep separate the two accounts, despite the overlap, and not read Lukan characteristics into the Johannine account. This is particularly important in the characterization of the sisters. In the Lukan account, Martha is somewhat negatively portrayed in relation to her sister—anxious about practical realities, resentful at her sister's inactivity, and jealous of Mary's position. Although she serves the meal in 12:2, the Johannine Martha is not in conflict with her sister, nor is she portrayed as jealous and resentful.[8] Noting the similarities and differences between the Johannine and Synoptic accounts in both the anointing and Martha and Mary traditions helps us to read the Fourth Gospel in its own terms, without (consciously or unconsciously) amalgamating the Gospels.

THE RAISING OF LAZARUS

The anointing is arguably not a separate pericope standing by itself, as is generally assumed, but is one scene in a larger unit, the raising of Lazarus, artificially divided by the chapter break between John 11 and 12. Already the narrator has created an inclusion by the proleptic reference to Mary's anointing at the beginning of the Lazarus story, puzzlingly referred to as if it has already taken place: "Now Mary was the one who anointed the Lord with myrrh and dried his feet with her hair, whose brother Lazarus was ill" (11:2). Awkward though this reference is, it acts as a prolepsis, a narrative anticipation, and has the literary effect of entwining the story of the anointing with the Lazarus story.[9] The reader will not have finished with Lazarus until the anointing has taken place; indeed the anointing will play a critical role in unfolding and completing Lazarus's tale. The drama does not end until the Bethany family gathers together in joyous union around Jesus, counteracting the separation, confusion, and pain of the opening episode.[10]

The narrative begins with Lazarus's illness (11:1–16) and concludes with the renewed threat to his life after the anointing (12:9–11).[11] In between these episodes, Martha and Mary take center stage, the one sister confessing her faith in Jesus as the resurrection and the life (11:17–27) and the other sister pointing symbolically to his death and resurrection (12:1–8). Meanwhile, the response of "the Jews" is a subplot within the narrative,[12] subtly interweaving the story of Jesus' own death and resurrection, which is the inner meaning of the Lazarus story (11:28–37; 11:45–57). At the center of the sequence is the actual raising of Lazarus from the dead (11:38–44). From this perspective, the narrative can be read as a chiasm, the center of which is the vivid picture of Lazarus emerging from the tomb—itself a symbolic and highly stylized account (11:38–44). The narrative consists of seven scenes:

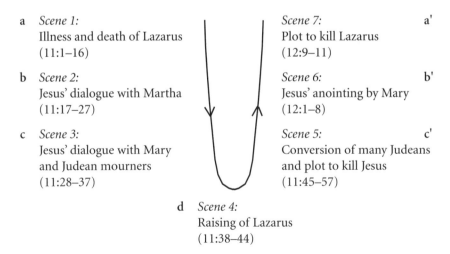

a   *Scene 1:*   *Scene 7:*   a'
    Illness and death of Lazarus   Plot to kill Lazarus
    (11:1–16)   (12:9–11)

b   *Scene 2:*   *Scene 6:*   b'
    Jesus' dialogue with Martha   Jesus' anointing by Mary
    (11:17–27)   (12:1–8)

c   *Scene 3:*   *Scene 5:*   c'
    Jesus' dialogue with Mary   Conversion of many Judeans
    and Judean mourners   and plot to kill Jesus
    (11:28–37)   (11:45–57)

            d   *Scene 4:*
                Raising of Lazarus
                (11:38–44)

If this structure is right, it means that the parallel to Martha's dialogue with Jesus is not Mary's conversation in the next scene—which, though appearing to begin in the same way, proceeds in a very different direction—but rather Mary's anointing of Jesus' feet. In parallel scenes, the sisters confess their faith in Jesus in different ways, the first before the raising of Lazarus and the second after it (and after the plot to kill Jesus).[13] Each faith confession represents symbolic words and actions that are crucial to the Gospel's understanding of eternal life.

Seen as a whole sequence that encompasses all these elements, the raising of Lazarus is the centerpiece of the Fourth Gospel, bringing to a climax the themes and symbols of the first half of the Gospel. It contains the greatest of the "I am" sayings (11:25–26), has its center in the major Johannine theme of life (*zōē aiōnios*, e.g., 1:4; 3:15–18; 5:21–29; 10:10b),[14] and completes the "signs" ministry of Jesus, where the divine glory is made manifest in the flesh through his symbolic words and works. At the same time, if the sequence is seen to include the plot to kill Jesus (11:45–53), the raising of Lazarus sets in motion the second half of the Gospel, where the divine glory is again manifest in the flesh, this time through the cross. The dramatic response of "the Jews" to Jesus' action in raising Lazarus (11:45–46) is the immediate catalyst for this event: the authorities are politically threatened by the enthusiastic response of the people to Jesus and determine to do away with him (11:47a–50). The decision of the Sanhedrin leads in a straight line to Jesus' arrest, conviction, and death (11:55–57)—although ironically the authorities, for all their posturing, cannot lay hands on him until Jesus himself, at his Father's behest, determines the coming of the "hour" (12:23; 13:1; 17:1). On a deeper level, the narrative reveals the evangelical purpose of Jesus' coming, and therefore the Father's sending: to give life to believers at the cost of Jesus' death (3:16). In this program, the anointing plays a key symbolic role, signifying, on the one hand, the interplay of life and death and the triumph of the one over the other and, on the other hand, the intimacy that holds the community together in the Father's love.

THE ANOINTING AND ITS SOCIAL BACKGROUND

As with the feeding story, the anointing is set within the context of Passover ("it was near the Passover," 6:4; "six days before the Passover," 12:1a), a connection that is made also at the beginning of the footwashing ("before the feast of the Passover," 13:1). The link with the raising of Lazarus from the dead is also made (12:1b): Jesus once more returns to Bethany. The reader cannot be unaware of the danger of this visit to Judea, which has been alluded to in the opening episode (11:15–16; cf. 10:39), now intensified by the plot to kill Jesus and the watchfulness and readiness of the authorities (11:47–57). The dinner is given in Jesus' honor ("they made for him a dinner," 12:2), and Lazarus is conspicuously present, restored to health; his presence emphasizes the reality of his rising from the dead (Augustine, *In Joannis Evangelium* 50.5). It is unclear whether the home is that of the Bethany family or a neighbor's at which Lazarus is a guest; the reference to Martha serving suggests that it is their own home.[15] Martha is a minor character in the scene, described only as serving the meal, though the language is possibly suggestive of Christian service,[16] and reflects other Gospel references to women's service of Jesus (cf. Mark 15:40–41 par.; Luke 8:1–3). The opening verses set the scene for what is to happen (12:1–3), taking the dinner party in a completely unexpected direction.

Nothing as yet has been said of Mary in the introduction to the scene. She now appears rather abruptly and begins to anoint Jesus' feet; though she does not speak, what she does is a "sign act" in the prophetic style.[17] The narrator describes Mary's action and its immediate effect in three sentences, each of which expresses something that is palpable and sensual:

- The narrator describes carefully yet succinctly the aromatic oil Mary uses to anoint Jesus' feet: "Mary having taken a pound of myrrh, of genuine nard, very costly, anointed the feet of Jesus" (12:3a). The perfumed oil is extraordinary for its richness and rarity, its genuineness, its costliness and quantity.[18] It is hard to imagine an ordinary family possessing so expensive an item—let alone being willing to lavish it, all at once, on a guest at dinner.

- Mary then wipes Jesus' feet with her hair. This means presumably that Mary wipes away the excess oil, which is pouring over Jesus' feet and the couch on which he reclines (12:3b).[19] The unbinding of Mary's hair is unusual, to say the least, but it is unclear just how disreputable this gesture might appear in a private or semiprivate setting such as this, especially for a single woman; certainly for a married woman, it would be scandalous.[20] In any event, it suggests both the intimacy and a level of unconventionality in what she does in anointing Jesus.

- The house, probably small, is flooded with the rich aroma of the scented oil (12:3c).

The immediate effect of the anointing is the objection of Judas Iscariot, ostensibly in support of the poor, whose cause is seemingly neglected in this extravagant and wasteful action (12:4–5). The evangelist, however, does not allow Judas's objection to stand: not only is he the betrayer; he is also a petty thief and wants the money for himself (12:6). In addition to the editorial dismissal of Judas's objection, Jesus also intervenes to defend Mary's action against the criticism and, in doing so, interprets it (12:7–8), relating the anointing to his own impending death. Yet the precise form of the wording is difficult. Literally it reads, "Leave her, in order that she might keep it for the day of my burial" (*aphes autēn, hina eis tēn hēmeran tou entaphiasmou mou tērēsē auto*, 12:7b). The sentence, though awkward, could theoretically stand in its own right. Alternatively, the reader may need to supply the main clause: "(she bought/saved/did it) in order that she might keep it for the day of my burial." In either case, it is hard to know what is meant by "keep," given that Mary has just poured the oil over Jesus' feet. Moreover, she does not anoint Jesus for burial in John's Gospel after his death—though he is sumptuously anointed by others (cf. 19:39–40). Barrett suggests that the verb "keep" (*tērein*) be paraphrased as "keep in mind" rather than "retain [for burial]"—that is, Mary will remember at the time of Jesus' burial.[21] It is more likely that John's clumsy wording means much the same as Mark 14:8, which is clearer: "she has anointed my body beforehand for burial."[22] Whatever the precise meaning, the overall significance is plain—John is linking Mary's action to Jesus' death and burial.

What is the background of Mary's action in the cultural terms of the day? Nowadays, with the widespread use of aromatherapy in the Western world, what Mary does in anointing Jesus makes some sense, although there are still puzzling elements. The ancient world is familiar with two related practices—footwashing and anointing with oil. In an earlier chapter we saw that footwashing is common in the ancient world, often in the context of a banquet, as a gesture of cleansing and hospitality; it could also have cultic overtones. In most cases, footwashing in water was performed by a slave/servant at the instigation of the host with water, but in exceptional circumstances a woman could perform such an act for her lover (as Aseneth does for Joseph); in wealthy circles the feet could be washed in spiced wine rather than water.[23] There are elements that suggest footwashing in what Mary does for Jesus: the pouring of liquid onto the feet of a guest and wiping them dry afterwards, the context of the banquet and thus hospitality, the lavish welcome of Jesus after what he has done to restore the family's life together. On the other hand, a woman's long, unbound hair is not normally used as a towel to dry the feet after footwashing. Nor is oil used for footwashing. Yet there are exceptions: in the Odyssey, for example, Odysseus is recognized on his return home by his old nurse, Eurycleia, who, while washing his feet and anointing them with oil, sees the familiar scar on his leg.[24] There is also a story within Judaism of a Jewish master who instructs his slave girl to wash his feet and those of his Gentile guest in olive-oil in order to demonstrate his abundance of oil.[25]

Anointing, on the other hand, is a more diverse activity in the ancient world and in Judaism. It is used in various contexts, more usually with oil (whether or not it is scented), but is particularly important in the biblical world and Judaism:[26]

- Domestic: for cooking, massage, moisturizing in a dry climate, and the cosmetic perfuming of the body to make it attractive, sometimes for sexual reasons (Ruth 3:3; 2 Sam. 12:20; Esth. 2:12; Cant. 1:3).

- Hospitality: as a sign of hospitality and honor to a guest at a banquet, usually on the head (Ps. 23:5; Luke 7:46); also more generally as a symbolic expression of joy and celebration (Isa. 61:3; cf. Matt. 6:16–17).

- Therapy: for medicinal purposes, where it is applied to wounds, skin complaints, aches and pains (Isa. 1:6; Jer. 8:22; Mark 6:13; Luke 10:34; Jas. 5:14; Apoc. 3:18; Josephus, *Jewish War* 1.657 = *Antiquities* 17.172; Philo, *De Som-*

niis 2.58–59; *Acts of Thomas* 67); it is also used in exorcisms for its magical-
therapeutic properties (*Testament of Solomon* 18:34), including in Gnostic
and Christian circles for baptism.[27]

- Status: to signify wealth and royal status, where expensive, perfumed oil
  would be used (1 Sam. 10:1; 16:12–13; Ps. 45:7); this includes consecration,
  either of persons or of sacred objects (Gen. 28:18; Exod. 30:22–33; Ps. 133:2).

- Death: to embalm the bodies of the dead at their interment (Mishnah, *Shab-
  bat* 23:5), a task often associated with women (Mark 16:1; Luke 23:56; 24:1;
  Gospel of Peter 12.50).

One other rather unusual use of anointing with oil in Judaism is worth mention-
ing—namely, its power to transfigure. In a narrative commentary on the life of
Enoch (Gen. 5:21–32), the patriarch is divested of his clothing by the archangel
Michael and covered in oil: "the appearance of that oil is greater than the greatest
light, and its ointment is like sweet dew, and its fragrance myrrh; and it is like the
rays of the glittering sun" (*2 Enoch* 22:8–10). When Enoch sees himself transfigured, he realizes that he has "become like one of his glorious ones." Obviously not
all of these are necessarily present in the Johannine story of the anointing, but they
do illustrate the wealth of symbolic association on which John might draw.

SYMBOLISM IN THE ANOINTING

Bearing in mind the connection between the larger narrative which precedes it
and the passion story which is to follow, we can ask the question of how Mary's
action in anointing Jesus is to be interpreted symbolically in the Fourth Gospel.
Symbols, as we have already seen, rarely limit themselves to one meaning, often
moving between different associations. This makes them difficult to interpret,
because it is never entirely clear which aspects of the symbolism belong within the
text and which are imported by the reader. Not all is obscure, however: there are
some dimensions that are clearly present and can be supported from other symbolic usage within the same text; and there are other readings that are arguably
alien to the text. Nevertheless between the two extremes is an uncertain area. The
question we need to ask is what features of the anointing are consonant with
John's overall symbolic perspective. There are no other episodes that include a
similar act of anointing with oil, so that our discussion will be more constricted
than with other symbols that span the whole Gospel. Nevertheless, the story of the
anointing belongs in so central a place within the literary structure of the Fourth
Gospel that it should not surprise us if its symbolic yield is large.

First of all, at the literal level, the anointing within its narrative context functions as an expression of gratitude for Jesus' gift of life to Lazarus. In the previous

scenes, the evangelist has told the story of Lazarus's death and the grief of the two
sisters. We learn of Jesus' love for the two women and their brother, and their love
for him as disciples (11:3, 5). After Lazarus's death, Jesus visits the grieving sisters
and holds conversation with Martha, where he reveals himself to her and she
responds in faith (11:25–27).[28] In what at first seems a parallel to the meeting with
Martha, Jesus encounters Mary with a crowd of mourners (11:28–37). Significantly, as the later narrative will reveal, she falls at his feet in grief and disappoint-
ment. While she too loves Jesus, she shares with Martha the sense of being
abandoned by him in her hour of need; yet it is possible that her desperation is
greater than Martha's. Indeed the whole scene is beset with grief, unlike scene 2,
where the emphasis is on the hope which transfigures death.[29] The harmony of
Mary's love for Jesus has broken down: because he delays his coming, because
Lazarus dies as a consequence, because the reality of death is so tragic and final.
Mary, though one of his disciples, is alienated. She weeps and the mourners weep,
and Jesus too begins to weep, seeming to share their grief (11:35).[30] In this manner, they proceed to the tomb where Martha reappears and Jesus—unexpectedly
for those present, yet not surprisingly for the attentive reader (11:4, 11–15)—
turns the tables on the grief, horror, tragedy, and captivity of death.

The banquet described in John 12 belongs to the same story. Once again, as in
scene 3, we find Mary at Jesus' feet; this time everything could not be more different. Now she can express her love without reservation or qualification. Now she
pours out her gratitude for the gift of her brother's life. For John, the communion
of this meal begins in the loving and grateful recognition that, for these people,
Jesus is the radiant giver of life. The family circle, broken by sickness and death in
the first scene of the narrative, is restored in the sixth scene around the table where
the members of the family gather with Jesus and his disciples. Mary's action
expresses the gratitude of the family now miraculously reunited through the life-
giving power of Jesus.[31] The anointing is fundamentally the expression of festiv-
ity and joy.[32]

Second, and paradoxically, the anointing is also "a proleptic burial ritual,"
linked not just to Lazarus's death but also to that of Jesus.[33] Mary's action is more
than an expression of gratitude, important though that is. The interpretation
given at the end of the scene presents the anointing as the perceptive recognition
of Jesus' forthcoming death: "She bought it [the perfume] so that she might keep
it for the day of my burial (12:7)." The wording of Jesus' defense is awkward, as we
have seen, but the meaning makes sense in the context of what has gone before:
Jesus' death is the consequence of what he has done in risking the return to Judea
and in raising Lazarus from the dead. Mary has anointed Jesus precisely for the
death which results from the gift of life bestowed on Lazarus. Thus, the anointing
"casts a long shadow forward to Jesus' imminent arrest, trial, condemnation, crucifixion and burial."[34] Mary's action, however, need not be interpreted as an
unconscious one: against a number of commentators, Hoskyns argues that Mary

performs an act of "intelligent devotion."[35] Similarly, Léon-Dufour comments that Mary "is the only person in the Fourth Gospel who has a sense of the mystery of the Hour."[36] Jesus defends Mary because she realizes that Jesus has given life at the cost of his own life. She knows that the journey to Lazarus's tomb is the journey to his own death (11:7–16). The cross lies at the heart of Jesus' mission to the world and Mary, perhaps alone of those present, recognizes that reality.[37] The life-giving journey to Bethany, for Jesus, is the journey to death. It may not be the last word for the Johannine Jesus, but it is a word that must be spoken. Jesus' death is the subtext of the raising of Lazarus.

At the end of scene 1, Thomas's suggestion that they accompany Jesus is courageous, recognizing that it is the pathway to death (cf. 11:8): "let us also go so that we might die with him" (11:16). In scene 6, the perfumed oil is the beginning of Jesus' embalming, the wrapping of his body in unguents that will soothe the sting of death, articulate the love of his friends, and enable them to touch his body and grieve over the loss of his presence. Mary is one of the "myrrh-bearing women," friends of Jesus, loving his body before the pain and torment of the end has even begun. Her action, anticipated at the beginning of the Lazarus story, is itself anticipatory of the end of the Johannine story in the passion and death of Jesus. Mary of Bethany joins hands with Joseph of Arimathea and Nicodemus across a barrier of days, a festival, an arrest, a trial, a crucifixion (19:39–40). As if he were already dead, she anoints his feet with costly oil, with unbound hair, with unrestrained love.

The nexus beneath life and death—the life given to Lazarus, the death faced by Jesus—is emphasized in the perfume that Mary spills over the feet of Jesus: "And the house was filled with the fragrance of the myrrh" (*hē de oikia eplērōthē ek tēs osmēs tou myrou*, 12:3). The odor is so strong that it pervades the house. In the period of Second Temple Judaism, women anointed the bodies of their beloved dead with spices and fragrant oils as a way of mourning their death and expressing their grief. But the same burial customs also pointed to life. In the second burial one year later, after the putrefaction of the flesh, the bones were laid carefully in an ossuary in hope of the resurrection of the dead: something of the soul of the departed was held to reside still in the bones (see Ezek. 37:1–14).[38] In the same way, Mary's anointing is as much about life as about death.[39] The jar of perfume, broken open in her hands, is a symbol of life and hope, the fragrance pointing symbolically to salvation.[40] The fine perfume wafting through the house contrasts with the smell of death at the tomb of Lazarus (11:39).[41] In the previous scene Martha, for all her faith, wants to protect against the smell of death, the unbearable stench of mortality. But Jesus reveals to her that, unless it is faced, the odor of death can never be transfigured into the fragrance of life. Here in scene 6, the transformation has already begun: the descent into death is paradoxically the finest moment of radiance and glory, releasing the bands of death. As in the Bethany story, the reek of death is transmuted into the fragrant odor of life. The

Bethany family has faced the reality of death and found life at its center, a life whose fragrance is infinitely stronger than the cloying stench of death. Jesus stands once more before the reader as Resurrection and Life.

In more senses than one, Judas Iscariot symbolizes in this story the forces of death, which are inimical to life (12:4–6). There is a powerful contrast drawn between the two main characters of the story (apart from Jesus himself). Both are disciples of Jesus, and both are present at the restored intimacy of the family's life. Both, in an ironic way, are connected with Jesus' death: Mary because she proclaims Jesus' death in faith and love through the anointing, and Judas because he betrays Jesus and brings about his death (13:21–30; 18:2–3). Just as Mary is exemplary as a disciple—one who "articulates the right praxis of discipleship"[42]—so Judas is the type of the false disciple. Mary is "the positive counterpart to Judas; the true female disciple is an alternative to the unfaithful male disciple."[43] But Judas's objection is not allowed to stand, as we have seen; it is neither sincere nor valid. Judas is a thief and has no concern for the poor, and the departure of Jesus is frighteningly near.[44] Even if Judas were sincere, his words would not lessen the greatness of Mary's action. Instead his response reveals the way in which evil infiltrates the life of the community. True communion is threatened here not by the external powers of death but by internal forces of petty-mindedness and greed coming from one who claims to be a follower of Jesus. The evangelist warns the reader that, even in the community of faith, there are ungenerous and destructive forces at work that would turn the fragrance of life back into the smell of decay. Jesus defeats the attempt to destroy the harmony of the family. The one who gives the gift also protects and nourishes it. In defending Mary, Jesus defends the unity of the community. Once again, life triumphs over the forces of death.[45]

At the same time, Mary of Bethany contrasts not only with Judas, but also with Caiaphas in scene 5. Once more the "contrast-parallel" is ironic.[46] Caiaphas plays a significant role in Jesus' death. On the one hand, he brings it about through the plot he instigates, justifying it on the grounds of political expediency (11:49–50, 53); on the other hand, he unwittingly prophesies Jesus' death and its true meaning "on behalf of the people," which the evangelist enlarges upon (11:51–52). Like Mary, Caiaphas indicates the significance of Jesus' death, pointing to its symbolic meaning, even if in his case unknowingly. Unlike Mary, his response to Jesus arises from fear, hatred, and political pragmatism. Just as she represents those who love Jesus and venerate him, perceiving his gift of life through death, so Caiaphas is the representative of those who hate Jesus and thus symbolize death. Friend contrasts starkly with enemy. The tragedy is that Judas finally engages on the side of Caiaphas rather than of Mary; his final decision to betray Jesus links him inexorably with the forces of darkness (cf. 13:30).

There is a further christological dimension to the theme of life and death. Edgar Bruns has argued persuasively for a royal interpretation of the anointing, partly on the basis of a story told by the second-century B.C.E. Greek historian

Polybius, in which Antiochus Epiphanes, bathing in the public baths, jokingly pours "a jar of precious ointment" (*keramion polytelestatou myrou*) over a commoner to make him smell like a king (*Histories* 36.1.12–14).[47] Bruns links this motif to the burial scene in which Nicodemus, "bearing a mixture of myrrh and aloes, about a hundred liters," anoints Jesus' body (19:39). The kingly overtones of the burial in the Johannine narrative are pronounced: the new community around Jesus "handles his body in a royal way."[48] The link with the burial is already indicated in the anointing. What the burial does is to draw out the royal significance of Jesus' identity, an identity confirmed in the passion narrative, where, with an irony that is in part intended to score off the "Jews" who have manipulated him, Pilate has Jesus scourged and crucified as a king (18:33–37; 19:2–5, 15, 19–22). The crucifixion is a kind of royal enthronement, prefigured in the anointing of his feet by Mary of Bethany.[49] Beasley-Murray sees the anointing of the *feet* as also significant in this regard, making of the event "a consecration of Jesus to royal service, i.e. to a death by which the saving sovereignty comes."[50] There are also overtones of the perfumed oil "like sweet dew and its fragrance myrrh" with which Enoch is anointed by Michael, signifying his transfiguration into the divine life (*2 Enoch* 22:9). Similarly in the vision of Isaiah, when he encounters the Lord in the temple, the prophet speaks in language that seems to be echoed in John 12:3: "the house [of the temple] was full of his glory" (*kai plērēs ho oikos tēs doxēs autou*, Isa 6:1 LXX). Both motifs, the royal and the divine, point to the Johannine crucifixion as the climax of the glorification of Jesus.

Third, Mary symbolizes the response of the community of faith to the gift of life which Jesus gives. She not only recognizes the cost of what Jesus has done in raising her brother from the dead; she also mirrors it in the costliness of her action (12:3).[51] It is not some cheap scent that she pours over Jesus' feet, but the best perfume money can buy—perhaps the whole of her life's savings.[52] As a true disciple, Mary responds to the costliness of Jesus' gift of life with the costliness of her own gift in an act of "self-giving extravagance."[53] John's theology of mutual love is exemplified in this symbolic action. Disciples are not slaves, as we have already observed, but friends and beloved of Jesus (15:15);[54] yet even so Mary illustrates the freedom of humility in her loving action.[55] The extravagance and humility of Jesus' self-gift, behind which lies the Father's bountiful love for the world, call for a response that, however feeble or inadequate in objective terms, is subjectively of the same type: self-giving love calls forth a self-giving response. Mary responds as the faith-community to the dying and undying love of Christ: pouring, in the flow of the myrrh, her own self in love for Jesus. Although at one level the two gestures hardly compare, at another level, they are comparable acts of self-sacrificing, extravagant love. Mary responds to the death of Jesus on behalf of the community of faith, in the fullness of love and adoration.

There is a fourth dimension to the story of the anointing that, while not immediately apparent, is nevertheless part of its symbolic ambience. As becomes clear in the Johannine narrative, Mary's anointing is linked symbolically to the foot-washing (13:1–17). The symbolism is too close to be coincidental—as is the near location of the two narratives and their explicit connection to Jesus' death. The parallels are striking when the two stories are placed side by side:

- Both narratives are set within the context of Passover (12:1; 13:1; cf. 19:28; 19:14, 31, 42).

- In both accounts, the meal is shared with Jesus among intimate friends and disciples and has possible sacramental overtones (12:2; 13:1, 2a, 23).

- Judas, the betrayer, is present at both and identified as treasurer of the band of disciples (12:4–6; 13:2, 11, 21–30).

- Both narratives involve the anointing/washing and drying/wiping of feet as an act of loving service and self-giving, normally performed by a slave or servant (12:3; 13:4–5).

- Both narratives are linked profoundly to Jesus' imminent death and are concerned with union between Jesus and his disciples (12:7; 13:8b–10).

- In each case, the language and symbols are extravagant and unconventional.

The one who washes the disciples' feet in water as an act of cleansing, preparation, and union (13:8) has thus already had his own feet "washed" in perfumed oil by a devoted disciple. The two acts have a similar, though not identical, quality. The vital connection between them is part of the way the narrator layers the Gospel narrative and allows one symbolic action to fold into another, revealing the interconnections. However we interpret it, Mary's anointing of Jesus' feet cannot be seen in isolation from Jesus' washing of the disciples' feet. Each assists the reader to understand and interpret the other. In this sense, the anointing prefigures the footwashing.[56] It prepares Jesus for his own death, as the narrator makes clear (11:7), and it enables the reader to interpret the footwashing aright. This is an important point, since in popular understanding, the footwashing is generally misinterpreted despite its subsequent liturgical place on Maundy Thursday. As we have already noted in an earlier chapter, the story of the anointing helps us see that the primary impulse and symbolic power of the footwashing lies in the union it forges between Jesus and the disciples, precisely as a consequence of Jesus' death; it demonstrates that "the crucifixion was Jesus' consummate act of complete self-giving love."[57] The connection with the anointing—as well as its own place in the Gospel narrative—makes clear that the footwashing is concerned first and foremost with the love between Jesus and his friends, and only in a secondary sense the outflow of love within the community of faith. This is no less than the new commandment that Jesus gives to the community he will leave behind (yet not abandon): "love one another as I have loved you" (13:34–35).

SYMBOLISM AND NEGLECT
IN THE STORY OF MARY OF BETHANY

The story of Mary's anointing is a more complex symbol than is at first apparent. In this seemingly small event, John is able to unfold a rich symbolic meaning that casts light on the meaning of discipleship and the response of faith to God's love for the world. Yet this symbolism, until more recent times, has been largely ignored. Mary's story has been left in the shadows and its symbolic meaning diminished. There are a number of reasons for this neglect of the Johannine anointing. Exegetically, the narrative has not generally been interpreted as part of the raising of Lazarus. Not being seen adequately within its narrative context has meant that, as a small pericope in the larger narrative of Jesus' impending death, it is all too easy to bypass. But unless the anointing is seen as integral both to the Lazarus story and to Jesus' own story, the subtle dynamics between life and death are lost. Only within the larger story does Mary's action come into its own and unfold its true, symbolic meaning.

Second, the relative obscurity of this Johannine episode, divorced from its narrative context, is underlined when Mary of Bethany's action is viewed as an unconscious one. We are on difficult ground here, since the text says nothing overt about Mary's own knowledge of what is taking place; Mary herself does not speak. Yet, if we interpret her action as a prophetic sign, there is no reason to doubt that she is unaware of what she is doing. If the disciples can perceive that Jesus' visit to Bethany will result in his death (11:8), why cannot Mary? This is especially so considering the extraordinary response to the raising of Lazarus by "the Jews" with whom Mary herself is associated in scenes 3 and 5. The threat to Lazarus's life in the final scene of the narrative likewise accentuates the danger of Jesus' action and its repercussions both for himself and for others. It does not take an extraordinary degree of intelligence to perceive something of the political implications of what Jesus has done in raising Lazarus from the dead. Indeed, one could argue that only such intelligent knowledge on Mary's part makes sense of the extravagance of what she does. Instead Mary has been interpreted as someone who responds only to immediate feelings, without forethought, reinforcing the stereotype of women as emotionally volatile and reactive rather than proactive. In the context of her first meeting with Jesus (11:32), for example, she is described as "nothing but a complaining woman" and "hysterical."[58] Yet John's portrait of Mary, on the contrary, highlights her role as an exemplary disciple—particularly in the contrast between her response to Jesus and that of Caiaphas and Judas—whose love for Jesus is perceptive and intelligent as well as intuitive.

Third, subsequent church tradition has exacerbated the problem and diminished even further the symbolic meaning of this Johannine story. The early church, particularly in the Western tradition, conflated all the anointing stories and merged them with the character of Mary Magdalene, the supposedly penitent whore. Perhaps this is easy to understand when there are so many Marys in the Gospels, but there is also an androcentric note to this harmonizing: the tendency to sideline female characters and not take the trouble to read their stories with the same care and attention accorded to male characters. As a result, Mary is seen not as an exemplary disciple, revealing the authentic response of the true disciple to Jesus, but as a sinner whose repentance is articulated in the anointing of his body. Without demeaning the Lukan story, which has its own distinctive power, it is vital that the Johannine story be accorded its own integrity and read with its own symbolic associations, very different from its Synoptic equivalents. Once that is done, its fully symbolic meaning can emerge, along with its vital role in the unfolding drama of Jesus' glorification.

CONCLUSION

The anointing of Jesus' feet by Mary of Bethany, once it has stepped from the shadows and been given its rightful place within the narrative of the Fourth Gospel, is a vibrant symbol of the life that comes through death. The story works on two levels, that of death and that of life. The oil is myrrh for anointing the body of the beloved dead, yet its fragrance points to the joyful and festive overcoming of death: the hope of a life that transcends death and replaces the stench of decay with the fragrant odor of life. In this sense, it points to and anticipates the glorification of Jesus on the cross.[59] The oil becomes a symbol of the life-giving journey from death to life. In this sense the sequence of the larger narrative (11:1–12:11) is "not only the story of Lazarus raised to life, it is also the story of Jesus going to face death in order to conquer death."[60] Mary's symbolic action reveals once more the presence of divine glory within the flesh.

The anointing symbolizes also the communion that disciples share with Jesus. That this relationship is mutual and reciprocal is made clear in the symbolism: the costliness of Jesus' gift of life is reciprocated by Mary's extravagant gesture. There are both ritual and sensuous overtones in her gestures and actions. Her caressing of Jesus' feet is the ritual adoration directed to the one who, in the Johannine view, replaces the temple as the locus of true worship (2:13–22; 4:19–26). The unashamed nature of the physical contact confirms the incarnation and the sanctity of the flesh. Hair, feet, hands are offered to the beloved in response to his divine self-giving in the flesh. The very tangibility of the symbolism opens a meaning that is both spiritual and embodied. Desire and intimacy lie at the core of discipleship. Mary's action exemplifies the love of the true disciple for the divine Lover who has given himself, body and soul, for the life of his friends

(15:13).[61] In this sense, Mary of Bethany represents the community of faith in its love and abiding.

At the same time, Mary's anointing prepares the reader for the footwashing, when Jesus will turn to the feet of his disciples, as Mary has placed herself at his. In his washing of their feet, Jesus will draw them into union with himself, purifying and transfiguring them in relationship with him. The same love is to be the basis of their life as a community in their "washing" of one another's feet (whether we are to understand this ritually and/or metaphorically). Just as Mary of Bethany exemplifies the love and devotion of the true disciple for Jesus, so disciples are to extend the same love and hospitality toward one another. Such love is the gift of the Spirit-Paraclete, who will not leave the disciples orphaned but will be made manifest in their love for one another (14:16–18), making dynamically present the one who is absent. The anointing is a powerful symbol of that paternal yet maternal love into which disciples are called, a love that has its origins and goal in the intimate life of God.

CHAPTER 9

Resurrection and Life: Symbols of Easter

I was a nest
built of old stolen things, hidden amongst thorns,
you sought me out
and made your home in me.
Let the sunlight grow upon the rocks,

for I was cold
until I felt your touch, I was the coldest stone
before I saw you rise in rising hands.
I was blind as stone
and you have made me into your eye.[1]

S O FAR WE HAVE EXAMINED various symbols in the Fourth Gospel that reveal the meaning of salvation in John's understanding. Mostly these symbols have stretched across the Gospel narrative, although in the case of the anointing the symbolism is restricted (more or less) to the one story. The presence of Easter symbolism is more complicated. On the one hand, it is confined to two narrative contexts: the raising of Lazarus (11:1–12:11) and the resurrection narratives (John 20–21). On the other hand, the whole Gospel is permeated with the closely related concept of life, which is the central theme of the Fourth Gospel and probably represents a reworking of the Synoptic understanding of the *basileia* (reign/realm) of God:

> In him was life, and the life was the light of human beings.
> And the light shines in the darkness,
> and the darkness has not apprehended it. (1:4–5)

> These things are written that you may believe
> that Jesus is the Christ the Son of God,
> and that, believing, you may have life in his name. (20:31)

The Johannine understanding of life is multidimensional, incorporating material and spiritual, human and natural, present and future, human and divine. "Eternal life" (*zōē anōnios*), although in continuity with physical life, nonetheless has a divine power that defies death and transforms present existence in the shape of resurrection. The great paradox, for John, is that the one who is the source of the life of creation has become incarnate, entering into the natural world and trans-figuring its life with divine glory. Within a broad, Johannine perspective, this chapter explores Easter symbols through the lens of two stories: the meeting of Martha with Jesus after the death of her brother, which is the second scene in the raising of Lazarus (11:17–27),[2] and the meeting of Mary Magdalene with Jesus after his resurrection (20:1–18).[3]

It may seem strange to link Martha and Mary Magdalene in this way, especially given the closer literary connection between Martha and Mary of Bethany, who occupy parallel places in a chiastic structure and make confession of their faith in word and deed. Nevertheless, though separated by a narrative gulf, the stories of Martha and Mary Magdalene are interlinked theologically by the explicit theme of resurrection. In the first story, the meeting with Jesus takes place toward the end of Jesus' public ministry in a narrative that is in many respects the watershed of the Gospel, bringing the first half to a climax and setting in motion the second half. In the second story, almost at the end of the Gospel, the occasion is the first in which a grieving disciple is transformed by the discovery of Easter. In both, the women confront death and struggle to comprehend that it is not the last word. Jesus takes seriously the sincerity of their desire to understand the symbols denot-ing his risen presence. In both, Jesus reveals himself as sovereign over life and death, the one who has unique authority to "lay down my life in order that I might take it up again" (10:17). In John's Gospel, Easter symbolism is given initially to women.

RESURRECTION AND ITS BACKGROUND

The Old Testament affirms unquestionably that God is the source of life: not only Israel's life but also the life of creation. All life—human, animal, plant, mineral—has its origins in God's creative word and is sustained by that dynamic word from day to day. There is no life that exists outside the provenance of God: unlike later forms of Gnostic thought, creation in its inherent goodness has its origin in divine power and generativity and its final destiny in the eternal being and covenant love of God. Life is the supreme good, lived before the face of a gracious God.[4] Despite this unswerving commitment to God as the giver of life, the Old Testament is slow to develop a belief in the resurrection of the dead; for the most part, death is "the end of any meaningful existence for the individual."[5] Sheol is the place of the dead, "a vast underground region, dark and dusty," where the shades of the departed live a shadowy and forgotten life, a mere glimmering of mortal life that is a nonlife, separated from the living and from God (Eccl. 3:19–21; Pss. 6:5; 30:3; 86:13; 104:29).[6] Salvation has a this-wordly quality to it, a vigorous concern with the here and now and the realities of life in the present. As God's supreme gift, life is disconnected from any notion of resurrection; in fact, no doctrine of the resurrection "could have been arrived at by reflection on the Old Testament."[7] Resurrection is a relatively late belief in Jewish thought.

Those references which seem to indicate a notion of resurrection in the Old Testament are surprisingly diverse and need to be interpreted with caution: it is too easy to read back later notions into the text.[8] The earliest occurrences use resurrection as a metaphor for the restoration of Israel as a nation, in the context of exile, without any sense of individual survival or revival after death, as in Ezekiel's vision of the valley of dry bones (Ezek. 37:1–14). Yet, though late in coming, in another sense belief in the resurrection is far from alien to the spirit of Old Testament theology. Whatever Persian or other influence there has been on the development of the concept, when it finally appears within Israel it is grounded in much older Old Testament understandings of God's covenant love, faithfulness, and saving justice.[9]

The notion of the individual dead rising again emerges during the Maccabæan period, appearing first in the apocalypse of Daniel, where it refers to faithful Jews and their oppressors:

> Many of those who sleep in the dust of the earth shall awake,
> some to everlasting life,
> and some to shame and everlasting contempt. (Dan. 12:2; cf. Isa. 26:19)

The experience of persecution and martyrdom under Antiochus Epiphanes in the second century B.C.E.—who tried to outlaw the Torah and bring Judaism under Hellenistic domination—gave rise to the need for a belief that the death of the martyrs was not in vain: that their deeds would be rewarded and their self-sacrifice vindicated by God. This belief was part of an apocalyptic outlook in which hope was seen to be grounded in the final intervention of God at the end of history to overpower evil and inaugurate God's reign. In the apocalyptic writings of the intertestamental period, belief in personal resurrection became more prominent (e.g., *1 Enoch* 22–27; 92–105; 2 Macc. 7), sometimes alongside belief in the immortality of the soul (e.g., Wis. 3:1–6).[10] This apocalyptic perspective was shared by a number of groups within Judaism, particularly the Pharisees, who held to belief in the resurrection of the dead as God's final word on creation and history (as opposed to the Sadducees, who denied any life beyond death: Mark 12:18–27 pars.; Acts 23:6–9; Josephus, *Jewish War* 2.162–66). Resurrection beliefs were diverse within the Judaism of the intertestamental period, rejected by some altogether and accepted by others in various forms. Some believed only in the resurrection of the righteous; others included the wicked; some believed in a universal resurrection of the dead, with rewards and punishment after death; others in the immortality of the soul.

Under the influence of these later Jewish developments, the New Testament believes that the final, eschatological intervention of God—the inbreaking of God's reign and the giving of eternal life—has already begun to take place. Jesus of Nazareth in his life, death, and resurrection is the definitive sign of that apocalyptic, divine presence. Pheme Perkins shows that "Resurrection comes into prominence in Christianity," creating a new sense of hope and expectation that is by no means universal within the diverse world of pre–70 C.E. Judaism.[11] For the New Testament, God's eschatological future has already burst in upon the world, overcoming evil and vindicating goodness, signified above all in the Easter events. In Christ, the end of the old age and the beginning of the new has arrived. Yet the New Testament struggles to make sense of that eschatological conviction alongside awareness of the ongoing reality of the world in which the early communities must make their way. Different New Testament theologies have different ways of understanding the impact of the eschatological advent of Christ.

The Fourth Gospel represents one strand in New Testament theology, emphasizing the capacity of God's future in Jesus Christ to transform the present moment. The future coming of the Son of Man in glory is already realized in the incarnation (1:14, 51); the final judgment has arrived (3:18–21; 5:24–25). The resurrection is a dynamic, existential reality for the believing community (11:25–26); the unbelieving *kosmos* is already overcome (16:33b), and the community now lives in celestial peace, joy, love, and unity (13:34; 14:27). In short, as the central theme of the Fourth Gospel, eternal life is not primarily a future experience for the individual believer after death but a "present possession" (3:16).[12] As Schnackenburg outlines it, the uniquely Johannine concept of eternal life is grounded in Christology, overcomes mortality in the present, gives life on earth its meaning, signifies a sharing in the life of God, and possesses both moral and sacramental dimensions.[13] Yet, while holding strongly to this perspective, John is not without awareness of that which is unfinal and still awaiting eschatological consummation (5:28–29; 15:18–16:4a), the two dimensions often intertwined. The narratives we are about to examine, reflecting the influence of Jewish apocalypticism and Synoptic traditions,[14] illustrate the Johannine concern with resurrection as a distinctly (though not exclusively) present reality.

MARTHA AND RESURRECTION

Jesus' self-revelation to Martha is not the first reference to the resurrection in the Fourth Gospel (cf. 2:19–22; 10:17–18), but it is the first time Jesus reveals himself as "resurrection and life" in an "I am" saying and within the actual context of death. Martha's story begins with the illness of the sisters' beloved brother, Lazarus (11:1), and their summoning of Jesus to attend the sickbed of "the one whom you love" (11:3). Mary's name is mentioned first at the beginning, perhaps because of the reference to the anointing which will immediately follow (11:1–2), but a little later it is "Martha and her sister" (11:5). The response to the request is mysterious, but—given earlier examples of Jesus' reaction to the request for a "sign" (2:5; 4:47)—not entirely unexpected: first, Jesus uses characteristic glory language to imply that a "sign" is about to take place (cf. 2:11), and, second, he delays his departure for two days (11:6). The narrator clearly feels it necessary to assure the reader, however, that the delay is not due to lack of love for the family (11:5); Jesus' motivation is very different. The inscrutable delay is somehow linked to the revelation of glory we are about to witness.

The scene that follows is of vital importance (scene 2), disclosing the Johannine understanding of the "sign" which is about to occur.[15] Unusually, the dialogue occurs before rather than after the "sign." Despite the Johannine language which challenges the seeming hopelessness of the situation (11:4, 9, 11–15), the reader is not surprised that Jesus' arrival, four days after the burial (11:17), meets with reproach. The grieving Martha goes out to meet him, convinced that his delay has cost her brother his life: "Lord, if you had been here, my brother would not have died" (11:21). Not being present to hear what Jesus has to say about her brother's illness and death, Martha has missed the crucial Johannine pointers to the true significance of the delay (although later the Johannine Jesus will speak as if she has not, 11:40): "This illness is not for death [*pros thanaton*] but for the sake of God's glory [*tēs doxēs tou theou*], that the Son of God might be gloried through it" (11:4); "Lazarus our friend [*ho philos hēmōn*] has fallen asleep; but I am going to wake him up" (11:11).

Yet Martha's reproach to Jesus, for all the grief and anger it contains, is also a partial statement of faith.[16] This is clear not just in her conviction of Jesus' healing power but also in her openness to the future and her confident belief that God's presence is still operative in Jesus: "even now I know that whatever you ask of God, God will give you" (11:22).[17] When Jesus introduces Easter symbols, Martha's faith, though real, is limited to the future: like the Samaritan woman in 4:25, she is restricted in her sense of divine timing or eschatology (cf. "and now is," 4:23). As a result, her understanding of Jesus' identity, in Johannine terms, is deficient. Symbols of life for Martha are confined to the structures of human experience and, at least in the present age, within the bounds of mortality. The issue is not the lack of a religious or faith perspective but rather the inability to see how the incarnation has radically reshaped the human agenda: its structures, timetable, hopes, and expectations. Martha's faith reflects both Jewish apocalyptic thinking and more futuristic Christian accounts of the significance of Easter; it is not yet Johannine. Like Mary Magdalene later in the narrative, we are presented with a woman of faith whose distress is comprehensible but whose cramped vision of God's advent in human history is about to be enlarged beyond her dreams. Martha is imprisoned within her conviction of the finality of death in the here and now as much as Lazarus is bound in the fetters of the tomb. Her understanding of Jesus is caged in mortal bounds.

As often in Johannine narrative, Martha's misunderstanding serves an important function in facilitating the revelation. Jesus clarifies her misapprehension on both levels, the eschatological and the christological, in the central affirmation of the narrative:

> I am the resurrection and the life.
> The one believing in me, even if he [she] dies will live,
> and everyone living and believing in me will never die.

> *egō eimi hē anastasis kai hē zōē;*
> *ho pisteuōn eis eme kan apothanę zēsetai,*
> *kai pas ho zōn kai pisteuōn eis eme ou mē apothanę*
>   *eis ton aiōna.* (11:25–26)[18]

Several aspects of this self-revelation are immediately apparent. Unlike most of the Old Testament, resurrection and life are inextricably interwoven, the one inseparable from the other: "eternal life" and "resurrection life" are one and the same thing. Unlike Jewish apocalyptic thinking, the word order, in placing resurrection first, indicates that Jesus is not speaking of the future when earthly life is ended but rather the present, in the midst of mortal life. Moreover, the meaning of the whole is bound up with Jesus' identity as the Son who has divine authority to give life (5:19–30).

The couplet in the second and third lines is a form of Hebrew parallelism, but it is unclear in what sense "life" and "death" are to be understood. In one interpretation, the two lines reflect "synonymous parallelism," in which both statements say much the same thing. Life and death are vividly contrasted in this view, yet with different nuances of meaning: physical death contrasts with eternal life in the first, and physical life contrasts with eternal death in the second.[19] In each case, life and death move between the literal and the metaphorical. The problem with this reading, however, is that the phrase "the one living" (in the sense of earthly life) in the second line seems redundant and clumsy. A better view is that of "synthetic parallelism" in which the second line does not simply repeat the first but advances it significantly.[20] In this interpretation, whereas death is used literally in the first line, it is more comprehensive in the second; "life" means "eternal life" in both cases. Thus we have a kind of staircase effect, familiar already from the Prologue (1:1–2), in which the second line takes the first further. For those who believe, death in an eternal sense can have no power:

> The believer who dies will live; the living believer will never die.... In both cases the life in question is eternal life ... which does not yield to either physical death, however real, or the "death forever" which cannot touch the believer.[21]

Death in the first case is literal and in the second symbolic. Life in both instances signifies life in Christ. In the simplicity yet complexity of Jesus' self-revelation, death is presented literally and symbolically, the evangelist pointing to the different levels at which resurrection life is to be understood. Though it has a future dimension in the final overthrow of death through faith ("whoever believes in me, even though they die, will live," 11:25), resurrection is already bountifully present; even now death cannot quench the life which Jesus gives and embodies (11:26).

Martha's response to the revelation is eager and unhesitating: "Yes, Lord, I have come to believe [*pepisteuka*] that you are the Messiah/Christ, the Son of God, the one coming into the world" (11:27). The problem is whether Martha has understood Jesus' self-revelation and grasped its meaning or still misunderstands. On the one side, Sandra Schneiders has argued that Martha's confession of faith is "the most fully developed in the Fourth Gospel"; she needs no "sign" to convince her who Jesus is.[22] That is why, later in the narrative, she falters at the tomb (11:34), according to Schneiders: not because of inadequacy in her faith, but because she cannot imagine that the resurrection embodied in Jesus will be anticipated for her brother.[23] At the other extreme, Moloney argues that Martha's response to Jesus' self-revelation is arrogant and closed-minded, based on inadequate titles that fail dismally to convey the plenitude of Johannine Christology.[24]

It may well be that Martha's confession of faith is more complex than either of these positions suggests. On the one hand, Martha's use of the titles is not in itself problematic. The critical issue with christological titles is not their use in Judaism or early Christianity but the way their meaning is shaped and developed in the Johannine narrative. The ending of John 20 uses the two main titles Martha employs—the Christ, the Son of God (*ho Christos, ho huios tou theou*, 20:31)—in its summary of the evangelical purpose of the Gospel. Their meaning has been expanded by John's unfolding narrative and Christology. Martha's third "title"— if it is a title—corresponds to the Prologue where the true Light is described as "coming into the world" (*to phōs to alēthinon . . . erchomenon eis ton kosmon*, 1:9; *ho eis ton kosmon erchomenos*, 11:27). On the basis of the titles alone, therefore, we cannot reject Martha's understanding as deficient. On the other hand, her lack of enthusiasm at the tomb needs to be taken seriously as suggesting a limited faith: "Lord, he already smells [*ēdē ozei*], for it is the fourth day" (11:39). It is more likely that Martha is unsure whether Jesus' authority extends to death than that her faith has become so otherworldly that earthly "signs" and symbols are no longer needful. Such a reading seems overly spiritualized in a Gospel that confirms the centrality of the flesh in its christological understanding.

There is one conclusion to be drawn from this seemingly conflicting evidence: Martha both understands and fails to understand at the same time. Her objection at the tomb suggests that she still does not fully comprehend the "now" of his presence. She fails to understand that the raising of her brother is a symbol pointing to Jesus' eschatological identity in the here and now, and thus to his own resurrection. She does not perceive that death has been challenged by the advent of Jesus and now represents a penultimate rather than an ultimate reality. In this sense, she has not yet grasped in full the radical nature of Jesus' self-revelation.

This need not imply that Martha's faith has not developed in the dialogue with Jesus or that her confession is insincere, misguided, or shallow. Her emphatic "yes" (*nai*) indicates that, to a considerable extent, she has grasped what Jesus is saying, even if not its full implications. Like other characters in the Gospel of John, Martha is still learning. Her confession of faith is like that of Peter in the Synoptic Gospels, in more ways than one (Mark 8:30 pars.).[25] Just as Peter confesses his faith in Jesus as the Messiah/Christ, yet moments after—at least in Mark and Matthew—is attempting to turn Jesus from the way of the cross (Mark 8:32 par.), so Martha comprehends something vital of Jesus' identity but attempts to turn him away from the tomb (and thus his own destiny). She is able to make the basic Christian confession yet is still discovering its meaning. Like Peter's in the Synoptics, Martha's confession of faith is one of the most important in the Gospel, indicated by its central place in the Johannine narrative and by its proximity to Jesus' dramatic self-revelation.

As elsewhere in the Fourth Gospel, the narrative operates on two levels, the literal and the symbolic. In John's symbolic world, the physical/carnal level is essential in order to open up the eternal; it is in no sense irrelevant. For Martha, the symbol of resurrection is the raising of her brother, the central section of the chiasm (11:28–44) and part of the core revelation of the Gospel. As the story unfolds, this event becomes the physical "sign" that points to and conveys the symbolic meaning. Relevant to this are the parallels between the raising of Lazarus and the resurrection of Jesus, apparent not only theologically but also in the narrative similarities:

- the arrival at the tomb (11:38; 20:1)
- the grief and faith of the women present
- the cavelike tomb with its heavy stone, which has first to be removed (11:38–39, 41; 20:1)
- the reference to the headcloth (*soudarion*, 11:44; 20:7)
- the need to be freed from the grave-clothes (11:44; 20:6–7)[26]

Suggestions of the death of Jesus are already present from the beginning of the Lazarus story: in the danger of Jesus' presence so close to Jerusalem and his opponents (11:16; cf. 10:39), and in his sudden grief and anger as he approaches the tomb (11:33, 35, 38).[27] The theme of Easter faith pervades both narratives. Just as the other "signs" in the first half of the Gospel reveal the eternal through the physical—the divine glory through the structures of the flesh—so the death of Lazarus and his emergence from the tomb, at the authoritative summons of Jesus (11:43; cf. 5:25), symbolize the dying and rising Christ, who is the seed that is buried in order to bear "much fruit" (*polyn karpon*, 12:24). The narrator does not tell us whether Martha in the end comes to understand this message fully, although it may be inferred from her active presence at the dinner afterwards (12:2). In some respects, her faith story is taken up and completed by her sister Mary in the anointing.

THE RESURRECTION AND MARY MAGDALENE

These parallels attest to the importance of reading the one "Easter" narrative in relation to the other. Mary Magdalene's story, though in one sense very different, is similar in a number of respects to that of Martha. In John 20:1–18 we encounter another woman of faith who comes face-to-face with the reality of death and struggles to understand how the "I am" of Jesus' self-revelation overcomes nature's last and final word. Both women move from a less adequate to a fuller and more comprehensive faith in Jesus as "the resurrection and the life." While Martha's narrative may seem more obviously symbolic, Mary Magdalene is also confronted by the symbols of Easter. Yet not till she grasps the divine reality to which the symbols point can she respond appropriately and receive the message of the resurrection.

There are a number of literary problems with the narrative of 20:1–18 that indicate the presence of editorial seams:

- Mary says that "we" have discovered the tomb empty (11:2), even though she has gone alone.

- The mini-story of the race to the tomb is surprising in itself, yet also left strangely unresolved: the beloved disciple is said to believe (apparently on the basis of seeing the headcloth, 11:8), but the narrator then tells us that neither yet "believed the Scripture that it was necessary for him to rise from the dead" (11:9).

- Mary's presence at the tomb is abrupt and, oddly enough, the other two disciples do not address her; nor does the beloved disciple communicate his "faith" to her; instead they return home and she is left alone at the tomb (20:11).

- Apart from the grave-clothes, the tomb seems otherwise empty when Peter and the beloved disciple investigate, but when Mary Magdalene stoops to look in (for the first time?) she sees two angels present and the text says nothing about the grave-clothes or headcloth (20:6–7, 12).

It is likely that John is drawing on earlier Synoptic traditions of the empty tomb (Mark 16:1–8 pars.), but has modified them: first to exclude reference to the other women at the tomb and second to include the story of the race to the tomb. The evangelist's reason for the former is not difficult to surmise: there is a preference throughout the Johannine narrative to depict Jesus encountering individuals rather than the group. Why John has included the race to the tomb, and in so awkward a way, is more complex. Part of the evangelist's agenda throughout the Farewell Discourse and passion narrative is to situate the beloved disciple in the places of honor, thus vindicating the Johannine tradition (13:23; 19:25–27). The beloved disciple achieves status here through his association with both Peter and Mary Magdalene. Yet the narrator seems anxious not to disturb what may be the format of the original tale: Peter's (the apostles'?) lack of faith and Magdalene's belief in the risen Lord (cf. Matt. 28:8–10; Luke 24:8–10). To retain the full impact of Mary's story in its Johannine form, moreover, requires that she be the first to reach Easter faith: "recognition stories" in the Gospels are not nearly as convincing where they come later in the series of appearances.[28] At the same time, the evangelist wants to find a way of incorporating the beloved disciple into the domain of Easter faith and in a position of some superiority to Peter). The resultant narrative is confused, torn between conflicting requirements: the two men run to the tomb; the beloved disciple reaches it first but does not enter (20:4–5); Peter arrives and goes straight in (20:5); Peter does not believe, but the beloved disciple does on the basis of the headcloth (20:8);[29] neither believes the Scriptures about the resurrection from the dead (20:9); the beloved disciple does not tell Mary of his "faith"; the two men go home without speaking to Mary; she is the first to meet and believe in the risen Christ.

This literary awkwardness, despite various imaginative attempts to explain it, is finally irresolvable, serving also to explain why John 21 is needed in order to clarify the confusion. What is interesting, however, is the desire of many to rescue the beloved disciple from his literary uncertainty—usually at the cost of Mary Magdalene. In this reading, she contrasts unfavorably with the beloved disciple and he emerges as superior to her.[30] Whereas he exemplifies the true faith that needs no sight (cf. 20:29), Mary tends to be depicted as a helpless, dependent woman who seeks Jesus but foolishly misses her cues, only reaching Easter faith after her sight has been bombarded with symbols of new life. The gender dimensions of this misreading of the Johannine narrative are of some significance, although it must be added that Thomas too shares a similar fate. In John 21, however, the gender problem moves from its interpreters to the text itself: the meeting of the risen Lord with the seven disciples is counted as the "third" resurrection narrative, presumably discounting the appearance to Mary Magdalene (21:14).[31]

Despite these qualifications and the awkwardness of the Johannine text, the story of Mary Magdalene has a recognizable literary integrity that manages to survive the inconsistencies. Along with the Thomas story (20:24–30), the narrative of John 20:1–18 frames the giving of the Spirit (20:19–23), which exercises a centripetal force on the narrative of John 20.[32] Each scene in this literary frame is linked directly to the glorification/exaltation of Jesus, and each contains Easter symbols that the characters struggle to understand within the context of the giving of the Spirit-Paraclete by the risen Christ:

a   *At the empty tomb on Easter morning* (20:1–18)

   • Magdalene finds the tomb empty
   • Peter and the beloved disciple come to the tomb and return home

- Magdalene encounters the risen Christ at the tomb
- She receives the "apostolic" commission

b *In a room in Jerusalem on Easter night* (20:19–23)

- The risen One comes to the waiting disciples and shows his wounds
- He gives them the gift of peace
- They receive the commission for mission
- They are empowered with the life-giving Spirit

a¹ *In a room in Jerusalem one week later* (20:24–29)

- Thomas is absent on Easter night
- He does not believe the testimony of the others
- He encounters the risen Christ one week later
- Through confession of faith, he opens the door to future believers

c *Summation of the Gospel* (20:30–31)

It could be argued that this schema relegates Peter and the beloved disciple to minor roles have, despite their importance elsewhere in the Fourth Gospel. However, to claim that the faith of the beloved disciple is central to John 20 ignores what we have already seen of the ambiguity of 20:8–9. We know already that he has a unique relationship to Jesus and that he believes more than Peter at this point, but what that "more" is we do not yet know.[33] This interpretation is strengthened by the fact that the beloved disciple's response in 20:8 has, surprisingly, no narrative impact.[34]

From the beginning of the first scene, we recognize Mary Magdalene as a woman of faith whose credentials have been established at the foot of the cross (19:25). She is one in a group of four women disciples who, along with the beloved disciple, have witnessed Jesus' exaltation on the cross. The Easter narrative thus begins with a disciple who has shown herself faithful, who has seen Jesus' life-giving glory in death and whose fidelity has brought her to the tomb. Unlike the Synoptics, the narrator gives no reason for her coming: either to anoint the body (Mark 16:1; Luke 23:55–24:1) or to view the tomb (Matt. 28:1). Yet Mary's understanding, like that of other disciples at this point, is limited (see 19:38–42). As with Martha, Mary Magdalene sees death as an ultimate reality rather than penultimate; she does not realize that Jesus is "the resurrection and the life." She too is bound by the chains and fetters of mortality. In the darkness, upon her first arrival at the tomb, she presumably cannot see inside the tomb but surmises that it is empty from the position of the stone.[35] But the stone rolled away is paradoxically the sign of a living presence that she fails to perceive; the garden likewise has symbolic overtones of life that are lost on her. For Mary, the emptiness, even in the garden, underlines only the dull sense of a dead absence. Her only explanation is that "they" (an unspecified group) have robbed the tomb (20:2). Thus Mary responds to the empty tomb as Martha does when confronted by the tomb filled with her brother's corpse (11:34). Mary's reaction is to turn to others with the dreadful news of the despoliation of the grave. But though her brothers in faith try to assist, in the end they have nothing to say (20:3–10).[36] Their inadequate response in this respect acts as a foil to Mary: Peter's lack of faith and the beloved disciple's silence contrast with her persistence (20:11). Their departure instead focuses the reader's attention on Mary's faith and the determination of her search.

The ambivalence of Mary's faith is demonstrated in her tears, which begin once her fellow disciples leave (20:10). The weeping suggests frustration as well as grief and creates in turn further misunderstanding. Because she is overcome by tears, Mary fails to recognize the Easter symbols which point to a transformed existence, just as she has failed to interpret aright the symbolism of the stone rolled away from the tomb. The angels inside the tomb sympathetically question her, implying that her tears are extraordinary enough to warrant explanation: "Woman, why do you weep?" (20:13a). Their raiment is celestial, its "whiteness" signifying divine light, and their posture, at either end of the stone slab on which the body lay (20:12), suggests symbolically the ark of the covenant: at each end golden cherubim faced each other, their outstretched wings covering the mercy seat (Exod. 37:7–9).[37] Mary's tears blind her to these symbols and she reiterates her misapprehension of the significance of the empty tomb (20:13b). The drama of misunderstanding rises as the Easter symbols intensify. When she comes face-to-face with the Lord himself, she likewise fails to recognize his living presence. Instead she mistakes him for the gardener, in a very literal sense, so set is she in her conviction that the body has been stolen (20:14; cf. Gen. 2:8–9). The garden symbolism is as lost to her as is that of the angels or the presence of the divine "Gardener": all the symbols of vibrant, resurrection life confirm her only in the conviction of death and desecration. Yet, despite misunderstanding, Mary at no point abandons her search to leave for home. Behind her tears are love and determination as well as misunderstanding.[38] It is this persistence in exploring the symbols—even though she does not at first recognize them as such—which is finally rewarded when Magdalene, hearing her name, turns back and joyfully recognizes the Lord (20:16).

The simple, double naming in this encounter, *Mariam* and *Rabbouni* ("my teacher"), is of great significance for the evangelist. Mary Magdalene's naming of Christ occurs in response to his naming of her, which is itself symbolic—names in the ancient world having the power to evoke identity and presence, as well as relationship (20:16). Behind this lies the pastoral symbolism of John 10:1–18.[39] Mary reveals herself as one of the flock, responding in faith to the voice of the Good Shepherd (10:3); she enters the fold of which he is the Gate (10:7, 9). "The true life-giving ruler of the Paradise (Garden) of God has called his own sheep by name, and she knows His voice."[40] In John 10, the Shepherd is good (*kalos*) because he gives life to the sheep through the laying down and taking up of his life (10:15, 17–18). Because of her presence at the cross and empty tomb, Mary implicitly perceives this: she recognizes the authority (*exousia*) of the one who, in obedience to the Father, has laid down his life in order to take it up again. It is on this basis that she responds with "Rabbouni," expressing love for Jesus as well as understanding of his teaching. Some have seen Mary's response as inadequate, particularly in comparison to Thomas's words to the risen Christ (20:28).[41] Yet Mary's declaration is affectionate rather than confessional at this point, as her reversion to the mother tongue (Aramaic) suggests: it is the reunion with her beloved Teacher that is uppermost in her mind.[42] In her study of Mary Magdalene, Carla Ricci emphasizes Mary's extraordinary depth and intensity of feeling and sees the image of double naming as a numinous moment in the narrative. Here Magdalene discovers her true self in relationship to Jesus:

> in hearing herself called, the woman finds at the same time the voice she knows, the voice of the other, and now here of the Other, and finds herself, her perception and understanding of her own depths. The relationship, this contemporaneous double meeting with the other with herself, in which otherness and identity are both present, this unity that includes duality, could be comprehensively such only in the manifestation of the Risen Christ to a woman . . . Mary, after the uncontainable sorrow of losing, is now completely filled with the joy of finding what she sought.[43]

Mary's depth of experience enables us to feel both the desolation at the beginning and later the overpowering joy of rediscovery and awakening. Mary's name has been spoken by the one whose voice she assumed to be silent for ever. Like Martha, her loved one has been restored to her. She is like the lover in the Song of Songs who loses, seeks, and finally recovers her beloved (Cant. 3:1–4).[44]

The self-revelation of the Shepherd to Mary is unfolded in the following verses. Jesus uses the language of ascent to clarify further misunderstanding (20:17).[45] What is revealed to her is the confirmation of Jesus' promise in the Farewell Discourse: his final presence with the community is to be symbolically through the Paraclete (see 14:26; 15:26; 16:7–11, 13–15). The revelation to Mary relates to the promised sending of the Spirit. The Good Shepherd reveals himself to her and Mary responds with faith and understanding, as the witness to his crucifixion and resurrection/ascension.[46] The result of her meeting with Jesus is that she comes to Easter faith. This is based on misunderstanding and struggle, yet arises from the response of faith to which she gives expression. She becomes the recipient of revelation for the reader—a revelation communicated by the Lord himself.

Further misunderstanding is implied by Jesus' command that Mary not "touch" him (*mē mou haptou*, 20:17). Exegetically the problem is why Jesus, after Mary's search and suffering, seems to repel her. Moreover, why, having asked her not to touch him, does he later invite Thomas to do so (20:27)? The problem is largely resolved by noting the present tense of the imperative, which conveys the sense of ongoing aspect: literally, "do not go on touching me."[47] Again the narrative presents Mary in a positive and sympathetic light: what she does in reaching out to Jesus is a natural response. In one sense she is right to assume that Jesus is to remain with her; what she still misunderstands is the symbolic mode of that presence. Jesus distances himself because his abiding with Mary is not to be in the old way, as she supposes, but rather in the Spirit and through the life of the apostolic community (cf. 20:22).[48] The problem is not with her touching him, therefore, but rather with her holding to him.[49] As before, understanding coalesces with misunderstanding. Both aspects are intrinsic to the revelation which follows, and both enable Jesus to unfold the symbolic meaning of Easter. His return to the Father is incomplete until he confirms in full the gift of the Spirit. His risen flesh remains a symbolic reality (*symbolum et verum*, "symbol and truth"), even in his resurrection.

There is a further symbolic dimension to the revelation Mary Magdalene receives, arising from the commission of 20:17. The expression "my brothers and sisters" (*adelphoi*), which, as we have already seen, is generic rather than confined to the Twelve—not a major category in the Fourth Gospel's understanding of the community (cf. 6:67, 70, 71; 20:29)—signifies a new relationship for believers through the Easter events.[50] The term recalls the birthing imagery of the Prologue, where those who accept the incarnate Word become God's children (*tekna theou*, 1:12; also 3:3, 5) and therefore brothers and sisters to one another, and to Jesus (cf. 15:15). Closely linked are the covenantal overtones: "to my Father and your Father, and my God and your God" (cf. Jer. 31:33; Ezek. 37:28; Ruth 1:16).[51] The symbolic language expresses the strong identification between Jesus and disciples in relation to God. But it is also carefully nuanced to reflect the difference in status between them (John Chrysostom, *Homily* 81).[52] The covenant relationship in which believers become God's "family" is dependent on Jesus as Son (14:6; also 10:7, 9). Here again the symbol of community as the people of God, and as sisters and brothers, comes to life in and through the Easter events (see 19:26–27). The risen Lord reveals this new relationship to Mary Magdalene as she meets him in faith.

In this respect, the role of Mary Magdalene parallels that of the mother of Jesus at the foot of the cross. Just as the one who is named "woman" at the cross is a founding member of the new community inaugurated by Jesus' death, so too the one named "woman" at the empty tomb belongs to the same foundational event, stretched over three days. Indeed, there is a similar self-communication to the Samaritan woman, likewise named "woman" by Jesus (4:21). "Significantly, for the last time in the Gospel, a woman will once again be privy to the self-revelation of Jesus."[53] Theologically, the crucifixion, resurrection, and ascension make up the one event of "glorification" in the Fourth Gospel—which explains, in part, the Johannine muddle over chronology as to when Jesus is actually "exalted." Nevertheless, both the mother of Jesus and Mary Magdalene, along with the beloved disciple, are crucial figures for the new community as it confesses its nascent faith in the glorified Jesus. The language of mother and son, brothers and sisters, is performative, bringing the church into being—born from the death of Jesus and sustained by his risen presence. Neither event makes sense without the other. The mother of Jesus and Mary Magdalene share a common connection to the vital "hour" which issues in the creation of life.

Mary's task is now that of witness to the resurrection. The commission she is given is more than confirming the presence of the risen Lord, though that is the basis for her witness. Like any other witness in the Fourth Gospel, she is to announce to the community the symbolic significance of the event (*angellousa tois mathētais*, v. 18a).[54] The purpose of being sent is to unfold the inner meaning of Jesus' risen presence in relation to his ascension and the establishing of a new, covenant community. Mary prepares the reader of the Gospel for the giving of the Spirit in the following scene, by which Jesus' ascension is made complete. Her role as witness to the resurrection is unique, yet it also stands in a long line of witnesses in the Fourth Gospel, beginning with John the Baptist (1:7–8, 15, 19; 3:26–30), and including the Samaritan woman (4:39–42), the beloved disciple (19:35; 21:24), and the other women at the cross (19:25–27). While the Gospel makes no specific reference to "apostles," Mary Magdalene is given a "quasi-apostolic" role;[55] she is "portrayed as an apostle, as the first one to know and understand the full significance of the empty tomb and to bear witness to others."[56] As the "first disciple of the risen Lord," she is comparable in status to Peter elsewhere in the New Testament (cf. Luke 24:34; 1 Cor. 15:5).[57] The christophany she receives is a "protophany," a prior appearance that, in a sense, is set apart from subsequent apparitions.[58] No other disciple in John's Gospel, male or female, plays this role.[59]

Throughout the narrative of John 20, a centripetal force is at work. Jesus' appearance to Magdalene leads into the central scene in which the Spirit-Paraclete is given. Similarly, the appearance to Thomas flows out of 20:19–23, bringing the Gospel to its climax. The commission to Magdalene is the precondition for the giving of the Spirit; in proclaiming the message she prepares the way for the risen Lord to manifest his presence to the apostolic community. Everything that occurs in the first scene, therefore, represents an inclining toward the Spirit, into which the other disciples, including Thomas, are drawn. His confession of faith and the blessing on future believers that it evokes (20:28–29) are vivid signs of the Spirit's activity. The same dynamic is operative for the reader. By identifying with the faith of Mary Magdalene, readers are drawn into the center, where, in company with the gathered disciples, they meet the risen Christ behind locked doors, hear the words of peace, see the wounds, receive the Spirit, and are given the mandate for mission and the authority to forgive sins. The reader encounters the symbols of Easter faith and is invited to reinterpret his or her own struggle with death from a radically new perspective.

EASTER SYMBOLISM

This brief survey of the two narratives raises questions, for our purpose, concerning the figurative and theological meaning of resurrection. Where precisely do we locate the Easter symbols and in what way do they emerge from the Johannine narrative? How do the two stories relate to each other in a metaphorical reading? In what way is resurrection symbolic in this Gospel? There are several ways in which the symbolism functions within the two stories:

1. Martha's dialogue represents her struggle to believe in Jesus as the resurrection and the life. Unusually, the "sign" occurs after its meaning is disclosed. The real meaning of what is said relates to Jesus and only in a secondary sense to Lazarus. His experience of being raised from the dead, unlike that of Jesus, is not an experience of resurrection but rather of resuscitation, a physical symbol that points to the glory of the resurrection. His body remains mortal (cf. 12:9–11). In this sense, Lazarus's rising from the dead becomes a christological symbol, revealing Jesus' identity as "the resurrection and the life," an identity confirmed in Jesus' own resurrection. The body of Lazarus is the physical symbol which points to the transformed body of Christ.[60] The physical raising of the body discloses the glory of God. It presents Jesus as the giver of life, the one who possesses that "Sabbath" power over life and death which is uniquely divine. Martha's story, in this sense, points forward symbolically to that of Magdalene, foreshadowing its meaning and anticipating its symbols.

2. In John 20, the empty tomb is symbolic of the living, resurrected Jesus, as are also the angels seated in the tomb. In both cases, the absence becomes paradoxically a divine presence, indicated also by the garden, which is a symbol of fecundity and life. The symbolism relates to Mary Magdalene's desire to hold on to Jesus' physical presence. She does not realize that his presence is not to be with her in that way. He will be absent, in one sense, in the flesh; yet that fleshly presence will continue in the community, through the Spirit, in the living out of the love command and in its sacramental life. Mary takes literally Jesus' physical presence, not realizing that it will be communicated from now on in other, symbolic ways, though no less palpable and substantial. This means that her "touching" of Jesus is to be differently construed from that of Thomas, who touches in order to perceive in the wounds the symbols of life.

3. All this means that the symbolism associated with resurrection and life is complex and not easily unraveled. Essentially, physical life becomes symbolic of eternal life: that is, resurrection life. Physical life is subject to death and decay, is limited and finite. John does not dismiss this life. What he does do, however, is to

make of it a symbol of a life that is greater, a life that embraces and transcends the finitude of mortal life, a life that in one sense moves in the very opposite direction to mortality, yet in another sense gathers it in. Because physical life is symbolic of eternal life, what is needed is the transfiguration of one to the other, not the letting go of one in order to seize upon the other. The physical is taken up into the eternal, just as flesh is transfigured in the person of Jesus to reveal divine glory. Flesh, therefore, even in its risen form is still symbolic of divine glory. The incarnation is not bypassed; it is not a temporary event that is no longer relevant once the ascension is complete. The risen Christ, in the flesh, remains the definitive Symbol of God, the true Icon sustaining all life, mortal and eternal. The life which he unites within himself, against all human expectation, is both natural life and resurrection life: the two are held together as one.

4. The relation of this to Johannine eschatology is not easy to decipher—partly because John's eschatological picture seems uneven and at times inconsistent. The calling forth of Lazarus from the tomb symbolizes a power over death that already takes effect in the present (5:25). It is not simply a "sign" for the future: that is where Martha's faith is partial and incomplete (11:24, 34). Like Mary Magdalene, she does not at first perceive that Jesus *is* the resurrection and life in the here and now. There is a profound sense in which ordinary human life is now to be lived in the shadow of resurrection, particularly in the love and unity of the Christian community, symbolized in the restored communion of the Bethany family after the raising of their brother from the dead (12:1–2). Yet resurrection has an unmistakably future dimension: or, better, that which is experienced in the present will follow through to the end, will never fail, will complete its task of overcoming all that is represented by death and darkness. In the end, all things are restored. Death itself, though suggesting the undefeated powers of darkness, has already yielded to a greater power. Now even suffering and death can disclose the presence and the glory of God, just as they have—and precisely because they have—in Jesus.

5. John is not just concerned about death in a literal sense, the decay of the physical body, but is using "death" to speak symbolically of all that inhibits, constrains, captivates, and destroys human life. The evangelist acknowledges that death in some sense remains a reality for the community: Christians still become ill and die, especially since the Lord is "absent" (symbolized, for the evangelist, by Jesus' delay in coming to Lazarus); they still have to confront on a daily basis their own mortality and finitude. Yet Jesus himself has overcome death by entering mortal flesh, by dying in that flesh, and by rising to a new life, translating "this Jack, joke, poor potsherd, patch, matchwood, mortal diamond" into "immortal diamond."[61] The transformation is recognizably fleshly and palpable (as the scenes involving both Martha and Mary Magdalene make plain). Although this theme points to a future reality in which "all flesh" becomes like that of Jesus, it is more truly experienced in the present, where death and all that it stands for now

becomes the pathway to life. Death itself is transformed to yield life: the dark tomb becomes the womb of life. In its metaphorical sense, death becomes a symbol leading not to decay and disintegration but rather to community, solidarity and life.

6. There is a further dimension to this, namely, the symbolic role played by the women themselves in the two narratives. In both cases, Martha and Mary symbolize the Christian community in its struggle to believe and its transfiguring reception of Easter faith. Both are witnesses to the central meaning of Christian faith, even though on different sides of Easter. Martha makes the Christian confession, "you are the Christ," not only for herself but also on behalf of the Christian community in the light of Jesus' self-revelation as "resurrection and life."[62] Magdalene receives the first epiphany of the risen Christ and the apostolic commission, accepting it both in joy and in faith—a faith and witness that belong to the whole community.[63] In the transformation of her meeting with the risen Lord, Mary becomes for the community of faith a symbol pointing to his living presence, even in absence. Although the two women are by no means the only Johannine characters who play such a representative role, they illustrate that the evangelist uses women as well as men in a central position, to represent the community in its struggle to believe.

MARTHA AND MARY MAGDALENE: A LIVING TRADITION

In the light of what we have seen of Martha and Mary Magdalene in the Fourth Gospel, it is instructive to glimpse something of their subsequent history beyond the Johannine text. At least in the West, it is a chequered history of both holding to, yet also relinquishing the Johannine tradition. It is sometimes assumed that Mary Magdalene fares better at the hands of the Gnostic writings of the second century C.E. than in orthodox Christian circles. Certainly, in a number of these texts, Mary is presented as a prominent disciple of Jesus and a leader in the early community. In the Gospel of Mary, after she has comforted the grief of the apostles, Peter asks Magdalene to reveal the mysteries disclosed only to her. She proceeds to enlighten them, but they do not believe that the risen Lord would speak to a woman and not to them. Levi defends her: "if the Savior made her worthy, who are you indeed to reject her? Surely the Savior knows her very well. That is why he loved her more than us" (*Gospel of Mary* 10–19). Elsewhere Mary is Jesus' partner and companion, who has inherited the kingdom because she has become pure spirit (*Pistis Sophia* 61, 87).[64] The greater prominence given to Magdalene (and other females) in the diverse Gnostic texts, according to Elaine Pagels, goes along with a more balanced use of feminine and masculine language for God.[65] However, as Ingrid Maisch argues, the high place of Magdalene within Gnosticism is dearly bought: her position, though reflecting a distinctive social place for women in Gnostic circles, derives from a dualistic anthropology that diminishes the body and is liable to cancel out Magdalene's femaleness, regarding her as quasi-male (see *Gospel of Thomas* 114).[66] The asceticism of Gnosticism in fact separates women from their sexuality, depicting the world as the creation not of God but of an evil demiurge.[67]

In the earliest orthodox traditions, Mary Magdalene is also highly regarded: she is one of the "myrrh-bearing women" (*myrophoroi*) who find the tomb empty and witness to the risen Lord—an interpretation still maintained in the East.[68] Susan Haskins's study of Mary Magdalene in the history of Western art points out that the image of the women visiting the tomb on Easter morning is one of the most popular in early Christian art.[69] The first known painting of Mary Magdalene, at Dura-Europos (240 C.E.), depicts her in such a role.[70] For Hippolytus of Rome (ca. 170–235 C.E.), Mary is presented as the figure of John 20, discovering the risen Christ in the garden, like the Shulammite woman seeking her beloved in the Song of Songs. Interestingly, Hippolytus connects Mary in this exposition with the figure of Martha. Most importantly, he makes a link between Mary Magdalene and Eve, a connection more often made of the mother of Jesus:

> As the old Eve had forfeited her right to the tree of life in the Garden of Eden, Mary Magdalen/Martha-Mary now cling passionately to Christ having found him, the Tree of Life, in the Easter garden where life rises anew. . . . Mary Magdalen mistakes Christ for the gardener, and then recognizes him, thereby repairing Eve's fault.[71]

More than that, Hippolytus also appears to be the first to ascribe to Mary Magdalene the title of *apostola apostolorum* ("apostle of/to the apostles"), because of her role as witness to the resurrection and her commission to proclaim the message to the other apostles.[72] Hippolytus interprets this language in terms of the Eve typology: the connection with Song of Songs leads to the identification of Mary Magdalene with the Bride of Christ, because she is first to meet the risen Christ, thus representing the church's Easter faith. The same perspective is present in a number of patristic writers who do not confuse her with the women of the anointing:[73] rather, they acknowledge her as "equal to the apostles" and significant for her leading role in the Easter narratives.[74]

Later harmonization arose as a result of confusion in the West over the identities of Mary Magdalene, Mary of Bethany, and the repentant sinner. The conflation was made by Gregory the Great in the late sixth century: the "seven devils" cast out of Mary Magdalene in Luke 8:3 are now interpreted as sins of the flesh, and it is she, therefore, who washes Jesus' feet with tears of penitence and also comes to the tomb on Easter morning.[75] Particularly in popular understanding, Mary Magdalene becomes more and more separated from her Johannine characterization and her role as the "apostle to the apostles" and primary witness to the resurrection. The Lukan portrait of the sinful woman (Luke 7:36–50) comes to dominate over the Johannine picture, and indeed over the Synoptic depiction of the resurrection narratives. The conflating of the Lukan and Johannine accounts of Martha has a similar effect: strangely enough, we are left with the Lukan account as the more dominant. Martha the fussy housekeeper, jealous and resentful, though hardworking and good-hearted—if somewhat unappreciated—is the image most Western Christians have retained. The Johannine portrait of a believer who makes the basic Christian confession, "you are the Christ," yet struggles to grasp its fuller dimensions, in parallel to the Synoptic version of Peter who likewise makes confession of his faith but needs to grow in understanding, is largely lost to us. For both women, the Lukan narratives have dominated over the Johannine.

There are exceptions to this Western tendency of interpretation, even where the image of Mary Magdalene as the penitent whore thrives. Medieval mysticism, for example, retains a sense of Magdalene representing the church in the Easter garden; she is the bride, seeking her divine lover in the tradition of Song of Songs, and the new Eve. She symbolizes the coming of the Gentiles into the believing community and witnesses to the divine and human natures of Christ.[76] Ingrid Maisch argues that, at this point, the image of the penitent whore has not yet fully taken over the character of Mary Magdalene.[77] She and her supposed sister, Martha, are regarded as images of the church—along Lukan lines—with Mary Magdalene signifying its contemplative side and Martha its temporal, secular side. It is interesting to observe the version of both characters in medieval French legends. According to these stories, Mary Magdalene (= Mary of Bethany), Martha and Lazarus set out from Palestine in a boat and safely reach the coast of Provence, where they convert Marseilles and many of its surrounding inhabitants to the Christian faith.[78] Though Mary Magdalene feels compelled to repent of the sins of her youth for the rest of her life in harsh asceticism and self-denial, both she and Martha are credited with important roles as missionaries and preachers of the gospel (though never bishops like their brother Lazarus), leaders in the church of Provence, active in performing miracles and caring for the poor, and spiritual guides to the faithful. Martha is even credited with overcoming a terrifying dragon.[79] Something of the Johannine characterization is retained in these legends, both for Martha and for Mary Magdalene, particularly in their preaching of resurrection faith. In the baroque period, however, the image of Magdalene as the penitent whore becomes dominant. She is now a highly ambivalent archetype of true sanctity and penitential love, "a time-bound symbol that endures only in partial aspects: the beautiful sinner as object of male lust."[80] For the most part, the Johannine presentation of the two women as carriers of the Easter gospel is lost within the West. With that loss comes also the loss of something of the Easter symbolism.

In contrast to the later Latin tradition, the two Johannine resurrection narratives—the one in the middle and the other at the end of the Gospel—portray two women struggling, in the face of death and bereavement, to expand their understanding of faith beyond mortal bounds. Martha is not a fussy, pragmatic housekeeper, nor is Mary Magdalene a weak, helpless woman moving blindly from one misapprehension to another. Both women, in different ways, bear witness to Jesus' identity as "the resurrection and the life," the Word-made-flesh, the definitive symbol and revelation of God, the Son who has divine authority over life and death. Both women develop in faith through encounter with Jesus in the harsh and tragic context of death. It is this mortal context which the Johannine Easter symbols address. The signs pointing to death, decay, and desecration as the last word in human affairs—the illness, the tomb, the smell of putrefaction, the large stone laid across the entrance, the grave-clothes bound around and around the corpse, the presence of the mourners, the grief and anger of the loved ones, the chilling darkness and emptiness of the tomb's seeming profanation—all these signs, in the hands of the evangelist are transformed. Now they become symbols of life: not life in an escapist sense, but life in spite of death, life on the other side of death, life unable to be conquered by death. It is not nature that has the final say in these narratives, but rather the God of life:

> The Christ who was consigned, in haste, and with grief and alarm, by those who got his wrecked body down from the cross, to the tomb, that darkly private place, was also the one of whom the later natural processes could not take command. The earth, and the air, and the fire, and the water, had in effect to stand back. Paintings show soldiers reeling: but we are talking about nature reeling. In the face of fate's claims, resurrection prevailed.[81]

The signs of the natural world are helpless and ineffective in the presence of death. Only those symbols which open up another world, within yet also beyond the structures of the present, have any power. In the dramatic experience of both women, the fourth evangelist lays before us Easter symbols that need to be recaptured. Mistaken turnings, confused demands, inadequate understanding, and unfocused longings are all part of the Easter journey for this narrator. The characterization of both women draws the reader onto the path of faith and witness. Signs that in human terms denote death and darkness in these two narratives are transfigured to become radiant symbols of eternal life. In the end, even death (despite itself) reveals the glory of God, for through its dread signs, the Son of God gives birth to life and brings salvation to the world.

Reading for Transformation

W HATEVER WE MAY SAY of other New Testament writings, John's theological perspective at its core is a symbolic one. Beginning with the understanding of God as holy and transcendent, the Fourth Gospel presents the advent of God within the world through the primary symbol of incarnation. The flesh of Jesus, with its sense of continuity not only with human beings (male and female) but with all creation, is the locus of divine glory, the eschatological place of God's self-revelation. The symbol of flesh is not just the first in a series of Johannine symbols. It is the controlling or determining symbol that makes room for all the others. Because God in Christ has taken flesh, sharing mortal life and destiny, the whole world becomes replete with divine glory: everything now possesses the capacity to bear the beauty and splendor of God. Paradoxically, by pursuing the same glory, human beings find their true identity as children of God, giving them access to the ultimate source of life—rich, fecund, and joyful. John's eschatology—his understanding of ultimate meaning—radiates through the present moment, filling it already with that which is to come. At the same time, this eschatology is also protology, a return to the beginnings. In the transfiguration of flesh to reflect divine glory, the lost image is restored through the one who is the Image of the Father, and creation becomes what it was always intended to be— what it was created for—formed in the shape of an original beatitude.

In this reading of the Gospel of John, symbols, whether in metaphorical, iconic, or other form, are not incidental to the narrative structures and theological meaning of the Fourth Gospel. They are not included to decorate the plain meaning of the text. On the contrary, they stand at the center of the evangelical proclamation, shaping both the text and the reader. The function of the Johannine symbols is threefold. In the first place, they make palpable the spirituality of the divine realm, giving it form and shape that are comprehensible in human terms and witnessing to the self-revelation of Jesus. In this sense, they are real and substantial, possessing content and making claims to truth. They do not stand over against truth or reality, but convey divine substance through the textures of human life. Second, while disclosing the true nature of God, they make no attempt to capture the divine being but are implicitly open-ended, drawing into themselves yet never exhausting the inexhaustible life of God. This is particularly so of the core symbols of the Gospel, which stand close to the heart of Johannine revelation. Third, the symbols have the capacity to engage the reader at both a cognitive and intuitive level: cognitively, because they play a substantial and incremental role; intuitively, because they appeal to the reader's affective faculties.

Of like interest in the Gospel of John is the position assigned to women in the narrative. The five women of the Gospel are centrally placed, conveying the symbolic meaning of the text through their struggle to understand. They are present at the beginning, the middle, and the end of Jesus' ministry: at the wedding, which sets the tone of celebration, new life, and manifested glory; through the ministry, where they engage with Jesus to comprehend the life he offers; at the cross and in the Easter garden. Their vibrant presence serves as a point of identification for the reader, showing the way in which the physical and material fall open to reveal divine glory. The Johannine women do not always understand, but they do not cease the attempt at understanding; and finally all five become founding figures of the Johannine community, exemplary disciples and "apostolic" leaders who confess their faith in Jesus, the Word of God incarnate. They are not alone in this witness; they stand alongside the men of the Gospel—the disciples, the supplicants— who share a similar faith and love and show a parallel struggle to open themselves to the meaning of the revelation.

Our study of Johannine symbolism has observed particularly the way in which gender and symbol interact. The flesh of Jesus, in its expanded Johannine meaning, gathers women as well as men into its embrace, recapitulating their humanity and bestowing glory—a glory that extends to all creation. The image of living water, which crisscrosses the Johannine narrative at various points, has a strong focus in the story of the Samaritan woman, a focus that the reader retains as the symbolism develops. Although the symbols of abiding and friendship do not dwell particularly on female characters, their usage demonstrates that relationship and intimacy lie at the core of evangelical faith—a perspective that is grounded in the Fourth Gospel's understanding of God as a communion of "persons." Parenting symbols are also vital for this Gospel's understanding of God and the church. Our study of the father symbol suggests that it is not an oppressive conception of the divine being, but derives from a personal understanding of God as the gracious and kindly author of life, in every sense. Motherhood symbols, though less palpable, are nevertheless discernible within the Johannine text, crossing the boundary between human and divine. The mother of Jesus, the Spirit-Paraclete, and Jesus himself all share maternal imagery that unites them in giving birth to the community of faith. The symbol of anointing, though more discrete in its occurrence within the Gospel narrative, displays the mirroring of true discipleship, which repays divine, costly self-giving with a similarly unrestrained and generous self-giving. Finally, the "Easter" narratives of Martha and Mary Magdalene, through their potent symbolism, reveal that resurrection lies at the heart of the life that Jesus gives, drawing the community into a new understanding of eternal life in the here and now, with implications extending far beyond mortal limits.

The reader has a vitally important role to play in discerning meaning and embracing the transformation that the text evokes. Meaning emerges in the interaction between text and reader in which the reader is an *active* listener, an engaged presence within the borders formed by the symbolic structure of the text. Merging with the implied reader, the real reader is drawn into the drama of the narrative and becomes a conversation partner in a dialogue that the text itself creates and shapes. Only by appreciating the active participation of the reader is transformation possible. To argue in this way need not buy into a postmodern relativism that encourages arbitrary, subjective readings without any sense of objective reference point. In many respects, postmodernism, with its fragmentation and parochialism, represents the other side of the coin to Enlightenment objectivity and empiricism. Yet, while the reader may not be the arbiter of final meaning and cannot displace the otherness of the text, there is still the need for positive engagement with the Gospel as integral to a hermeneutics of transformation.

There is a further dimension to the role of the reader in interpreting biblical symbolism. The reader is never a solitary figure but, within Christian understanding, lives and reads within the context of the believing community. Reading belongs first and foremost to the household of faith. The image of the lonely reader, struggling in solitude to interpret the text, bespeaks the tragedy of post-Enlightenment isolation and is neither the way the texts arose nor how, at least in the early centuries, they were embraced. A community perspective implies that the reader is also in dialogue with a living tradition. The wider context is a vital part of reading, engaging the reader not only with the text but also with the voices of other interpreters down through the centuries who have opened themselves to the gospel in active listening: through creed and confession, through contemplation and theology, through liturgy and prayer, through mission and service.

In what ways might this study of Johannine symbols open the reader to the transformation offered by the Fourth Gospel? There are three issues that suggest how a transformative reading might operate. In the first place, while awareness of gender is important, it is not a restrictive category in reading. Although it is sometimes claimed that the Bible was written by men and for men, there is insufficient evidence to substantiate this view. Undoubtedly the Bible emerges from a male world and reflects the assumptions of such a world—including its androcentrism —but there is no evidence to support the claim that biblical writers were unaware of a female as well as male readership. The Gospel of John, in particular, with its focus on the partnership of women and men in discipleship and ministry, does not appear to assume male-only readers. Nor are the symbols it offers directed toward male experience rather than female.

There are two seemingly contradictory implications that follow from this. On the one hand, the presence of women characters creates a space for the female reader that enables her to engage with the text, making it possible for her to recognize her own needs and longings within the characterization provided by the evangelist. At the same time, while female presence in terms of characterization guarantees female presence in readership, it does not direct the reader's own interactive reading of the text. We cannot assume that female readers turn exclusively to female characters—despite the general sense of welcome that their presence denotes. Nor can we assume that male readers identify only with male characters. Once the welcome is assured, the reader is free to move toward those characters whose experience engages most forcefully with his or her own. Such a decision on the part of the reader—directed as much by unconscious forces as conscious—is influenced certainly by gender but also by other factors that may be unrelated to gender. The presence of women as vivid characters in the Johannine text enables them to function symbolically not only for the female but also for the male reader.

Second, while symbols arise from their own cultural context and reflect the experience of their specific situations, they possess a universal quality that enables them to speak across cultures and contexts. For the reader of the Fourth Gospel—male or female—core symbols such as flesh, water, friendship and love, fatherhood and motherhood evoke common experiences that create a bridge between the world of the text and that of the reader, despite the gulf that divides them. The Johannine symbols evoke a common humanity, a knowledge and experience that are not defined by the narrow limits of contextuality. On the contrary, such symbolism opens doors between worlds, allowing the insights of one age and culture to speak powerfully and evocatively to another. A pathway opens up between worlds that are otherwise closed to each other by distance, time, and cultural diversity.

Third, and related to the second point, symbol and metaphor appeal to the experience of the reader more effectively than abstract, discursive prose is able to do. The pain of past suffering, the knowledge of incompleteness, the awareness of a restless spirit, the sense of inner emptiness and isolation, the longing for wholeness and cleansing: these resist articulation in most people's experience and can often be touched only at a level deeper than the conscious or cognitive. It is this level which the symbols of the Fourth Gospel address, drawing the reader into that dual experience of knowing which is the purpose of the Revealer's coming: the knowledge of the self and the knowledge of God. The symbols open the heart to the deepest longings and fill the reader with hope, drawing him or her into a divine world that transfigures through love and understanding. The symbols function to open mortal wounds and provide resources for their healing.

In the end, what the symbols of the Fourth Gospel offer is a pathway to divine glory, which is both the location and the means of transformation. The road is paved by the Logos himself, who becomes flesh, sharing in that which he first created. In the incarnation, the Word takes on mortality and reveals the glory of the Immortal within the shape and form of human life. The pathway begins and ends in divine love: in the radical movement of glory to flesh, heaven to earth, eternity to time. Because divine glory becomes manifest within the flesh of Jesus, so now flesh in its widest expanse possesses the capacity to bear the glory. The reader who lives in darkness is drawn into the radiance of the light, enticed toward God along a pathway created by Jesus himself, who is "the way, the truth, and the life." Eastern Orthodox Christians call this pathway to glory "deification": the restoration of the Fall and the recovery of an original, divine identity once lost. On this road, flesh does not fall away and become irrelevant. On the contrary, it is transformed to reflect glory, just as that of the Logos radiates the true life-giving and loving nature of the Father. Thus flesh already begins to partake of resurrection, already reflects its immortal destiny, is already embraced by the knowledge of an eternity from which it derives. Flesh and glory are not alternatives, in the Johannine symbolic worldview. In the end, it is the union of the two which spells out for the reader the meaning and experience of salvation.

Notes

INTRODUCTION

1. Milbank, Ward, and Pickstock, "Introduction: Suspending the Material: The Turn of Radical Orthodoxy," in *Radical Orthodoxy,* ed. Milbank et al., 1.

2. See the critique of Vanhoozer, *Is There a Meaning in This Text?* 15–35.

3. Culpepper, *Anatomy of the Fourth Gospel.*

4. Ibid., 180–202.

5. See, for example, Talbert, *Reading John;* Stibbe, *John;* Moloney, *John;* idem, *Belief in the Word;* idem, *Signs and Shadows;* idem, *Glory not Dishonor;* and Culpepper, *Gospel and Letters.* See also the collection of articles in Culpepper and Segovia, eds., *The Fourth Gospel from a Literary Perspective.*

6 Lee, *Symbolic Narratives.*

7. Koester, *Symbolism.*

8. Schneiders, *Written That You May Believe;* eadem, *Revelatory Text.*

9. Van der Watt, *Family of the King.*

10. Brown, "Roles of Women in the Fourth Gospel," appendix 2 in *Community of the Beloved Disciple,* 183–98, originally printed in *Theological Studies* 36 (1975): 688–99. On this, see further, for example, Schneiders, "Women in the Fourth Gospel"; Seim, "Roles of Women," 16-19; Scott, *Sophia and the Johannine Jesus,* 174–240; and Conway, *Men and Women in the Fourth Gospel.* See also Schüssler Fiorenza, *In Memory of Her,* 323–33; O'Day, "John," in *Women's Bible Commentary,* ed. Newsom and Ringe, 294–302; Reinhartz, "John," in *Searching the Scriptures,* vol. 2, *A Feminist Commentary,* ed. Schüssler Fiorenza, 561–600; van Tilborg, *Imaginative Love,* 167–208; and Kitzberger, "Mary of Bethany and Mary of Magdala."

11. For example, Davies, *Rhetoric and Reference in the Fourth Gospel;* Fehribach, *Women in the Life of the Bridegroom;* and Kitzberger, "'How Can This Be?' (John 3:9): A Feminist-Theological Re-Reading of the Gospel of John," in *"What Is John?"* vol. 2, *Literary and Social Readings of the Fourth Gospel,* ed. Segovia, 19–41; also, to a lesser extent, Maccini, *Her Testimony Is True.*

12. It is most likely that there are four women present in this scene, corresponding to the four soldiers (19:23–25). See Hoskyns and Davey, *Fourth Gospel,* 2:630–31; and Ricci, *Mary Magdalene and Many Others,* 174.

238

13. On this, see further chapter 7 below, 177–78.

14. See Conway, *Men and Women in the Fourth Gospel*, 203.

15. Reinhartz, "John," 594–95.

16. For a comparative study of male and female characters in the Fourth Gospel, see Conway, *Men and Women in the Fourth Gospel*. See also the recent study on Johannine gender pairings by Margaret Beirne, "Women and Men in the Fourth Gospel."

17. The term "biblical theology" is used here in a limited sense to refer to the theologies of individual biblical writers.

18. The use of the term "Old Testament" is problematic, but no less so than other designations such as "Hebrew Bible." "Old Testament" is retained in this study, but the adjective is used in the sense of "ancient" rather than superseded.

19. Ricoeur, *Interpretation Theory*, 55. Ricoeur is speaking more narrowly of metaphor and symbol.

20. Against this, compare Vanhoozer, who is critical of Ricoeur's position, arguing for the objectivity of the author's intention and the singularity of meaning (*Is There a Meaning in This Text?* 106–11, 201–80); see also Hirsch, *Aims of Interpretation*, esp. 74–92.

21. Breck, *Shape of Biblical Language*, 13–14.

22. See Schneiders, *Revelatory Text*, 27–43; also Chopp, *Power to Speak*, 40–70.

23. Ricoeur, *Interpretation Theory*, esp. 71–88.

24. Ibid., 74.

25. Ricoeur, *Rule of Metaphor*, 254.

26. Stylianopoulos, *New Testament: An Orthodox Perspective*, vol. 1, *Scripture, Tradition, Hermeneutics*, 187–238.

27. The translations of Greek and Latin texts are my own (unless otherwise indicated), and are intended to be literal rather than elegant. Apart from the Septuagint and the New Testament, the English Bible used is the New Revised Standard Version.

28. See Christiaan Mostert, "Is a Non-contextual Theology Viable?" In *Mapping the Landscape*, ed. Emilsen and Emilsen, 118–33.

CHAPTER 1
THE MEANING OF SYMBOL IN THE FOURTH GOSPEL

1. Ricoeur, *Symbolism of Evil*, 347.

2. On the controlling principles set out by Origen, see Stylianopoulos, *New Testament: An Orthodox Perspective*, vol. 1, *Scripture, Tradition, Hermeneutics*, 111.

3. Young, *Biblical Exegesis*.

4. Ibid., 76–96.

5. Ibid., 116.

6. Ibid., 161–85.

7. Ibid., 120; see also Stylianopoulos, *New Testament*, 118.

8. Brock, "Introduction," in *St. Ephrem the Syrian: Hymns on Paradise*, introduced and translated by Sebastian Brock (New York: St. Vladimir's Seminary Press, 1990), 42.

9. Stylianopoulos, *New Testament*, 111.

10. Young, *Biblical Exegesis*, 119.

11. Stylianopoulos, *New Testament*, 109.

12. Ibid., 115–22.

13. Young, *Biblical Exegesis*, 137, 116, 115–22..

14. Brock, *Luminous Eye*, 43.

15. Stylianopoulos, *New Testament*, 120.

16. *Hymns on Paradise*, 77–188.

17. Stylianopoulos, *New Testament*, 158.

18. See, for example, Elizabeth Struthers Malbon and Janice Capel Anderson, "Literary-Critical Methods" (p. 251), and Claudia V. Camp, "Feminist Theological Hermeneutics: Canon and Christian Identity" (pp. 166–69), both in *Searching the Scriptures*, vol. 1, *A Feminist Introduction,* ed. Schüssler Fiorenza. See also Moore, who speaks of turning the text against its author ("Are There Impurities in the Living Water," 215).

19. Rahner, *Theological Investigations,* 4:224, 229.

20. Ibid., 235.

21. See, for example, Barth, *Church Dogmatics,* 2.1:75–84.

22. Tillich, *Systematic Theology,* vol. 1, *Reason and Revelation, Being and God,* 239–41.

23. Ibid., 239.

24. Ibid., 177.

25. Ibid., 240.

26. Rahner, *Theological Investigations,* 4:244–45.

27. Léon-Dufour, *Lecture,* 1:19.

28. Tillich, "Religious Symbol," 301–3.

29. Tillich, "Meaning and Justification of Religious Symbols," 4–5; also idem, *Dynamics of Faith,* 41–43.

30. Tillich, "Meaning and Justification," 8–9.

31. Ibid., 10.

32. Brock, *Luminous Eye*, 53–84, esp. 80, 54.

33. Schneiders, *Written That You May Believe,* 65–69, esp. 66. See also Jones, *Symbol of Water,* 14–26.

34. Schneiders, *Revelatory Text,* 27–43; eadem, "The Bible and Feminism," in *Freeing Theology,* ed. LaCugna, 37–40.

35. R. Alan Culpepper agrees with the distinction between sign and symbol, but argues that Schneiders's definition fails to distinguish between different kinds of symbol (*Anatomy of the Fourth Gospel,* 187).

36. Culpepper, *Anatomy of the Fourth Gospel,* 189–97; see also van der Watt, *Family of the King,* 101.

37. Culpepper, *Anatomy of the Fourth Gospel,* 189–90.

38. Koester, *Symbolism,* 4–12.

39. Ibid., 4.

40. Soskice, *Metaphor and Religious Language,* 15.

41. Robert Kysar, "The Making of Metaphor: Another Reading of John 3:1-15," in *"What Is John?"* ed. Segovia, 37.

42. Van der Watt, *Family of the King,* 151. In his extensive study of metaphor in the Fourth Gospel, van der Watt agrees that metaphor creates meaning, but his insistence on the priority of the message tends to weaken this view, threatening to drive a wedge between form and content (pp. 143–49).

43. Ibid., 162.

44. See Richards, *Philosophy of Rhetoric;* also Ricoeur, *Rule of Metaphor,* 80–81.

45. On the importance of interpreting Johannine metaphors within their literary and sociohistorical framework, see van der Watt, *Family of the King,* 11–13.

46. Dead metaphors have lost this tension and are easy to paraphrase (Soskice, *Metaphor,* 73).

47. Ricoeur, *Rule of Metaphor,* 247–56. Soskice is critical of Ricoeur's notion of "split reference" within metaphor (*Metaphor,* 88).

48. Van der Watt is right to see water in 4:10–11 as a "suspended metaphor" (*Family of the King*, 231).

49. Frye, *Great Code*, 61.

50. Soskice, *Metaphor*, 58–60.

51. Jones, *Symbol of Water*, 14–15.

52. On this, see further Lee, *Symbolic Narratives*.

53. McFague, *Metaphorical Theology*, 35.

54. Ibid., 13–14.

55. Ibid., 1–6.

56. Ibid., 12.

57. Ibid., 1–2.

58. Ibid., 6.

59. See McFague, *Models of God*, 69–78; eadem, *The Body of God*.

60. On this, see further chapter 2 below, 52–66.

61. See Lee, "Touching the Sacred Text," 249–64.

62. See, for example, Ouspensky, "The Meaning and Language of Icons," in *The Meaning of Icons,* ed. Ouspensky and Lossky, 23–49; Limouris, "Microcosm and Macrocosm of the Icon," in *Icons,* ed. Limouris, 93–123; and Quenot, *Icon,* 11–64.

63. See Léon-Dufour, *Lecture*, 1:133–35.

64. Harrison, "Word as Icon in Greek Patristic Theology," 60. Harrison argues that Nicaea II makes "a direct parallel between the Gospel narrative and the painted representation of the icon," both having their theological roots in the incarnation (p. 58).

65. Limouris, "Microcosm and Macrocosm of the Icon," 111 (emphasis added).

66. Ibid., 115.

67. Rahner, *Theological Investigations*, 4:237.

68. Schneiders, "History and Symbolism in the Fourth Gospel," 373–75.

69. Schneiders, *Written That You May Believe*, 74.

70. See Nicolas Ozoline, "La théologie de l'icône," in *Nicée II, 787–1987*, ed. Boespflug and Lossky, 403–20.

71. Graham Ward, "Bodies: The Displaced Body of Jesus Christ," in *Radical Orthodoxy,* ed. Milbank et al., 170.

72. "To be able to stammer about God is after all more important than to speak exactly about the world" (Rahner, *Theological Investigations,* 3:395).

73. See Ruether, *Introducing Redemption in Christian Feminism*, 83–85.

74. On this, see further Ince, "Judge for Yourselves," 59–71.

75. See Soskice, "Trinity and Feminism," in *Cambridge Companion to Feminist Theology,* ed. Parsons, 141.

76. On this, see further chapter 7 below.

77. So Catherine M. LaCugna, "God in Communion With Us," in *Freeing Theology,* ed. LaCugna, 83–114.

78. See the three treatises of John of Damascus, *Apologetic Discourses on Those Who Defame the Holy Icons,* 1231–1420.

79. See, for example, E. A. Johnson, *She Who Is,* 17–57.

80. Young, *Biblical Exegesis*, 140–60.

81. Ibid., 140.

82. Translated in *The Nicene and Post-Nicene Fathers,* second series (Edinburgh: T. & T. Clark, 1892), 5:264; see also Young, *Biblical Exegesis*, 141.

83. Young, *Biblical Exegesis*, 140–44.

84. Frye, *Great Code*, 3–30; see Young, *Biblical Exegesis*, 144–45.

85. Frye, *Great Code*, 7.

86. Ibid., 15.

87. Translated in *Nicene and Post-Nicene Fathers*, 5:221.

88. Presumably it is the evangelist speaking editorially, although there is no direct indication in the text; indeed John the Baptist is the speaker in 3:30. On this, see further Lee, *Symbolic Narratives*, 42.

89. Grese, "'Unless One Is Born Again,'" 692.

90. Ricoeur, "Interpretation Theory," 52.

91. Ephrem the Syrian, *Hymns on Faith* 9.16, quoted in Brock, *Luminous Eye*, 26.

92. Ward, "Bodies," 173.

93. Ricoeur, "Biblical Hermeneutics," 30.

CHAPTER 2
RESTORING GLORY: THE SYMBOL OF JESUS' FLESH

1. From W. H. Auden, "For the Time Being: A Christmas Oratorio," in *W.H. Auden: Collected Poems*, ed. Mendelson, 359.

2. On this translation, see de la Potterie, "L'emploie de *eis* dans Saint Jean"; and Moloney, "'In the Bosom of' or 'Turned towards' the Father?"; also Léon-Dufour, *Lecture*, 1:68–72. For a different view, see Schnackenburg, *Gospel*, 1:234.

3. See Brown, *Gospel*, 1:lii–lxvi; see also Dunn, *Christology in the Making*, 215–30.

4. This need not imply that Christology is the center of Johannine theology. Behind the portrait of Jesus Christ lies the divine purpose of salvation, which places God at the heart of John's theology. See C. K. Barrett, "Christocentric or Theocentric? Observations on the Theological Method of the Fourth Gospel," in *Essays on John*, 1–18; see also Moloney, *John*, 41.

5. On the Tabernacles Discourse as a literary unit, see Corley, "Wisdom's Rescue"; and Motyer, *Your Father the Devil?* 141–59.

6. See Lieu, "Mother of the Son in the Fourth Gospel."

7. Culpepper, *Gospel and Letters*, 116–20.

8. See, for example, Brown, *Gospel*, 1:18–23; and Schnackenburg, *Gospel*, 1:224–32. For the view that the Prologue was composed by the evangelist himself, see Barrett, *St. John*, 149–51; and Harris, *Prologue and Gospel*; also Brodie, *Gospel*, 134.

9. See Brodie, *Gospel*, 133–34.

10. See especially the detailed study by Harris, *Prologue and Gospel*, which argues for the integrated relationship between the Prologue and the Gospel narrative on the basis of a number of common themes: the figure of John the Baptist (pp. 26–62), the role of Moses and the Law (pp. 63–90), and in particular Johannine Christology (pp. 91–172). See also Hooker, "Johannine Prologue and the Messianic Secret."

11. It is not entirely clear what "his own" refers to in 1:11. In Greek there is a distinction between (literally) "his own things" and "his own people." If the parallel with 1:10a is strictly synonymous, then "his own" means the same as "the world"—that is to say, creation in general. If the parallelism is looser, "his own" might refer to Israel as God's chosen people. As John does not specify and either meaning is possible, it is likely that the ambiguity is deliberate: "his own" refers to the world in general and, most poignantly of all, to Israel, which fails to recognize its Creator and Redeemer. See Schnackenburg, *Gospel*, 1:259–61.

12. See, for example, Isa. 9:8–10:11; Jer. 1:4–19; Ezek. 2:1–3:11; Hos. 4; Amos 1:2–2:16; Mic. 2.

13. Philo identifies Word and Wisdom, for example, in *Allegorical Interpretation* 1.65, where wisdom is described as the word of God (*ho de estin ho theou logos*).

14. See, for example, Schnackenburg, *Gospel,* 1:481–93; Léon-Dufour, *Lecture,* 1:57–62; E. A. Johnson, *She Who Is,* 86–93; Willett, *Wisdom Christology;* Edwards, *Jesus the Wisdom of God,* 19–43; Witherington, *John's Wisdom;* McKinlay, *Gendering Wisdom the Host,* 179–237; Ringe, *Wisdom's Friends.*

15. E. Johnson, *She Who Is,* 95, 97.

16. See Willett, *Wisdom Christology,* 49–126.

17. Ibid., 125.

18. Note that the Latin *caro* ("flesh") from which we derive "in-*carn*-ation," has a similar range of meanings.

19. See E. Schweizer, "*sarx,*" *Theological Dictionary of the New Testament,* ed. Kittel, 8:99–110.

20. For example, Gen. 6:3; Isa. 3:3; Jer. 17:5; Ps. 78:39; Sir. 14:7-8; also 1QH 4:29.

21. An alternative reading has the verb in the singular: "who was born . . . ," referring not to believers but to the Light (1:9) and his miraculous birth. The witnesses to this reading, however, are not sufficiently strong to overturn the weight of Greek manuscripts. See Metzger, *Textual Commentary,* 168–69.

22. Bernard, *Commentary,* 1:18; see also Augustine, *In Joannis Evangelium* 2.14.

23. Beasley-Murray, *John,* 13.

24. Malina and Rohrbaugh, *Social-Science Commentary on John,* 32–33. On 1:13, see further chapter 6 below, 140–42.

25. Ibid., 32.

26. Schnackenburg, *Gospel,* 1:267.

27. The term "world" (*kosmos*), however, can be used in either sense (Bultmann, *Gospel,* 62). John's use of "world" is complex, with different shades of meaning, positive and negative. There is no ontological dualism in this understanding of *kosmos*: the distinction is primarily eschatological; see Bultmann, *Gospel,* 54–55. On this, see further chapter 7 below, 182.

28. Bultmann sees this as the turning point of the Prologue (*Gospel,* 60–61). According to Dunn (*Christology,* 241), prior to v. 14, no Hellenistic Jew would find the Logos hymn alien or unfamiliar. See also Ringe, *Wisdom's Friends,* 51.

29. See Schnackenburg, *Gospel,* 1:267–68.

30. See John 1:14 [2x]; 2:11; 5:41, 44 [2x]; 7:18 [2x]; 8:50, 54; 9:24; 11:4, 40; 12:41, 43 [2x]; 17:5, 22, 24.

31. See John 7:39; 8:54 [2x]; 11:4; 12:16, 23, 28 [3x]; 13:31 [2x]; 32 [2x?]; 14:13; 15:8; 16:14; 17:1 [2x], 4, 5, 10; 21:19.

32. Witherington, *John's Wisdom,* 55.

33. Kittel, "*doxa,*" *Theological Dictionary,* ed. Kittel, 2:245.

34. Schnelle, *Antidocetic Christology,* 81.

35. Compare Exod. 40:34–35; 1 Kgs. 8:10–11; Pss. 24:7–10; 63:2; 102:16; Isa. 4:5; 60:1–7; Ezek. 43:4–5; 44:4. On the language for "tabernacle," see Koester, *Dwelling of God,* 102–4.

36. On the temple theme, see further Coloe, *God Dwells with Us.*

37. Barrett, *St. John,* 165.

38. Cf. Culpepper's chiastic structure for the Prologue which places 1:12b—"he gave authority to become children of God"—at the center ("Pivot of John's Prologue").

39. Moloney describes the structure of the Prologue as like a series of waves on the seashore, each wave carrying the message further forward (*John,* 34).

40. Note that Craig R. Koester does not discuss directly "flesh" as a Johannine symbol, although he sees Jesus' identity—human, messianic, and divine—as lying at the heart of Johannine symbolism (*Symbolism in the Fourth Gospel,* 5, 13–15, 39–45).

41. Schnelle, *Antidocetic Christology,* 81, 175.

42. Ibid., 166.

43. See Thompson, *Humanity of Jesus*, 53–86.

44. Hans Weder, "Deus Incarnatus: On the Hermeneutics of Christology in the Johannine Writings," in *Exploring the Gospel of John*, ed. Culpepper and Black, 334.

45. Against this view, see Schnelle, *Antidocetic Christology*, 82, 173–74.

46. The phrase is either appositional or explicative: "the temple, namely, his body" or "the temple that is his body"; see Moloney, *John*, 82.

47. It is most likely that the verb *gennan* means "to give birth" in this context; see Lee, *Symbolic Narratives*, 43–48. For the meaning "to beget," see Brown, *Gospel*, 1:129.

48. See Lee, *Symbolic Narratives*, 49–52.

49. On this, see further chapter 3 below.

50. See, for example, his discussion of the wedding at Cana or the feeding of the multitude (Augustine, *In Joannis Evangelium* 9.1; 24.1).

51. This view goes back to Irenaeus, *Against Heresies* 4.15.2, ed. Harvey; see also Barrett, *St. John*, 355; and Lee, *Symbolic Narratives*, 185–86.

52. Most commentators accept this reading of the Nicodemus story; for a different view, which sees Nicodemus remaining in darkness, see, for example, Bassler, "Mixed Signals"; Goulder, "Nicodemus."

53. Käsemann, *Testament of Jesus*, 25–26.

54. On this, see further Lee, *Symbolic Narratives*, 94–97.

55. In contrast to the Synoptic accounts, where Jesus gives the divided loaves and fish to the disciples to distribute to the people (Mark 6:32–44 pars.; Mark 8:1–9 par.).

56. Despite the literary awkwardness, this seems to be one and the same group in dialogue with Jesus, creating a rough but discernible narrative line; see Lee, *Symbolic Narratives*, 130–31.

57. Brown, *Gospel*, 1:272, 290–91.

58. For the view that the discourse is only sapiential and not eucharistic, see Dunn, "John VI, A Eucharistic Discourse?"

59. Against Bultmann (*Gospel*, 234–37), who argues that this section is a later addition, P. Borgen sees these verses as a midrashic expansion of the "quotation" in 6:31 (*Logos Was the True Light*, 21–22, 23–24).

60. There is no "I am" saying for the water to parallel the "I am" saying for the bread (6:34), precisely because of the link with the Spirit. In John's theology, Jesus is the giver of the Spirit but also distinct from the Spirit, whereas with the bread Jesus is both giver and gift.

61. As, for example, Bultmann does (*Gospel*, 234–37); see also Haenchen, *Commentary*, 1:296-300. Against this, see Schnackenburg, *Gospel*, 2:56–59.

62. See Lee, *Symbolic Narratives*, 155–57.

63. According to Bernard (*Commentary*, 1:283), in the Old Testament *koilia* is "the seat of man's emotional nature." See also Léon-Dufour, *Lecture*, 2:237.

64. The NRSV follows the punctuation of the first alternative, but still regards the "belly" as referring to the believer. See also Witherington, *John's Wisdom*, 174.

65. For this reading, see, for example, Barrett, *St. John*, 326–27; Haenchen, *Commentary*, 2:17; and Lindars, *Gospel*, 299–300.

66. On the wisdom overtones here, see Witherington, *John's Wisdom*, 173–74; and Corley, "Wisdom's Rescue," 100–102.

67. For the christological reading, see, for example, Brown, *Gospel*; Moloney, *John*, 256; and Schnackenburg, *Gospel*, 2:153–54.

68. The contradiction is purely formal. As Schnackenburg points out, "God's saving will always prevails over his judgment" (*Gospel*, 2:105).

69. On this, see further chapter 7 below.

70. In between the Tabernacles Discourse and the Farewell Discourse, there is also the raising of Lazarus, which makes reference to Jesus' emotional response upon meeting the mourners on the way to the tomb (anger, tears, 11:33, 35, 38). The question is whether these emotions are part of the depiction of Jesus' humanity—the normal expression of grief and anger at the death of a friend (11:36). That hardly makes sense of the narrative: Jesus' response to Lazarus's illness and death has been to delay his coming (11:6), and he expresses joy at the prospect of raising Lazarus from the dead (11:15). The narrative is concerned with resurrection and life, not death. The glory revealed in the flesh is in the "sign" itself: the authoritative calling of Lazarus from the tomb and the releasing of his body (11:38–44). On this, see further chapter 9 below.

71. Hoskyns and Davey, *Fourth Gospel*, 2:519.

72. Léon-Dufour, *Lecture*, 3:45; and Talbert, *Reading John*, 195. Note that this is the first formal reference to the beloved disciple in the Fourth Gospel. Witherington suggests the possibility that he is a Judean disciple who is, in fact, hosting the banquet (*John's Wisdom*, 239), but this ignores the symbolic significance of the beloved disciple's relationship to Jesus at the level of the fourth evangelist (as opposed to the historical level).

73. Brouwer, *Literary Development of John 13–17*, 9–10, 117–18; see also Moloney, *John*, 477–79. On chiasmus in the Farewell Discourse, see further Breck, *Shape of Biblical Language*, 213–29.

74. A better title than the traditional "high priestly prayer"; so Schnackenburg, *Gospel*, 3:167–202.

75. On this, see Bultmann, *Gospel*, 407–8.

76. Dodd, *Interpretation*, 419–20.

77. For a similar, though not identical structure, see Perkins, *John*, 197–98.

78. See, e.g., Brown, *Gospel*, 2:740; Schnackenburg, *Gospel*, 3:171; Bernard, *Commentary*, 2:560–61; and Kysar, *John*, 255. Léon-Dufour argues that "all flesh" and "everything you have given him" present the same opposition between natural and redeemed humanity that is found at 1:12 (*Lecture*, 3:281–82).

79. See Gen. 6:18, 20; 7:15, 16, 21; 8:17; 21; 9:11, 15, 19; cf. 1 Cor. 15:39.

80. Note the textual problems with both verses in John 17, precisely on this point of the neuter, which suggests that scribes were puzzled by John's seemingly erratic movement (here and elsewhere) between masculine and neuter. The most difficult, textually speaking, is 10:29, where the relative pronoun *ho* ("that which") has a plethora of textual variants, although the most likely text reads: "What my Father has given me is greater than all and no one can snatch [it? them?] out of the Father's hand."

81. A textual variant in v. 39 has "him" rather than "it" but is not well attested.

82. Blass-Debrunner-Funk §1.1 argues that the neuter may be used "if it is not the individuals but a general quality that is to be emphasized."

83. So Brown, *Gospel*, 2:741; Barrett, *St. John*, 502; and Moloney, *John*, 463.

84. Moloney concedes that 6:37 could refer to all creation, although the focus is on human beings (*John*, 216).

85. Perkins, *John*, 198.

86. Whitacre, *John*, 404. See, for example, John 3:35; 5:19–29; (12:32); 13:3; 14:26; 15:15; 16:15, 30; 17:7, 10; 19:28.

87. As Barrett notes (*St. John*, 201).

88. The textual problem in 19:38 is minor and makes no difference to the meaning.

89. Here the word used is *psychē*, which in some instances means "life" (see 10:11, 15, 24) and not "soul," as it is sometimes used elsewhere (e.g., Matt. 10:38; cf. John 12:27). Later

in the Johannine narrative, Simon Peter will claim that he is prepared to "lay down his life [*psychē*]" for Jesus, but Jesus disabuses him of his illusions (13:37–38; cf. 15:13).

90. We need to beware of a linguistic fundamentalism that associates a concept definitively with a single word; on this, see further Barr, *Semantics of Biblical Language,* especially 206–62. As a parallel, note that Logos, though central to John's theology, is not found in direct, christological form outside the Prologue.

91. Moloney relates *anthrōpos* to the Son of Man title elsewhere in the Fourth Gospel (*John,* 495).

92. Brodie, *Gospel,* 537.

93. Schnackenburg, *Gospel,* 3:257.

94. The Passover connotations of the hyssop are found in Exod. 12:22–23. On this scene, see further chapter 3 below.

95. The climactic nature of this scene is indicated by the reference to the one who sees and bears witness to the truth (19:35) and the two quotations from Scripture (19:36–37).

96. Schnelle, *Antidocetic Christology,* 209.

97. On the further symbolic associations of this scene, and particularly its feminine iconography, see chapters 3 (pp. 82–83) and 6 (pp. 158–59) below.

98. The Johannine Epistles are close to the Gospel in their use of language for the incarnation, although there are also differences. "Flesh" refers in two out of three instances to the corporeality of Jesus, which is central to the author's antidocetic Christology (1 John 4:2; 2 John 7); this is reinforced by the remarkably tangible language found in the opening words of 1 John: "that which we have *heard,* that which we have *seen with our eyes,* that which we have *gazed upon* and *our hands have handled*" (1 John 1:1). Later, the same Epistle speaks of "the water and the blood" as witnesses alongside the Spirit (1 John 5:6–8), with reference presumably to the flow of blood and water in the Gospel (John 19:34), which has both incarnational and sacramental overtones. However, the Epistles seem to depart from Johannine usage in at least two respects: blood is now explicitly regarded as cleansing (1 John 1:7) and, on one occasion, *sarx* is used pejoratively, with reference to concupiscence, in the phrase "the desire of the flesh" (1 John 2:16). Bultmann sees this as closer to the Pauline sense of "a power hostile to God" (*Johannine Epistles,* 33). Yet even in Johannine terms, the flesh unenlivened by the Spirit does become inimical to God (cf. 8:15, 59).

99. On the appearance to Mary Magdalene, see further chapter 9 below, 220–26.

100. Graham Ward, "Bodies: The Displaced Body of Jesus Christ," in *Radical Orthodoxy,* ed. Milbank et al., 163–81.

101. Ibid., 167.

102. We need to note that strictly speaking the Greek fathers tried to distinguish between "image" and "likeness," arguing that only the latter is lost in the Fall. See especially J. P. Smith, *St. Irenaeus,* 126 n. 70. While the distinction cannot be sustained linguistically, the attempt to present the Fall as partial rather than total is of great theological importance.

103. The Orthodox understanding of "deification" derives, at least in part, from the Johannine notion of glorification. On "*theōsis,*" see C. Stavropoulos, "Partakers of Divine Nature," in *Eastern Orthodox Theology: A Contemporary Reader,* ed. Clendenin, 183–92.

104. On the distinction between the verbs "to be" (*einai*) and "to become" (*ginesthai*) in the Prologue, see Frank Kermode, "John," in *Literary Guide to the Bible,* ed. Alter and Kermode, 443–48; also John Chrysostom, *Homilies on John* 40.

105. See Lee, *Symbolic Narratives,* 21, 62–63, 94–97, 230–35.

106. For an opposing view, see Käsemann, *Testament of Jesus,* esp. 9–13, 25–26. Against Käsemann, see G. Bornkamm, "Towards the Interpretation of John's Gospel: A Discussion of *The Testament of Jesus* by Ernst Käsemann," in *The Interpretation of John,* ed. J. Ashton, 97–119; and Thompson, *Humanity of Jesus,* 1–11, 33–53, 87–115. On the antidocetism of

John in general, see Hoskyns and Davey, *Fourth Gospel*, 1:45–55; Lindars, *Gospel*, 61–63; and Schnelle, *Antidocetic Christology*.

107. To call this "Christology from above" is an unhelpful distinction for John's Gospel, ignoring the essentially symbolic character of its theology in which the "flesh" is central; J. Moltmann rejects the distinction between Christology "from above" and "from below" as simplistic and misleading (*Way of Jesus Christ*, 69).

108. Schneiders, *Written That You May Believe*, 69–74, especially 71–72.

109. The danger of divorcing Jesus from the theologies that shape his presentation in the Gospels is that he becomes ideologically a child of our own times and remarkably attuned to contemporary Western liberal-democratic values: sharing our ideological concerns about imperialism and democracy, our postmodern unease toward organized religion, and our discomfort with anything that seems overtly "supernatural." Even Elisabeth Schüssler Fiorenza argues that the latest quest of the historical Jesus, in which she too has an interest, has a kind of historicism that takes little or no account of interpretative bias (*Miriam's Child*, 82–88; eadem, *Jesus: The Politics of Interpretation*, 82–114). Despite concerns to revalorize the humanity of Jesus, such reconstructions—including among feminists—can easily dismiss the Johannine Jesus as at best a subjective extrapolation of the human figure or at worst a distortion of Jesus' simple moral teaching and political insight. Against this, see Luke Timothy Johnson, who argues that the "real Jesus" is the Jesus of the Gospels, "who is now alive and powerfully present, through the Holy Spirit, in the world and in the lives of human beings" (*Real Jesus*, 144).

110. Jasper, *Shining Garment of the Text*. Jasper examines Augustine, Hildegard of Bingen, Luther, Bultmann, and Adrienne von Speyr, concluding that each—although to different degrees—promotes "a view of the flesh in terms of a contaminating, perverse otherness, symbolised by woman and the feminine" (p. 23).

111. Ibid., pp. 162–82, 183–209.

112. Ibid., 209.

113. Ibid., 207. Jasper herself attempts a feminist rereading of flesh in the Fourth Gospel, using Julia Kristeva's psychoanalytic categories (pp. 210–33).

114. The term is used by Carter Heyward throughout *Touching Our Strength*.

115. Irigaray, "Equal to Whom?"; also Casey, "Luce Irigaray," 51–53.

116. See especially Ruether, *To Change the World*, 45–56; eadem, *Sexism and God-Talk*, 116–38; eadem, *Introducing Redemption in Christian Feminism*, 81–94. For a succinct theological summary of the issues in the way the maleness of Christ has been used, see Elizabeth Johnson, "Redeeming the Name of Christ," in *Freeing Theology*, ed. LaCugna, 118–20.

117. Moltmann-Wendel, "Christ in Feminist Context," in *Christ and Context*, ed. Regan and Torrance, 105.

118. Ruether, *Women and Redemption*, 277.

119. Daly, *Beyond God the Father*, 72, 69–97.

120. Hampson, *Theology and Feminism*, 50–80, especially 50, 53–66.

121. McFague, *Models of God*, 70; see also 69–87, 93.

122. Ibid., 136.

123. Ibid., 137.

124. For a critique of Christa and works of art in a similar vein, see D'Costa, *Sexing the Trinity*, 61–75.

125. Heyward, *Touching Our Strength*, 114–18.

126. Brock, *Journeys by Heart*.

127. Ibid., 50–70.

128. Carter Heyward, "Christa," in *Dictionary of Feminist Theologies*, ed. Russell et al., 40.

129. Brock, *Journeys by Heart*, 52.

130. Heyward, *Touching Our Strength*, 94.

131. Schüssler Fiorenza, *Miriam's Child,* especially 20–24.

132. See, for example, her critique of Ruether (*Miriam's Child*, 43–47); also *Jesus: The Politics of Interpretation*, 145–49.

133. Schüssler Fiorenza, *Miriam's Child*, 131–62. It is ironic that, having rejected the notion of Jesus as the unique, revealed, divine Word/Son of God, Schüssler Fiorenza in her discussion of Mariology (*Miriam's Child*, 180) suggests that mythological Marian language needs to be relocated in all three persons of the Trinity!

134. On this, see further Schüssler Fiorenza, *Jesus: The Politics of Interpretation*, 145–74.

135. Ruether, *Sexism and God-Talk*, 137.

136. Ruether, *Introducing Redemption*, 85.

137. Ruether, *Sexism and God-Talk*, 137.

138. Ruether, *Introducing Redemption*, 93.

139. See also Kelly Brown Douglas (*The Black Christ,* 97–117), who argues that black Christology is based not on Christ's metaphysical identity but rather on his prophetic ministry and his friendship and empathy with black women in their struggles against oppression; thus, for them, the christological question is not Who? but Where? and With whom? Jacqueline Grant gives an excellent summary of feminist Christologies (*White Women's Christ*, 91–194) but argues that they are deeply flawed in being white and racist (p. 195).

140. See Schüssler Fiorenza, *Miriam's Child*, 119–21, 143–53.

141. Soskice, "Blood and Defilement," 288–89.

142. D' Costa, *Sexing the Trinity*, 59.

143. See, for example, E. Johnson, "Redeeming the Name of Christ," in *Freeing Theology,* ed. LaCugna, 115–37; Soskice, "Blood and Defilement," 285–303; Wilson-Kastner, *Faith, Feminism and the Christ;* and Carr, *Transforming Grace,* 158–88. From a womanist perspective, Grant argues that black women traditionally saw Jesus as "the divine co-sufferer" and that their belief in Jesus as God "meant that White people were not God" (*White Women's Christ*, 212–13).

144. E. Johnson, "Redeeming the Name of Christ," 130.

145. Ibid., 127–31; also Soskice, "Blood and Defilement," 285–89; Wilson-Kastner, *Faith, Feminism and the Christ*, 114–16. Ray S. Anderson's otherwise insightful critique of Sallie McFague unfairly associates her depersonalized Christology with that of Johnson and Wilson-Kastner ("The Incarnation of God in Feminist Christology," in *Speaking the Christian God,* ed. Kimel, 288–312).

146. Janet Martin Soskice, "Response" (to Moltmann-Wendel, "Christ in Feminist Context"), in *Christ in Context*, ed. Regan and Torrance, 121.

147. D'Costa, *Sexing the Trinity*, 74.

148. See A. Y. Collins, "New Testament Perspectives," 50–51.

149. E. Johnson, *She Who Is*, 97. On this see further chapter 6 below.

150. For the former view, see Schüssler Fiorenza, *Miriam's Child*, 152–54; and McKinlay, *Gendering Wisdom*, 179–207; for the latter view, see Scott, *Sophia and the Johannine Jesus*, 172; and E. Johnson, *She Who Is*, 99. See also Ringe, *Wisdom's Friends*, 62.

151. See Lightfoot, *St. John's Gospel*, 321–22.

152. See Caroline Walker Bynum, who demonstrates that, throughout much of the Western tradition, Christianity was not, strictly speaking, dualistic—as witnessed in the persistence of a very physical and literal belief in the resurrection of the body (*Resurrection of the Body*). On the Eastern Christian tradition, see Ware, "My Helper and My Enemy," 90–110.

153. On the role of eros alongside other forms of love in Christian theology, see Tillich, *Love, Power and Justice*, 24–34, 116–18.

154. Schnelle, *Antidocetic Christology*, 167.

155. Schnackenburg, *Gospel*, 1:267.

156. Irigaray, *Speculum of the Other Woman;* see also D'Costa, *Sexing the Trinity*, 64.

157. Rahner, *Theological Investigations*, 4:239.

158. Gerard Loughlin, "Erotics: God's Sex," in *Radical Orthodoxy*, ed. Milbank et al., 158.

CHAPTER 3
QUENCHING THIRST: THE SYMBOL OF LIVING WATER

1. Hymn from the Orthodox Liturgy on the Feast of St. Photini and St. Phota, 26 February.

2. So Culpepper, *Anatomy of the Fourth Gospel*, 189–90; Koester, *Symbolism*, 4–12; and van der Watt, *Family of the King*, 101.

3. Larry Paul Jones sees water as not yet symbolic, even in outline, at this point in the narrative (*Symbol of Water*, 50–51).

4. See Moloney, "From Cana to Cana."

5. Jones, *Symbol of Water*, 64.

6. Although this is not strictly a supersessionist view of the relationship between Christianity and Judaism, it is typological, regarding the Old Testament and Judaism as possessing no independent existence outside the revelation of God in Christ.

7. See chapter 2 above.

8. See Richard, "Expressions of Double Meaning," 102–4; and Wead, "Johannine Double Meaning," 106–8.

9. The narrative prefers to use *pneuma* for "wind" rather than the more common noun, *anemos*, creating deliberate ambiguity.

10. See, for example, Pamment, "John 3.5," 189–90; and Witherington, *John's Wisdom*, 97.

11. So Jones, *Symbol of Water*, 70.

12. Ibid., 74; see also Léon-Dufour, *Lecture*, 1:292, who quotes Ezek. 36:25–27.

13. Jones, *Symbol of Water*, 75.

14. On the birth overtones throughout 3:1–21, see Lee, *Symbolic Narratives*, 43–48.

15. It is difficult to know the precise meaning of 3:31–36: either the speaker or the overall significance of the imagery. This reading presupposes that the Johannine Jesus is the speaker, not John the Baptist, and that the incident concerning baptism (3:22–30) has been deliberately inserted into the discourse with Nicodemus (3:10–21); see Lee, *Symbolic Narratives*, 42, 60–61.

16. It is as a reference to baptism that Bultmann excludes the words "of water" as a later, editorial intrusion—an attempt by a later redaction to insinuate sacraments into the supposedly antisacramental theology of the Fourth Gospel (*John*, 138–39). Against this, see Schnackenburg, *Gospel*, 1:369; and I. de la Potterie, "'Naître de l'eau et naître de L'Esprit': Le texte baptismal de Jean 3.5," in *La vie selon l'Esprit*, ed. de la Potterie and Lyonnet, 31–63.

17. As Jones does (*Symbol of Water*, 75–76).

18. See Schnackenburg, *Gospel*, 1:368–74; Bultmann, *Gospel*, 135–38; Lindars, *Gospel*, 150–54; and Dodd, *Interpretation*, 303–5; see also Lee, *Symbolic Narratives*, 43–48. Against this, see Brown (*Gospel*, 1:129) and Haenchen (*Commentary*, 1:200), who see the basic

image as paternal rather than maternal. See also van Tilborg, *Imaginative Love,* 33-53, who argues that "water" means seed.

19. Sandra Schneiders, "Born Anew," 192.

20. Ben Witherington III, "The Waters of Birth," 155–60, especially 158; also idem, *John's Wisdom,* 97.

21. On the birth imagery, see further chapter 6 below, 140–59.

22. On the betrothal/wedding imagery, see Alter, *Art of Biblical Narrative,* 51–62; Schneiders, *Revelatory Text,* 187; and Fehribach, *Women in the Life of the Bridegroom,* 47–58.

23. Pazdan, "Nicodemus and the Samaritan Woman," 145–48; and Conway, *Men and Women in the Fourth Gospel,* 103–6.

24. On the religious significance of Jacob's well, see Neyrey, "Jacob Traditions."

25. See Allison, "Living Water," 144–46, 151–52.

26. Bultmann, *Gospel,* 186.

27. For a different reading that argues that, whereas Jesus is inconsistent in separating the physical and the spiritual, the woman refuses to do so, see Moore, "Are There Impurities?" 222–25; for Moore, "the female student has outstripped her male teacher" (p. 225).

28. Bultmann, *Gospel,* 188. It is unlikely that these verses are related allegorically to the idolatry of the Samaritans (see 2 Kgs. 17:29–34); so Barrett, *St. John,* 235–36; and Schnackenburg, *Gospel,* 1:433. Against this, see Léon-Dufour, *Lecture,* 1:362–64; and Schneiders, *Revelatory Text,* 190–91. See chapter 7 below.

29. For a discussion of the nonjudgmental attitude of Jesus to the woman, see Conway, *Men and Women in the Fourth Gospel,* 116–19; and Jones, *Symbol of Water,* 101–2; also chapter 7 below.

30. So Calvin, *St. John,* 1:20.

31. There are various theories to explain the woman's action: her eagerness to go home (Schnackenburg, *Gospel,* 1:443; and Bultmann, *Gospel,* 193) or her intention to return (Lindars, *Gospel,* 28; Beasley-Murray, *John,* 63; O'Day, *Revelation in the Fourth Gospel,* 75; and Moloney, *John,* 134–35) or it provides a parallel with the disciples in the Synoptics (e.g., Mark 1:16-20 par.), who leave behind their occupations to follow Jesus (John Chrysostom, *Homily on John* 34.1; and Schneiders, *Revelatory Text,* 192). Most likely, the woman has moved from a literal understanding (cf. 4:15) to a symbolic one, taking on a new role as witness (see Conway, *Men and Women in the Fourth Gospel,* 122–23).

32. For Moloney (*John,* 29) and Maccini (*Her Testimony Is True,* 140–42), the woman's understanding is still partial; Teresa Okure argues, however, that the woman speaks with the openness of the true missionary (*Johannine Approach to Mission,* 174–75).

33. O'Day, *Revelation in the Fourth Gospel,* 89.

34. See John Painter, "John 9," 47; and idem, *John: Witness and Theologian,* 140–41.

35. It is this tensive dynamic that Moore fails to grasp in his conviction that the Johannine Jesus speaks inconsistently against his own being, separating the physical and the spiritual in his words to the Samaritan woman, whereas they are intermingled—mutually "contaminating"—in his person ("Are There Impurities?" 218–25). Throughout the Gospel, however, the two levels are not identical yet are ultimately inseparable, both in the Johannine Jesus himself and in his message.

36. On this interpretation, see Barrett, *St. John,* 233–34; Beare, "Spirit of Life and Truth," 113–14, 120; and McKinlay, *Gendering Wisdom the Host,* 182–92.

37. A formal contradiction with John 4:13–14, which is nevertheless making much the same point; so Bultmann, *Gospel,* 186–87.

38. Calvin captures this dynamic well: "without knowledge of self there is no knowledge of God" and "without knowledge of God there is no knowledge of self" (*Institutes,* ed. McNeill, I.1.1 and 2).

39. For this view, see Bultmann, *Gospel,* 184–85.

40. McKinlay, *Gendering Wisdom the Host,* 210.

41. So Schnackenburg, *Gospel,* 1:426; Brown, *Gospel,* 1:178–79; and Olsson, *Structure and Meaning,* 214–18.

42. See chapter 2 above, 41–42.

43. The evening ritual for the feast was the lighting of the lamps in the temple, illuminating the whole city of Jerusalem; see Moloney, *Signs and Shadows,* 66–70.

44. According to Moloney, throughout John 5–10 the evangelist uses the feasts as "signs and shadows" to present Jesus as "the perfection of Jewish liturgy and theology" (*Signs and Shadows,* ix) and the one who "fulfills, universalizes and transcends all the symbols and expectations" of Judaism (p. 102).

45. Jones, *Symbol of Water,* 136.

46. "Siloam" could well be derived from the Hebrew verb *šālaḥ,* meaning "send" (cf. Gen. 49:10; Isa. 8:6), though the actual etymology is a Johannine construction.

47. Jones, *Symbol of Water,* 160.

48. Brown (*Gospel,* 2:559–62), following M.-E. Boismard, sees the footwashing as having two separate but parallel interpretations: the first ritual (13:6–11) and the second paraenetic or moral (13:12–17). Yet the example that Jesus sets his disciples is grounded in relationship and salvation: disciples wash each other's feet because, and only because, they have been drawn into the radical love of Jesus. On the literary unity of the passage, see Thomas, *Footwashing,* 116–25.

49. See Moloney's structure (*John,* 477–79); see also chapter 2 above.

50. See Lee, "Presence or Absence?"

51. Moloney, *John,* 383–84.

52. For a survey of different exegetical interpretations of the footwashing, see Thomas, *Footwashing,* 11–17.

53. On the Jewish and Roman-Hellenistic background of the practice of footwashing, see Thomas, *Footwashing,* 26–60.

54. Assuming the longer text of 13:10: "The one who bathes (*louein*) has no need to wash (*niptein*) except for the feet, but is entirely clean," as opposed to the shorter reading, which omits "except for the feet." While many commentators support the shorter ending (e.g., Brown, *Gospel,* 2:552; and Moloney, *John,* 378–79), the longer ending is well attested and makes sense of Jesus' insistence on the necessity of footwashing in 13:8 (in this context, distinguishing the verb *louein*—meaning a complete bath—from *niptein,* denoting a partial wash). For the longer ending, see Metzger, *Textual Commentary,* 240; and Thomas, *Footwashing,* 19–25.

55. In the Jewish apocryphal romance, Aseneth washes Joseph's feet as an act of love and hospitality ("Joseph and Aseneth," in *Old Testament Pseudepigrapha,* ed. Charlesworth, vol 2, chap. 20); see Thomas, *Footwashing,* 38–40.

56. Philo, *Questions and Answers on Exodus,* Suppl. 2, p. 7; on the cultic aspect of footwashing, see Thomas, *Footwashing,* 27–31.

57. So Thomas, *Footwashing,* 149–72.

58. Witherington, *John's Wisdom,* 310–11.

59. Jones, *Symbol of Water,* 204–5.

60. Moore argues that Jesus' thirst in the story of the Samaritan Woman has as its purpose "to arouse *her* thirst" ("Are There Impurities?" 208). However, Moore also goes on to suggest that Jesus desires to be desired by the woman, thus filling his own lack. Such a reading ignores Jesus' explicit intention throughout the Gospel to do not his own will but the Father's will (4:34; 5:19–30; 19:28). On Jesus' thirst in the context of his death, see further chapter 2 above, 46–47.

61. Heil, *Blood and Water,* 106; also Jones, *Symbol of Water,* 211.

62. On this passage, see further chapter 2 above.

63. Witherington, who does not make the connection with birth (or sacraments) here, says of John 3 that we fail to perceive the birth imagery because we live "in an antiseptic age, where birth is . . . hidden from view" ("Waters of Birth," 160).

64. See chapter 6 below, 158–59.

65. On the relationship between John 21 and the rest of the Gospel, see chapter 9 below, 221, 271.

66. For this view, see Koester, *Symbolism,* 156.

67. John is most often interpreted as a sectarian Gospel, with a sense of being cut off from the world, and (to a certain extent) from the rest of the church. Yet there is also a universalism in the message of the Gospel which stands in some tension with this view.

68. On the exegetical problems of 4:22, see de la Potterie, "'Nous adorons,'" 77–85.

69. Note the Samaritan terminology of the woman's outlook—particularly its view of messianism—which Jesus seems to confirm (4:25).

70. As Moore mistakenly reads it ("Are There Impurities?" 207–27); see also McKinlay, *Gendering Wisdom the Host,* 182–84.

71. On this theme, see further R. F. Collins, "Representative Figures of the Fourth Gospel." Augustine interprets the woman in this story as representative of the church (*In Joannis Evangelium* 15.10.1, 2; 15.22.2).

72. On the woman's independence and public role here (which parallels that of Mary Magdalene), see van Tilborg, *Imaginative Love,* 171–77.

CHAPTER 4
ABIDING ON THE VINE: SYMBOLS OF LOVE AND FRIENDSHIP

1. From Christina Rossetti, "After Communion," in *Women in Praise of the Sacred,* ed. Hirschfield, 189.

2. See F. Hauck, "*menō,*" in *Theological Dictionary of the New Testament,* 4:574–76; and Brown, *Gospel,* 1:510–11; also Heise, *Bleiben,* 22–28. Both the sense of God abiding forever (God's word, dominion, covenant, counsel—e.g., LXX [*menein*] Pss. 9:8; 111:3, 9; Isa. 40:8; Wis. 7:27) and God's indwelling in Zion (e.g., LXX [*kataskēnoun*] Ezek. 43:7; Zech. 2:11; Joel 4:17; Sir. 24:4) are relevant for John's heightened usage of *menein* and its synonyms. See also Lee, "Abiding in the Fourth Gospel."

3. On the two broad meanings of *menein,* see Heise, *Bleiben,* 47–103.

4. Ibid., 44.

5. Assuming "Son of God" as the more likely reading than "elect one of God"; against this, see Schnackenburg, *Gospel,* 1:305–6.

6. Léon-Dufour, *Lecture,* 1:189.

7. Barrett, *St. John,* 181.

8. Ibid., 243.

9. Brown proposes that the participle *trōgōn* ("eating") here has a distinct meaning from the normal verb "to eat" (*esthiein*) (*Gospel,* 1:283). Since the verb *trōgein* in classical Greek is used of the eating of animals, Brown suggests that it is deliberately chosen "to emphasize the realism of the eucharistic flesh." By this stage, however, the verb *trōgein* seems to have lost its original force; see Barrett, *St. John,* 299; and Schnackenburg, *Gospel,* 2:62.

10. Willett, *Wisdom Christology,* 112. On the Wisdom/Sophia overtones of "abiding," see Scott, *Sophia and the Johannine Jesus,* 157–59.

11. On the influence of Wisdom traditions in the discourse, see Catherine Cory, "Wisdom's Rescue, 95–116.

12. On the complex question of the eschatology of the Farewell Discourse, see Brown, *Gospel*, 2:601–3. Schnackenburg rather overstates the case for realized eschatology when he speaks of "the magnificent one-sidedness of Johannine eschatology," which is nevertheless corrected by the evangelist's disciples (*Gospel*, 2:426–37, especially 437).

13. Brown defines the Johannine Paraclete as "the Holy Spirit in a special role namely, as the personal presence of Jesus in the Christian while Jesus is with the Father" (*Gospel*, 2:1139). The definition is helpful, but overly individualistic.

14. Segovia, *Farewell of the Word*, 123–35.

15. Brouwer, *Literary Development*. Brouwer's literary reading does not deny the complex prehistory of the present Johannine text.

16. Ibid., 9–10, 117–18.

17. Moloney, *John*, 417.

18. For the structure, see Brodie, *Gospel*, 479–84, with some amendments.

19. As Witherington points out (*John's Wisdom*, 257–58), early Judaism makes no clear distinction between parable and allegory. See also Brown, *Gospel*, 2:668–72; and D. Moody Smith, *John*, 279–80.

20. See Brown, *Gospel*, 2:665–68. Note the presence of both sets of imagery in Psalm 80.

21. Culpepper, *Gospel and Letters*, 213–15.

22. On the parallelism with the symbolism and rites of Dionysius, see Sanford, *Mystical Christianity*, 284–85.

23. Witherington, *John's Wisdom*, 258.

24. "[T]he overriding theme of the Fourth Gospel is . . . the revelation of God in Jesus and the way in which it was and should be received" (Ashton, *Understanding the Fourth Gospel*, 383).

25. Beasley-Murray, *John*, 272. See also Augustine, *In Joannis Evangelium* 80.2.

26. O'Day, "John," 303.

27. Brodie, *Gospel*, 482.

28. Witherington rejects the interpretation that the pruning refers to "the Jews": "This Gospel is not interested in pitting the Christians over against the Jews as the true people of God" (*John's Wisdom*, 256).

29. Brodie, *Gospel*, 475.

30. The two Greek verbs "thrown out" and "withered" are both in the aorist, giving a vivid sense of action completed: as if the pruning of dead branches has already happened. See Lagrange, *Évangile*, 404.

31. Schnackenburg, *Gospel*, 3:99.

32. Dodd, *Interpretation*, 187; see also Brown, *Gospel*, 1:511.

33. Dodd, *Interpretation*, 194.

34. See Segovia, *Farewell of the Word*, 179–212. In Brouwer's chiasmus, 15:18–16:4a is paralleled by 14:27–31 under the rubric of "troubling encounter with the world" (*John 13-17*, 9–10, 117–18).

35. Barrett captures the nuanced sense of "the world" in the Fourth Gospel, commenting on Jesus' prayer in 17:9: "John, having stated (3.16) the love of God for the *kosmos*, does not withdraw from that position in favour of a narrow affection for the pious. . . . But to pray for the *kosmos* would be almost an absurdity, since the only hope for the *kosmos* is precisely that it should cease to be the *kosmos*" (*St. John*, 506). On this, see further chapter 7 below, 182–84.

36. See Rensberger, *Overcoming the World*, 15–36.

37. This is the pattern of the narrative of the man born blind in John 9, opposition and hostility ironically leading the man to faith.

38. Gruenler, *Trinity*, 107.

39. The proportionate usage of the two word groups is a little more than one to three. Further on the *phil-* words, see G. Stählin, "*Phileō, Kataphileō, Philēma, Philos, Philē, Philia,*" in *Theological Dictionary of the New Testament* 9:113–71.

40. Stählin, "*Phileō*," 147, 151–54.

41. See, in particular, Cicero, *De Amicitia;* also Aristotle, *Nicomachean Ethics,* books 8 and 9; and Plutarch, "*De Multitudine Amicorum,*" in *Moralia* 2.93–97.

42. Van Tilborg, *Imaginative Love,* 149.

43. G. E. Sterling, "The Bond of Humanity," in *Greco-Roman Perspectives on Friendship,* ed. Fitzgerald, 203–23.

44. On this theme, see further Willett, *Wisdom Christology,* 105–13.

45. On background ideas of friendship in the Greco-Roman, Jewish, and early Christian worlds, see Ford, *Redeemer, Friend and Mother,* 76–92.

46. Ringe, *Wisdom's Friends,* 93, 65.

47. See John 13:23–26; 19:25–27; 20:2–10; 21:7, 20, 23–24; the beloved disciple may also be the unnamed disciple of 1:37 and 18:15, and the witness in 19:35. For a survey of the vast amount of material on the identity of this disciple, see Charlesworth, *Beloved Disciple,* 127–224, who later in the same book identifies the beloved disciple with Thomas. See also Grassi, *Secret Identity;* and Culpepper, *John, the Son of Zebedee,* 56–88, both of whom regard the identity of the beloved disciple as unknown. On the beloved disciple and authorship of the Fourth Gospel from a feminist perspective, see Schneiders, *Written That You May Believe,* 211–32, who argues that the gender and the identity of the beloved disciple remain enigmatic.

48. Culpepper, *John, the Son of Zebedee,* 84.

49. See Brown, *Community of the Beloved Disciple,* 31–34.

50. See chapter 2 above, 42–43.

51. Van Tilborg, *Imaginative Love,* 131.

52. Ringe, *Wisdom's Friends,* 76.

53. On the relationship between Peter and the beloved disciple, see Quast, *Peter and the Beloved Disciple.*

54. Van Tilborg suggests a wider group than the Twelve but proposes it is all male (*Imaginative Love,* 111–12); see chapter 3 above.

55. See Schneiders, "Foot Washing," 140–43; also van Tilborg, *Imaginative Love,* 110–68, especially 148–54.

56. See, for example, Mark 13:32–37 par.; Luke 12:35–48; 17:1–10; Rom. 1:1; Phil. 1:1; Jas. 1:1; 2 Pet. 1:1; Apoc. 1:1; 19:2, 5.

57. Barrett, *St. John,* 477.

58. On the chiastic structure, see Brown, *Gospel,* 2:857–59.

59. Luce Irigaray, "The Fecundity of the Caress: A Reading of Levinas, *Totality and Infinity,*" in *An Ethics of Sexual Difference,* 206, 194.

60. Irigaray, "Questions to Emmanuel Levinas," in *Irigaray Reader,* ed. Whitford, 187.

61. Irigaray, "Fecundity," 210.

62. Keller, *Reflections on Gender and Science,* 8.

63. Ibid., 117. Keller makes a valuable distinction between authentic objectivity, which implies our connectedness to the world of objects, and "objectivist epistemology, in which truth is measured by its distance from the subjective" (p. 87).

64. Zizioulas, *Being as Communion,* 102.

65. Ibid., 53–59, 143–69.

66. Ibid., 50, 44.

67. Dunne, *Homing Spirit,* 83–91. On the literary and theological use of "I am" in the Fourth Gospel, see especially Ball, *'I am' in John's Gospel.*

68. O'Day, "John," 303.
69. Grey, *Redeeming the Dream*, 31.
70. E. Johnson, *Friends of God and Prophets*, 41.
71. Ibid., 61.
72. Ibid., 79–85, 105, 136–37.
73. Ibid., 138.
74. Ibid., 262.
75. See chapter 2 above.
76. Grey, *Redeeming the Dream*, 51.
77. Johnson, *Friends of God*, 217–18.
78. Irigaray, "Questions," 186.
79. Irigaray, "The Envelope: A Reading of Spinoza, *Ethics*," in *Ethics of Sexual Difference*, 83–94.
80. Keller, *Reflections on Gender and Science*, 99.
81. Wilson-Kastner, *Faith, Feminism and the Christ*, 62.

CHAPTER 5
AUTHORING LIFE: THE SYMBOL OF GOD AS FATHER

1. From "Prayer," in *Carmina Gadelica*, ed. Carmichael, 207.
2. Paul W. Meyer, "'The Father': The Presentation of God in the Fourth Gospel," in *Exploring the Gospel of John*, ed. Culpepper and Black, 255–73.
3. On this, see further Lee, "Beyond Suspicion?" and eadem, "Symbol of Divine Fatherhood."
4. G. Schrenk, "*patēr, patrǭos, patria, apatōr, patrikos,*" in *Theological Dictionary of the New Testament*, 5:952–53.
5. According to C. J. H. Wright ("Family," in *Anchor Bible Dictionary*, 2:767–68), Israelite children were not legally the property of their fathers, so that the *patria potestas* is not nearly as dominant in ancient Israel.
6. Schrenk, "*patēr*," 951–54.
7. Ibid., 954.
8. Plato, *Timaeus* 28c, in R. G. Bury, ed., *Plato*, vol. 9.
9. Schrenk, "*patēr*," 954–56.
10. Thompson, *Promise of the Father*, 35–55; eadem, *God of the Gospel of John*, 64–69.
11. Thompson, *Promise of the Father*, 18, 39, 54–55, 71–72, 134–35; eadem, *God of the Gospel of John*, 58–64.
12. Cf. Schrenk, who denies any link between divine fatherhood and the covenant in Old Testament usage—indeed sees the title as originally alien to belief in Yʜᴡʜ ("*patēr*," 965–69).
13. On *abba*, see Jeremias, *New Testament Theology*, 61–68; and idem, *Prayers of Jesus*, 11–65; Hamerton-Kelly, *God the Father*; idem, "God the Father in the Bible and in the Experience of Jesus: The State of the Question," in *God as Father?* ed. Metz and Schillebeeckx, 95–102. Thompson does not deny Jesus' unique use of the Aramaic *abba* (*Promise of the Father*, 21–34, 67–71), which is not baby talk but an adult form of address (so Barr, "*Abba* Isn't Daddy"). For a critique of the view that *abba* was central to Jesus' self-understanding, see D'Angelo, "*Abba* and 'Father.'" For a sober assessment, see Meier, *Marginal Jew*, 2:358–59 n. 20.
14. Thompson, *Promise of the Father*, 134–35.
15. For example, John 1:18; 6:27; 8:41, 42; 13:3; 16:27; 20:17. See Schrenk, "*patēr*," 996; and Schnackenburg, *Gospel*, 2:173–77; also Juel and Keifert, "'I Believe in God,'" 49–52.

16. See John 3:35; 4:21; 5:17–26; 6:27; 10:30; 12:26; 14:6–13; 16:28; 18:11; 20:17.

17. For example, John 2:16; 8:19; 10:18; 14:2; 15:1; 20:17.

18. John 11:41; 12:27–28; 17:1, 3, 5, 24.

19. See, for example, John 6:44; 8:16, 18; 12:49; 14:24; cf. 6:57; 20:21. On the absolute use of "Father," see Schnackenburg, *Gospel*, 2:174–77 (Excursus 9).

20. Thompson, *Promise of the Father*, 134.

21. On this, see further Thompson, *Promise of the Father*, 133–34.

22. Gail R. O'Day rightly points out the importance of reading the title "Father" within its narrative context, rather than separating it ("'Show Us the Father'").

23. The preferred, although more difficult, reading is *monogenēs theos* ("only Son, God") rather than *monogenēs huios* ("only/only-begotten Son"), although the meaning is much the same; see Barrett, *St. John*, 169; and D. Moody Smith, *John*, 61–62.

24. Thompson, *Promise of the Father*, 135.

25. Barrett argues for the latter on the basis of Johannine theological usage elsewhere (*St. John*, 166).

26. Moloney, *John*, 39–41.

27. Soskice, "Naming God at Sinai," in *Naming God*.

28. So Brown, *Gospel*, 1:34–35. Hoskyns points out that "only-begotten" and "beloved" in the LXX both translate the same Hebrew word ("only") (Hoskyns and Davey, *Fourth Gospel*, 1:146–47).

29. See chapter 1 above, 15–16.

30. The Judaism of the period believed that God could be "seen" by human beings only in the world to come (Schnackenburg, *Gospel*, 1:278).

31. Thompson, *Promise of the Father*, 153; eadem, *God of the Gospel of John*, 72.

32. Thompson argues that divine fatherhood needs to be seen in terms of authority and kinship rather than "emotional intimacy" (*Promise of the Father*, 153–54), but it is hard to see why it must be one or the other, particularly given the metaphorical language of closeness and reciprocal love, both in the Prologue and elsewhere in the Gospel.

33. Sanders and Mastin, *Commentary*, 116–17.

34. Brown, *Gospel*, 1:147. Bultmann says: "Unbelief, by shutting the door on God's love, turns his love into judgment. For this is the meaning of judgement, that man shuts himself off from God's love" (*Gospel*, 154).

35. Schnackenburg, *Gospel*, 1:436–37.

36. Brown, *Gospel*, 1:199–204; and Moloney, *John*, 164–65.

37. Moloney, *Signs and Shadows*, 152.

38. On the parallels between John 5 and 9, see Lee, *Symbolic Narratives*, 105–7.

39. On this, see further Whitacre, *John*, 121–24.

40. Brown describes the discourse as "one of the most exalted in John" (*Gospel*, 1:216).

41. Lee, *Symbolic Narratives*, 111–13.

42. Dodd, "A Hidden Parable in the Fourth Gospel," in *More New Testament Studies*, 30–40; see also Talbert, *Reading John*, 121–30. Against this view, see Beasley-Murray, *John*, 75; and Schnackenburg, *Gospel*, 2:102, 462.

43. Schrenk, "*patēr*," 983.

44. The two verbs for sending, *pempein* and *apostellein*, are used synonymously with virtually no difference of meaning, although there is some stylistic difference; see especially 20:21, where both verbs are found.

45. Loader, *Christology*, 30–32; also P. Borgen, "God's Agent in the Fourth Gospel," in *Religions in Antiquity*, ed. Neusner, 137–48. See also Anderson, "The Having-Sent-Me Father."

46. Thompson, *Promise of the Father*, 143; eadem, *God of the Gospel of John*, 78–79.

47. P. Borgen sees 6:32–33 as a threefold correction of the misunderstanding implied in the biblical quotation used by the crowds in 6:31 ("Observations on the Midrashic Character of John 6," in *Logos Was the True Light*, 24–25): not Moses but God, not "gave" but "gives," not just for the ancestors but also for "the world."

48. As Moloney points out (*John*, 285), the main celebrations of the feast are each given a christological orientation in the Tabernacles Discourse.

49. On the theme of fickle faith in John's Gospel, see Carson, *Gospel*, 346–51; and Moody Smith, *John*, 184–85.

50. See Schnackenburg, *Gospel*, 2:224.

51. The link with Hanukkah is not as transparent as the link with the other feasts in this section of the Gospel; on the background and christological significance, see Moloney, *John*, 312–18.

52. Schnackenburg, *Gospel*, 3:48. For an illuminating discussion of Johannine ecclesiology in this context, see also Schnackenburg, *Gospel*, vol. 2 (Excursus 17), who speaks here of the "fundamentally ecclesial tendency of Johannine thinking" (p. 213).

53. See chapter 4 above, 88–99.

54. Witherington, *John's Wisdom*, 250.

55. See chapter 3 above. On "perichoresis," see further LaCugna, *God For Us*, 270–78.

56. Dodd, *Interpretation*, 262.

57. Barrett is not unusual in interpreting "the Father is greater than I" (14:28) as a reference to the period of Jesus' earthly existence, rather than his eternal Sonship (*St. John*, 468): "John's thought is focused on the humiliation of the Son in his earthly life, a humiliation which now, in his death, reached both its climax and its end." According to Maurice Wiles, the late fourth century saw an increasing rejection of subordination within the *homoousios* ("one being") of Father and Son (see *Spiritual Gospel*, 122–27).

58. On the covenant language of this declaration, see Schneiders, *Written That You May Believe*, 199–200.

59. On this, see Thompson, *Promise of the Father*, 135–36, 144; eadem, *God of the Gospel of John*, 70–71, 96–97.

60. Jan van der Watt argues that the Johannine narrative builds up a network of family relationships around the fatherhood of God (though he calls it "the family of the King"), incorporating many of the themes of the Gospel: kinship, love, birth, children, brothers and sisters, sustenance, care, obedience, and so on (*Family of the King*, 161–439). The Gospel, for him, "unfolds as part of the family history of the Father and the Son" (p. 399).

61. On this structure, see further Schüssler Fiorenza, *But She Said*, 114–20, especially the chart of Greek patriarchal democracy on p. 117.

62. E. Johnson, *She Who Is*, 34–40; see also A. Swidler, "The Image of Woman in a Father-Oriented Religion," in *God as Father?* ed. Metz and Schillebeeckx, 75–80.

63. S. B. Thistlethwaite, "Every Two Minutes: Battered Women and Feminist Interpretation," in *Feminist Interpretation of the Bible*, ed. Russell; and Russell, *Sex, Race, and God*, 110–14; also Moltmann, "I Believe in God the Father," 19–21.

64. See Schnackenburg, *Gospel*, 2:175.

65. On the Sabbath question in John 5, see Lee, *Symbolic Narratives*, 111–12, 114–18.

66. See Marianne Meye Thompson, "Thinking about God: Wisdom and Theology in John 6," in *Critical Readings of John 6*, ed. Culpepper, 239–40.

67. Jacobs-Malina, *Beyond Patriarchy*, 92–93.

68. On the political implications of Jesus' kingship in John, see Rensberger, *Overcoming the World*, 87–106.

69. See Brown, *Gospel,* 1:503–4; Thompson, *Humanity of Jesus,* 94–97; and Painter, *John: Witness and Theologian,* 50–60.

70. On "glory," see Brown, *Gospel,* 1:503–4; Thompson, *Humanity of Jesus,* 94–97; and Painter, *John: Witness and Theologian,* 50–60.

71. Schrenk, "*patēr,*" 999–1001.

72. See Schüssler Fiorenza, *In Memory of Her,* 267–70.

73. T. E. Pollard, "The Father-Son and God-Believer Relationships according to St. John: A Brief Study of St. John's Use of Prepositions," in *L'Evangile de Jean,* ed. de Jonge, 367–69.

74. Schneiders, *Women and the Word,* 11–14.

75. Schneiders, "Symbolism and the Sacramental Principle"; and eadem, *Written That You May Believe,* 53–54. See also Jacobs-Malina, *Beyond Patriarchy,* 96.

76. See Gruenler, *Trinity in the Gospel of John,* 122–31.

77. O'Day, "John," 303–4.

78. Widdicombe, *Fatherhood of God;* idem, "Fathers on the Father," 105–25.

79. Widdicombe, *Fatherhood of God,* 97–101.

80. Ibid., 255.

81. Ibid., 121.

82. LaCugna, *God For Us,* 53–79, 243–317; see also eadem, "God in Communion With Us: The Trinity," in *Freeing Theology,* ed. LaCugna, 85–88. See, for example, Gregory of Nyssa, *Against Enomius* 1.14–16, and 5.3.

83. LaCugna, *God For Us,* 209–41; see Rahner, *Trinity.*

84. LaCugna, *God For Us,* 221; see Rahner, *Trinity,* 21–24.

85. LaCugna, *God For Us,* 400.

86. La Cugna, "God In Communion With Us," 94.

87. For a defense of this view, see in particular Janet Martin Soskice, "Can a Feminist Call God 'Father'?" in *Speaking the Christian God,* ed. Kimel, 81–109.

88. Reinhartz, "'And the Word was Begotten,'" 83–103.

89. The language of "coherence" and "contingency" is used of the Pauline Epistles by Beker, *Paul the Apostle,* 23–36.

90. Thompson, "'God's Voice You Have Never Heard,'" 189.

91. Widdicombe, *Fatherhood of God,* 258.

92. LaCugna, "God In Communion With Us," 93–94.

93. Translated in *Nicene and Post-Nicene Fathers of the Christian Church* (Edinburgh: T. & T. Clark, 1892, 1988), vol. 5, II.3; see also *Contra Eunomium* III.6.32–41, vol. 2, and *Nicene and Post-Nicene Fathers,* VIII.4, vol. 5.

94. See, for example, Gregory of Nyssa, *Refutatio Confessionis Eunomii* 4–7, and *Contra Eunomium* III.1.126–41; translated in *Nicene and Post-Nicene Fathers,* II.2, III.7, vol. 5.

95. Note the subtlety of Gregory's usage in *Against Eunomius,* in *Gregory of Nyssa, Part 4,* 238–43 (825–32); also *Nicene and Post-Nicene Fathers,* X.1.

96. Barth, *Church Dogmatics,* I.1, 384–98, especially 392–93.

97. *Speaking the Christian God,* ed. Kimel, especially the articles by Elizabeth Achtemeier ("Exchanging God for 'No Gods': A Discussion of Female Language for God," pp. 1–16) and Robert W. Jenson ("The Father, He . . . ," pp. 95–109).

98. Widdicombe, *Fatherhood of God,* 256–59.

99. Thompson, *Promise of the Father,* 170.

100. Translated in *Nicene and Post-Nicene Fathers,* I.39.

101. LaCugna, "God In Communion With Us," 100.

102. This accusation certainly cannot be leveled at Garrett Green's article in Kimel's collection, since its basic argument is that "genderless theology" or alternatives such as

those of Sallie McFague fail precisely because, despite their rhetoric, they fail to take metaphor seriously (Green, "The Gender of God and the Theology of Metaphor," in *Speaking the Christian God*, ed. Kimel, 44–64).

103. See chapter 1 above, 14–15.

104. Pannenberg, *An Introduction to Systematic Theology,* 31; idem, "Feminine Language about God?" 27–29. See also Robert W. Jenson, "'The Father, He . . . ,'" in *Speaking the Christian God*, ed. Kimel, 95–109; and Thomas F. Torrance, "The Christian Apprehension of God as Father" in *Speaking the Christian God*, ed. Kimel, 129–30.

105. Green, "Gender of God," 52.

106. Translated in *Nicene and Post-Nicene Fathers*, III.5.

107. Translated in *Nicene and Post-Nicene Fathers*, VII.4.

108. Thomas Hopko, "Apophatic Theology and the Naming of God in Eastern Orthodox Tradition," in *Speaking the Christian God*, ed. Kimel, 159–60.

CHAPTER 6
GIVING BIRTH TO BELIEVERS: SYMBOLS OF MOTHERHOOD

1. Hildegard of Bingen, "Alleluia-Verse for the Virgin," in *Women in Praise of the Sacred,* ed. Hirschfield, 71.

2. It is interesting that the *Theological Dictionary of the New Testament* devotes seventy pages to discussing "father," whereas there are virtually only two devoted to a discussion of "mother": W. Michaelis, "*mētēr*," 4:644–46.

3. See Malina, *New Testament World,* 25–50, 94–121.

4. On the subordination of women within the Israelite family, see P. A. H. de Boer, *Fatherhood and Motherhood,* 3–13.

5. C. J. H. Wright, "Family," in *Anchor Bible Dictionary*, 2:766; also Michaelis, "*mētēr*," 643.

6. Wright, "Family," 762.

7. On this theme in the Old Testament, see further J. Cheryl Exum, "Mother in Israel: A Familiar Figure Reconsidered," in *Feminist Interpretation of the Bible*, ed. Russell, 73–82; and Esther Fuchs, "The Literary Characterization of Mothers and Sexual Politics in the Hebrew Bible," in *Feminist Perspectives on Biblical Scholarship*, ed. A. Y. Collins, 117–36. On its relevance to the Fourth Gospel, see Fehribach, *Women in the Life of the Bridegroom*, 25–28.

8. Michaelis, "*mētēr*," 644.

9. P. A. H. de Boer, *Fatherhood and Motherhood,* 37.

10. Massyngbaerde Ford, *Redeemer—Friend and Mother,* 37–49.

11. On this imagery and its significance, see Gruber, *Motherhood of God,* 3–15.

12. Massyngbaerde Ford, *Redeemer—Friend and Mother,* 39–43.

13. Gruber, *Motherhood of God*, 11.

14. Massyngbaerde Ford, *Redeemer—Friend and Mother,* 43–45, 124–27.

15. See P. W. Skehan and A. A. Di Lella, *The Wisdom of Ben Sira,* 262–66.

16. On this, see further especially Sandelin, *Wisdom as Nourisher,* 177–85; Scott, *Sophia and the Johannine Jesus,* 116–19; also McKinlay, *Gendering Wisdom the Host,* 179–207.

17. See, for example, E. Johnson, *She Who Is,* 92–93.

18. Ironically, this is at variance with the misogyny of Apuleius's presentation of female characters.

19. See Lee, "Heavenly Woman," 202–8, 213–14.

20. The textual variant in 1:13 ("he who was begotten not of blood"), implying the virgin birth, is not found in the Greek manuscripts and is unlikely to be original; see Brown et al., *Mary in the New Testament*, 181–82.

21. It may be that the third phrase (and perhaps even the second phrase) is a later addition, but it is more likely to be omitted rather than added.

22. See chapter 2 above, 33–34.

23. Lindars argues that the three phrases are in reverse order—conception, sexual desire, male decision—but this is probably too wooden a distinction (*Gospel*, 92).

24. See van Tilborg, *Imaginative Love*, 34–38.

25. On this see chapter 2 above.

26. Does 1:11 refer to "the Jews" or to the world in a more general sense? John's ability to move between the "world" and "his own" as those who reject the Light suggests that, at this stage, it is the world's rejection that is in mind. So Schnackenburg, *Gospel*, 1:258–61. On this, see further chapter 7 below.

27. Brodie, *Gospel*, 142.

28. Brown, *Gospel*, 1:129; also Haenchen, *Commentary*, 1:200.

29. For more details, see the discussion in chapter 3 above, 68–71.

30. The term *adelphoi* is probably generic (cf. Mark 6:3 par.); so Schneiders, *Written That You May Believe*, 219.

31. Cf. Judg. 11:12; 2 Sam. 19:22; 1 Kgs. 17:18; 2 Chr. 35:21; Mark 1:24; 5:7. See Brown et al., *Mary in the New Testament*, 191; and Gaventa, *Mary*, 84–85.

32. Culpepper, *Gospel and Letters*, 233.

33. This could be read as a question, but is more likely a statement linked to Jesus' glorification. See Brown et al., *Mary in the New Testament*, 191–92.

34. Ibid., 188–89. Fehribach, however, argues that, while there is a literary *inclusio*, the characterization of the mother of Jesus is different in the two narratives; in both cases, her function is patriarchal and androcentric: to draw attention to the male characters, on whom females are dependent (*Women in the Life of the Bridegroom*, 25, 32–40, 140–41).

35. Brown et al., *Mary in the New Testament*, 192.

36. McHugh, *Mother of Jesus*, 393–94.

37. See Brown, *Gospel*, 1:95–96; and Moloney, *John*, 63–65.

38. Moloney, *John*, 68. Contra Witherington who seems to ignore the significance of this verse when he argues that the mother of Jesus only enters the family of faith at the cross (*John's Wisdom*, 79).

39. On the view that the mother of Jesus represents faith, see, for example, McHugh, *Mother of Jesus*, 399–403; and R. Collins, "Representative Figures of the Fourth Gospel," 120. Against this, see Maccini, who argues that the mother of Jesus is not presented here in the role of witness (*Her Testimony Is True*, 112–17).

40. On this pattern, see further Giblin, "Suggestion, Negative Response," 197–211. For a careful parallel reading of 2:1–12 and 4:46–54, see Maccini, *Her Testimony Is True*, 107–12.

41. Barrett, *St. John*, 191; and O'Day, "John," 295. Against this reading, see Conway, *Men and Women in the Fourth Gospel*, 75–78.

42. Witherington, *John's Wisdom*, 79. Against this view, see Judith Lieu, "Mother of the Son," 67.

43. Gaventa, *Mary*, 85; and Lieu, "Mother of the Son," 67.

44. As Lieu points out ("Mother of the Son," 66), it is the reader who is baffled and made uncomfortable by the exchange, not the mother of Jesus.

45. Gaventa, *Mary*, 82, 89.

46. Contra Lieu, "Mother of the Son," 71.

47. Alison Jasper sees the absence of Jesus' mother in the Prologue as part of the Johannine devaluation of femaleness and flesh; her role, in Jasper's view, is replaced by the male figure of John the Baptist (*Shining Garment of the Text,* 174–79, 194–96).

48. Moloney, *John,* 237.

49. Gaventa, *Mary,* 88.

50. On the feminine imagery, see chapter 2 above, 70–71.

51. Dodd, *Interpretation,* 308.

52. John appears to be silent on the tradition of the virginal conception, despite the ambiguity of 8:41. Of more significance is the dual identity of Jesus as Son of the Father and son of Joseph and Mary. On this, see further Brown, *Birth of the Messiah,* 518–21.

53. Assuming that these are probably synonymous groups; see Lee, *Symbolic Narratives,* 154–55.

54. The unity of the discourse is a contentious issue, with Bultmann's relegation of 6:52–59 to a later ecclesiastical redaction (*Gospel,* 234–37). Peder Borgen has given the most comprehensive account of how these verses explicate the significance of the Old Testament quotation concerning the manna in 6:31b; see "The Unity of the Discourse in John 6," in *Logos Was the True Light,* 21–22; idem, "Observations on the Midrashic Character of John 6," in *Logos Was the True Light,* 23–24. More fundamental, however, are the narrative significance and the drawing out of the meaning of the feeding.

55. Massyngbaerde Ford, *Redeemer—Friend and Mother,* 128–31.

56. Ibid., 134–35.

57. See chapter 2 above, 41–42.

58. J. Behm, "*koilia,*" *Theological Dictionary of the New Testament,* 3:786–89.

59. Massyngbaerde Ford, *Redeemer—Friend and Mother,* 135.

60. Moloney, *John,* 402.

61. Contra H. Seesemann, "*orphanos,*" *Theological Dictionary of the New Testament,* 5:488, who argues that, because Jesus does not portray himself here as a father, the reference to "orphans" really means "abandoned."

62. On Paul's use of the metaphor of motherhood to describe his relation to the churches he founded, see Gaventa, "Our Mother St. Paul."

63. Segovia, *Farewell of the Word,* 253.

64. Witherington, *John's Wisdom,* 265.

65. So Lieu, "Mother of the Son," 71–72.

66. For example, Isa. 21:3; 26:16–17; Jer. 13:21; 22:23; Hos. 13:13–15. See Hoskyns and Davey, *Fourth Gospel,* 2:576–78; Fehribach, *Women in the Life of the Bridegroom,* 132–33.

67. Massyngbaerde Ford, *Redeemer—Friend and Mother,* 165.

68. Ibid.

69. Lieu sees a link between "the woman" of 16:21 and Eve (Gen. 3:16), in which the *lypē* (pain, grief) of Eve is relived and broken by the advent of the new *anthrōpos* ("Mother of the Son," 74–75).

70. It is probable that there are four women rather than three: it is inconceivable that the sister of Jesus' mother would also be called Mary, and the four women parallel the four soldiers and four divisions of the clothing at 19:23–24. See Hoskyns and Davey, *Fourth Gospel,* 2:630–31; also above, Introduction.

71. Schneiders argues that we cannot assume the maleness of the beloved disciple here (*Written That You May Believe,* 216–24); see chapter 4 above, 100–101, 254.

72. Contra O'Day ("John," 300), who argues that, whereas the beloved disciple represents the community of faith (future), the mother of Jesus represents his earthly ministry (past), thus creating continuity between past and future.

73. Gaventa, *Mary*, 90–91.

74. Ibid., 91.

75. So van der Watt, *Family of the King*, 334.

76. Culpepper, *Gospel and Letters*, 234.

77. For an overview of various interpretations of the mother of Jesus at this point, see Conway, *Men and Women in the Fourth Gospel*, 80–81. Conway sees the interpretation of the new family as the most plausible (pp. 81–85); see also Seim, "Roles of Women," 62–65; and O'Day, "John," 300.

78. Brown et al., *Mary in the New Testament*, 218.

79. So Bultmann, *Gospel*, 672–73.

80. For a succinct survey of representative interpretations of the mother of Jesus, see Fehribach, *Women in the Life of the Bridegroom*, 23–25.

81. Reinhartz, "John," 592.

82. For a moderate reading of this view, see, for example, Brown, *Gospel*, 2:925–26.

83. Lieu, who argues against symbolic connotations of Eve at the cross in the figure of Mary, does perceive a link with Eve in 16:21, where the pattern of the old is broken with the birth of the new *anthrōpos* ("Mother of the Son," 74–75).

84. See Seim, "Roles of Women," 60–62.

85. For Léon-Dufour, Mary represents Israel, both at the wedding at Cana (*Lecture*, 1:226–28) and at the foot of the cross (4:144–46).

86. Whether this imagery can be pushed in a more specifically mariological direction is not a question for exegesis, but rather is an extrapolation from the Johannine text. That also applies to the question of Eve symbolism (Gen. 3:15). According to Brown et al., such symbolism is at best secondary (*Mary in the New Testament*, 217–18).

87. Writing from a Roman Catholic perspective, Gavin D' Costa argues that the Johannine portrait of Mary gives the church, which she represents, the role of co-Redemptor with Christ, a role that reinforces the "feminine" characteristics of Jesus' flesh and mitigates somewhat against the maleness of the iconography for redemption (*Sexing the Trinity*, 68–75).

88. Lieu, "Mother of the Son," 70.

89. On this, see further chapter 9 below, 220–26.

90. See chapter 2 above, 47.

91. On this, see further chapter 3 above, 68–71.

92. Massyngbaerde Ford, *Redeemer—Friend and Mother*, 193.

93. Ibid., 195–99.

94. On this, see further Kathleen P. Rushton, *The Parable of John 16:21: A Feminist Socio-Rhetorical Reading of a (Pro)creative Metaphor for the Death-Glory of Jesus* (Ph.D. thesis, Griffith University, Australia, 2000).

95. Maccini, *Her Testimony Is True*, 203–6. For a survey of views on the identity of the witness, see Brown, *Death of the Messiah*, 2:1182–84; and Schnackenburg, *Gospel*, 3:293–94.

96. It is hard to know whether the quotation from Zechariah 12:10 is to be read in the sense of judgment—Jesus' executioners will gaze in remorse on what they have done—or with the meaning of salvation—Jesus' followers will gaze in faith on the streaming side and find salvation. It is most likely that both meanings are intended. On this, see Brown, *Gospel*, 2:1186–88.

97. For a negative reading of Nicodemus in this scene, see, for example, Sylva, "Nicodemus"; and Bassler, "Mixed Signals."

98. Take, for example, the image of the Lamb in the book of Revelation, which appears variously as martyr, cultic sacrifice, slaughtered and risen, pictured with seven horns and seven eyes, the object of worship, opener of the seven-sealed books, redeemer, sovereign,

wrathful warrior-hero, and triumphant bridegroom wedded to a bride who is a city (Apoc. 5:6, 8, 12–14; 6:1, 16; 7:14; 14:4; 17:14; 19:7).

99. Quoted in Brock, *Luminous Eye,* 137.

100. Brock, *Luminous Eye,* 168–72.

101. Quoted in Brock, *Luminous Eye,* 171.

102. In *St. Ephrem the Syrian: Selected Prose Works,* ed. McVey.

103. Brock, *Luminous Eye,* 39.

104. Quoted in Massyngbaerde Ford, *Redeemer—Friend and Mother,* 196.

105. On the development and use of the image of Christ as mother in the twelfth century, see especially Bynum, *Jesus as Mother,* 111–68.

106. Ibid., 129, 131–34.

107. Bynum, *Fragmentation and Redemption,* 100.

108. Bynum, *Jesus as Mother,* 133. At the same time, Bynum cautions that motherhood language in the Middle Ages did not necessarily lead to increased status for women: a high view of motherhood could often go hand in hand with fear of actual women (pp. 140–46).

109. See John-Julian, "Introduction," in *A Lesson of Love,* xi–xiii.

110. Ibid., chap. 58, p. 153.

111. Ibid., chap. 60, pp. 157–58.

112. Ward, *Prayers and Meditations of St. Anselm,* 153 (lines 397–404). Anselm in this prayer describes both Paul and Jesus as the mothers of his soul.

113. Bynum, *Fragmentation and Redemption,* 79–117. See especially figures 3.10 and 7.6, both of which depict pictorially the femininity of Jesus' body (pp. 110, 278).

114. *Katharina Schütz Zell: Pamphlet on the Lord's Prayer, 1532,* trans. Matheson.

115. So André Cabusset in 1949 of the image of Christ as Mother in the twelfth century, quoted in Bynum, *Jesus as Mother,* 2.

116. Massyngbaerde Ford, *Redeemer—Friend and Mother,* 37.

117. The intimate connection between Jesus and the mother of Jesus can, and has been, interpreted in ways not necessarily benevolent to women. See, for example, the summary in Anne E. Carr, "Mary: Model of Faith," in *Mary, Woman of Nazareth,* ed. Donnelly, especially pp. 8-10.

CHAPTER 7

WALKING IN DARKNESS: SYMBOLS OF EVIL

1. From Wright, "Eli, Eli," in *Judith Wright: Selected Poems,* 31.

2. On this, see further Lee, "Women as 'Sinners.'"

3. Although etymology is a poor guide to semantic meaning, it is nonetheless of some significance to note that the Greek word "symbol" has to do with "putting/throwing together" (*syn* + *ballein*), whereas the word "devil" has to do with dividing, "putting/throwing apart" (*dia* + *ballein*).

4. Brown supports the first two of these, rejecting the third (*Gospel,* 1:58–63).

5. Beasley-Murray, *John,* 24–25.

6. So Barrett, *St. John,* 176–77.

7. Schnackenburg, *Gospel,* 1:299. See especially Metzner, who sees the main evidence for the paschal interpretation in the crucifixion (*Das Verständnis der Sünde,* 115–58).

8. On the reasons for avoiding a Gentile establishment, see Beasley-Murray, *John,* 327–28.

9. Moloney argues that the center of the title lies in the phrase "of God," since in the Old Testament only God can remove sin (*John,* 58–59).

10. Brown, *Gospel,* 1:56.

11. Schnackenburg, *Gospel,* 1:298.

12. For example, 1 Sam. 2:9; Job 10:21–22; 24:14–17; Pss. 23:4; 82:5; 88:6, 12; 139:11–12; Prov. 2:13; 4:18–19; Isa. 8:21–22; 42:6–7; 59:9–10; 60:1–3; Joel 2:1–2, 31; Amos 5:18; Sir. 22:11; *2 Bar.* 18:2; 56:5–10; 1QS 3:13–26.

13. Koester, *Symbolism,* 127–29.

14. Ibid., 125–26.

15. Brown sees 1:5 as a reference to the Fall (*Gospel,* 1:26–27), but the present tense of the verb ("shines") indicates an ongoing reality (so Moloney, *John,* 36–37).

16. See chapter 2 above, 300, 242.

17. Léon-Dufour, *Lecture,* 1:182.

18. Moloney, *John,* 90–91.

19. So Koester, *Symbolism,* 134–35.

20. Schnackenburg, *Gospel,* 1:401.

21. In 1 John, the same imagery of walking in the light rather than the darkness is used of the love between members of the believing community (e.g., 1 John 2:8–11).

22. On this, see further Yee, *Jewish Feasts,* 70–82.

23. Koester, *Symbolism,* 136.

24. Brodie points out that John 7–8 contains two groups: those who believe genuinely (7:40, 41a; 8:30) and those "who cling to what is superficial" and so reject Jesus (7:41b–42; 8:31, 33) (*Gospel,* 328).

25. Koester, *Symbolism,* 145–47.

26. On this passage, see further chapter 8, pp. 198–200, and chapter 9, pp. 215–19 below.

27. Schneiders, *Written That You May Believe,* 153, 154.

28. On the background of this quotation—which is closer to the Hebrew than the Greek Old Testament—see Barrett, *St. John,* 431–32.

29. See further chapter 4 above.

30. The reference to "*their* law" at 15:25 does not distance Jesus himself from the Torah but rather emphasizes that it is this law which the authorities are supposed to revere: "the law which they claim to possess" might be a loose paraphrase. Note also that there is no "but" in 1:17 in the distinction between Moses and Jesus: "because the Law was given through Moses; grace and truth came into being through Jesus Christ." See Moloney, *John,* 46.

31. Metzner, *Das Verständnis der Sünde,* 246.

32. On these verbs and their link to Matt. 18:18, see Beasley-Murray, *John,* 382–84.

33. So Brown, *Gospel,* 2:1043–44.

34. O'Day, "John," 296.

35. See especially Schneiders, *Revelatory Text,* 180–99.

36. Bernard, *Commentary,* 1:143–44; Brown, *Gospel,* 1:171; Schnackenburg, *Gospel,* 1:433, Léon-Dufour, *Lecture,* 1:362–64; and Schneiders, *Revelatory Text,* 190–91; see especially Fehribach, *Women in the Life of the Bridegroom,* 45–81. Against this interpretation, see Barrett, *St. John,* 235; and Schnackenburg, *Gospel,* 1:433.

37. See chapter 3 above, 71–77.

38. Bultmann, *Gospel,* 188.

39. For a discussion of the nonjudgmental attitude of Jesus to the woman, see Conway, *Men and Women in the Fourth Gospel,* 116–19; and Jones, *Symbol of Water,* 101–2.

40. So Calvin, *Gospel According to St. John,* 1:20.

41. See chapter 3 above, 68–71.

42. Lightfoot, *St. John's Gospel*, 135.

43. Metzner, *Das Verständnis der Sünde*, 50.

44. See Metzner, *Das Verständnis der Sünde*, 61.

45. Ibid., 52–53, 61; Metzner understands death in the Fourth Gospel as punishment for sin (judgment).

46. For example, Hoskyns and Davey, *Fourth Gospel*, 2:673–78; Brown, *Gospel*, 1:335–36; and Barrett, *St. John*, 589–91. Against this view, see Heil, "Story of Jesus and the Adulteress"; also the response of Wallace, who argues against Heil for the majority view ("Reconsidering 'The Story of Jesus'").

47. The story is absent from the oldest and best manuscripts (e.g., $P^{66, 75}$, $\aleph$, B, et al.), and also a wide variety of other ancient authorities. See the discussion in Metzger, *Textual Commentary*, 219–22.

48. Brown, *Gospel*, 1:335.

49. Schnackenburg, *Gospel*, 2:164.

50. O'Day, "John 7:53–8:11."

51. See Brown, *Gospel*, 1:338; and Barrett, *St. John*, 591–92; also Witherington, *Women in the Ministry of Jesus*, 22.

52. This feature seems closer to the Lukan depiction of women than the Johannine. On Luke and women, see further especially, Seim, *Double Message*.

53. Witherington, *Women in the Ministry of Jesus*, 22–23.

54. Schnackenburg, *Gospel*, 2:167.

55. On sin in the narrative of John 9, see further Hasitschka, *Befreiung von Sünde*, 283–342, especially 338–42.

56. For different interpretations of the man's expulsion from the synagogue, see Martyn, *History and Theology*, 37–62; Goodman, *State and Society in Galilee*, 106–7; and D. Moody Smith, "Judaism and the Gospel of John," in *Jews and Christians*, ed. Charlesworth, 83–88, 97–98.

57. Though Judas is not named here, it is probably he who is meant; so Barrett, *St. John*, 543. Against this, see Beasley-Murray, who suggests that it is Caiaphas who is referred to here (*John*, 340).

58. On the parallels with John 21, see Minear, who argues for the coherence of this chapter with the rest of the Fourth Gospel (*John: The Martyr's Gospel*, 156–59).

59. So Bultmann, *Gospel*, 86–87, 144–45.

60. See Lowe, who argues that "Judeans" should translate *Ioudaioi* throughout the Fourth Gospel ("Who Were the IOUDAIOI?"). For a critique of this view, see Ashton, *Understanding the Fourth Gospel*, 133–34.

61. See, for example, Martyn, *History and Theology*; and Ashton, *Understanding the Fourth Gospel*, 131–37, 151–59.

62. Motyer, *Your Father the Devil?* 122–220. See also Sigfred Pedersen, "Anti-Judaism in John's Gospel: John 8," in *New Readings in John*, ed. Nissen and Pedersen, 172–93.

63. Motyer, *Your Father the Devil?* 212.

64. Culpepper, *Gospel and Letters*, 173.

65. For example, John 1:10, 29; 3:16–17; 4:42; 12:19; 17:18, 21, 23.

66. See John 1:9; 3:19; 6:14, 33, 51; 9:5; 10:36; 11:27; 16:21, 28; 17:24; 18:20, 37; 21:25.

67. For example, John 1:10; 7:7; 8:23; 12:25; 13:1; 14:17, 22, 27, 30; 15:18–19; 16:8, 11, 20, 33; 17:6, 9, 14, 25; 18:36. In order to avoid a metaphysical form of dualism in which matter is viewed as evil, I have used the Greek *kosmos* to indicate those places where the word has a distinctively negative connotation, as opposed to "world," where the meaning is either positive or neutral. See chapter 7 above, 182.

68. Koester, *Symbolism*, 249.

69. Ashton, *Understanding the Fourth Gospel*, 136.

70. Barrett, *St. John*, 506.

71. On the wider issue of John's treatment of "the Jews," see Culpepper, "Gospel of John and the Jews"; see also von Wahlde, "Johannine 'Jews'"; Ashton, "Identity and Function"; D. Moody Smith, "Judaism and the Gospel of John"; Ashton, *Understanding the Fourth Gospel*, 131–59; and Motyer, *Your Father the Devil?*

72. Culpepper, *Anatomy of the Fourth Gospel*, 125–32.

73. On the irony of this scene, see further Duke, *Irony in the Fourth Gospel*, 87–89.

74. As Brown argues, reflecting a general scholarly consensus (*Gospel*, 2:794–95, 860).

75. On this negative reading of Pilate's character, see Rensberger, *Overcoming the World*, 87–106.

76. On the structure, see Brown, *Gospel*, 2:857–59; see chapter 4 above, 104.

77. Barrett, *St. John*, 80.

78. Bultmann, *Gospel*, 551.

79. See chapters 8–9 below.

80. So Byrne, *Lazarus*, 87.

81. Jan A. Du Rand, "A Syntactical and Narratological Reading of John 10 in Coherence with Chapter 9," in *Shepherd Discourse*, ed. Beutler and Fortna, 94–115.

82. Metzner, *Das Verständnis der Sünde*, 112.

83. G. von Rad and G. Kittel, "*doxa* et al.," *Theological Dictionary of the New Testament*, 2:233–51.

84. John 1:14; 2:11; 7:18; 11:4, 40; 12:28, 41; 17:4, 10.

85. John 7:39; 12:16, 23, 28; 13:31–32; 17:1, 5.

86. John 14:13; 15:8; 16:4; 17:22, 24; see also 21:19.

87. So Brown, *Gospel*, 1:225–26; and Barrett, *St. John*, 269.

88. Bultmann, *Gospel*, 268–69 n. 6; and Schnackenburg, *Gospel*, 2:127.

89. Culpepper, *Gospel and Letters*, 195.

90. See Metzner, *Das Verständnis der Sünde*, 231, 246–47.

91. See chapter 4 above, 99–104.

92. Ricoeur, *Symbolism of Evil*, 54.

93. Metzner, *Das Verständnis der Sünde*, 113.

94. Koester, *Symbolism*, 143.

95. Saiving, "Human Situation."

96. Plaskow, *Sex, Sin, and Grace*.

97. McFadyen, *Bound to Sin*, 136; see also his wider discussion of pride in the tradition and in feminist critique (pp. 134–38).

98. Plaskow, *Sex, Sin, and Grace*, 92; see also Moltmann-Wendel, *Land Flowing with Milk and Honey*, 151–65; eadem, "Self-Love and Self-Acceptance."

99. Saiving, "Human Situation," 37.

100. See, for example, Russell, *Human Liberation*, 50–71; eadem, "Authority and the Challenge of Feminist Interpretation," in *Feminist Interpretation of the Bible*, ed. Russell, 138–40; eadem, *Household of Freedom*, 59–72; also Ruether, *Sexism and God-Talk*, 22–33.

101. Steinem, *Revolution from Within*, 25.

102. West, *Deadly Innocence*.

103. Ibid., xiii–xviii, 1–13, 208–15.

104. Ibid., 208.

105. Ibid., 105–13.

106. Ibid., 87–200.

107. Ibid., 38–48.

108. Ibid., 69–70; see Hampson, *Theology and Feminism,* 123.

109. West, *Deadly Innocence,* 197.

110. See Russell, *Household of Freedom,* 29–41.

111. See, for example, Schüssler Fiorenza, "Transforming the Legacy of *The Woman's Bible,*" in *Searching the Scriptures,* vol. 1, *A Feminist Introduction,* ed. Schüssler Fiorenza, 11–16.

112. McFadyen, *Bound to Sin,* 136–37.

113. The parallel imagery is pointed out by Schnackenburg, *Gospel,* 2:383.

114. Coll, *Christianity and Feminism,* 124.

115. Hampson, *Theology and Feminism,* 123.

116. McFadyen, *Bound to Sin,* 139; for the whole discussion of sloth, see pp. 139–54.

117. Ibid., 141. See also the list of verbs that McFadyen gleans from feminist writings on women's sin (pp. 141–42).

118. Ibid., 150.

119. Beverly R. Gaventa, "Romans," in *Women's Bible Commentary,* ed. Newsom and Ringe, 316.

120. Ricoeur, *Symbolism of Evil,* 74.

121. See chapter 4 above, 88–99.

122. Coll, *Christianity and Feminism,* 121–24.

CHAPTER 8

COSTLY SELF-GIVING: THE SYMBOL OF ANOINTING

1. Irigaray, *Elemental Passions,* 104.

2. Léon-Dufour, *Lecture,* 2:445.

3. On the similarities and differences between the Gospel accounts, see Brown, *Gospel,* 1:449–52; D. Moody Smith, *John,* 233–35; and Culpepper, *Gospel and Letters,* 191–92. It is likely that the different stories go back to one or two original episodes in the life of Jesus. The strange intertwining of similarities and differences between the three basic narrative lines suggests one original event (so Holst, "One Anointing of Jesus," 435–46). On the other hand, it is possible that Mark and Luke have drawn on two separate episodes—the one prophetic and the one signifying repentance—while John has used an amalgam of the two traditions, giving it his own characteristic emphasis (see Brown, *Gospel,* 1:450–51).

4. On this, see further chapter 9 below, 220–26.

5. On the possibility that the Lukan story is about different forms of ministry (cf. Acts 6:1–6) and women's exclusion from leadership, see Seim, *Double Message,* 97–112.

6. Note that, in antiquity, people reclined on couches around a low table, leaving their sandals outside. The woman who washes/anoints Jesus' feet is not groveling on the floor under the table, but is visible as she kneels (probably) at the end of a couch. See Haskins, *Mary Magdalen,* 17–18.

7. But compare the parable of the Rich Man and Lazarus, where the fact that one of the characters is given a name is unprecedented among the parables (Luke 16:19–31).

8. On the character of Martha, see further chapter 9 below, 215–19.

9. Marchadour, *Lazare,* 73–75, 77–79.

10. See P. Mourlon-Beernaert, "Parallelisme entre Jean 11 et 12: Etude de structure littéraire et théologique," in *Génèse et structure d'un texte du Nouveau Testament,* ed. Descamps et al., 132–34.

11. Lee, *Symbolic Narratives,* 188–97. Most commentators regard the raising of Lazarus as consisting of 11:1–44. A few, however, extend it to include the plot against Jesus; for

example, Lindars, *Gospel,* 378, and Beasley-Murray, *John,* 187; Morris takes it to the end of the chapter (*Gospel,* 532–70). Witherington discusses 11:1–12:11 in one chapter, but subdivides it at the end of John 11 (*John's Wisdom,* 196–213); see also J. N. Suggit, who divides the narrative of 11:1–12:11 into two sections, 11:1–46 and 12:1–11, with 11:47–53 as a bridge holding them together ("Raising of Lazarus"). P. F. Ellis regards 10:40–12:11 as a chiasm (*Genius of John,* 177–96).

12. For the possibility that the term *hoi Ioudaioi* means "Judeans" in the context of John 11–12, see D. Moody Smith, *John,* 221. The term is certainly not used in this narrative in a negative way. See further chapter 7 below, 181–82.

13. For a different view that sees Martha's faith as inferior to Mary's, see Schillebeeckx, "This Sickness Does not Lead to Death (John 11)," in *God Among Us,* 328–30.

14. Moule, "Meaning of 'Life.'"

15. Culpepper, *Gospel and Letters,* 193. Women were permitted to be present at small dinner parties with a limited guest list; see Fehribach, *Women in the Life of the Bridegroom,* 98–100.

16. See Schneiders, "Women in the Fourth Gospel," 41–42; Schüssler Fiorenza, *In Memory of Her,* 230; and Scott, *Sophia and the Johannine Jesus,* 212–14. Against this view, see Maccini, *Her Testimony Is True,* 176–78.

17. Conway, *Men and Women in the Fourth Gospel,* 151.

18. Nard is an herb with aromatic qualities imported from the East. A liter (*litra,* Latin *libra*) is a Roman pound, the equivalent of 327.45 grams or 12 ounces; see Bultmann, *Gospel,* 414. The word translated "genuine" (*pistikēs*) is unclear in its meaning; on the various possibilities, see Morris, *John,* 551–52 n. 14. The price suggested by Judas, three hundred denarii, represents about a year's wages for a day laborer (Matt. 20:2).

19. Coakley, "Anointing at Bethany," 249–52. Contra Maccini, who interprets the wiping of Jesus' feet as an act of devotion (*Her Testimony Is True,* 173–74).

20. Coakley, "Anointing at Bethany," 250 n. 51.

21. Barrett, *St. John,* 414.

22. Schnackenburg, *Gospel,* 2:369. The textual variant in 12:7 makes the point clear (though it is thereby less likely to be correct).

23. On footwashing, see further chapter 3 above, 78–81.

24. Homer, *Odyssey,* 19.503–7, vol. 2.

25. *Sifre* to Deuteronomy 355:15.2 on Deut. 33:24, in *The Components of the Rabbinic Documents,* ed. Neusner.

26. On anointing in antiquity, see H. Schlier, "*aleiphō,*" *Theological Dictionary of the New Testament,* 1:229–32; and J. A. Thompson, "Ointment," *Interpreter's Dictionary of the Bible,* 3:593–95.

27. In 1 John 2:20, 27, anointing is linked to the teaching of the Holy Spirit.

28. On this, see further chapter 9 below, 215–19.

29. Culpepper sees in the narrative a loose parallel to the Pauline cardinal virtues of faith, hope, and love: Martha epitomizing faith, Lazarus hope, and Mary love (*Anatomy of the Fourth Gospel,* 142).

30. For a survey of different interpretations of Jesus' emotions (distress and anger), see Lee, *Symbolic Narratives,* 208–12. It is arguable that Jesus' intense emotions, which make little sense if interpreted literally within a Johannine framework, represent symbolically the imminence of the "hour." See Byrne, *Lazarus,* 57–60. See further chapter 2 above, 244–45.

31. Koester, *Symbolism,* 112–13.

32. Morris, *John,* 514.

33. Witherington, *John's Wisdom,* 198.

34. Köstenberger, *Encountering John,* 132.

35. Hoskyns and Davey, *Fourth Gospel*, 2:416. Against this, see Brown, *Gospel*, 1:449; Lindars, *Gospel*, 419; Gnilka, *Johannesevangelium*, 97; and Maccini, *Her Testimony Is True*, 183.

36. Léon–Dufour, *Lecture*, 2:446.

37. According to Moloney, Mary is "the first person to understand the significance of the death of Jesus" (*John*, 349).

38. See Rachel Hachlili, "Burials," *Anchor Bible Dictionary*, 1:787–94; and Malina and Rohrbaugh, *Social-Science Commentary on John*, 276–77.

39. Lightfoot sees this signified in the wiping of Jesus' feet (*St. John's Gospel*, 237).

40. Bultmann, *Gospel*, 415; and Gnilka, *Johannesevangelium*, 97.

41. Lee, *Symbolic Narratives*, 222 n. 2; also O'Day, "John," 299.

42. Schüssler Fiorenza, *In Memory of Her*, 330. Against the view that Mary is portrayed as a disciple, see Fehribach, *Women in the Life of the Bridegroom*, 83–85.

43. Reinhartz, "John," 583.

44. John 12:8 is missing from several witnesses, including D, though its inclusion is more likely given its support in P[66] A B et al.

45. On the theme of darkness and death, see further chapter 7 above.

46. Bultmann, *Gospel*, 416.

47. Bruns, "A Note on Jn 12,3," 21.

48. Moloney, *John*, 511; see also Koester, *Symbolism*, 114–15.

49. The royal overtones are present also in the Markan anointing story—made stronger by the fact that it is Jesus' head that the woman anoints (Mark 14:3 par.).

50. Beasley-Murray, *John*, 209.

51. See Byrne, *Lazarus*, 59–60.

52. According to Malina and Rohrbaugh, Mary is a "rather wealthy mistress of the house" (*Social-Science Commentary on John*, 205), but Koester is right to point out that Martha's serving of the meal, rather than a servant, shows no indication of wealth (*Symbolism*, 113).

53. Koester, *Symbolism*, 114.

54. See chapter 4 above, 102–4.

55. Witherington, *John's Wisdom*, 207–8.

56. O'Day, "John," 111–18; and Scott, *Sophia and the Johannine Jesus*, 209–12.

57. Koester, *Symbolism*, 116.

58. Respectively, Schnackenburg, *Gospel*, 2:333; and T. E. Pollard, "The Raising of Lazarus [John xi]," in *Studia Evangelica, Vol. IV*, ed. Livingstone, 440. Beasley-Murray is right to argue that she is a woman of faith, even if grief has temporarily clouded that faith (*John*, 192); see also Bultmann, *Gospel*, 405.

59. Moloney, *John*, 350.

60. Dodd, *Interpretation*, 367.

61. Contra Fehribach, who argues that Mary of Bethany is sidelined and marginalized in the Johannine narrative (*Women in the Life of the Bridegroom*, 107–11).

CHAPTER 9
RESURRECTION AND LIFE: SYMBOLS OF EASTER

1. From Kevin Hart, "Easter Psalm," in *Anthology of Australian Religious Poetry*, ed. Murray, 128.

2. See chapter 8 above, 198–200.

3. Ingrid Rosa Kitzberger sees the parallelism between Mary of Bethany and Mary Mag-

dalene rather than Martha ("Mary of Bethany and Mary of Magdala," 564–86). For her, the two women are so positively portrayed that there is no need to "read against the grain" (p. 585).

4. Martin-Achard, *From Death to Life,* 3–15.

5. J. Jarick, "Questioning Sheol," in *Resurrection,* ed. Porter et al., 31.

6. Robert Martin-Achard, "Resurrection (OT)," *Anchor Bible Dictionary,* 5:680.

7. Evans, *Resurrection and the New Testament,* 14.

8. See, for example, Job 19:25–27; Pss. 16:9–11; 49:15; 73:23–28; Isa. 25:8; 26:19; 53:10b–12; Ezek. 37:1–14; Hos. 6:1–3; 13:14; Dan. 12:2–3. For a survey of individual Old Testament texts, see Martin-Achard, *From Death to Life,* 74–181. See also Schaper, who shows how the Greek Old Testament has subtly introduced resurrection themes into the Psalter (*Eschatology in the Greek Psalter,* 152–58).

9. Martin-Achard, *From Death to Life,* 186–205.

10. See George W. E. Nickelsburg, "Resurrection (Early Judaism and Christianity)," *Anchor Bible Dictionary,* 5:684–91.

11. Perkins, *New Testament Witness,* 63.

12. Ashton, *Understanding the Fourth Gospel,* 216.

13. Schnackenburg, *Gospel,* 2:355–56 (Excursus 12).

14. Ashton, *Understanding the Fourth Gospel,* 214–20, 383–406.

15. For the view that the evangelist's editorial perspective is carried by Martha in this scene, see Fortna, *Fourth Gospel,* 94–109; and Wagner, *Auferstehung und Leben,* 95–334. Others have argued that source and editing are inseparable in the Lazarus story; e.g., Henneberry, *Raising of Lazarus,* 1–64.

16. Schnackenburg, *Gospel,* 2:329; Gnilka, *Johannesevangelium,* 91; and Barrett, *St. John,* 395.

17. Colleen N. Conway stresses Martha's confidence in the dialogue with Jesus (*Men and Women in the Fourth Gospel,* 140–41).

18. The words "and the life" in 11:25 (*kai hē zōē*) are omitted in some witnesses (e.g., P[45]) but are probably authentic, for both textual and exegetical reasons.

19. See Schnackenburg, *Gospel,* 2:331–32; and Barrett, *St. John,* 396.

20. So Dodd, *Interpretation,* 365; Brown, *Gospel,* 1:434; and Henneberry, *Raising of Lazarus,* 138–41.

21. Schneiders, "Death in the Community of Eternal Life," 51; see also Lee, *Symbolic Narratives,* 203–5.

22. Schneiders, *Written That You May Believe,* 159; so also Conway, *Men and Women in the Fourth Gospel,* 141–43; Reinhartz, "John," 581; and Seim, "Roles of Women," 71.

23. Schneiders, *Written That You May Believe,* 159–60.

24. Moloney, *John,* 328–29, 339.

25. So Schneiders, "Women in the Fourth Gospel," 41; also R. E. Brown, "The Roles of Women in the Fourth Gospel" in *Community of the Beloved Disciple,* 190–91; Schüssler Fiorenza, *In Memory of Her,* 329–30; and Seim, "Roles of Women," 71–72.

26. On the parallels with the raising of Lazarus (11:44), see Schnackenburg, *Gospel,* 3:311; Beasley-Murray, *John,* 372; Talbert, *Reading John,* 250; and Stibbe, *John,* 109–10, 204–5.

27. See chapter 8 above, 244–45.

28. That is why the narrative of John 21:1–14 seems strange in the light of what has already taken place in John 20. For this and other reasons, John 21 is often regarded as a later addition to the Fourth Gospel, although using material that may have derived from the evangelist. See, for example, Brown, *Gospel,* 2:1077–82; Schnackenburg, *Gospel,* 3:341–51; and Moloney, *John,* 545–47, 562–66. Yet it is possible to argue for some sense of

literary unity between John 20 and 21, without denying the awkwardness, probably because the final text has tried to be sensitive to the narrative of John 20: tying up its loose ends and adding information. For the view that John 21 forms a literary unity with the rest of the Fourth Gospel, see Minear, "Original Functions of John 21"; Staley, *Print's First Kiss,* 111–16; Schneiders, "John 21:1–14"; Breck, *Shape of Biblical Language,* 229–32; and Brodie, *Gospel,* 574–76. Culpepper points out that, even though the Fourth Gospel was probably composed over a period of time, and in more than one edition, John 21 plays a vital role, particularly in relation to Peter and the beloved disciple (*Gospel and Letters,* 244–45).

29. For the view that the headcloth is a Johannine "sign," see Byrne, "Faith of the Beloved Disciple"; and Schneiders, "The Veil."

30. See Barrett, *St. John,* 561; Talbert, *Reading John,* 250; and Haenchen, *Commentary,* 2:211–12. Brown identifies four different kinds of faith in John 20, of which the beloved disciple's is the greatest and that of Thomas the least (*Gospel,* 2:1004–5, 1045–46); also Byrne, "Faith of the Beloved Disciple." Adeline Fehribach, who agrees with this interpretation, sees it as a patriarchal diminishing of the role of the women in the Synoptic tradition at the tomb (*Women in the Life of the Bridegroom,* 163–64). Against this interpretation, see Conway, *Men and Women in the Fourth Gospel,* 188–92.

31. D. Moody Smith, *John,* 389.

32. See Lee, "Partnership in Easter Faith."

33. Witherington, *Women in the Ministry of Jesus,* 177; and Minear, "'We Don't Know Where . . . ,'" 127–28.

34. See Scott, *Sophia and the Johannine Jesus,* 226–27.

35. Fehribach, *Women in the Life of the Bridegroom,* 152–53.

36. Conway raises the question of why, if the beloved disciple does believe, he fails to communicate his faith to anyone else (*Men and Women in the Fourth Gospel,* 189–90).

37. Brown, *Gospel,* 2:989. See also Graham Ward, "Bodies: The Displaced Body of Jesus Christ," in *Radical Orthodoxy,* ed. Milbank et al., 173.

38. T. Okure, "The Significance of Jesus' Commission to Mary Magdalene," *International Review of Mission* 81 (1992): 180.

39. Brown, *Gospel,* 2:1009–10; Barrett, *St. John,* 564; and Schüssler Fiorenza, *In Memory of Her,* 333.

40. Hoskyns and Davey, *Fourth Gospel,* 2:646.

41. So Brown, *Gospel,* 2:991–92, 1010; and Bernard, *Commentary,* 2:667. Cf. Conway, who argues that Mary's use of "Teacher" and "Lord" shows her depth of understanding, particularly in the context of the resurrection (*Men and Women in the Fourth Gospel,* 187–88).

42. So Maccini, *Her Testimony Is True,* 212–13; and Moloney, *John,* 528; see Okure, "Jesus' Commission," 181. Hoskyns sees it as a divine title, but there is no real evidence for this view (Hoskyns and Davey, *Fourth Gospel,* 2:648).

43. Ricci, *Mary Magdalene,* 143.

44. See Feuillet, "La recherche du Christ," 93–112; Léon-Dufour, *Lecture,* 4:220; and Okure, "Jesus' Commission," 181. Against this parallel, see Minear, "'We Don't Know Where . . . ,'" 129–30.

45. The present tense of the verb (*anabainō*) indicates process here rather than a single event; so Brown, *Gospel,* 2:993; Schnackenburg, *Gospel,* 3:319; and Lightfoot, *St. John's Gospel,* 331.

46. Contra Maccini, who, while conceding that Mary Magdalene does function as a witness in this scene, claims that she is not the primary witness of the resurrection nor presented in an apostolic role; as with Jewish witnesses in general, her testimony needs corroboration, which is provided, he argues, by Peter and the beloved disciple (*Her Testi-*

mony Is True, 206–33). Note that Maccini argues against the common view that women in Judaism could not testify under any circumstances (pp. 63–97).

47. So Barrett, *St. John*, 565; Schnackenburg, *Gospel*, 3:318; Beasley-Murray, *John*, 366; Bultmann, *Gospel*, 687; Léon-Dufour, *Lecture*, 4:223–24; and Lee, "Partnership," 42; also Blass-Debrunner-Funk §336.3. Against this, see Fowler, "Meaning of 'Touch me not.'" Brown (*Gospel*, 2:992) and Dodd (*Interpretation*, 443) prefer the translation, "Don't cling to me!" despite its stereotyped gender associations; so also Senior, *Passion of Jesus*, 137; and Minear, "'We Don't Know Where . . . ,'" 129–30. Another explanation is that Jesus is in too numinous a state to be touched at this point; see D'Angelo, "Critical Note"; and Conway, *Men and Women in the Fourth Gospel*, 195–97.

48. See O'Day, "John," 302.

49. It is likely that Mary is embracing him at this point, though it is possible that she is holding onto his feet, as in Matt. 28:9 (see Léon-Dufour, *Lecture*, 4:224); however, the language there is quite different.

50. Against reading *adelphoi* as generic, see Fehribach, *Women in the Life of the Bridegroom*, 165–66; and Davies, *Rhetoric and Reference*, 254.

51. Feuillet, "La recherche du Christ," 101–2; Hoskyns and Davey, *Fourth Gospel*, 2:647; and Brown, *Gospel*, 2:1016–17.

52. Lindars, *Gospel*, 608; Hoskyns and Davey, *Fourth Gospel*, 2:647; and Watson, *Easter Faith and Witness*, 100. On the paternal imagery here, see chapter 5 above, 122.

53. Conway, *Men and Women in the Fourth Gospel*, 194.

54. See Okure, "Jesus' Commission," 185.

55. Brown, "Roles of Women," 189–90; Schüssler Fiorenza, *In Memory of Her*, 326, 332–33; Scott, *Sophia and the Johannine Jesus*, 225; and Witherington, *John's Wisdom*, 332–33.

56. Reinhartz, "John," 592.

57. O'Day, "John," 302.

58. Schneiders, "Women in the Fourth Gospel," 43.

59. O'Day, "John," 301–2.

60. See Byrne, *Lazarus*, 51–53, 64–65, 86–89; and Lee, *Symbolic Narratives*, 224–26.

61. Gerald Manley Hopkins, "That Nature is a Heraclitean Fire, and of the Comfort of the Resurrection." In *Poems and Prose*, selected and edited by W. H. Gardner (Harmondsworth: Penguin Books, 1963), 65–66.

62. Léon-Dufour, *Lecture*, 2:419–20. Against this, see Maccini, who argues that, unlike Peter, Martha is speaking for herself alone (*Her Testimony Is True*, 155). However, the use of the first person does not necessarily eliminate a representative function.

63. See R. F. Collins, "Representative Figures," in *'These Things Have Been Written,'* 33–35.

64. Maisch, *Between Contempt and Veneration*, 19–29.

65. Pagels, *Gnostic Gospels*, 48–69.

66. Maisch, *Between Contempt and Veneration*, 27–28.

67. Heine, *Women and Early Christianity*, 106–23.

68. Esther de Boer, *Mary Magdalene*, 11–12.

69. Haskins, *Mary Magdalen*, 61.

70. Ibid., figure 7, p. 59.

71. Quoted in ibid., 65.

72. Hippolytus, *On the Song*, in *Hippolytus Werke*, ed. Bonwetsch and Achelis, XV, p. 353.

73. Atwood, *Mary Magdalene*, 147–84.

74. See Haskins, *Mary Magdalen*, 90–93.

75. Atwood, *Mary Magdalene*, 184–85.

76. Maisch, *Between Contempt and Veneration,* 30–42. See Augustine, *De Joannis Evangelium* 121.

77. Maisch, *Between Contempt and Veneration,* 27–28.

78. See David Mycoff, ed., *Life of Saint Mary Magdalene.*

79. Ibid., chap. XL; also Moltmann-Wendel, *Women Around Jesus,* 39–48.

80. Maisch, *Between Contempt and Veneration,* 79.

81. Steele, "And Buried," 2.

Bibliography

Allison, D. C. "The Living Water (John 4:10–14; 6:35c; 7:37–39)." *St. Vladimir's Theological Quarterly* 30 (1986): 143–57.

Alter, Robert. *The Art of Biblical Narrative.* New York: Basic Books, 1981.

Alter, Robert, and Frank Kermode, eds. *The Literary Guide to the Bible.* London: Fontana Press, 1987.

Anchor Bible Dictionary, The. Edited by David Noel Freedman. 6 volumes. New York: Doubleday, 1992.

Anderson, Paul N. "The Having-Sent-Me Father: Aspects of Agency, Encounter, and Irony in the Johannine Father-Son Relationship." *Semeia* 85 (1999): 33–57.

Apuleius. *Metamorphoses.* Edited by J. A. Hanson. 2 volumes. Loeb Classical Library. Cambridge, Mass.: Harvard University Press, 1989.

Aristotle. *The Nicomachean Ethics.* Loeb Classical Library. Cambridge, Mass.: Harvard University Press, 1982.

Ashton, John. "The Identity and Function of the *Ioudaioi* in the Fourth Gospel." *New Testament Studies* 27 (1985): 40–75.

———. *Understanding the Fourth Gospel.* 2nd ed. Edinburgh: T. & T. Clark, 1997.

Ashton, John, ed. *The Interpretation of John.* 2nd ed. Edinburgh: T. & T. Clark, 1997.

Athanasius. *De Incarnatione: An Edition of the Greek Text.* Edited by F. L. Cross. Texts for Students 50. London: SPCK, 1957.

Atwood, Richard. *Mary Magdalene in the New Testament Gospels and Early Tradition.* Bern: Peter Lang, 1993.

Auden, W. H. *Collected Poems.* Edited by E. Mendelson. London: Faber & Faber, 1976, 1991.

Augustine. *In Joannis Evangelium Tractatus CXXIV.* In *Patrologiae Cursus Completus. Series Latina.* Edited by J.-P. Migne, vols. 34–35. Paris: Garnier, 1846–91.

———. *Sermones.* In *Patrologiae Cursus Completus. Series Latina.* Edited by J.-P. Migne, vols. 38–39. Paris: Garnier, 1846–91.

_____. *De Trinitate.* In *Patrologiae Cursus Completus. Series Latina.* Edited by J.-P. Migne, vols. 42–43. Paris: Garnier, 1846–91.

Ball, David Mark. *'I am' in John's Gospel: Literary Function, Background and Theological Implications.* Journal for the Study of the New Testament Supplement Series 124. Sheffield: JSOT Press, 1996.

Barr, James. *The Semantics of Biblical Language.* Oxford: Oxford University Press, 1961.

———. "*Abba* Isn't Daddy." *Journal of Theological Studies* 39 (1988): 28–47.

Barrett, C. K. *Essays on John.* London: SPCK, 1982.

———. *The Gospel According to St. John: An Introduction with Commentary and Notes on the Greek Text.* 2nd ed. London: SPCK, 1978.

Barth, Karl. *Church Dogmatics*. 13 volumes. Edited by G. W. Bromiley and T. F. Torrance. Edinburgh: T. & T. Clark, 1936–1977.

Bassler, J. "Mixed Signals: Nicodemus in the Fourth Gospel." *Journal of Biblical Literature* 108 (1989): 635–46.

Bauer, W., W. F. Arndt, and F. W. Gingrich. *A Greek-English Lexicon of the New Testament and Other Early Christian Literature*. Chicago/London: University of Chicago Press, 1957, 1979.

Beare, F. W. "Spirit of Life and Truth: The Doctrine of the Holy Spirit in the Fourth Gospel." *Toronto Journal of Theology* 3 (1987): 110–25.

Beasley-Murray, G. R. *John*. Word Biblical Commentary 36. Waco, Tex.: Word Books, 1987.

Beirne, Margaret. "Women and Men in the Fourth Gospel: A Genuine Discipleship of Equals." Dissertation, Melbourne College of Divinity, 2000.

Beker, J. Christiaan. *Paul the Apostle: The Triumph of God in Life and Thought*. Philadelphia: Fortress, 1980.

Bernard, J. H. *A Critical and Exegetical Commentary on the Gospel According to St. John*. 2 volumes. International Critical Commentary. Edinburgh: T. & T. Clark, 1928.

Beutler, J., and R. T. Fortna, eds. *The Shepherd Discourse of John 10 and its Context: Studies by Members of the Johannine Writings Seminar*. Society for New Testament Studies Monograph Series 67. Cambridge: Cambridge University Press, 1991.

Blass, F., and A. Debrunner. *A Greek Grammar of the New Testament and Other Early Christian Literature*. Translated and edited by R. W. Funk. Chicago/London: University of Chicago Press, 1961.

Boespflug F., and N. Lossky, eds. *Nicée II, 787–1987: Douze siècles d'images religieuses*. Paris: Cerf, 1987.

Borgen, Peder. *Logos Was the True Light and Other Essays on the Gospel of John*. "Relieff": The Department of Religious Studies, University of Trondheim. Trondheim: Tapir, 1983.

Bornkamm, G. "Towards the Interpretation of John's Gospel: A Discussion of *The Testament of Jesus* by Ernst Käsemann." In *The Interpretation of John*, edited by J. Ashton, 97–119. 2nd ed. Edinburgh: T. & T. Clark, 1997.

Breck, John. *The Shape of Biblical Language: Chiasmus in the Scriptures and Beyond*. Crestwood, N.Y.: St. Vladimir's Seminary Press, 1994.

Brock, Rita Nakashima. *Journeys by Heart: A Christology of Erotic Power*. New York: Crossroad, 1988, 1992.

Brock, Sebastian. *The Luminous Eye: The Spiritual World Vision of Saint Ephrem*. Kalamazoo, Mich.: Cistercian Publications, 1985.

Brodie, T. L. *The Gospel According to John: A Literary and Theological Commentary*. Oxford: Oxford University Press, 1993.

Brouwer, Wayne. *The Literary Development of John 13–17: A Chiastic Reading*. Atlanta: Society of Biblical Literature, 2000.

Brown, Raymond E. *The Birth of the Messiah: A Commentary on the Infancy Narratives in the Gospels of Matthew and Luke*. 2nd ed. New York: Doubleday, 1993.

———. *The Community of the Beloved Disciple: The Life, Loves, and Hates of an Individual Church in New Testament Times*. New York: Paulist, 1979.

———. *The Death of the Messiah*. 2 volumes. London: Geoffrey Chapman, 1994.

———. *The Gospel According to John*. 2 volumes. Anchor Bible 29–29A. Garden City, N.Y.: Doubleday, 1966.

Brown Raymond E., et al., eds. *Mary in the New Testament: A Collaborative Assessment by Protestant and Roman Catholic Scholars*. Philadelphia: Fortress, 1978.

Bruns, J. Edgar. "A Note on Jn 12,3." *Catholic Biblical Quarterly* 28 (1966): 219–22.

Bultmann, Rudolf. *The Gospel of John: A Commentary*. Translated by G. R. Beasley-Murray. Oxford: Blackwell, 1971.

———. *Johannine Epistles*. Translated by P. O'Hara. Hermeneia. Philadelphia: Fortress, 1973.

Bynum, Caroline Walker. *Fragmentation and Redemption: Essays on Gender and the Human Body in Medieval Religion*. New York: Zone Books, 1991.

———. *Jesus as Mother: Studies in the Spirituality of the High Middle Ages*. Berkeley: University of California Press, 1982.

———. *The Resurrection of the Body in Western Christianity, 200–1336*. New York: Columbia University Press, 1995.

Byrne, Brendan. "The Faith of the Beloved Disciple and the Community in John 20." *Journal for the Study of the New Testament* 23 (1985): 83–97.

———. *Lazarus: A Contemporary Reading of John 11:1–46*. Zacchaeus Studies. Collegeville, Minn.: Liturgical Press, 1991.

Calvin, John. *The Gospel According to St. John*. Translated by T. H. L. Parker. 2 volumes. Grand Rapids: Eerdmans, 1959.

———. *Institutes of the Christian Religion*. Edited by J. T. McNeill. 2 volumes. Philadelphia: Westminster, 1960.

Carmichael, Alexander, ed. *Carmina Gadelica: Hymns and Incantations*. Edinburgh: Floris Books, 1992, 1994.

Carr, Anne E. *Transforming Grace: Christian Tradition and Women's Experience*. San Francisco: Harper & Row, 1988.

Carson, D. A. *The Gospel According to John*. Leicester: InterVarsity Press; Grand Rapids: Eerdmans, 1991.

Casey, Damien. "Luce Irigaray and the Advent of the Divine." *Pacifica* 12 (1999): 29–54.

Charlesworth, J. H. *The Beloved Disciple: Whose Witness Validates the Gospel of John?* Valley Forge, Pa.: Trinity Press International, 1995.

Charlesworth, J. H., ed. *Jews and Christians: Exploring the Past, the Present, and Future*. New York: Crossroad, 1990.

———. *The Old Testament Pseudepigrapha*. 2 volumes. London: Darton, Longman & Todd, 1985.

Chopp, Rebecca S. *The Power to Speak: Feminism, Language, God*. New York: Crossroad, 1989.

Cicero. *De Amicitia*. Loeb Classical Library. London: Heinemann, 1953.

Clement of Alexandria. *Paedagogus*. In *Patrologia Cursus Completus. Series Graeca,* edited by J.-P. Migne, vol. 9. Paris: Garnier, 1844–1891.

Clendenin, D. B., ed. *Eastern Orthodox Theology: A Contemporary Reader*. Grand Rapids: Baker Books, 1995.

Coakley, J. F. "The Anointing at Bethany and the Priority of John." *Journal of Biblical Literature* 107 (1988): 241–56.

Coll, Regina. *Christianity and Feminism in Conversation*. Mystic, Conn.: Twenty-Third Publications, 1994.

Collins, Adela Yarbro. "New Testament Perspectives: The Gospel of John." *Journal for the Study of the Old Testament* 22 (1982): 47–53.

Collins, Adela Yarbro, ed. *Feminist Perspectives on Biblical Scholarship*. Chico: Scholars Press, 1985.

Collins, R. F. "Representative Figures of the Fourth Gospel." *Downside Review* 94 (1976): 26–46, 118–32.

———. *'These Things Have Been Written': Studies on the Fourth Gospel*. Louvain: Peeters Press, 1990.

Coloe, Mary. *God Dwells with Us: Temple Symbolism in the Fourth Gospel*. Collegeville, Minn.: Michael Glazier, Liturgical Press, 2001.

Conway, Colleen M. *Men and Women in the Fourth Gospel: Gender and Johannine Characterization*. Society of Biblical Literature Dissertation Series 167. Atlanta: Society of Biblical Literature, 1999.

Cory, Catherine. "Wisdom's Rescue: A New Reading of the Tabernacles Discourse (Jn 7:1–8:50)." *Journal of Biblical Literature* 116 (1997): 95–116.

Culpepper, R. Alan. *Anatomy of the Fourth Gospel: A Study in Literary Design*. Philadelphia: Fortress, 1983.

———. "The Gospel of John and the Jews." *Review and Expositor* 84 (1987): 273–88.

———. *The Gospel and Letters of John*. Interpreting Biblical Texts. Nashville: Abingdon, 1998.

———. *John, the Son of Zebedee: The Life of a Legend*. Columbia: University of South Carolina Press, 1994.

———. "The Pivot of John's Prologue." *New Testament Studies* 27 (1981): 1–31.

Culpepper, R. Alan, ed. *Critical Readings of John 6*. Leiden: Brill, 1997.

Culpepper, R. Alan, and C. C. Black, eds. *Exploring the Gospel of John: In Honor of D. Moody Smith*. Louisville: Westminster John Knox, 1996.

Culpepper R. Alan, and F. F. Segovia, eds. *The Fourth Gospel from a Literary Perspective*, Semeia 53. Atlanta: Scholars Press, 1991.

Daly, Mary. *Beyond God the Father: Towards a Philosophy of Women's Liberation*. Boston: Beacon, 1973, 1985.

Danby, H., ed. *The Mishnah: Translated from the Hebrew with Introduction and Brief Explanatory Notes*. Oxford: Oxford University Press, 1933–1985.

D'Angelo, Mary Rose. "*Abba* and 'Father': Imperial Theology and the Jesus Traditions." *Journal of Biblical Literature* 111 (1992): 611–30.

———. "A Critical Note: John 20.17 and Apocalypse of Moses 21." *Journal of Theological Studies* 41 (1990): 529–36.

Davies, Margaret. *Rhetoric and Reference in the Fourth Gospel*. Journal for the Study of the New Testament Supplement Series 69. Sheffield: JSOT Press, 1992.

D' Costa, Gavin. *Sexing the Trinity: Gender, Culture and the Divine*. London: SCM, 2000.

de Boer, Esther. *Mary Magdalene: Beyond the Myth*. London: SCM, 1997.

de Boer, P. A. H. *Fatherhood and Motherhood in Israelite and Judean Piety*. Leiden: Brill, 1974.

de Jonge, M., ed. *L'Evangile de Jean: Sources, rédaction, théologie*. Leuven: University Press, 1977.

de la Potterie, Ignace. "L'emploie de *eis* dans Saint Jean et ses incidences théologiques." *Biblica* 43 (1962): 366–87.

———. "'Nous adorons, nous, ce que nous commaissons, car le salut vient des Juifs': Histoire de l'exégèse et interprétation de Jean 4,22." *Biblica* 64 (1983): 77–85.

de la Potterie, Ignace, and S. Lyonnet, eds. *La vie selon l'Esprit: Condition du chrétien*. Paris: Cerf, 1965.

Descamps, A.-L., et al. *Génèse et structure d'un texte du Nouveau Testament: Etude interdisciplinaire du chapitre 11 de l'Evangile de Jean*. Paris: Cerf; Louvain-la-Neuve: Cabay, 1981.

Dodd, C. H. *The Interpretation of the Fourth Gospel*. Cambridge: Cambridge University Press, 1953.

———. *More New Testament Studies*. Manchester: Manchester University Press, 1968.

Donnelly, Doris, ed. *Mary, Woman of Nazareth: Biblical and Theological Perspectives*. New York: Paulist, 1989.

Duke, Paul D. *Irony in the Fourth Gospel*. Atlanta: John Knox, 1985.

Dunn, J. D. G. *Christology in the Making*. 2nd ed. London: SCM, 1989.

———. "John VI: A Eucharistic Discourse?" *New Testament Studies* 17 (1970–71): 328–38.

Dunne, John S. *The Homing Spirit: A Pilgrimage of the Mind, of the Heart, of the Soul*. New York: Crossroad, 1987.

Edwards, Denis. *Jesus the Wisdom of God: An Ecological Theology*. Homebush, NSW: St. Paul's, 1995.

Ellis, P. F. *The Genius of John: A Composition-Critical Commentary on the Fourth Gospel*. Collegeville, Minn.: Liturgical Press, 1984.

Ephrem the Syrian, St. *Hymns on the Nativity* III. In *The Nicene and Post-Nicene Fathers*. Second Series, volume 13. Edinburgh: T. & T. Clark, 1892.

———. *Hymns on Paradise*. Introduced and translated by Sebastian Brock. New York: St. Vladimir's Seminary Press, 1990.

Evans, C. F. *Resurrection and the New Testament*. London: SCM, 1970.

Fehribach, Adeline. *The Women in the Life of the Bridegroom: A Feminist Historical-Literary Analysis of the Female Characters in the Fourth Gospel*. Collegeville, Minn.: Liturgical Press, 1998.

Feuillet, A. "La recherche du Christ dans la nouvelle alliance d'après la christophanie de Jo 20,11–18." In *L'homme devant Dieu: Mélanges H. de Lubac*, 1:92–112. Paris: Aubier, 1963.

Fitzgerald, J. T., ed. *Greco-Roman Perspectives on Friendship*. Atlanta: Scholars Press, 1997.

Ford, J. Massyngbaerde. *Redeemer—Friend and Mother: Salvation in Antiquity and in the Gospel of John*. Minneapolis: Fortress, 1997.

Fortna, R. T. *The Fourth Gospel and its Predecessor: From Narrative Source to Present Gospel*. Edinburgh: T. & T. Clark, 1988.

Fowler, D. C. "The Meaning of 'Touch me not' in John 20:17." *Evangelical Quarterly* 47 (1975): 16–25.

Freedman, David Noel, ed. *The Anchor Bible Dictionary*. 6 volumes. New York: Doubleday, 1992.

Frye, Northrop. *The Great Code: The Bible and Literature*. London: Routledge & Kegan Paul, 1981.

García Martínez, F., and E. J. C. Tigchelaar, eds. *The Dead Sea Scrolls: Study Edition*. 2 volumes. Leiden: Brill, 1997.

Gaventa, Beverly Roberts. *Mary: Glimpses of the Mother of Jesus*. Edinburgh: T. & T. Clark, 1999.

———. "Our Mother St. Paul: Toward the Recovery of a Neglected Theme." *Princeton Seminary Bulletin* 17 (1996): 29–44.

Giblin, C. H. "Suggestion, Negative Response, and Positive Action in St. John's Portrayal of Jesus (John 2.1–11; 4.46–54; 7.2–14; 11.1–44)." *New Testament Studies* 26 (1980): 197–211.

Gnilka, J. *Johannesevangelium*. Die Neue Echter Bibel, Kommentar zum Neuen Testament mit der Einheitsübersetzung. Würzburg: Echter-Verlag, 1983.

Goodman, Martin. *State and Society in Galilee, A.D. 132–212*. Totowa, N.J.: Rowman & Allanheld, 1983.

Goulder, M. "Nicodemus." *Scottish Journal of Theology* 44 (1991): 153–68.

Grant, Jacqueline. *White Women's Christ and Black Women's Jesus: Feminist Christology and Womanist Response*. American Academy of Religion Series 64. Atlanta: Scholars Press, 1989.

Grassi, Joseph. *The Secret Identity of the Beloved Disciple*. New York: Paulist, 1992.

Gregory of Nazianzus. *In Sanctum Pascha*. In *Patrologia Cursus Completus. Series Graeca*, edited by J.-P. Migne, vol. 36. Paris: Garnier, 1844–1891.

Gregory of Nyssa. *Contra Eunomium Libri*. In *Gregorii Nysseni Opera*, edited by W. Jaeger, vols. 1–2. Leiden: Brill, 1960.

———. *In Canticum Canticorum. Oratio VII*. In *Gregorii Nysseni Opera*, edited by W. Jaeger and H. Langerbeck, vol. 6. Leiden: Brill, 1960.

———. *Refutatio Confessionis Eunomii*. In *Gregorii Nysseni Opera*, edited by W. Jaeger, vol. 2. Leiden: Brill, 1960.

Grese, W. C. "'Unless One Is Born Again': The Use of a Heavenly Journey in John 3." *Journal of Biblical Literature* 107 (1988): 677–93.

Grey, Mary. *Redeeming the Dream: Feminism, Redemption and Christian Tradition*. London: SPCK, 1989.

Gruber, Mayer I. *The Motherhood of God and Other Studies*. Atlanta: Scholars Press, 1992.

Gruenler, R. G. *The Trinity in the Gospel of John: A Thematic Commentary on the Fourth Gospel*. Grand Rapids: Baker Book House, 1986.

Haenchen, Ernst. *A Commentary on the Gospel of John.* Translated by R. W. Funk. 2 volumes. Hermeneia. Philadelphia: Fortress, 1984.

Hamerton-Kelly, R. *God the Father: Theology and Patriarchy in the Teaching of Jesus.* Philadelphia: Fortress, 1979.

Hampson, Daphne. *Theology and Feminism.* Oxford: Blackwell, 1990.

Harris, Elizabeth. *Prologue and Gospel: The Theology of the Fourth Evangelist.* Journal for the Study of the New Testament Supplement Series 107. Sheffield: JSOT Press, 1994.

Harrison, Verna E. F. "Word as Icon in Greek Patristic Theology." In *Constructive Christian Theology in the Worldwide Church,* edited by W. R. Barr, 58–70. Grand Rapids: Eerdmans, 1997.

Hartman, L., and B. Olsen, eds. *Aspects of the Johannine Literature.* Uppsala: Almqvist & Wiksell International, 1987.

Hasitschka, M. *Befreiung von Sünde nach dem Johannesevangelium: Eine bibeltheologische Untersuchung.* Innsbruck: Tyrolia-Verlag, 1989.

Haskins, Susan. *Mary Magdalen: Myth and Metaphor.* London: HarperCollins, 1993.

Heil, J. P. *Blood and Water: The Death and Resurrection of Jesus in John 18–21.* Catholic Biblical Quarterly Monograph Series 27. Washington: Catholic Biblical Association, 1995.

———. "The Story of Jesus and the Adulteress (John 7,53–8,11) Reconsidered." *Biblica* 72 (1991): 182–91.

Heine, Susanne. *Women and Early Christianity: Are the Feminist Scholars Right?* Translated by J. Bowden. London: SCM, 1987.

Heise, Jürgen. *Bleiben: Menein in den Johanneischen Schriften.* Tübingen: J. C. B. Mohr (Paul Siebeck), 1967.

Henneberry, B. *The Raising of Lazarus: An Evaluation of the Hypothesis that a Written Tradition Lies behind the Narrative.* Leuven: Katholieke Universeteit, 1983.

Heyward, Carter. *Touching Our Strength: The Erotic as Power and the Love of God.* San Francisco: Harper & Row, 1989.

Hippolytus. *On the Song.* In *Hippolytus Werke,* edited by G. N. Bonwetsch and H. Achelis. Leipzig: J. C. Hinrichs, 1897.

Hirsch, E. D. *The Aims of Interpretation.* Chicago: University of Chicago Press, 1976.

Hirschfield, Jane, ed. *Women in Praise of the Sacred.* New York: HarperCollins, 1994.

Holst, R. "The One Anointing of Jesus: Another Application of the Form-Critical Method." *Journal of Biblical Literature* 95 (1976): 435–46.

Homer. *The Odyssey of Homer.* Edited by W. B. Stanford. With General and Grammatical Introductions, Commentary, and Indexes. Classical Series. 2 volumes. London: Macmillan, 1965.

Hooker, Morna D. "The Johannine Prologue and the Messianic Secret." *New Testament Studies* 21 (1975): 40–58.

Hoskyns, Edwyn, and F. N. Davey. *The Fourth Gospel.* 2 volumes. 2nd ed. London: Faber & Faber, 1947.

Ince, Gwen. "Judge for Yourselves: Teasing out Some Knots in 1 Corinthians 11:2–16." *Australian Biblical Review* 48 (2000): 59–71.

Interpreter's Dictionary of the Bible, edited by G. A. Buttrick. 4 vols. Nashville: Abingdon, 1962.

Irenaeus. *Five Books Against Heresies.* Edited by W. Wigan Harvey. 2 volumes. Cambridge: Typis Academicis, 1857.

———. *Proof of the Apostolic Preaching.* Translated by J. P. Smyth. Westminster: Newman Press, 1952.

Irigaray, Luce. *Elemental Passions.* Translated by J. Collie and J. Still. New York: Routledge, 1992.

———. "Equal to Whom?" In N. Schor and E. Weed, *The Essential Difference,* 63–81. Translated by R. L. Mazzola. Bloomington: Indiana University Press, 1994.

———. *An Ethics of Sexual Difference.* Translated by C. Burke and G. C. Gill. Ithaca, N.Y.: Cornell University Press, 1993.

———. *Speculum of the Other Woman*. Translated by G. C. Gill. Ithaca, N.Y.: Cornell University Press, 1985.

Jacobs-Malina, D. *Beyond Patriarchy: The Images of Family in Jesus*. New York: Paulist, 1993.

Jasper, Alison. *The Shining Garment of the Text: Gendered Readings of John's Prologue*. Gender, Culture and Theology 6. Sheffield: JSOT Press, 1998.

Jeremias, Joachim. *New Testament Theology*. Translated by J. Bowden. London: SCM, 1971.

———. *The Prayers of Jesus*. Studies in Biblical Theology, Second Series 6. Translated by J. Bowden, C. Burchard, and J. Reumann. London: SCM, 1967.

John Chrysostom. *Homilies on John*. In *Patrologia Cursus Completus. Series Graeca*, edited by J.-P. Migne, vol. 59. Paris: Garnier, 1844–1891.

John-Julian. *A Lesson of Love: The Revelations of Julian of Norwich*. London: Darton, Longman & Todd, 1988.

John of Damascus. *Apologetic Discourses on Those Who Defame the Holy Icons*. In *Patrologiae Cursus Completus. Series Graeca*, edited by J.-P. Migne, vol. 94. Paris: Garnier, 1844–1891.

Johnson, Elizabeth A. *Friends of God and Prophets: A Feminist Theological Reading of the Communion of Saints*. London: SCM, 1998.

———. *She Who Is: The Mystery of God in Feminist Theological Discourse*. New York: Crossroad, 1992.

Johnson, Luke Timothy. *The Real Jesus: The Misguided Quest for the Historical Jesus and the Truth of the Traditional Gospels*. New York: HarperSanFrancisco, 1996.

Jones, Larry Paul. *The Symbol of Water in the Gospel of John*. Journal for the Study of the New Testament Supplement Series 145. Sheffield: JSOT Press, 1997.

Josephus. *Jewish Antiquities. Books I–XX*. Translated by H. St. J. Thackeray. Loeb Classical Library. London: William Heinemann, 1930. Volumes IV–IX.

———. *The Jewish War. Books I–VII*. Translated by H. St. J. Thackeray. Loeb Classical Library. London: William Heinemann, 1928. Volumes II–III.

Juel, D., and P. Keifert. "'I Believe in God': A Johannine Perspective." *Horizons in Biblical Theology* 12 (1990): 39–60.

Käsemann, Ernst. *The Testament of Jesus: A Study of the Gospel of John in the Light of John 17*. Translated by G. Krodel. 2nd ed. Philadelphia: Fortress, 1968.

Keller, Evelyn Fox. *Reflections on Gender and Science*. New Haven: Yale University Press, 1985.

Kimel, A. F., ed. *Speaking the Christian God: The Holy Trinity and the Challenge of Feminism*. Grand Rapids: Eerdmans, 1992.

Kittel, G., ed. *Theological Dictionary of the New Testament*. Translated and edited by G. W. Bromiley. 10 volumes. Grand Rapids: Eerdmans, 1964–1976.

Kitzberger, Ingrid Rosa. "Mary of Bethany and Mary of Magdala." *New Testament Studies* 41 (1995): 564–86.

Koester, Craig R. *The Dwelling of God: The Tabernacle in the Old Testament, Intertestamental Jewish Literature, and the New Testament*. Washington: Catholic Biblical Association of America, 1989.

———. *Symbolism in the Fourth Gospel: Meaning, Mystery, Community*. Minneapolis: Fortress, 1995.

Köstenberger, Andreas J. *Encountering John: The Gospel in Historical, Literary, and Theological Perspective*. Grand Rapids: Baker Books, 1999.

Kysar, Robert. *John*. Augsburg Commentary on the New Testament. Minneapolis: Augsburg, 1986.

LaCugna, Catherine Mowry, ed. *Freeing Theology: The Essentials of Theology in Feminist Perspective*. San Francisco: Harper, 1993.

———. *God For Us: The Trinity and Christian Life*. San Francisco: Harper, 1991.

Lagrange, M.-J. *Évangile selon Saint Jean*. 2nd ed. Paris: Librairie Victor LeCoffre, 1925.

Lee, Dorothy A. "Abiding in the Fourth Gospel: A Case-Study in Feminist Biblical Theology." *Pacifica* 10 (1997): 123–36.

———. "Beyond Suspicion? The Fatherhood of God in the Fourth Gospel." *Pacifica* 8 (1995): 140–54.

———. "The Heavenly Woman and the Dragon: Rereadings of Revelation 12." In *Feminist Poetics of the Sacred: Creative Suspicions,* edited by F. D. Glass and L. McCredden, 198–220. AAR. Oxford: Oxford University Press, 2001.

———. "Partnership in Easter Faith: The Role of Mary Magdalene and Thomas in John 20." *Journal for the Study of the New Testament* 58 (1995): 37–49.

———. "Presence or Absence? The Question of Women Disciples at the Last Supper." *Pacifica* 6 (1993): 1–20.

———. *The Symbolic Narratives of the Fourth Gospel: The Interplay of Form and Meaning.* Society for New Testament Studies Supplement Series 95. Sheffield: JSOT Press, 1994.

———. "The Symbol of Divine Fatherhood." *Semeia* 85 (1999): 177–87.

———. "Touching the Sacred Text: The Bible as Icon in Feminist Reading." *Pacifica* 11 (1998): 249–64.

———. "Women as 'Sinners': Three Narratives of Salvation in Luke and John." *Australian Biblical Review* 44 (1996): 1–15.

Léon-Dufour, X. *Lecture de l'évangile selon Jean.* 4 volumes. Paris: Éditions du Seuil, 1988–1996.

Lieu, Judith. "The Mother of the Son in the Fourth Gospel." *Journal of Biblical Literature* 117 (1998): 61–77.

Lightfoot, R. H. *St. John's Gospel: A Commentary.* Oxford: Clarendon, 1956.

Limouris, Gennadios, ed. *Icons: Windows on Eternity. Theology and Spirituality in Colour.* Faith and Order Paper 147. Geneva: WCC Publications, 1990.

Lindars, Barnabas. *The Gospel of John.* New Century Bible. Grand Rapids: Eerdmans, 1981.

Livingstone, E. A., ed. *Studia Evangelica.* Volume 4, *Papers Presented to the Fourth International Congress on New Testament Studies.* Berlin: Akademie-Verlag, 1973.

Loader, William. *The Christology of the Fourth Gospel.* Frankfurt am Main: Peter Lang, 1989.

Lowe, Malcolm. "Who Were the IOUDAIOI?" *Novum Testamentum* 18 (1976): 101–30.

Maccini, Robert Gordon. *Her Testimony Is True: Women as Witnesses According to John.* Sheffield: JSOT Press, 1996.

Maisch, Ingrid. *Between Contempt and Veneration: Mary Magdalene. The Image of a Woman through the Centuries.* Collegeville, Minn.: Liturgical Press, 1998.

Malina, Bruce J. *The New Testament World: Insights from Cultural Anthropology.* London: SCM, 1981.

Malina, Bruce J., and Richard L. Rohrbaugh. *Social-Science Commentary on the Gospel of John.* Minneapolis: Fortress, 1989.

Marchadour, A. *Lazare: Histoire d'un récit, récits d'une histoire.* Paris: Cerf, 1988.

Martin-Achard, Robert. *From Death to Life: A Study of the Development of the Doctrine of the Resurrection in the Old Testament.* Edinburgh/London: Oliver & Boyd, 1960.

Martyn, J. L. *The Gospel of John in Christian History.* New York: Paulist, 1979.

———. *History and Theology in the Fourth Gospel.* 2nd ed. Nashville: Abingdon, 1979.

McFadyen, Alistair. *Bound to Sin: Abuse, Holocaust and the Christian Doctrine of Sin.* Cambridge: Cambridge University Press, 2000.

McFague, Sallie. *The Body of God: An Ecological Theology.* Minneapolis: Fortress, 1993.

———. *Metaphorical Theology: Models of God in Religious Language.* London: SCM, 1982.

———. *Models of God: Theology for an Ecological, Nuclear Age.* London: SCM, 1987.

McHugh, John. *The Mother of Jesus in the New Testament.* London: Darton, Longman & Todd, 1975.

McKinlay, Judith E. *Gendering Wisdom the Host: Biblical Invitations to Eat and Drink.* Journal for the Study of the New Testament Supplement Series 216. Sheffield: JSOT Press, 1996.

McVey, Kathleen, ed. *St. Ephrem the Syrian: Selected Prose Works.* Washington: Catholic University of America Press, 1994.

Meier, John P. *A Marginal Jew.* 2 volumes. New York: Doubleday, 1994.

Metz J.-B., and E. Schillebeeckx, eds. *God as Father? Concilium* 143 (1981).

Metzger, Bruce M. *A Textual Commentary on the Greek New Testament.* 3rd ed. London/New York: United Bible Societies, 1975.

Metzner, Rainer. *Das Verständnis der Sünde im Johannesevangelium.* Tübingen: Mohr Siebeck, 2000.

Migne, J.-P., ed. *Patrologia Cursus Completus. Series Graeca.* Paris: Garnier, 1844–1891.

Milbank, John, Graham Ward, and Catherine Pickstock, eds. *Radical Orthodoxy.* London/New York: Routledge, 1999.

Minear, Paul S. *John: The Martyr's Gospel.* New York: Pilgrim Press, 1984.

———. "The Original Functions of John 21." *Journal of Biblical Literature* 102 (1983): 85–98.

———. "'We Don't Know Where . . . ,' John 20.1." *Interpretation* 30 (1976): 125–39.

Moloney, Francis J. *Belief in the Word: Reading John 1–4.* Minneapolis: Fortress, 1993.

———. "From Cana to Cana (John 2:1–4:54) and the Evangelist's Concept of Correct (and Incorrect) Faith." *Salesianum* 40 (1978): 817–43.

———. *Glory not Dishonor: Reading John 13–21.* Minneapolis: Fortress, 1998.

———. *The Gospel and Letters of John.* Nashville: Abingdon, 1998.

———. *The Gospel of John.* Sacra Pagina Series 4. Collegeville, Minn.: Liturgical Press, 1998.

———. "'In the Bosom of' or 'Turned towards' the Father?" *Australian Biblical Review* 31 (1983): 63–71.

———. *Signs and Shadows: Reading John 5–12.* Minneapolis: Fortress, 1996.

Moltmann, Jürgen. "I Believe in God the Father: Patriarchal or Non-Patriarchal Reference." *Drew Gateway* 59 (1990): 3–23.

———. *The Way of Jesus Christ: Christology in Messianic Dimensions.* London: SCM, 1990.

Moltmann-Wendel, Elisabeth. *A Land Flowing with Milk and Honey: Perspectives on Feminist Theology.* Translated by J. Bowden. London: SCM, 1986.

———. "Self-Love and Self-Acceptance." *Pacifica* 5 (1992): 288–300.

———. *The Women Around Jesus: Reflections on Authentic Personhood.* Translated by J. Bowden. London: SCM, 1982.

Moore, S. D. "Are There Impurities in the Living Water that the Johannine Jesus Dispenses? Deconstruction, Feminism and the Samaritan Woman." *Biblical Interpretation* 1 (1993): 207–27.

Morris, Leon. *The Gospel According to John: The English Text with Introduction, Exposition and Notes.* Grand Rapids: Eerdmans, 1971.

Mostert, Christiaan. "Is a Non-contextual Theology Possible?" In *Mapping the Landscape: Essays in Australian and New Zealand Christianity,* edited by S. Emilsen and W. Emilsen, 118–33. New York: Peter Lang, 2000.

Motyer, Stephen. *Your Father the Devil? A New Approach to John and "the Jews."* Carlisle, UK: Paternoster Press, 1997.

Moule, C. F. D. "The Meaning of 'Life' in the Gospel and Epistles of St. John: A Study in the Story of Lazarus." *Theology* 78 (1975): 114–25.

Murray, Les A., ed. *Anthology of Australian Religious Poetry.* Melbourne: CollinsDove, 1986.

Mycoff, David, ed. *The Life of Saint Mary Magdalene and of her Sister Saint Martha: A Medieval Biography.* Kalamazoo, Mich.: Cistercian Publications, 1989.

Nestlé-Aland. *Novum Testamentum Graece.* Edited by B. and K. Aland et al. 7th ed. Stuttgart: Deutsche Bibelgesellschaft, 1979, 1993.

Neusner, Jacob, ed. *The Components of the Rabbinic Documents: From the Whole to the Parts. VII, Part Two.* Atlanta: Scholars Press, 1997.

———. *Religions in Antiquity.* Leiden: Brill, 1968.

Newsom, Carol A., and Sharon H. Ringe, eds. *The Women's Bible Commentary.* Expanded edition. London: SCM, 1992, 1998.

Neyrey, Jerome. "Jacob Traditions and the Interpretation of John 4:10–26." *Catholic Biblical Quarterly* 41 (1979): 419–37.

Nicene and Post-Nicene Fathers of the Christian Church, edited by P. Schaff and H. Wace. Edinburgh: T. & T. Clark, 1892, 1988.

Nissen, J., and S. Pedersen, eds. *New Readings in John: Literary and Theological Perspectives.* Journal for the Study of the New Testament Supplement Series 182. Sheffield: JSOT Press, 1999.

O'Day, Gail R. "John." In *The Women's Bible Commentary,* edited by Carol A. Newsom and Sharon H. Ringe, 293–304. Expanded edition. London: SCM, 1998.

———. "John 7:53–8:11: A Study in Misreading." *Journal of Biblical Literature* 111 (1992): 631–40.

———. *Revelation in the Fourth Gospel: Narrative Mode and Theological Claim.* Philadelphia: Fortress, 1986.

———. "'Show Us the Father, and We Will be Satisfied' (John 14:8)." *Semeia* 85 (1999): 11–17.

Okure, Teresa. *The Johannine Approach to Mission: A Contextual Study of John 4:1–42.* Wissenschaftliche Untersuchungen zum Neuen Testament: Reihe 2/31. Tübingen: J. C. B. Mohr, 1988.

Olsson, Birger. *Structure and Meaning in the Fourth Gospel: A Text-Linguistic Analysis of John 2:1–11 and 3:1–42.* Lund: Gleerup, 1974.

Origen. *Commentary on S. John's Gospel.* Edited by A. E. Brooke. Cambridge: Cambridge University Press, 1896.

Ouspensky L., and V. Lossky, eds. *The Meaning of Icons.* New York: St. Vladimir's Seminary Press, 1989.

Pagels, Elaine. *The Gnostic Gospels.* New York: Random House, 1979.

Painter, John. *John: Witness and Theologian.* 3rd ed. London: SPCK, 1986.

———. "John 9 and the Interpretation of the Fourth Gospel." *Journal for the Study of the New Testament* 28 (1986): 31–61.

Pamment, Margaret. "John 3.5: 'Unless One is Born of Water and the Spirit, He Cannot Enter the Kingdom of God.'" *Novum Testamentum* 25 (1983): 189–90.

Pannenberg, Wolfhart. "Feminine Language about God?" *Asbury Theological Journal* 48 (1993): 27–29.

———. *An Introduction to Systematic Theology.* Grand Rapids: Eerdmans, 1991.

Pazdan, M. M. "Nicodemus and the Samaritan Woman: Contrasting Models of Discipleship." *Biblical Theology Bulletin* 17 (1987): 145–48.

Perkins, Pheme. "The Gospel According to John." In *The New Jerome Biblical Commentary,* edited by R. E. Brown et al., 942–85. Englewood Cliffs, N.J.: Prentice Hall, 1990.

———. *New Testament Witness and Contemporary Reflection.* London: Geoffrey Chapman, 1984.

Philo, *Allegorical Interpretation.* Translated by F. H. Colson and G. H. Whitaker. Loeb Classical Library. London: Heinemann, 1929. Vol. 1.

———. *On Dreams.* Translated by F. H. Colson and G. H. Whitaker. Loeb Classical Library. London: Heinemann, 1988. Vol. 5.

———. *Questions and Answers on Exodus.* Translated by R. Marcus. Loeb Classical Library. Cambridge, Mass.: Harvard University Press, 1970. Supplement 2.

Plaskow, Judith. *Sex, Sin and Grace: Women's Experience and the Theologies of Reinhold Niebuhr and Paul Tillich.* Washington: University Press of America, 1980.

Plato. *Timaeus, Critias, Cleitophon, Menesux, Epistles.* Edited by R. G. Bury. Loeb Classical Library. Cambridge, Mass.: Harvard University Press, 1929. Vol. 9.

Plutarch. *Moralia.* Loeb Classical Library. London: Heinemann, 1971.

Polybius. *Histories.* Edited by W. R. Paton. Loeb Classical Library. Cambridge, Mass.: Harvard University Press, 1978. Vol. 5.

Porter, S. E., M. A. Hayes, and D. Tombs, eds. *Resurrection.* Sheffield: JSOT Press, 1999.

Quast, Kevin. *Peter and the Beloved Disciple: Figures for a Community in Crisis.* Journal for the Study of the New Testament Supplement Series 32. Sheffield: JSOT Press, 1989.

Quenot, Michel. *The Icon: Window on the Kingdom.* New York: St. Vladimir's Seminary Press, 1991.

Rahner, Karl. *Theological Investigations.* Volume 3, *The Theology of the Spiritual Life.* London: Darton, Longman & Todd, 1967.

———. *Theological Investigations.* Volume 4, *More Recent Writings.* Translated by Kevin Smyth. London: Darton, Longman & Todd, 1966.

———. *The Trinity.* Tunbridge Wells: Burns & Oates, 1970.

Regan, H., and A. J. Torrance, eds. *Christ and Context: The Confrontation between Gospel and Culture.* Edinburgh: T. & T. Clark, 1993.

Reinhartz, Adele. "'And the Word was Begotten': Divine Epigenesis in the Gospel of John." *Semeia* 85 (1999): 83–103.

———. "The Gospel of John." In *Searching the Scriptures,* volume 2, *A Feminist Commentary,* edited by Elisabeth Schüssler Fiorenza, 561–600. New York: Crossroad, 1994.

Rensberger, D. *Overcoming the World: Politics and Community in the Gospel of John.* London: SPCK, 1988.

Ricci, Carla. *Mary Magdalene and Many Others: Women Who Followed Jesus.* Translated by P. Burns. Tunbridge Wells: Burns & Oates, 1994.

Richard, E. "Expressions of Double Meaning and their Function in the Gospel of John." *New Testament Studies* 31 (1985): 96–112.

Richards, I. A. *The Philosophy of Rhetoric.* New York: Oxford University Press, 1936.

Ricoeur, Paul. "Biblical Hermeneutics." *Semeia* 4 (1975): 27–148.

———. *Interpretation Theory: Discourse and the Surplus of Meaning.* Fort Worth: Texas Christian University, 1976.

———. *The Rule of Metaphor: Multi-Disciplinary Studies in the Creation of Meaning.* Translated by R. Czerny. London: Routledge & Kegan Paul, 1978.

———. *The Symbolism of Evil.* Translated by E. Buchanan. Boston: Beacon, 1967.

Ringe, Sharon H. *Wisdom's Friends: Community and Christology in the Fourth Gospel.* Louisville, Ky.: Westminster John Knox Press, 1999.

Ruether, Rosemary Radford. *Introducing Redemption in Christian Feminism.* Introductions in Feminist Theology 1. Sheffield: JSOT Press, 1998.

———. *To Change the World: Christology and Cultural Criticism.* New York: Crossroad, 1981.

———. *Sexism and God-Talk: Toward a Feminist Theology.* Boston: Beacon, 1983, 1993.

———. *Women and Redemption: A Theological History.* Minneapolis: Fortress, 1988.

Russell, Letty M. *Household of Freedom: Authority in Feminist Theology.* Philadelphia: Westminster, 1987.

———. *Human Liberation in a Feminist Perspective—A Theology.* Philadelphia: Westminster, 1974.

———. *Sex, Race, and God: Christian Feminism in Black and White.* London: Chapman, 1989.

Russell, Letty M., ed. *Feminist Interpretation of the Bible.* Oxford: Blackwell, 1985.

Russell, Letty M., and J. Shannon Clarkson, eds. *Dictionary of Feminist Theologies.* London: Mowbray, 1996.

Saiving, Valerie. "The Human Situation: A Feminine View." In *Womanspirit Rising: A Feminist Reader in Religion,* edited by C. P. Christ and J. Plaskow, 25–42. San Francisco: Harper & Row, 1979.

Sandelin, K.-G. *Wisdom as Nourisher: A Study of an Old Testament Theme, Its Development within Early Judaism and Its Impact on Early Christianity.* Abo: Abo Akademi, 1986.

Sanders, J. N., and B. N. Mastin. *A Commentary on the Gospel According to St. John.* London: A. & C. Black, 1968.

Sanford, John A. *Mystical Christianity: A Psychological Commentary on the Gospel of John.* New York: Crossroad, 1995.

Schaff P., and H. Wace, eds. *Nicene and Post-Nicene Fathers of the Christian Church.* Edinburgh: T. & T. Clark, 1892, 1988.

Schaper, J. *Eschatology in the Greek Psalter*. Tübingen: J. C. B. Mohr (Paul Siebeck), 1995.

Schillebeeckx, E. *God Among Us: The Gospel Proclaimed*. London: SCM, 1983.

Schnackenburg, Rudolf. *The Gospel According to St. John*. 3 volumes. Translated by K. Smyth. Herder's Theological Commentary on the New Testament. London: Burns & Oates, 1968–1982.

Schneiders, Sandra M. "Born Anew." *Theology Today* 44 (1987): 189–96.

———. "Death in the Community of Eternal Life: History, Theology and Spirituality in John 11." *Interpretation* 41 (1987): 44–56.

———. "The Foot Washing (John 13:1–20): An Experiment in Hermeneutics." *Ex Auditu* 1 (1985): 135–46.

———. "History and Symbolism in the Fourth Gospel." In *L'évangile de Jean: Sources, rédaction, théologie*, edited by M. de Jonge, 371–76. Louvain: University Press, 1977.

———. "John 21:1–14." *Interpretation* 43 (1989): 70–75.

———. *The Revelatory Text: Interpreting the New Testament as Sacred Scripture*. San Francisco: Harper, 1991.

———. "Symbolism and the Sacramental Principle in the Fourth Gospel." In *Segni e sacramenti nel Vangelo di Giovanni*, ed. P.–R. Tragan, 221–35. Rome: Editrice Anselmiana, 1977.

———. "The Veil: A Johannine Sign (John 20:1–10)?" *Biblical Theological Bulletin* 13 (1983): 94–97.

———. *Women and the Word: The Gender of God in the New Testament*. Madeleva Lecture in Spirituality. New York: Paulist, 1986.

———. "Women in the Fourth Gospel and the Role of Women in the Contemporary Church." *Biblical Theology Bulletin* 12 (1982): 35–45.

———. *Written That You May Believe: Encountering Jesus in the Fourth Gospel*. New York: Crossroad, 1999.

Schnelle, Udo. *Antidocetic Christology in the Gospel of John: An Investigation of the Place of the Fourth Gospel in the Johannine School*. Translated by L. Maloney. Minneapolis: Fortress, 1992.

Schüssler Fiorenza, Elisabeth. *But She Said: Feminist Practices of Biblical Interpretation*. Boston: Beacon, 1992.

———. *In Memory of Her: A Feminist Theological Reconstruction of Christian Origins*. 2nd ed. London: SCM, 1994.

———. *Jesus: The Politics of Interpretation*. London: Continuum, 2000.

———. *Miriam's Child, Sophia's Prophet: Critical Issues in Feminist Christology*. London: SCM, 1994.

Schüssler Fiorenza, Elisabeth, ed. *Searching the Scriptures*. Volume 1, *A Feminist Introduction*. New York: Crossroad, 1993.

———. *Searching the Scriptures*. Volume 2, *A Feminist Commentary*. New York: Crossroad, 1994.

Scott, Martin. *Sophia and the Johannine Jesus*. Journal for the Study of the New Testament Supplement Series 71. Sheffield: JSOT Press, 1992.

Segovia, Fernando F. *The Farewell of the Word: The Johannine Call to Abide*. Minneapolis: Fortress, 1991.

Segovia, Fernando F., ed. *'What Is John?' Readers and Readings of the Fourth Gospel*. Society of Biblical Literature Symposium Series 3. Atlanta: Scholars Press, 1996.

Seim, Turid Karlsen. *The Double Message: Patterns of Gender in Luke and Acts*. Studies of the New Testament and its World. Edinburgh: T. & T. Clark, 1994.

———. "Roles of Women in the Gospel of John." In *Aspects on the Johannine Literature*, edited by L. Hartman and B. Olsson, 56–73. Uppsala: Almqvist & Wiksell International, 1987.

Senior, Donald. *The Passion of Jesus in the Gospel of John*. Passion Series 4. Collegeville, Minn.: Liturgical Press, 1991.

Smith, D. Moody. *John.* Abingdon New Testament Commentaries. Nashville: Abingdon, 1999.

Smith, J. P. *St. Irenaeus: Proof of the Apostolic Preaching.* Westminster, Md.: Newman Press, 1952.

Soskice, Janet Martin. "Blood and Defilement: Reflections on Jesus and the Symbolics of Sex." In *The Convergence of Theology: Festschrift Honoring Gerald O'Collins,* edited by D. Kendell and S.T. Davis, 285–303. New York: Paulist, 2001.

———. *Metaphor and Religious Language.* Oxford University Press, 1987.

———. "Naming God at Sinai" in *Naming God.* Forthcoming.

———. "Trinity and Feminism." In *The Cambridge Companion to Feminist Theology,* edited by Susan Parsons, 141. Forthcoming.

Staley, J. L. *The Print's First Kiss: A Rhetorical Investigation of the Implied Reader in the Fourth Gospel.* Society of Biblical Literature Dissertation Series 82. Atlanta: Scholars Press, 1988.

Stavropoulos, C. "Partakers of Divine Nature." In *Eastern Orthodox Theology: A Contemporary Reader,* edited by D. B. Clendenin, 183–92. Grand Rapids: Baker Book House, 1995.

Steele, Peter. "And Buried." Unpublished homily. Newman College, University of Melbourne, 2000.

Steinem, Gloria. *Revolution from Within: A Book of Self-Esteem.* London: Corgi Books, 1992.

Stibbe, M. W. G. *John.* Readings: A New Biblical Commentary. Sheffield: JSOT Press, 1993.

Stylianopoulos, Theodore. *The New Testament: An Orthodox Perspective.* Volume 1, *Scripture, Tradition, Hermeneutics.* Brookline, Mass.: Holy Cross Orthodox Press, 1999.

Suggit, J. N. "The Raising of Lazarus." *Expository Times* 95 (1983–84): 106–8.

Sylva, D. D. "Nicodemus and His Spices (John 19.31)." *New Testament Studies* 34 (1988): 148–51.

Talbert, C. H. *Reading John: A Literary and Theological Commentary on the Fourth Gospel and the Johannine Epistles.* Reading the New Testament Series. London: SPCK, 1992.

Tertullian. *Treatise on the Incarnation.* Edited by E. Evans. London: SPCK, 1956.

Theological Dictionary of the New Testament. Edited by G. Kittel. Translated and edited by G. W. Bromiley. 10 volumes. Grand Rapids: Eerdmans, 1964–1976.

Thomas, J. C. *Footwashing in John 13 and the Johannine Community.* Journal for the Study of the New Testament Supplement Series 61. Sheffield: JSOT Press, 1991.

Thompson, Marianne Meye. *The God of the Gospel of John.* Grand Rapids: Eerdmans, 2001.

———. "'God's Voice You Have Never Heard, God's Form You Have Never Seen': The Characterization of God in the Gospel of John." *Semeia* 63 (1993): 171–204.

———. *The Humanity of Jesus in the Fourth Gospel.* Philadelphia: Fortress, 1988.

———. *The Promise of the Father: Jesus and God in the New Testament.* Louisville: Westminster John Knox Press, 2000.

Tillich, Paul. *Dynamics of Faith.* World Perspectives 9. London: George Allen & Unwin, 1957.

———. *Love, Power and Justice.* The Firth Lectures. New York: Oxford University Press, 1960.

———. "The Meaning and Justification of Religious Symbols." In *Religious Experience and Truth: A Symposium,* edited by S. Hook, 3–11. London: Oliver & Boyd, 1962.

———. "The Religious Symbol." In *Religious Experience and Truth: A Symposium,* edited by S. Hook, 301–21. London: Oliver & Boyd, 1962.

———. *Systematic Theology.* Volume 1, *Reason and Revelation, Being and God.* London: SCM, 1951.

Van der Watt, Jan. *Family of the King: Dynamics of Metaphor in the Gospel According to John.* Biblical Interpretation Series 47. Leiden: Brill, 2000.

Vanhoozer, Kevin J. *Is There a Meaning in This Text? The Bible, the Reader and the Morality of Literary Knowledge.* Leicester: Apollos, 1998.

van Tilborg, Sjef. *Imaginative Love in John*. Biblical Interpretation Series 2. Leiden: Brill, 1993.

von Wahlde, Urban C. "The Johannine 'Jews': A Critical Study." *New Testament Studies* 28 (1983): 33–60.

Wagner, J. *Auferstehung und Leben: Joh 11,1–12,19 als Spiegel johanneischer Redaktions- und Theologiegeschichte*. Regensburg: Verlag Friedrich Pustet, 1988.

Wallace, D. B. "Reconsidering 'The Story of Jesus and the Adulteress Reconsidered.'" *New Testament Studies* 39 (1993): 290–96.

Ward, Benedicta. *The Prayers and Meditations of St. Anselm*. Middlesex: Penguin Books, 1973.

Ware, Kallistos. "'My Helper and My Enemy: The Body in Greek Christianity." In *Religion and the Body*, edited by Sarah Coakley, 90–110. Cambridge: Cambridge University Press, 1997.

Watson, Nigel. *Easter Faith and Witness*. Melbourne: Desbooks, 1990.

Wead, D. W. "The Johannine Double Meaning." *Restoration Quarterly* 13 (1970): 106–20.

West, Angela. *Deadly Innocence: Feminism and the Mythology of Sin*. London: Cassell, 1995.

Whitacre, Rodney A. *John*. Leicester: InterVarsity Fellowship, 1999.

Whitford, M., ed. *The Irigaray Reader*. Oxford: Blackwell, 1991.

Widdicombe, Peter. *The Fatherhood of God from Origen to Athanasius*. Oxford Theological Monographs. Oxford: Clarendon, 1994.

———. "The Fathers on the Father in the Gospel of John." *Semeia* 85 (1999): 105–25.

Wiles, Maurice. *The Spiritual Gospel: The Interpretation of the Fourth Gospel in the Early Church*. Cambridge: Cambridge University Press, 1960.

Willett, Michael E. *Wisdom Christology in the Fourth Gospel*. San Francisco: Mellen Research University Press, 1992.

Wilson-Kastner, Patricia. *Faith, Feminism and the Christ*. Philadelphia: Fortress, 1983.

Witherington, Ben, III. *John's Wisdom: A Commentary on the Fourth Gospel*. Cambridge: Lutterworth Press, 1995.

———. "The Waters of Birth: John 3:5 and 1 John 5:6–8." *New Testament Studies* 35 (1989): 155–60.

———. *Women in the Ministry of Jesus: A Study of Jesus' Attitudes to Women and Their Role as Reflected in his Earthly Life*. Cambridge/New York: Cambridge University Press, 1984.

Wright, Judith. *Selected Poems*. Sydney: Angus & Robertson, 1990.

Yee, Gale A. *Jewish Feasts and the Gospel of John*. Wilmington, Del.: Michael Glazier, 1989.

Young, Frances. *Biblical Exegesis and the Formation of Christian Culture*. Cambridge: Cambridge University Press, 1997.

Zell, Katharine Schütz. *Pamphlet on the Lord's Prayer, 1532*. Unpublished translation by Peter Matheson.

Zizioulas, John. *Being as Communion: Studies in Personhood and the Church*. Contemporary Greek Theologians 4. New York: St. Vladimir's Seminary Press, 1985.

Indexes

Subjects

Passages